Nancy Bell

Manners and monuments of prehistoric peoples

The Marquis de Nadaillac

Nancy Bell

Manners and monuments of prehistoric peoples
The Marquis de Nadaillac

ISBN/EAN: 9783744640626

Printed in Europe, USA, Canada, Australia, Japan

Cover: Foto ©ninafisch / pixelio.de

More available books at **www.hansebooks.com**

MANNERS AND MONUMENTS

OF

PREHISTORIC PEOPLES

BY

THE MARQUIS DE NADAILLAC

CORRESPONDENT OF THE INSTITUTE

AUTHOR OF "L'AMÉRIQUE PRÉHISTORIQUE," "LES PREMIERS HOMMES ET LES TEMPS PRÉHISTORIQUES," ETC.

WITH 113 ILLUSTRATIONS

TRANSLATED BY

NANCY BELL (N. D'ANVERS)

AUTHOR OF "THE ELEMENTARY HISTORY OF ART," "THE LIFE-STORY OF OUR EARTH," "THE STORY OF EARLY MAN," ETC.

G. P. PUTNAM'S SONS
NEW YORK   LONDON
27 WEST TWENTY-THIRD STREET   24 BEDFORD STREET, STRAND
The Knickerbocker Press
1892

TRANSLATOR'S NOTE

The present volume has been translated, with the author's consent, from the French of the Marquis de Nadaillac. The author and translator have carefully brought down to date the original edition, embodying the discoveries made during the progress of the work. The book will be found to be an epitome of all that is known on the subject of which it treats, and covers ground not at present occupied by any other work in the English language.

NANCY BELL (N. D'ANVERS).

SOUTHBOURNE-ON-SEA,
1891.

ILLUSTRATIONS.

FIGURE		PAGE
	Fossil man from Mentone	*Frontispiece*
1.	Stone weapons described by Mahudel in 1734 .	8
2.	Copper hatchets found in Hungary and now in national museum of Budapest	20
3.	Copper beads from Connett's Mound, Ohio (natural size)	21
4.	Stone statues on Easter Island .	37
5.	Fort-hill, Ohio	39
6.	Group of sepulchral mounds	40
7.	Ground plan of a pueblo of the Mac-Elmo valley .	41
8.	Cliff-house on the Rio Mancos	42
9.	House in a rock of the Montezuma cañon . .	43
10.	1. Fragments of arrows made of reindeer horn from the Martinet cave (Lot-et-Garonne). 2. Point of spear or harpoon in stag-horn (one third natural size). 3. and 4. Bone weapons from Denmark. 5. Harpoon of stag-horn from St. Aubin. 6. Bone fish-hooks pointed at each end, from Waugen.	61
11.	Bear's teeth converted into fish-hooks.	62
12.	Fish-hook made out of a boar's tusk.	
13.	A. Large barbed arrow from one side of the Plantade shelter (Tarn-et-Garonne). B. Lower part of a barbed harpoon from the Plantade deposit.	65
14.	Ancient Scandinavian boat found beneath a tumulus at Gogstadten	73
15.	Ancient boat discovered in the bed of the Cher .	75

FIGURE		PAGE
16.	A lake pirogue found in the Lake of Neuchâtel. 1. As seen outside. 2. and 3. Longitudinal and transverse sections.	76
17.	Stones used as anchors, found in the Bay of Penhouet. 1, 2, 3. Stones weighing about 160 lbs. each. 4. and 5. Lighter stones, probably used for canoes.	78
18.	Scraper from the Delaware valley.	
19.	Implement from the Delaware valley.	82
20.	Worked flints from the Lafaye and Plantade shelters (Tarn-et-Garonne)	83
21.	1. Stone javelin-head with handle. 2. Stone hatchet with handle.	89
22.	1. Fine needles. 2. Coarse needles. 3. Amulet. 4 and 6. Ornaments. 5. Cut flints. 7. Fragment of a harpoon. 8. Fragments of reindeer antlers with signs or drawings. 9. Whistle. 10. One end of a bow (?). 11. Arrow-head. (From the Vache, Massat, and Lourdes caves)	91
23.	Amulet made of the penien bone of a bear and found in the Marsoulas cave	92
24.	Various stone and bone objects from California .	93
25.	Dipper found in the excavations at the Chassey camp	95
26.	Pottery of a so far unclassified type found in the Argent cave (France).	98
27.	1. Lignite pendant. 2. Bone pendant. (Thayngen cave)	107
28.	Round pieces of skull, pierced with holes (M. de Baye's collection)	110
29.	Part of a rounded piece of a human parietal. Stiletto made of the end of a human radius. Disk, made of the burr of a stag's antler.	111
30.	Whistle from the Massenat collection . . .	112
31.	Staff of office	113
32.	Staff of office, made of stag-horn pierced with four holes	114
33.	Staff of office found at Lafaye.	
34.	Staff of office in reindeer antler, with a horse engraved on it (Thayngen).	115

ILLUSTRATIONS.   ix

FIGURE		PAGE
35. Staff of office found at Montgaudier		117
36. Carved dagger-hilt (Laugerie-Basse).	⎫	
37. The great cave-bear, drawn on a pebble found in the Massat cave (Garrigou collection).	⎬	118
	⎭	
38. Mammoth or elephant from the Léna cave.	⎫	119
39. Seal engraved on a bear's tooth, found at Sordes.	⎭	
40. Fragment of a bone, with regular designs. Fragment of a rib on which is engraved a musk-ox, found in the Marsoulas cave		120
41. Head of a horse from the Thayngen cave.	⎫	
42. Bear engraved on a bone, from the Thayngen cave.	⎬	121
43. Reindeer grazing, from the Thayngen cave		122
44. Head of *Ovibos moschatus*, engraved on wood, found in the Thayngen cave		123
45. Young man chasing the aurochs, from Laugerie		124
46. Fragment of a staff of office, from the Madelaine cave.	⎫	125
47. Human face carved on a reindeer antler, found in the Rochebertier cave.	⎬	
48. The glyptodon		128
49. *Mylodon robustus*		129
50. Objects discovered in the peat-bogs of Laybach, A. Earthenware vase. B. Fragment of ornamented pottery. C. Bone needle. D. Earthenware weight for fishing-net. E. Fragment of jawbone		152
51. Small terra-cotta figures found in the Laybach pile dwellings.		153
52. Small terra-cotta figures from the Laybach pile dwellings.		154
53. Nurhag at Santa Barbara (Sardinia)		168
54. "Talayoti" at Trepuco (Minorca)		170
55. Dolmen of Castle Wellan (Ireland)		175
56. The large dolmen of Careoro, near Plouharnel		176
57. Dolmen of Arrayalos (Portugal)		177
58. Megalithic sepulchre at Acora (Peru)		178
59. The great broken menhir of Locmariaker with Cæsar's table		186

FIGURE		PAGE
60.	Covered avenue of Dissignac (Loire-Inférieure), view of the chamber at the end of the north gallery	189
61.	Covered avenue near Antequera	190
62.	Ground plan of the Gavr'innis monument	191
63.	Monoliths at Stennis, in the Orkney Islands	193
64.	Cromlech near Bône (Algeria)	196
65.	Dolmen at Pallicondah, near Madras (India)	201
66.	Dolmen at Maintenon, with a table about 19½ feet long	204
67.	Part of the Mané-Lud dolmen	208
68.	Sculptures on the menhirs of the covered avenue of Gavr'innis	210
69.	Dolmen with opening (India)	211
70.	Dolmen near Trie (Oise)	212
71.	Bronze objects found at Krasnojarsk (Siberia)	237
72.	Prehistoric polisher near the ford of Beaumoulin, Nemours	239
73.	Section of a flint mine	242
74.	Plan of a gallery of flint mine	243
75.	Picks, hammers, and mattocks made of stag-horn	245
76.	Cranium of a woman from Cro-Magnon (full face)	249
77.	Skull of a woman found at Sordes, showing a severe wound, from which she recovered	250
78.	Fragment of human tibia with exostosis enclosing the end of a flint arrow	252
79.	Fragment of human humerus pierced at the elbow-joint (Trou d'Argent)	253
80.	Mesaticephalic skull, with wound which has been trepanned	259
81.	Trepanned Peruvian skull	268
82.	Skull from the Bougon dolmen (Deux-Sèvres), seen in profile	273
83.	Trepanned prehistoric skull	274
84.	Prehistoric spoon and button found in a lake station at Sutz	287
85.	General view of the station of Fuente-Alamo	293
86.	Group at Liberty (Ohio)	299
87.	Trenches at Juigalpa (Nicaragua)	300
88.	Vases found at Santorin	313

ILLUSTRATIONS. xi

FIGURE		PAGE
89.	Vase ending in the snout of an animal, found on the hill of Hissarlik	325
90.	Funeral vase containing human ashes. .	326
91.	Large terra-cotta vases found at Troy . . .	327
92.	Earthenware pitcher found at a depth of 19½ feet.	328
93.	Vase found beneath the ruins of Troy.	
94.	Terra-cotta vase found with the treasure of Priam.	329
95.	Vase found beneath the ruins of Troy.	
96.	Earthenware pig found at a depth of 13 feet . .	330
97.	Vase surmounted by an owl's head, found beneath the ruins of Troy . . .	331
98.	Copper vases found at Troy	333
99.	Vases of gold and electrum, with two ingots (Troy),	334
100.	Gold and silver objects from the treasure of Priam,	335
101.	Gold ear-rings, head-dress, and necklace of golden beads from the treasure of Priam .	336
102.	Terra-cotta fusaïoles	339
103.	Cover of a vase with the symbol of the swastika .	340
104.	Stone hammer from New Jersey bearing an undeciphered inscription	341
105.	Chulpa near Palca.	357
106.	Dolmen at Auvernier near the lake of Neuchâtel .	359
107.	A stone chest used as a sepulchre . . .	361
108.	Example of burial in a jar	363
109.	Aymara mummy	365
110.	Peruvian mummies	367
111.	Erratic block from Scania, covered with carvings .	379
112.	Engraved rock from Massibert (Lozère) . .	380

MANNERS AND MONUMENTS OF PREHISTORIC PEOPLES.

CHAPTER I.

THE STONE AGE: ITS DURATION AND ITS PLACE IN TIME.

THE nineteenth century, now nearing its close, has made an indelible impression upon the history of the world, and never were greater things accomplished with more marvellous rapidity. Every branch of science, without exception, has shared in this progress, and to it the daily accumulating information respecting different parts of the globe has greatly contributed. Regions, previously completely closed, have been, so to speak, simultaneously opened by the energy of explorers, who, like Livingstone, Stanley, and Nordenskiöld, have won immortal renown. In Africa, the Soudan, and the equatorial regions, where the sources of the Nile lie hidden; in Asia, the interior of Arabia, and the Hindoo Koosh or Pamir mountains, have been visited and explored. In America whole districts but yesterday inaccessible are now intersected by railways, whilst in the other hemisphere Australia and the islands of Polynesia have been colonized; new societies have rapidly sprung into being, and even the unmelting ice of the polar regions no longer checks the advance of the intrepid explorer. And all this is but a small portion of the work on which the present generation may justly pride itself.

Distant wars too have contributed in no small measure to the progress of science. To the victorious march of the French army we owe the discovery of new facts relative to the ancient history of Algeria; it was the advance of the English and Russian forces that revealed the secret of the mysterious lands in the heart of Asia, whence many scholars believe the European races to have first issued, and of this ever open book the French expedition to Tonquin may be considered at present one of the last pages.

Geographical knowledge does much to promote the progress of the kindred sciences. The work of Champollion, so brilliantly supplemented by the Vicomte de Rougé and Mariette Bey, has led to the accurate classification of the monuments of Egypt. The deciphering of the cuneiform inscriptions has given us the dates of the palaces of Nineveh and Babylon; the interpretation by savants of other inscriptions has made known to us those Hittites whose formidable power at one time extended as far as the Mediterranean, but whose name had until quite recently fallen into complete oblivion. The rock-hewn temples and the yet more strange dagobas of India now belong to science. Like the sacred monuments of Burmah and Cambodia they have been brought down to comparatively recent dates; and though the palaces of Yucatan and Peru still maintain their reserve, we are able to fix their dates approximately, and to show that long before their construction North America was inhabited by races, one of which, known as the Mound Builders, left behind them gigantic earthworks of many kinds, whilst another, known as the Cliff Dwellers, built for themselves houses on the face of all but inaccessible rocks.

Comparative philology has enabled us to trace back the genealogies of races, to determine their origin, and to follow their migrations. Burnouf has brought to light the ancient Zend language, Sir Henry Rawlinson and Oppert have by their magnificent works opened up new methods of research, Max Müller and Pictet in their turn by availing themselves of the most diverse materials have done much to make known to us the Aryan race, the great educator, if I may so speak, of modern nations.

To one great fact do all the most ancient epochs of history bear witness: one and all, they prove the existence in a yet more remote past of an already advanced civilization such as could only have been gradually attained to after long and arduous groping. Who were the inaugurators of this civilization? Who were the earliest inhabitants of the earth? To what biological conditions were they subject? What were the physical and climatic conditions of the globe when they lived? By what flora and fauna were they surrounded? But science pushes her inquiry yet further. She desires to know the origin of the human race, when, how, and why men first appeared upon the earth; for from whatever point of view he is considered, man must of necessity have had a beginning.

We are in fact face to face with most formidable problems, involving alike our past and future; problems it is hopeless to attempt to solve by human means or by the help of human intelligence alone, yet with which science can and ought to grapple, for they elevate the soul and strengthen the reasoning faculties. Whatever may be their final result, such studies are of enthralling interest. "Man," said a learned member of the French Institute, "will ever be for man the grandest of all mysteries, the most absorbing of all objects of contemplation." [1]

Let us work our way back through past centuries and study our remote ancestors on their first arrival upon earth; let us watch their early struggles for existence! We will deal with facts alone; we will accept no theories, and we must, alas, often fail to come to any conclusion, for the present state of prehistoric knowledge rarely admits of certainty. We must ever be ready to modify theories by the study of facts, and never forget that, in a science so little advanced, theories must of necessity be provisional and variable.

Truly strange is the starting-point of prehistoric science. It is with the aid of a few scarcely even rough-hewn flints, a few bones that it is difficult to classify, and a few rude stone monuments that we have to build up, it must be for our readers to say with what success, a past long prior to any written history, which has left no trace in the memory of man, and during which our globe would appear to have been subject to conditions wholly unlike those of the present day.

The stones which will first claim our attention, some of them very skilfully cut and carefully polished, have been known for centuries. According to Sueto-

---
[1] M. Gaston.

nius, the Emperor Augustus possessed in his palace on the Palatine Hill a considerable collection of hatchets of different kinds of rock, nearly all of them found in the island of Capri, and which were to their royal owner the weapons of the heroes of mythology. Pliny tells of a thunder-bolt having fallen into a lake, in which eighty-nine of these wonderful stones were soon afterwards found.[1] Prudentius represents ancient German warriors as wearing gleaming *ceraunia* on their helmets; in other countries similar stones ornamented the statues of the gods, and formed rays about their heads.[2]

A subject so calculated to fire the imagination has of course not been neglected by the poets. Claudian's verses are well known:

> Pyrenæisque sub antris
> Ignea flumineæ legere ceraunia nymphæ.

Marbodius, Bishop of Rennes, in the eleventh century, sang of the thunder-stones in some Latin verses which have come down to us, and an old poet of the sixteenth century in his turn exclaimed, on seeing the strange bones around him:

> Le roc de Tarascon hébergea quelquefois
> Les géants qui couroyent les montagnes de Foix,
> Dont tant d'os successifs rendent le témoignage.

With these stones, in fact, were found numerous bones of great size, which had belonged to unknown creatures. Latin authors speak of similar bones found in Asia Minor, which they took to be those of giants

---

[1] Pliny calls them *ceraunia gemma* ("Natural History," book ii., ch. 59; book xxxvii., ch. 51).

[2] S. Reinach proves clearly enough that the collections of the Emperor Augustus were from Capri.

of an extinct race. This belief was long maintained; in 1547 and again in 1667 fossil remains were found in the cave of San Ciro near Palermo; and Italian savants decided that they had belonged to men eighteen feet high. Guicciadunus speaks of the bones of huge elephants carefully preserved in the Hôtel de Ville at Antwerp as the bones of a giant named Donon, who lived 1300 years before the Christian era.

In days nearer our own the most cultivated people accepted the remains of a gigantic batrachian[1] as those of a man who had witnessed the flood, and it was the same with a tortoise found in Italy scarcely thirty years ago. Dr. Carl, in a work published at Frankfort[2] in 1709, took up another theory, and, such was the general ignorance at the time, he used long arguments to prove that the fossil bones were the result neither of a freak of nature, nor of the action of a plastic force, and it was not until near the end of his life that the illustrious Camper could bring himself to admit the extinction of certain species, so totally against Divine revelation did such a phenomenon appear to him to be.

Prejudices were not, however, always so obstinate. For more than three centuries stones worked by the hand of man have been preserved in the Museum of the Vatican, and as long ago as the time of Clement VIII. his doctor, Mercati, declared these stones to have been the weapons of antediluvians who had been still ignorant of the use of metals.

---

[1] This skeleton was discovered in 1726 by Scheuchzer, a doctor of Œningen, and by him placed in the Leyden Museum, with the pompous inscription: *Homo diluvii testis* (*Philosophical Transactions*, vol. xxxiv.). Cuvier, by scraping away the stone, revealed the true nature of the fossil.

[2] " Ossium Fossilium Docimasia."

During the early portion of the eighteenth century a pointed black flint, evidently the head of a spear, was found in London with the tooth of an elephant. It was described in the newspapers of the day, and placed in the British Museum.

In 1723 Antoine de Jussieu said, at a meeting of the *Académie des Sciences*, that these worked stones had been made where they were found, or brought from distant countries. He supported his arguments by an excellent example of the way in which savage races still polish stones, by rubbing them continuously together.

A few years later the members of the *Académie des Inscriptions* in their turn, took up the question, and Mahudel, one of its members, in presenting several stones, showed that they had evidently been cut by the hand of man. "An examination of them," he said, "affords a proof of the efforts of our earliest ancestors to provide for their wants, and to obtain the necessaries of life." He added that after the re-peopling of the earth after the deluge, men were ignorant of the use of metals. Mahudel's essay is illustrated by drawings, some of which we reproduce (Fig. 1), showing wedges, hammers, hatchets, and flint arrow-heads taken, he tells us, from various private collections.[1]

Bishop Lyttelton, writing in 1736, speaks of such weapons as having been made at a remote date by savages ignorant of the use of metals,[2] and Sir W. Dugdale, an eminent antiquary of the seventeenth century, attributed to the ancient Britons some flint

---

[1] "Mém. Acad. des Inscriptions," 1734, vol. x., p. 163.
[2] *Archæologia*, vol. ii., p. 118.

hatchets found in Warwickshire, and thinks they were made when these weapons alone were used.[1]

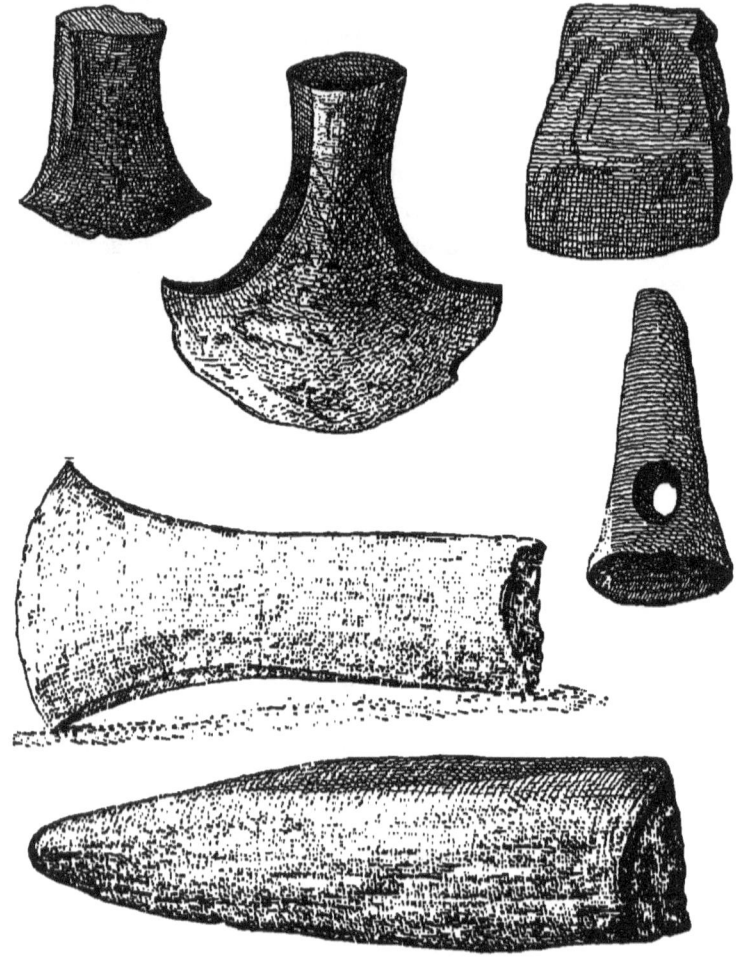

FIG. 1.—Stone weapons described by Mahudel in 1734.

A communication made by Frère to the Royal Society of London deserves mention here with a few supplementary remarks.[2]

---

[1] "The Antiquities of Warwickshire," vol. iv., 1656.
[2] *Archæologia*, vol. xiii., p. 105.

This distinguished man of science found at Hoxne, in Suffolk, about twelve feet below the surface of the soil, worked flints, which had evidently been the natural weapons of a people who had no knowledge of metals. With these flints were found some strange bones with the gigantic jaw of an animal then unknown. Frère adds that the number of chips of flint was so great that the workmen, ignorant of their scientific value, used them in road-making. Everything pointed to the conclusion that Hoxne was the place where this primitive people manufactured the weapons and implements they used, so that as early as the end of last century a member of the Royal Society formulated the propositions,[1] now fully accepted, that at a very remote epoch men used nothing but stone weapons and implements, and that side by side with these men lived huge animals unknown in historic times. These facts, strange as they appear to us, attracted no attention at the time. It would seem that special acumen is needed for every fresh discovery, and that until the time for that discovery comes, evidence remains unheeded and science is altogether blind to its significance.

But to resume our narrative. It is interesting to note the various phases through which the matter passed before the problem was solved. In 1819, M. Jouannet announced that he had found stone weapons near Périgord. In 1823, the Rev. Dr. Buckland published the "Reliquiæ Diluvianæ," the value of which, though it is a work of undoubted merit, was greatly lessened by the preconceived ideas of its author. A few years later, Tournal announced his discoveries in

---

[1] Castelfranco: *Revue d'Anthropologie*, 1887.

the cave of Bize, near Narbonne, in which, mixed with human bones, he found the remains of various animals, some extinct, some still native to the district, together with worked flints and fragments of pottery. After this, Tournal maintained that man had been the contemporary of the animals the bones of which were mixed with the products of human industry.[1] The results of the celebrated researches of Dr. Schmerling in the caves near Liège were published in 1833. He states his conclusions frankly: "The shape of the flints," he says, "is so regular, that it is impossible to confound them with those found in the Chalk or in Tertiary strata. Reflection compels us to admit that these flints were worked by the hand of man, and that they may have been used as arrows or as knives." Schmerling does not refer, though Lyell does, and that in terms of high admiration, to the courage required for the arduous work involved in the exploration of the caves referred to, or to the yet more serious obstacles the professor had to overcome in publishing conclusions opposed to the official science of the day.

In 1835, M. Joly, by his excavations in the Nabrigas cave, established the contemporaneity of man with the cave bear, and a little later M. Pomel announced his belief that man had witnessed the last eruptions of the volcanoes of Auvergne.

In spite of these discoveries, and the eager discussions to which they led, the question of the antiquity of man and of his presence amongst the great Quater-

---

[1] *Annales des Sciences Naturelles*, vol. xvii., p. 607. Cartailhac: *Matériaux*, 1884.
[2] "Recherches sur les Ossements Fossiles de la Province de Liège."

nary animals made but little progress, and it was reserved to a Frenchman, M. Boucher de Perthes, to compel the scientific world to accept the truth.

It was in 1826 that Boucher de Perthes first published his opinion; but it was not until 1846 and 1847 that he announced his discovery at Menchecourt, near Abbeville, and at Moulin-Quignon and Saint Acheul, in the alluvial deposits of the Somme, of flints shaped into the form of hatchets associated with the remains of extinct animals such as the mammoth, the cave lion, the *Rhinoceros incisivus*, the hippopotamus, and other animals whose presence in France is not alluded to either in history or tradition. The uniformity of shape, the marks of repeated chipping, and the sharp edges so noticeable in the greater number of these hatchets, cannot be sufficiently accounted for either by the action of water, or the rubbing against each other of the stones, still less by the mechanical work of glaciers. We must therefore recognize in them the results of some deliberate action and of an intelligent will, such as is possessed by man, and by man alone. Professor Ramsay[1] tells us that, after twenty years' experience in examining stones in their natural condition and others fashioned by the hand of man, he has no hesitation in pronouncing the flints and hatchets of Amiens and Abbeville as decidedly works of art as the knives of Sheffield. The deposits in which they were found showed no signs of having been disturbed; so that we may confidently conclude that the men who worked these flints lived where the banks of the Somme now are, when these deposits were in course of being laid down, and that he was the contemporary of the ani-

[1] *Athenæum*, 16 July, 1859.

mals whose bones lay side by side with the products of his industry.

This conclusion, which now appears so simple, was not accepted without difficulty. Boucher de Perthes defended his discoveries in books, in pamphlets, and in letters addressed to learned societies. He had the courage of his convictions, and the perseverance which insures success. For twenty years he contended patiently against the indifference of some, and the contempt of others. Everywhere the proofs he brought forward were rejected, without his being allowed the honor of a discussion or even of a hearing. The earliest converts to De Perthes' conclusions met with similar attacks and with similar indifference. There is nothing to surprise us in this; it is human nature not to take readily to anything new, or to entertain ideas opposed to old established traditions. The most distinguished men find it difficult to break with the prejudices of their education and the yet more firmly established prejudices of the systems they have themselves built up. The words of the great French fabulist will never cease to be true:

> Man is ice to truth;
> But fire to lies.

One of the masters of modern science, Cuvier, has said[1]: "Everything tends to prove that the human race did not exist in the countries where the fossil bones were found at the time of the convulsions which buried those bones; but I will not therefore conclude that man did not exist at all before that epoch; he may

---

[1] "Discours sur les Révolutions du Globe," third edition, p. 13, Paris, Didot, 1861.

have inherited certain districts of small extent whence he repeopled the earth after these terrible events." Cuvier's disciples went beyond the doctrines of their master. He made certain reservations; they admitted none, and one of the most illustrious, Élie de Beaumont, rejected with scorn the possibility of the co-existence of man and the mammoth.[1] Later, retracting an assertion of which perhaps he himself recognized the exaggeration, he contented himself with saying that the district where the flints and bones had been collected belonged to a recent period, and to the shifting deposits of the slopes contemporary with the peaty alluvium. He added—scientific passions are by no means the least intense, or the least deeply rooted—that the worked flints may have been of Roman origin, and that the deposits of Moulin-Quignon may have covered a Roman road! This might indeed have been the case in the *Département du Nord*, where a road laid down by the conquerors of Gaul has completely disappeared beneath deposits of peat, but it could not be true at Moulin-Quignon, where gravels form the culminating point of the ridge. Moreover, the laying down of the most ancient peats of the French valleys did not begin until the great watercourses had been replaced by the rivers of the present day; they never contain relics of any species but such as are still extant; whereas it was with the remains of extinct mammals that the flints were found.

It was against powerful adversaries such as this that the modest savant of Abbeville had to maintain his opinion. "No one," he says, "cared to verify the facts of the case, merely giving as a reason, that these

---

[1] *Acad. des Sciences*, 16th and 23d May, 1863.

facts were impossible." Weight was added to his complaint by the refusal in England about the same time to print a communication from the Society of Natural History of Torquay, which announced the discovery of flints worked by the hand of man, associated, as were those of the Somme, with the bones of extinct animals. The fact appeared altogether too incredible!

But the time when justice would be done was to come at last. Dr. Falconer visited first Amiens and then Abbeville, to examine the deposits and the flints and bones found in them. In January, 1859, and in 1860, other Englishmen of science followed his example; and excavations were made, under their direction, in the massive strata which rise, from the chalk forming their base, to a height of 108 feet above the level of the Somme. Their search was crowned with success, and they lost no time in making known to the world the results they had obtained, and the convictions to which these results had led.[1] In 1859 Prestwich announced to the Royal Society of London that the flints found in the bed of the Somme were undoubtedly the work of the hand of man, that they had been found in strata that had not been disturbed, and that the men who cut these flints had lived at a period prior to the time when our earth assumed its present configuration. Sir Charles Lyell, in his opening address at a session of the British Association, did not hesitate to support the conclusions of Prestwich. It

---

[1] Lubbock: "On the Evidence of the Antiquity of Man Afforded by the Physical Structure of the Somme Valley" (*Nat. Hist. Review*, vol. ii.). Prestwich: "On the Occurrence of Flint Implements Associated with the Remains of Extinct Species in Beds of a Late Geological Period" (*Phil. Trans.*, 1860). Evans: "Flint Implements in the Drift" (*Arch.*, 1860-62).

was now the turn of Frenchmen of science to arrive at Abbeville. MM. Gaudry and Pouchet themselves extracted hatchets from the Quaternary deposits of the Somme.[1] These facts were vouched for by the well-known authority, M. de Quatrefages, who had already constituted himself their advocate. All that was now needed was the test of a public discussion, and the meeting of the Anthropological Society of Paris supplied a suitable occasion. The question received long and searching scientific examination. All doubt was removed, and M. Isidore Geoffroy-Saint-Hilaire was the mouth-piece of an immense majority of his colleagues, when he declared that the objections to the great antiquity of the human race had all melted away. The conversion of men so illustrious was followed of course by that of the general public, and, more fortunate than many another, Boucher de Perthes had the satisfaction before his death of seeing a new branch of knowledge founded on his discoveries, attain to a just and durable popularity in the scientific world.

It must not, however, be supposed that popular superstition yielded at once to the decisions of science, and it is curious to meet with the same ideas in the most different climates, and in districts widely separated from each other.[2] Everywhere worked flints are attributed to a supernatural origin; everywhere they are looked upon as amulets with the power of protecting their owner, his house or his flocks. Russian peasants believe them to be the arrows of thunder, and fathers transmit them to their children as precious

---

[1] *Acad. des Sciences*, 1859, 1863.
[2] Cartailhac: "L'Age de Pierre dans les Souvenirs et les Superstitions Populaires."

heirlooms. The same belief is held in France, Ireland, and Scotland, in Scandinavia, and Hungary, as well as in Asia Minor, in Japan, China, and Burmah; in Java, and amongst the people of the Bahama Islands, as amongst the negroes of the Soudan or those of the west coast of Africa,[1] who look upon these stones as bolts launched from Heaven by Sango, the god of thunder; amongst the ancient inhabitants of Nicaragua as well as the Malays, who, however, still make similar implements.

The name given to these flints recalls the origin attributed to them. The Romans call them *ceraunia* from κεραυνός, thunder, and in the catalogue of the possessions of a noble Veronese published in 1656, we find them mentioned under this name.[2] Every one knows Cymbeline's funeral chant in Shakespeare's play:

Fear no more the lightning flash
Nor the all dreaded thunder-stone.

In Germany we are shown *Donner-Keile*, in Alsace *Donner-Axt*, in Holland *Donner-Beitels*, in Denmark *Tordensteen*, in Norway *Tordenkeile*, in Sweden *Thorsoggar*, Thor having been the god of thunder amongst northern nations; while with the Celts[3] the *Mengurun*, in Asia Minor the *Ylderim-tachi*, in Japan the *Rai-fu-seki-no-rui*, in Roussillon the *Pedrus de Lamp*, and in Andalusia the *Piedras de Rayo* have the same significa-

[1] A short time before his tragic end, the noble and patriotic Gordon sent to Cairo three hatchets or stone wedges found amongst the Niams-Niams, who said they had fallen from Heaven, and who worshipped them with superstitious rites (*Bull. Institut Égyptien*, 1886, No. 14).

[2] "Museo Moscardo," Padova, 1656.

[3] According to M. Pitre de Lisle, the Bretons think that these stones vibrate at every clap of thunder.

tion. The inhabitants of the Mindanao islands call these stones the teeth of the thunder animal, and the Japanese the teeth of the thunder.[1] In Cambodia, worked stones, celts, adzes, and gouges or knives, are known as thunder stones. A Chinese emperor, who lived in the eighth century of our era, received from a Buddhist priest some valuable presents which the donors said had been sent by the Lord of Heaven, amongst which were two flint hatchets called *loui-kong*, or stones of the god of thunder. In Brazil we meet with the same idea in the name of *corisco*, or lightnings, given to worked flints; whilst in Italy, by an exception almost unique, they are called *lingue san Paolo*.

May we not also attribute to the worship of stones some of the religious and funeral rites of antiquity? According to Porphyry, Pythagoras, on his arrival on the island of Crete, was purified with thunder-stones by the dactyl priests of Mount Ida. The Etruscans wore flint arrow-heads on their collars. They were sought after by the Magi, and the Indians gave them an honored place in their temples. According to Herodotus, the Arabs sealed their engagements by making an incision in their hands with a sharp stone; in Egypt the body of a corpse before being embalmed was opened with a flint knife; a similar implement was used by the Hebrews for the rite of circumcision; and it was also with cut stones that the priests of Cybele inflicted self-mutilation in memory of that of Atys. At Rome the stone hatchet was dedicated to Jupiter Latialis, and solemn treaties were ratified by the sacrifice of a pig, the throat of which was cut with a sharp flint. According to Virgil, this custom was

---

[1] Roulin : *Acad. des Sciences*, December 28, 1868.

handed down to the ancient Romans by the uncouth nation of the Equicoles. At the beginning of the Christian era, the heroes commemorated by Ossian still had in the centre of their shields a polished stone consecrated by the Druids, and a saga maintains that the *ceraunia* assured certain victory to their owners. On the other side of the Atlantic, the Aztecs used obsidian blades for the sacrifices, in which hundreds of human victims perished miserably; and similar blades are used by the Guanches of Teneriffe to open the bodies of their chiefs after death. At the present day, the Albanian Palikares use pointed flints to cut the flesh off the shoulder-blade of a sheep with a view to seeking in its fibres the secrets of the future, and when the god Gimawong visits his temple of Labode, on the western coast of Africa, his worshippers offer him a bull slain with a stone knife. Lumholtz,[1] in the second of his recent explorations in Queensland, tells us that the natives still use stone weapons, varying in form and in the handles used, and that the weapons of the Australians living near Darling River, as well as those of the Tasmanians, are without handles.

During the first centuries of the Christian era, strange rites were still performed in honor of dolmens and menhirs. The councils of the Church condemned them, and the emperors and kings supported by their authority the decrees of the ecclesiastics.[2] Childebert in 554, Carloman in 742, Charlemagne by an edict issued at Aix-la-Chapelle in 789,[3] forbid their subjects to practise these rites borrowed from heathenism. But

---

[1] "Congrès d'Anthropologie et d'Archéologie Préhistorique," Paris, 1889.

[2] Council of Arles in 452, of Tours in 567, of Nantes in 658, of Toledo in 681 and 692, and of Leptis in 743.

[3] Baluze: "Capitularia Regum Francorum," vol. i., pp. 518, 1234, 1237.

popes and emperors are alike powerless in this direction, and one generation transmits its traditions and superstitions to another. In the seventeenth century a Protestant missionary called in the aid of the secular arm to destroy a superstition deeply rooted in the minds of his people; in England, sorcerers were proceeded against for having used flint arrow-heads in their pretended witchcraft; in Sweden, a polished hatchet was placed in the bed of women in the pangs of labor; in Burmah, thunder-stones reduced to powder were looked upon as an infallible cure for ophthalmia; and the Canaches have a collection of stones with a special superstition connected with each. But why seek examples so far away and in a past so remote? In our own day and in our own land we find men who think themselves invulnerable and their cattle safe if they are fortunate enough to possess a polished flint.

Prehistoric times are generally divided into three epochs—the *Stone Age*, the *Bronze Age*, and the *Iron Age*. We owe this classification to the archæologists of Northern Europe.[1] It is neither very exact nor very satisfactory, and fresh discoveries daily tend to unsettle it.[2] Alsberg maintained that iron was the first metal used, founding his contention on the scarcity of tin, the difficulty of obtaining alloys, and on the sixty-one iron foundries of Switzerland which may date from prehistoric times. The rarity of the discovery of iron objects, he urged, is accounted for by the ease with which such objects are destroyed by rust. There has never been a Bronze or an Iron age in America, so

---

[1] Steenstrup, Forchhammer, Thomsen, Worsaae, and Nillsson. The commission appointed by the Copenhagen Academy of Sciences presented six reports on the subject between 1850 and 1856.
[2] "Die Anfang des Eisens Cultur," Berlin, 1886.

that it would seem very doubtful whether all races went through the same cycles of development. I myself prefer the division into the *Palæolithic* period, when men only used roughly chipped stones, and the *Neolithic* period, when they carefully polished their stone weapons. "There may," says Alexander Bertrand,[1] "be one immutable law for the succession of strata throughout the entire crust of the earth, but there is no corresponding law applicable to human

FIG. 2.—Copper hatchets found in Hungary, and now in the National Museum of Budapest.

agglomerations or to the succession of the strata of civilization. It would be a very grave error to adopt the theory according to which all human races have passed through the same phases of development and have gone through the same complete series of social conditions."

It may perhaps be convenient to introduce a fourth period when copper alone was used and our ancestors were still ignorant of the alloys necessary for the pro-

---

[1] "Archéologie Celtique et Gauloise," p. 46.

duction of bronze. Hesiod speaks of a third generation of men as possessing copper only, and although it does not do to attach undue importance to isolated facts, recent discoveries in the Cevennes, in Spain, in Hungary, and elsewhere, appear to confirm the existence of an age of copper (Fig. 2). We may add that the mounds of North America contain none but copper implements and ornaments, witnesses of a time when that metal alone was known either on the shores of the Atlantic or of the Pacific [1] (Fig. 3).

It is impossible to fix the duration of the Stone age. It began with man, it lasted for countless

FIG. 3.—Copper beads, from Connett's Mound, Ohio (natural size).

centuries, and we find it still prevailing amongst certain races who set their faces against all progress. The scenes sculptured upon Egyptian monuments dating from the ancient Empire represent the employment of stone weapons, and their use was continued throughout the time of the Lagidæ and even into that of the Roman domination. A few years ago, on the shores of the Nile, I saw some of the common people shave

---

[1] Dr. Much: "L'Age de Cuivre en Europe et son Rapport avec la Civilisation des Indo-Germains," Vienna, 1886. Pulsky: "Die Kupfer Zeit im Ungarn," Budapest, 1884. Cartailhac: "Ages Prehistoriques de l'Espagne et du Portugal," p. 211. E. Chantre: *Mat.*, June, 1887; and Berthelot: *Journal des Savants*, September, 1889.

their heads with stone razors, and the Bedouins of Gournah using spears headed with pointed flints. The Ethiopians in the suite of Xerxes had none but stone weapons, and yet their civilization was several centuries older than that of the Persians. The excavations on the site of Alesia yielded many stone weapons, the glorious relics of the soldiers of Vercingetorix. At Mount Beuvray, on the site of Bibracte, flint hatchets and weapons have been discovered associated with Gallic coins. At Rome, M. de Rossi collected similar objects mixed with the *Æs rude*. Flint hatchets are mentioned in the life of St. Éloy, written by St. Owen, and the Merovingian tombs have yielded hundreds of small cut flints, the last offerings to the dead. William of Poitiers tells us that the English used stone weapons at the battle of Hastings in 1066, and the Scots led by Wallace did the same as late as 1288. Not until many centuries after the beginning of the Christian era did the Sarmatians know the use of metals; and in the fourteenth century we find a race, probably of African origin, making their hatchets, knives, and arrows of stone, and tipping their javelins with horn. The Japanese, moreover, used stone weapons and implements until the ninth and even the tenth century A.D.

But there is no need to go back to the past for examples. The Mexicans of the present day use obsidian hatchets, as their fathers did before them; the Esquimaux use nephritis and jade weapons with Remington rifles. Nordenskiöld tells us that the Tchoutchis know of no weapons but those made of stone; that they show their artistic feeling in engravings on bone, very similar to those found in the caves of the south of France. In 1854, the Mqhavi, an Indian tribe of the Rio Colorado (California), possessed no metal objects; and it is the same with the dwellers on the banks of the Shingu River (Brazil), the Oyacoulets of French Guiana, and many other wandering and savage races. Père Pelitot tells us that the natives living on the banks of the Mackenzie River are still in the stone age; and Schumacker has given an interesting example of the manufacture of stone weapons by the Klamath Indians dwelling on the shores of the Pacific. It has been justly said: "The Stone age is not a fixed period in time, but one phase of the development of the human race, the duration of which varies according to the environment and the race."[1]

In thus limiting our idea of the stone age, we may conclude that alike in Europe and in America,[2] there has been a period when metal was entirely unknown, when stones were the sole weapons, the sole tools of man, when the cave, for which he had to dispute possession with bears and other beasts of prey, was his sole and precarious refuge, and when clumsy heaps of stones served alike as temples for the worship of his gods and sepulchral monuments in honor of his chiefs.

Excavations in every department of France have yielded thousands of worked flints, and there are few more interesting studies than an examination of the mural map in the Saint Germain Museum on which are marked with scrupulous exactitude the dwelling-places of our most remote ancestors, and the megalithic monuments which are the indestructible memorials of our forefathers.

---

[1] Irenée Cochut: "Thèse présentée à la Faculté de Théologie Protestante de Montauban."

[2] See my translation of the author's admirable and exhaustive work on "Prehistoric America," chapters i. and iv.—Nancy Bell.

In the Crimea were picked up a number of small flints cut into the shape of a crescent exactly like those found in the Indies and in Tunis, and the Anthropological Society of Moscow has introduced us to a Stone age the memory of which is preserved in the tumuli of Russia. On the shores of Lake Lagoda have been found some implements of argillaceous schist, in Carelia and in Finland tools made of slate and schist, often adorned with clumsy figures of men or of animals. The rigor of the climate did not check the development of the human race; in the most remote times Lapland, Nordland, the most northerly districts of Scandinavia, and even the bitterly cold Iceland, were peopled. The Exhibition of Paris, 1878, contained some stone weapons found on the shores of the White Sea.

On several parts of the coast of Denmark we meet with mounds of an elliptical shape and about nine feet high, with a hollow in the centre, marking the site of a prehistoric dwelling. It was not until about 1850 that the true nature of these mounds was determined. Excavations in them have brought to light knives, hatchets, all manner of stone, horn, and bone implements, fragments of pottery, charred wood, with the bones of mammals and birds, the skeletons of fishes, the shells of oysters and cockles buried beneath the ashes of ancient hearths. To these accumulations the characteristic name of *Kitchenmiddings*, or kitchen refuse, has been given.

Several caves have recently been examined in Poland, one of which, situated near Cracow, appears to belong to Palæolithic times. Count Zawiska has already given an account of his interesting discoveries to the

Prehistoric Congress at Stockholm. In the Wirzchow cave he identified seven different hearths, and took out of the accumulations of cinders various amulets, clumsy representations of fish cut in ivory, split bones, bears', wolves', and elks' teeth pierced with a hole for threading, and more than four thousand stone objects of a similar type to those found in Russia, Scandinavia, and Germany. We meet with similar traces of successive habitation in a cave near Ojcow; the valuable contents of which included some beautiful flint tools, some awls, bone spatulæ, and some gold ornaments, mixed, in the lower of the hearths, with the bones of extinct animals, and in the upper, with those of species still living.

The discoveries made in the Atter See and in the Salzburg lakes with those in the Moravian caves prove what had previously been very stoutly denied, the existence in those districts of ancient races at a very remote date.

The most ancient inhabitants of Hungary, however, cannot be traced further back than to Neolithic times. In that country have been found, with polished stone implements, thousands of objects made of stag-horn, or bone, almost all without exception finely finished off. The discovery of copper tools and ornaments of a peculiar form in the Danubian provinces, bears witness to a distinct civilization in those districts, and confirms what we have just said about a Copper age.

From the Lake Stations of Austria and Hungary, we pass naturally to those of Switzerland. We shall have to introduce to our readers whole villages built in the midst of the waters, and a people long completely forgotten. In many of these stations, none but stone implements have been found, and on the half-burnt piles on which the huts had been set up, it is still easy to make out the notches cut with flint hatchets.

We meet with similar pile dwellings, as these structures are called, in France, Italy, Germany, Ireland, and England, for from the earliest times man was constantly engaged in sanguinary contests with his fellow-men, and sought in the midst of the waters a refuge from the ever present dangers surrounding him.

The discoveries made in Belgium must be ranked amongst the most important in Europe, and we shall often have occasion to refer to them. Holland, on the other hand, having much of it been under the sea for so long, yields nothing to our researches but a few arrow-heads, hatchets, and knives made of quartz or diorite, and all of them of the coarsest workmanship.

No less fruitful in results to prehistoric science are the researches made in the south of Europe. The congress that met at Bologna, in 1871, showed us that in the Transalpine provinces man was witness of those physical phenomena which gave to Italy its present configuration; and the exhibition in connection with the congress enabled us to get a good idea of the primitive industry which has left relics behind it in every district of the peninsula.

Some hatchets of a similar type to the most ancient found in France were dug out of a gravel pit at San Isidro on the borders of the Mançanarès, associated with the bones of a huge elephant that has long been extinct; and a cave has recently been discovered near Madrid from which were dug out nearly five hundred skeletons, the greater number thickly coated with stalagmite. Near the bodies lay several flint weapons, and some fragments of pottery.[1] Cartailhac tells us of similar discoveries in various parts of Portugal.[2] The caves of Santander have yielded worked bones and barbed harpoons; and those of Castile, various objects resembling those of the Reindeer period of France. It is, however, an interesting and important fact that the reindeer never crossed the Pyrenees. Although so far excavations have been anything but complete, we are already able to assert that during Palæolithic times the ancient Iberia was occupied by races whose industrial development was similar to that of modern Europe.

It will be well to mention also the excavations made on the slopes of Mount Hymettus, and in the ever-famous plains of Marathon. Finlay has brought together in Greece a very interesting collection of stone weapons and implements which he picked up in great numbers at the base of the Acropolis of Athens. All these discoveries prove the existence of man at a time about which but yesterday nothing was known, and to which it is difficult as yet to give a name, this existence being proved by the most irrefragable of evidence, the work of his own hands.

Although the proofs of there having been a Stone age in Western Europe are absolutely convincing, it is difficult to feel equally sure with regard to the portions of the globe where so many districts are closed to the explorer. Everywhere, however, where excavations have been made, they have yielded the most remarkable results. M. de Ujfalvy has brought diorite and serpentine hatchets and wedges from the south of

---

[1] *Académie des Sciences*, May 23, 1881; "Antiquités du Musée de Minoussink," Tomsk, 1886-7.
[2] "Les Âges Préhistoriques en Espagne et en Portugal."

Siberia, and Count Ouvaroff tells us of a Quaternary deposit, the only one known at present at Irkutsk, in Eastern Siberia, containing cut flints. Near Tobolsk, Poliaskoff found some beautifully worked stones. Other archæologists tell us of having found, in the east of the Ural Mountains and on the shores of the Joswa, hammers, hatchets, pestles, nuclei the shape of polygonal prisms, and round or long pieces of flint, all pierced with a central hole, which are supposed to have been spindle whorls. Lastly, Klementz tells us that the lofty valleys of the Yenesei and its tributaries were inhabited in the most remote times by races who developed a special civilization.

At the other extremity of the great Asiatic continent, a deposit of cinders found at the entrance of a cave near the Nahr el Kelb yielded some flint knives or scrapers, and more recently a prehistoric station has been made out at Hanoweh, a little village of Lebanon, east of Tyre. The flints are of primitive shapes, not unlike the most ancient forms found in France. They were discovered in a mass of *débris* of all kinds, forming a very hard conglomerate. Some teeth, which had belonged to animals of the bovidæ, cervidæ, and equidæ groups, were got out with considerable difficulty, but the bones in the conglomerate were too much broken up to be identified. Worked flints and arrow- or spear-heads were also found in considerable quantities in various parts of the table-land of Sinai, and at the openings of the caves in which the ancient inhabitants took refuge. It was with stone tools that these people worked the mines riddling the sides of the mountains, and it is still easy to make out traces of their operations.

We have already alluded to Japan; for a long time the barbarian Aïnos, the earliest inhabitants of the country, were acquainted with nothing but stone. Flint arrows were presented to the Emperor Wu-Wang eleven hundred years before our era; the annals of one of the ancient dynasties speak of flint weapons, and an encyclopædia published in the reign of the Emperor Kang-Hi speaks of rock hatchets, some black and some green, and all alike dating from the most remote antiquity.

Agates worked by the hand of man are found in great quantities in the bone beds of the Godavery. Some javelin heads in sandstone, basalt, and quartz, with scrapers and knives, most of them flat on one side and rounded on the other, appear to be even more ancient than the agate implements. Some of the celts resemble those of European type, others the flint weapons found in Egypt, and the clumsiest forms may be compared to those still in use amongst the natives of Australia. We may also mention a somewhat rare type lately discovered in the island of Melas, which have been characterized as saw-bladed knives. A letter from Rivett-Carnac announces the discovery of weapons and stone implements in Banda, a wild mountain district on the northwest of India. The scrapers, he says, strangely resemble those of the Esquimaux, and the arrow-heads those of the most ancient inhabitants of America.[1]

Many megalithic monuments are met with in places widely removed from each other in the vast Indian Empire. Captain Congreve, after describing the cairns

[1] "Stone Implements from the Northwestern Provinces of India," *Journal of the Asiatic Society of Bengal*, Calcutta, 1883.

with their rows of stones ranged in circles, the kistvaens or dolmens, the huge rocks placed erect as at Stonehenge, the barrows hollowed out of the cliffs, declares with undisguised astonishment that there is not a Druidical monument of which he had not seen the counterpart in the Neilgherry Mountains.[1]

General Faidherbe divides Africa into two distinct regions—one north of the Great Desert, where the inhabitants and the fauna and flora have all alike certain characteristics in common with those of Europe; and the other south of the Sahara, which was at one time separated from that in the north by a vast inland sea. In this southern region we are in Nigritia, or the Africa of the negroes, where the inhabitants in their physical characteristics and in their language, the mammals, and the plants, differ altogether from those of the north. In one point, however, these two regions resemble each other: in both we recognize a Stone age, which existed in Algeria and in Egypt, as well as on the banks of the Senegal and at the Cape of Good Hope. The valley of the Nile from Cairo to Assouan has yielded a series of objects in flint, porphyry, and hornblendic rock, retaining traces of human workmanship, and reminding us of similar implements of European type. These objects,[2] says M. Arcelin, are always found either beneath modern deposits or at the surface of the upper plateaux at the highest point to which the river rises; nothing has, however, been found in the alluvial deposits of the Nile, in spite of the most persevering search. At the Prehistoric Congress held

---

[1] *Literary Journal of Madras*, vol. xiv.
[2] "L'Âge de Pierre et la Classification Préhistorique d'après les Sources Égyptiennes," Paris, 1879.

at Stockholm, some worked flints were produced that had been found in the Libyan Desert. This once inhabited district, now without water or vegetation, can only be reached at the present day with the greatest difficulty. Is not this yet another proof of the great changes which have taken place since the advent of man? Lastly, the Boulak Museum contains a whole series of stone weapons and implements, showing in their workmanship a progressive development similar to that we find in Europe. Many archæologists are of opinion that the worked flints found in the plains of Lower Egypt date from Neolithic times. Those alone are Palæolithic which have been found in a deposit hard enough for the hollowing out of tombs, which are certainly earlier than the eighteenth dynasty. We must add, however, that neither with the Palæolithic nor with the Neolithic relics have been found any bones of extinct animals. Some savants go yet further: they think that these worked stones are but chips split off by the heat of the sun.[1] A phenomenon of this kind is mentioned by Desor and Escher de la Linth in the Sahara Desert; Fraas quotes a similar observation made by Livingstone in the heart of Africa, and one by Wetzstein, who, not far from Damascus, saw hard basalt rocks split under the influence of the early morning freshness. I have myself noticed similar phenomena in the Nile valley, but it must be added that the fragments of rock broken off by the combined influence of heat and humidity present very notable differences to those worked by the hand of man, and cannot really be mistaken for them.

---

[1] Pitt Rivers: "On the Discovery of Chert Implements in the Nile Valley," British Association, York, 1881.

In Algeria have been preserved some most interesting relics of prehistoric times. If I am not mistaken, Worsaae was the first to note the worked stones in the French possessions in Africa. They have been picked up in great numbers, especially near the watercourses at which the ancient inhabitants of the country slaked their thirst, as do their descendants at the present day. The exploration of the Sahara daily yields unexpected discoveries; and already fifteen different stations formerly inhabited by man have been made out. In those remote days a large river flowed near Wargla, which was then an important centre, and a number of tools picked up bear witness to the former presence of an active and industrious population. At one place the flint implements, arrow-heads, knives, and scrapers are all of a very primitive type, and were found sorted into piles. This was evidently a *dépôt*, probably forming the reserve stock of the tribe. Wargla or perhaps Golea at one time appears to have been the extreme limit of the Stone age in Algeria, but quite recently traces of primitive man have been discovered amongst the Tuaregs. These relics are hatchets made of black rock, and arrow-heads not unlike those which the Arabs attribute to the Djinn; but as we approach the south we find the flints picked up more clumsily and unskilfully cut—a proof that they were the work of a more barbarous people with less practical skill. It is the megalithic monuments of Algeria, of which we shall speak more in detail presently, that are the most worthy of attention. As in India, we meet with them in thousands, and in certain parts of the continent they extend for considerable distances. They consist of long, square, circular, or oval enclosures—

dolmens similar to those of Western Europe,—and almost always surrounded by circles of upright stones. The silence of historians respecting them need not make us doubt their extreme antiquity, for did it not take a very long time to induce the scientific men of our day to turn their attention to Algeria at all?

The exploration of Tunisia has enabled us to study the Stone age in that district, and a few years ago it was announced that nearly three thousand objects of different types had been found in thirteen different localities.[1] My son found near Gabes an immense number of small worked flints not unlike a human nail, the origin and use of which no one has been able to determine. The association of weapons and implements roughly finished off, with chips and stones still in the natural state, bears witness to the existence at one time of workshops of some importance. The recent discoveries of Collignon correspond with those in Algeria, and complete our knowledge of the basin of the Mediterranean.

In the Cave of Hercules, in Morocco, which Pomponius Mela spoke of as of great antiquity in his day, have been found a great many worked flints, such as knives and arrow-heads. We shall refer later to the important monument of Mzora and the menhirs surrounding it, the builders of which certainly belonged to a race that lived much nearer our own day than did the inhabitants of the Cave of Hercules.

The south of Africa is not so well known as the north, and the difficulty of making explorations is a great obstacle to progress. For some centuries, how-

---

[1] Belluci: "L'Eta della Pietra in Tunisia," Roma, 1876, *Bol. della Soc. Geog. Italiana*, 1876.

ever, polished stone hatchets from the extreme south of the continent have been preserved in the museums of Leyden and Copenhagen, under the name of *thunder-stones*, or *stones of God*. A great many are found in British South Africa, especially at Graham's Town and Table Bay.[1] Gooch, after describing the physical configuration of the Cape, says that stone implements are found in all the terraces at whatever level of the Quaternary deposits. With these stone objects were found a good many fragments of coarse hand-made pottery, that had been merely baked in the sun, and was strengthened with good-sized pieces of quartz. Similar peculiarities are noticed in ancient European pottery. We shall have to refer again to these singular analogies, one of the chief aims of this book being to bring them into notice.

In the torrid regions between the Vaal and the Zambezi rivers, we find traces of a race of a civilization different from that of the savages conquered by the English. At Natal the gradual progress of these unknown people can be traced step by step. To the earliest period of all belong nothing but roughly hewn flints, and no traces of pottery have been found; then follow flint arrow-heads of more distinct form, and here and there fragments of sun-dried pottery. Of more recent date still are polished stone weapons and more finely moulded pottery; whilst to the latest date of all belong weapons of considerable variety of form, better adapted to the needs of man, and with these weapons were found huge stone mortars which had been used for crushing grain, and bear witness to the use of vegetable diet.

---

[1] "The Stone Age of South Africa," *Journ. Anth. Institute*, 1881.

We also meet with important ruins in the Transvaal. Some walls are still standing which are thirty feet high and ten thick, forming imperishable memorials of the past. They are built of huge blocks of granite piled up without cement. We know nothing of those who erected them; their name and history are alike effaced from the memory of man, and we know nothing either of their ancestors or of their descendants.

In the Antipodes certain curious discoveries point to the existence of man in those remote and mysterious times, to which, for want of a better, we give in Europe the name of the Age of the Mammoth and the Reindeer; and everything points to the conclusion that man appeared in the different divisions of the earth about the same time. Probably the first appearance of our race in Australia was prior to the last convulsions of nature which gave to that continent its present configuration. "Scientific studies," says M. Blanchard,[1] " lead us to believe that at one period a vast continent rose from the Pacific Ocean, which continent was broken up, and to a great extent submerged, in convulsions of nature. New Zealand and the neighboring islands are relics of this great land."

In the Corrio Mountains in New Zealand, at a height of nearly 4,921 feet above the sea-level, have been found flints shaped by the hand of man, associated with a number of bones of the Dinornis, the largest known bird. Other facts bear witness to an extinct civilization, which we believe to have been extremely ancient, but to which, in the present state of our knowledge, it is impossible to assign a date. In the island of Tonga-Taboo, one of the Friendly group, is a

---

[1] *Revue des Deux-Mondes*, March 1, 1878.

remarkable megalith, the base of which rests on uprights thirty feet high, and supports a colossal stone bowl which is no less than thirteen feet in diameter by one in height. In the same island is a trilithon consisting of a transverse bar resting on two pillars provided with mortises for its reception. The pillars weigh sixty-five tons, and a local tradition affirms that the coralline conglomerate out of which they were hewn was brought from Wallis Island, more than a thousand miles off. It is difficult to explain[1] how the makers of this trilithon managed to transport, to work, and to place such masses in position. In a neighboring island a circle of uplifted stones, covering an area of several hundred yards, reminds us of the cromlechs of Brittany. The so-called Burial-Mound of Oberea at Otaheite, if it really was constructed with stone tools, is yet more curious. Imagine a pyramid of which the base is a long square, two hundred and sixty feet long by eighty-seven wide. It is forty-three feet high. The top is reached by a flight of steps cut in the coralline rock, all these steps being of the same size and perfectly squared and polished.[2]

On a rock at the entrance to the port of Sydney a kangaroo is sculptured. In Easter Island (Rapa-Nui) La Pérouse discovered a number of coarsely executed bust statues (Fig. 4). There are altogether some four hundred of them, forming groups in different parts of the island. The excavations conducted by Pinart in 1887 have proved these figures to be sepulchral monuments. He managed to make a considerable collection of crania and human bones. Round about the crater

---

[1] De Quatrefages: *Rev. d'Ethnographie*, 1883, p. 97, etc.
[2] Sir J. Lubbock: "Prehistoric Times," pp. 483, 549.

FIG. 4.—Stone statues on Easter Island.

of the Rana-Raraku volcano, forty of these figures have been counted, all of a similar type, all cut in one piece of solid trachyte rock. In another place are eighty busts with longer noses and thicker lips, forming a group by themselves. The largest of them is some thirty-nine feet high. On the sides of the volcano, scattered about amongst the statues, have been picked up a considerable number of knives, scrapers, and pointed pieces of obsidian, which were probably tools thrown away by the sculptors of the figures.

These monuments and sculptures are certainly the work of a race very different from the present natives, who are altogether incapable of producing anything of the kind, and who retain absolutely no traditions respecting their predecessors. This complete oblivion, which may appear rather strange, is by no means rare amongst savage races, and Sir John Lubbock cites a great many very curious examples. "Oral traditions," says Broca, "are changed and distorted by each succeeding generation; and are at last effaced to give place to others as transitory, and thus the most important events are, sooner or later, relegated to oblivion."[1]

We have dwelt at considerable length in another volume[2] on the earliest inhabitants of America. Much still remains unknown in spite of the considerable and important work done of late years. The very name of the New World seems to be altogether out of place, America being as old, if not older, than any continent of the Eastern Hemisphere. Lund has brought forward weighty reasons for his theory that the central plateau of Brazil was already a country when the rest

---

[1] *Ass. française*, le Havre, 1877. *Discours d'Ouverture.*
[2] "Prehistoric America," Paris, New York, and London.

of the continent was still submerged or at least represented merely by a few small islets. This theory, however, even if it could be absolutely proved, would not help us to fix the date of the earliest presence of man in America, still less to say by what route he arrived there.

Certain facts, amongst which I would, in the first place, quote the discoveries of Dr. Abbott in the alluvial deposits of the Delaware and those recently announced

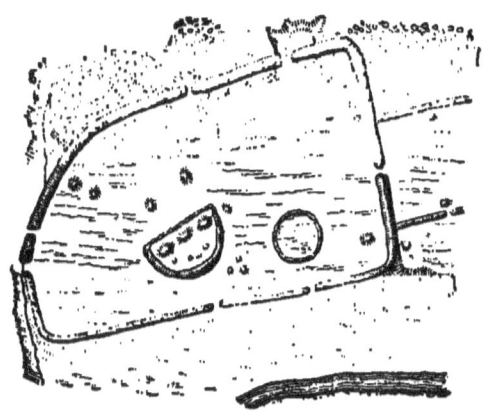

FIG. 5.—Fort Hill, Ohio.

in Nevada,[1] prove the contemporaneity of men like ourselves with the great edentate and pachydermatous mammals, which were the most characteristic creatures of the American fauna. The prehistoric inhabitants of North America were familiar with the mastodon, those of South America with the glyptodon, the shell of which on occasion served as a roof to the dwelling of primeval man, which dwelling was often but a den

---

[1] See my translation of "L'Amérique Préhistorique," chap. i., "Man and the Mastodon."—Nancy Bell.

hollowed out of the ground. As in Europe, the early inhabitants of America had to contend with powerful mammals and fierce carnivora; and in the West as in the East man made up in intelligence for his lack of brute force, and however formidable an animal might be, it was condemned to submit to, or disappear before, its master. In course of time Sedentary replaced Nomad races; shell heaps, some of marine, some of riverine and lacustrine species, but all alike mixed with a great

FIG. 6.—Group of sepulchral mounds.

variety of rubbish, were gradually piled up extending for many miles and covering many acres of ground, bearing witness to the existence of a population already considerable.

In other parts of America prehistoric races have left behind them huge earthworks, lofty masses which were probably fortifications (Fig. 5), temples, and sepulchral monuments (Fig. 6). These earthworks extend throughout North America from the Alleghany Mountains to the Atlantic, from the great lakes of Canada to the

Gulf of Mexico. The name of the people who erected them is lost, and we must be content with that of Mound Builders, which commemorate their vast undertakings.

At a period probably nearer our own, Arizona and New Mexico were occupied by other races, who built the so-called *pueblos*, which were regular phalansteries,

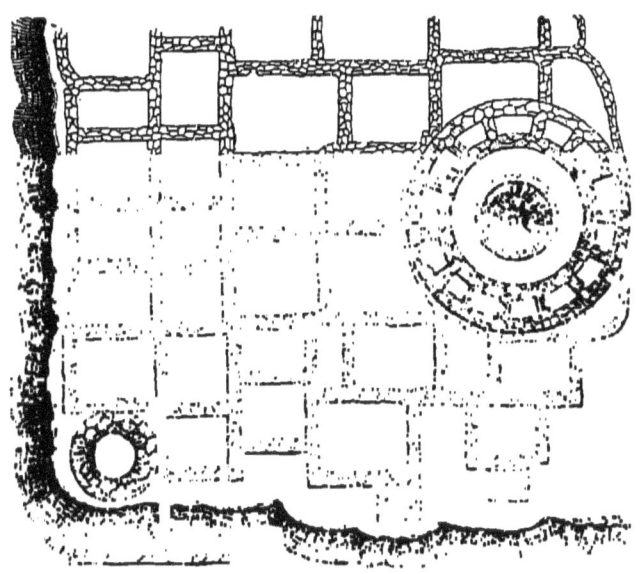

FIG. 7.—Ground plan of a pueblo of the Mac-Elmo Valley.

or communal dwellings, each member of the tribe having to be content with one wretched little cell (Fig. 7). At some distance from the men of the *pueblos* lived the Cliff Dwellers, about whom we know next to nothing; a few stone weapons and countless fragments of pottery being all they have left behind them. These men established themselves in situations which are now inaccessible, hewing out a dwelling in

Fig. 8.—Cliff-house on the Rio Mancos.

the rocks on the mountains (Figs. 8 and 9) with wonderful perseverance, and closing up the approaches with adobes or sun-dried bricks, making incredible efforts to obtain for their families what must have been at the best but a precarious shelter.[1] These prehistoric races were succeeded in America by the Toltecs, Aztecs, Chibcas, and Peruvians, all known in history, though their origin is as much involved in obscurity as that of their predecessors. Temples, palaces, and magnificent monuments tell of the wealth which gold gives, a wealth, alas, which also enervated the vital forces, so that the Spanish and Portuguese met with but little serious resistance in their rapid conquests.

Such are the facts with which we have to deal. In

---

[1] Many interesting details respecting the Cliff Dwellers are given in De Nadaillac's "L'Amérique Préhistorique," chap. v.—Nancy Bell.

the following chapters we shall consider more at length the problems they present, but already we are led to one important conclusion: in every part of the globe,

FIG. 9.—House in a rock of the Montezuma Cañon.

in every latitude, in every climate, worked flints, whether but roughly chipped or elaborately polished, present analogies which must strike the most superficial observer. "We find them," remarks an American author, "in the tumuli of Siberia, in the tombs of Egypt, in the soil of Greece, beneath the rude monuments of Scandinavia; but whether they come from Europe or Asia, from Africa or America, they are so much alike in form, in material, and in workmanship, that they might easily be taken for the work of the same men."

At a meeting of the British Association for the Advancement of Science in 1871, Sir John Lubbock showed worked flints from Chili and New Zealand with others found in England, Germany, Spain, Australia, the Guianas, and on the banks of the Amazon; which one and all belonged to the same type. More recently the Anthropological Society of Vienna compared the stone hatchets found near the Canadian lakes and in the deserts of Uruguay, with others from Catania in Italy, Angermünde in Brandenburg, and a tomb in Scandinavia, deciding that they were all exactly alike. Lastly, those who studied at the French Exhibition of 1878 the hatchets, hammers, and scrapers, the bone implements, pottery, and weapons brought from different places, the inhabitants of which had no communication with each other, could not fail to notice in their turn how impossible it was to distinguish between them. "So evident is this resemblance," says Vogt,[1] "that we may easily confound together implements brought from such very different sources."

The same observation applies to megalithic monuments. Everywhere we find these primitive structures assuming similar forms. It is difficult enough to believe that the wants of man alone, such as the craving for food, the need of clothing, and the necessity of defending himself, have led in every case to the same ideas and the same amount of progress. Even if this be

---

[1] *Congrès des Naturalistes Allemands*, Innsbruck, Sept., 1869,

proved by the worked flints, we cannot accept a similar conclusion with regard to the megalithic monuments, which imply reflection and a thought of the future far beyond the material needs of daily life. Is it not more reasonable to regard a similitude so striking as a proof of the unity of our race?

The human bones discovered are yet more convincing testimony. Excavations have yielded some which may date from the very earliest period of the existence of man upon the earth. They have been found in caves and in the river drift, beneath the mounds of America and the megalithic monuments of Europe, in the ice-clad districts of Scandinavia and of Iceland, and in the burning deserts of Africa, but not one of them owes its existence to men of a type different from those of historic times or of our own day.[1] MM. Quatrefages and Hamy in their magnificent work "Crania Ethnica," have been able to distinguish prehistoric races and indicate the area they occupied. These races are still represented, and their descendants of to-day retain the characteristics of their ancestors.

One final conclusion is no less interesting. These absolutely countless flints, these monuments of imposing size, these stones of immense weight often brought from afar, these marvellous mounds and tumuli, bear witness to the presence of a population which was already considerable at the time of which

---

[1] "Quaternary man is always man in every acceptation of the word. In every case in which the bones collected have enabled us to judge, he has ever been found to have the hand and foot proper to our species, and that double curvature of the spinal column has been made out, so characteristic that Serres made it the distinctive attribute of his human kingdom. In every case with him, as with us, the skull is more fully developed than the face. In the Neanderthal skull so often quoted as bestial, the cranial capacity is more than double that ever found in the largest gorilla." De Quatrefages: "Hommes Fossiles et Hommes Sauvages," p. 60.

we are endeavoring to make out the traces. A long series of centuries must have been needed for a people to increase to such an extent as to have spread over entire continents. And time was not wanting. Whatever antiquity may be attributed to the human race, whatever the initial date to which its first appearance may be relegated, this antiquity is but slight, this date is but modern, if we compare it with the truly incalculable ages of which geology reveals the existence. At every turn we are arrested by the immensity of time, the immensity of space, and yet our knowledge is still confined to the mere outer rind of the earth, and science cannot as yet even guess at the secrets hidden beneath that rind.

In concluding these introductory remarks, we must add that very great difficulties await those who devote themselves to prehistoric studies—difficulties such as none but those who have attempted to conquer them can realize. The rare traces of prehistoric man must be sought amongst the effects of the cataclysms that have devastated the earth, and the ruins piled up in the course of ages. We must show man wrestling with the ever-recurrent difficulties of his hard life, and gradually developing in accordance with a law which appears to be immutable. Such is the aim of this work, and it is with gratitude that we assert at the beginning that the *pianta uomo*, the human plant, as Alfieri calls our race, was endowed by the Creator from the first with a very vigorous vitality, to enable it to contend with the dangers besetting its steps in the early days of its existence, and with a truly marvellous spirit, to be able to make so humble a beginning the starting-point for a destiny so glorious.

CHAPTER II.

FOOD, CANNIBALISM, MAMMALS, FISH, HUNTING, AND FISHING.

THE first care of man on his arrival upon the earth was necessarily to make sure of food. Wild berries, acorns, and ephemeral grasses only last for a time, whilst land mollusca and insects, forming but a miserable diet at the best, disappear during the winter. Meat must certainly have been the chief food of prehistoric man; the accumulations of bones of all sorts in the caves and other places inhabited by him leave no doubt on that point. The horse, which in Europe was hunted, killed, and eaten for many centuries before it was domesticated, was an important article of diet, and was supplemented by the aurochs, the stag, the chamois, the wild goat, the boar, the hare, and failing them, the wolf, the fox, and above all the reindeer, which multiplied rapidly in districts suitable to it. The elephant bones picked up on Mount Dol and elsewhere are nearly all those of young animals; and it is probable that they had been killed for food by man. In the Sureau Cave in Belgium,[1] in that of Aurignac in

---

[1] In this cave were found the bones of 45 bears. In the Goyet Cave (which bears the number 3), were found complete sets of the bones of 12 mammoths, 8 rhinoceroses, 57 bears, 57 horses, 24 hyænas, 35 reindeer, 6 uruses, 2 lions, with the bones of a great number of goats, chamois, and boars. Dupont: "L'Homme pendant l'Âge de la Pierre," p. 86.

France, and Brixham in England, have been found complete skeletons of the *Ursus spelæus*, which had evidently been dragged in with the flesh still on them, for all the bones are in their natural position. In other caves, the thorax and the vertebræ of the skeletons were missing; the cave-man, having despatched his victim, had evidently taken only the more succulent parts into his retreat. Beasts of prey merely gnaw the comparatively tender and spongy tops of the bones, leaving the hard, compact parts untouched. In the caves that were inhabited by man, however, we find the apophyses neglected, whilst the diaphyses are split open. We cannot, therefore, make any mistake on this point, or attribute to the beast of prey what is certainly the work of man.

Whilst he evidently preferred to hunt and eat the larger mammals, man when pressed by hunger did not despise the small rodents, which were, of course, more easily captured. Amongst piles of the bones of horses and stags have been found the remains of martens, hedgehogs, and mice; and from the Thayngen Cave have been taken the bones of more than five hundred hares. In Belgium the water-rat seems to have been considered a dainty, and in the Chaleux Cave alone were found more than twenty pounds' weight of the bones of this creature, nearly all bearing traces of having been subjected to the action of fire.

The remains of birds are rarer, and Broca has remarked that the most ancient hunting implements which have come down to us; those from the Moustier Cave, for instance, were adapted rather to attack animals that would show fight than those that would simply fly or run away. The Gourdan Cave, however, has yielded the bones of the moor-fowl, the partridge, the wild duck, and even the domesticated cock and hen; the Frontal Cave, the thrush, the duck, the partridge, and the pigeon; and in other caves were found the bones of the goose, the swan, and the grouse. Milne-Edwards enumerates fifty-one species belonging to different orders found in the caves of France, and M. Rivière picked up the remains of thousands of birds in those of Baoussé-Roussé on the frontier of Italy.[1]

The skulls of the mammals had been opened, and the bones split. Brains and marrow probably figured at feasts as the greatest delicacies. Travellers, whose tales are a help to us in building up a picture of the remote past of our race, relate that the Laplanders, as soon as an animal is killed, break open its skull and devour the brain whilst it is still warm and bleeding. This was probably also the custom amongst prehistoric cave-men.

The flesh of animals was not, alas, the only meat eaten, and excavations in different parts of the globe have led to the discovery of traces of the practice of cannibalism which it is difficult not to accept.[2]

Dr. Spring noticed at Chauvaux a great many bones which were nearly all those of women and children, side by side with which lay others of ruminants belonging to species still extant. All these bones had alike been subjected to great heat, and none but those which had contained no marrow were left unbroken. This appears an incontrovertible proof of cannibalism, and

---

[1] These birds belonged to the rapaces, passeres, gallinaceous, wading, and web-footed groups. Every order is represented, and nearly all the bones were those of edible species, which had certainly served as food to man.

[2] Richard Andrée: "Die Anthropophagie eine Ethnographische Studie," Leipzig, 1887.

Dr. Spring concludes that it was certainly practised by the earliest inhabitants of Belgium. We must add, however, that other excavations in the same cave at Chauvaux prove that it was used as a burial-place, some skeletons being ranged in regular order with weapons and stone implements placed beside them.[1] M. Dupont mentions having found in the caves of the Lesse, which date from the Reindeer period, human bones mixed with other remains of a meal. He notes a similar fact in another cave that he considers belongs to Neolithic times. "But," he adds, "none of these bones bear any trace of having been struck with a flint or other tool with a view to their fracture. If any of them are broken it is transversely, and the cause of the fracture has been merely the weight of the earth above them; moreover, they show no trace of the action of fire."[2] M. Dupont, therefore, still retains some doubt of the cannibalism of the cave-men of the valley of the Lesse, and attributes the presence of the bones of the dead amongst the rubbish of all kinds accumulated by the living, to their idleness and indifference. One example at the present day tends to confirm this opinion, for travellers tell us of the same revolting carelessness amongst the Esquimaux, who cannot certainly be classed amongst cannibals.

The Abbé Chierici, speaking at the Brussels Congress[3] of the excavations in one of the Reggio caves, remarked that human bones were mixed with those of

---

[1] "Les Hommes de Chavaux et d'Engis" *Bul. Acad. Roy. de Belgique*, vol. xx., 1853; vol. xviii. (new series), 1863; vol. xxii., 1866; *Matériaux*, 1872, p. 517.
[2] "L'Homme pendant les Âges de la Pierre," p. 225.
[3] "Compte Rendu," p. 363.

animals, and that both showed traces of having been burnt. These bones date from the Neolithic period, and with them were picked up various objects of remarkable workmanship, including fragments of pottery, half a grindstone for crushing grain, and some admirably polished serpentine hatchets.

Other facts leave no doubt of the cannibalism of the earliest inhabitants of Italy. Moreover, hesitation on this point is impossible for other reasons, as Roman historians allude to the practice. Pliny,[1] in saying how little removed was a human sacrifice from a meal, adds, that it ought not to surprise us to meet with this monstrous custom amongst barbarian races, as it prevailed in ancient times in Italy and Sicily.

It is generally admitted that we can tell whether the fracture of long bones was intentional by the way in which they were broken. This fact, which is true alike with the bones of men and of animals, is the most important proof we have of the cannibalism of the men of the Stone age. To the examples already given, we can easily add others culled from France. In the Pyrenees and in the caves of Lourdes and Gourdan, for instance, human bones have been found mixed with the cinders and ashes of the hearth, and still bearing the marks of the implements with which they were broken.

At Bruniquel a human skull was found which had been opened in the same way as the heads of ruminants amongst which it was picked up, and on its external surface were deep notches, which appear to have been made with a flint hatchet. Similar traces of revolting feasts on human flesh are not at all rare; near Paris, at

---

[1] "Hist. Nat.," book vii., sec. 2.

Villeneuve-Saint-Georges, and at Varenne-Saint-Maur, for instance.[1]

The excavations in the Montesquieu-Avantès Cave, about six miles from Saint-Girons, have brought to light a hearth covered over with a layer of stalagmite; numerous fragments of human bones, crania, femora, tibiæ, humeri, and radii were found in this layer, and in that of the subjacent clay. In many cases the medullary orifice had been enlarged to make it easier to get out the marrow. It is impossible to attribute this to a rodent, for the bones gnawed by animals of that kind present a regular series of marks. The conclusion is inevitable : these bones, alike of men and of animals, were the remains of a meal.[2]

In Kent's Hole, the celebrated cave in Devonshire, amongst many objects dating from the Stone age, were found some human bones bearing traces of having been gnawed by man. The eminent anthropologist, Owen, came to a similar conclusion—that cannibalism had been practised—after examining the jaw-bone of a child found in Scotland ; and so did the Rev. F. Porter, after the excavations near Scarborough, where several skeletons were found under a tumulus, which had apparently been thrown where they were discovered by accident.

The Cesareda caves in Portugal have yielded some bones split lengthwise ; and beneath the dolmen near the village of Hammer, in Denmark, human bones and those of stags have been found half gnawed, and showing only too clearly the origin of the marks upon them. Worsaae quotes similar facts at Borreby, Chantres re-

---

[1] Belgrand : "Le Bassin Parisien," vol. i., p. 232.
[2] *Bull. Soc. Anth.*, 1869, p. 476.—*Ac. des Sciences*, 1870, first week, p. 167.

fers to the same thing in the caves of the Caucasus, Captain Burton at Beitsahur, near Jerusalem, Wiener in the *sambaquis* of Brazil, even in deposits which he considers of recent origin.[1]

Brazil is not the only part of the American continent in which we find traces of the use of this revolting food. In the kitchen-middings of Florida Wyman found human bones, which had been intentionally broken, mixed with those of deer and beavers. The marrow had been taken from all of them and eaten by man. Yet more recent discoveries of a similar kind have been made in New England.[2]

We must, however, add that many of these facts are contested. Every people considers it a point of honor to repudiate the idea that its ancestors fed on human flesh, and yet everywhere history tells us of the practice of cannibalism. Herodotus speaks of it amongst the Androphagæ and the Issedones, people of Scythian origin; Aristotle amongst the races living on the borders of the Pontus Euxinus; Diodorus Siculus amongst the Galatians; and Strabo, in his turn, says: "The Irish, more savage than the Bretons, are cannibals and polyphagous; they consider it an honor to eat their parents soon after life is extinct."[3]

From the ancient tombs of Georgia have been taken human bones that have been boiled or charred, which were doubtless those of the victims eaten by the assistants in the *fêtes* which have ever accompanied funeral rites.

In the fourth century of our era Jerome speaks of

---

[1] *Archives du Musée National de Rio de Janeiro*, vol. i., 1876.
[2] See my translation of De Nadaillac's "Prehistoric America," pp. 53, 58, and 59."—N. D'Anvers.   [3] "Geography," book iv.

having met in Gaul with the Attacotes, descended from a savage Scotch tribe, who fed on human flesh, and that though they possessed great herds of cattle and flocks of sheep, with numbers of pigs, for whom their vast forests afforded excellent grazing grounds [1]; and though the Scandinavian kitchen-middings have not so far yielded any traces of the practice of cannibalism, Adam of Bremen, who preached Christianity at the court of King Sweyn Ulfson, represents the Danes of his day as barbarians clad in the skins of beasts, chasing the aurochs and the eland, unable to do more than imitate the cries of animals and devouring the flesh of their fellow-men.[2]

Nothing could exceed the barbarity of the Mexican sacrifices, the numbers of the victims, and the refinements of torture to which they were subjected. Prisoners, who had often been fattened for months previously, perished by thousands on the altars. The palpitating flesh was distributed amongst the assistants, and a horrible custom compelled the priests to clothe themselves in the still bleeding skins of the unfortunate wretches, and to wear them until they rotted to pieces.

Without going back to an antiquity so remote, in how many different regions of Africa and America, and in how many islands of Polynesia have not our sailors and missionaries reported the practice of cannibalism in our own day? It is difficult, therefore, not to believe, although the fact cannot perhaps be very distinctly proved, that the first inhabitants of Europe

---

[1] "Opera," vol. ii., Migne edition, p. 335. Richard, of Cirencester, says that the Attacotes lived on the shores of the Clyde, beyond the great wall of Hadrian.

[2] Schweden's "Urgeschichte," p. 341.

degraded as were the conditions of their existence, did eat human flesh and acquire a depraved taste for it; impelled thereto not only by the pangs of hunger, but also by a revolting superstition.

Animals, however, were very plentiful all around. Stags, elks, aurochs, horses, and the large pachyderms multiplied very rapidly in the wide solitudes, the pasture lands of which afforded them a constantly renewed supply of food, and the beasts of prey in their turn found an easy prey in the ruminants.[1] The ways of animals do not change, and the travellers who are exploring the interior of Africa tell us that now, as in the day we are trying to recall, hundreds of elephants and rhinoceroses congregate in a limited area, whilst innumerable herds of giraffes, zebras, and gazelles graze peacefully in the presence of man, whose destructive powers they have not yet learnt to dread.

Delegorgue speaks of one lake peopled by more than one hundred hippopotami, and of a region less than three miles in diameter containing six hundred elephants. Livingstone tells us that he saw troops of more than four thousand antelopes pass at a time, and that these animals showed absolutely no fear. We may give a yet more curious instance. Captain Gordon

---

[1] The felidæ were very numerous in Europe in Quaternary times. We may mention two species of lions, *Leo nobilis* and *Leo spelæus*, the latter often confounded with the *Felis spelæus* of such frequent occurrence in French caves, two species of tigers, *Tigris Edwarsiana* and *Tigris Europæa*, the largest of the Quaternary felidæ, which was some twelve feet long. We also know of seven species of leopards, six species of cats, from the Serval to a little felis smaller than our domestic cat; two species of lynx, and lastly the *machairodus*, a beast of prey of considerable size, characterized by having exceptionally long upper canines serrated like a saw. Probably these beasts of prey were not all contemporaries, but succeeded each other. (Bourguignat: "Histoire des Felidæ Fossiles en France dans les Dépôts de la Période Quaternaire," Paris, 1879.)

Cumming, crossing the plains stretching away on the north of the Cape, saw troops of gazelles and antelopes, compelled by a long drought to migrate in search of the water indispensable to them, and he describes with enthusiasm one of these migrations, telling us that the plain was literally covered with animals, the hurrying herds defiling before him in an endless stream. On the evening of the same day, a yet more numerous herd passed by in the same direction, the numbers of which were absolutely incalculable, but which, according to Cumming, must have exceeded several hundred thousand.

Such must have been animal life in Europe in Quaternary times. "Grand indeed," cries Hugh Miller, "was the fauna of the British Isles in those days. Tigers, as large again as the biggest Asiatic species, lurked in the ancient thickets; elephants, of nearly twice the bulk of the largest individuals that now exist in Africa or Ceylon, roamed in herds; at least two species of rhinoceros forced their way through the primeval forest, and the lakes and rivers were tenanted by hippopotami as bulky and with as great tusks as those of Africa."[1]

Material proofs of the presence of animals are not wanting. The accumulation of coprolites in the cave of Sentenheim (Alsace) bears witness to the number of bears which once haunted it. Nordmann took from a cave near Odessa 4,500 bones of ursidæ, associated with no less numerous relics of the large cave-lion and cave-hyena.[2] The Külock Cave, now some six hundred

---

[1] "Testimony of the Rocks," p. 127, Edinburgh and Boston, 1857.
[2] *Ossements Fossiles Trouvés à Odessa.* The cave-hyena resembles that now living at the Cape.

and fifty feet above the river, contained the remains of no less than 2,500 bears, and similar relics occur by thousands in the osseous breccia of Santenay and in the cave of Lherm, where they form a regular ossuary. It would be easy to quote similar facts from Belgian, German, and Hungarian caves. In almost every case the position of the skeletons seems to show that the bears sought a last refuge in the caves, and that death had surprised them during their winter sleep. Pachyderms were no less numerous than bears. The remains of mammoths are found from the north of Europe to Greece and Spain, and we meet with them in Algeria, in Asia from the Altai Mountains to the Arctic Ocean, and in America in Mexico and Kentucky. They seem to have entrenched themselves especially in Siberia, whence tusks are still exported as an article of commerce. In the extreme North, those parts of Wrangel's Land which have been explored are strewn with the bones of mastodons, and in some parts of Sonora and Columbia these remains form almost inexhaustible deposits.

Animals of the cervine and equine groups were, if possible, yet more numerous. M. Piette estimates the number of reindeer whose bones he has picked up in the Gourdan Cave as over 3,000, and the number of cervidæ found at Hohlefels is positively incalculable.

In 1826, Marcel de Serres called attention to the great number of the bones of animals of the equine family found in the neighborhood of Lunel-Viel; at Solutré, the remains of horses cover a great portion of the slope which stretches from the eastern side of the mountain to the bottom of the valley. Here are found those vast accumulations to which the inhabitants of the valley give the characteristic name of *horse-walls*. The number of horses, the bones of which have gone to form these walls, may be estimated without exaggeration at 40,000. The bones are mixed together in the greatest confusion, many of them show traces of having been burnt, and the flesh of the horse was evidently the favorite diet of the people of Solutré.[1]

At first man obtained by force, often aided by strategy, the animals he coveted. He had not yet learnt to tame them and reduce them to servitude. Neither the reindeer nor the horse was as yet domesticated, and neither in the caves nor in the various deposits elsewhere has a complete skeleton been found, but only— a very significant fact—the bones on which had been the greater amount of flesh. The absence of any remains of the dog, so indispensable an animal in the keeping of flocks, is yet another proof that domestication was still unpractised.

It was with most miserable weapons, such as a few stones, scarcely even rough-hewn, and a few flint arrows, that the cave-man did not hesitate to attack the most formidable animals, and with such apparently inadequate means he succeeded in wounding and even killing them. The French Museum possesses mammoth and rhinoceros bones bearing fine scratches produced by the weapons which had been used to despatch the animals. The metacarpus of a large beast of prey, found at Eyziès, retains marks no less clear, and the skull of a bear from Nabrigas has in it a large wound which must have been made by a missile of some kind.

In Ireland a stone hammer was found wedged into

---

[1] Ducrost and Arcelin: "Stratigraphie de l' Éboulis de Solutré," *Mat.*, 1876, p. 403. *Archives du Muséum d'Hist. Nat. de Lyon*, vol. I.

the head of a *Cervus megaceros;* in Cambridgeshire, the skull of an *Ursus spelaeus* still containing the fragment of a celt which had given the animal his death-blow; at Richmond (Yorkshire) the bones of a large deer which had been sawn with a flint implement. The fine collection in the University of Lund, contains a vertebra of a urus pierced by an arrow, and the Copenhagen Museum, the jaw of a stag pierced by a fragment of flint. Steenstrup mentions two bones of a large stag into which stone chips had penetrated deeply, and in which the fracture had been gradually covered over by the bony tissue. A bone of some bovine animal with an arrow deeply imbedded in it has been taken from a bed of peat in the island of Moën, celebrated for its tumuli and the number of objects found in them. At Eyziès, a flint flake has been found firmly fixed in one of the lumbar vertebræ of a young reindeer, and M. de Baye mentions an arrow with a tranverse edge stuck in the bone of a badger.[1] The Abbé Ducrost found a flint arrow-head sticking in a vertebra of a horse.

Nor were those already mentioned the only animals on which man made war. We shall speak presently of the contests with each other, which began amongst men in the very earliest days of humanity. Human bones, perforated by arrows and broken by stone hatchets, bear ineffaceable traces to this day of homicidal struggles.

In many places fresh-water and marine fish were utilized as food by man. In the numerous caves of the Vezère, in those of Madeleine, Eyziès, and Bruniquel, excavations have brought to light the vertebræ and

---

[1] M. de Baye found a great many similar arrow-heads in the Petit-Morin caves.

other bones of fishes, amongst which predominate chiefly those of the jack, the carp, the bream, the chub, the trout, and the tench—in a word, all the fish which still people our rivers and lakes. In the Lake Stations of Switzerland, fish of all kinds are no less abundant. At Gardeole, amongst the bones of mammals have been found the shells of mollusca, and remains of the turtle and of goldfish. Fish was not, however, caught by all these primitive people, not even by all those who lived by the sea. In researches carefully carried on for years in the Maritime-Alps, M. Rivière found neither fishing-tackle nor fish-lines.

Whilst the cave-men of the south of France seem not to have utilized any but fresh-water fish, the Scandinavians, at a date probably less remote however, did not hesitate to brave the ocean. The kitchen-middings contain numerous remains of fish, amongst which those of the mackerel, the dab, and the herring are the most numerous. There, too, we meet with relics of the cod, which never approaches the coast, and must always be sought by the fisherman in the open sea.

Although we are in a position to assert that men were able to catch fish during every prehistoric period, if not in every locality, we can speak less positively of their mode of doing so. The earliest fishing-tackle was doubtless of the most primitive description: the bone of some animal, a fragment of hard wood, or even a fish-bone pointed at each end and pierced with a hole, served their purpose (Fig. 10). The Exhibition of Fishing-Tackle held at Berlin in 1880 contained several such implements, some of wood, others of bone. Others have also been found in the Madeleine Cave, and in different stations of the ancient inhabitants of Switzerland. It is interesting to note their resemblance to those still in use amongst the Esquimaux.

FIG. 10.—1. Fragments of arrows made of reindeer horn from the Martinet Cave (Lot-et-Garonne).—2. Point of spear or harpoon in stag-horn (one third natural size).—3. and 4. Bone weapons from Denmark.—5. Harpoon of stag-horn from St. Aubin.—6. Bone fish-hooks pointed at each end, from Wangen.

Prehistoric man also turned to account the teeth of animals. We may quote in this connection the molars of a bear from which the enamel and the crown have been removed, and the thickness of which has been lessened by rubbing (Fig. 11). The small flints picked up in great numbers in the department of the Gironde also date from a remote antiquity; they are sixteen millimetres long by four wide, and though we cannot assert it as a fact, they are supposed to have been used for catching fish.

The Museum of Lund possesses two flint fish-hooks of a curved shape, one of them, which is four centimetres long by nearly three wide, was found by the seashore; the other and smaller one came from the

FIG. 11.—Bears' teeth converted into fish-hooks.

FIG. 12.—Fish-hook made out of a boar's tusk.

shores of Lake Kranke.[1] Fish-hooks made of bone, which is more easily worked than flint, very soon replaced those in that material. They are numerous in the Lake Stations of Wangen, Mooseedorf, and St. Aubin. Some are cut out of the horns of oxen, others of stags' antlers; while others again are made of boars' tusks (Fig. 12), but all alike greatly resemble modern forms. The peat-bogs of Scania have yielded a bone fish-hook seven centimetres long, which is considered very ancient, and the Museum of Stettin possesses one, also very old, found in a marly deposit of Pomerania. We must not forget to mention, although it probably

---

[1] Nilsson: "The Primitive Inhabitants of Scandinavia."

belongs to a much more recent period, a fish-hook in reindeer horn, now in the Christiania Museum. It was found in a tomb in the island of Kjelnoë, not far from the Russian frontier. Numerous skeletons, wrapped up in swathings of birch-bark, repose in this tomb. All around lay fragments of pottery, lance- and arrow-heads,[1] and combs of reindeer horn, the date of which it is impossible to fix exactly.

In America, stone fish-hooks are rare. The most ancient are of bone, and resemble those now in use. They have been picked up in Dakota, and in the cinder-heaps of Madisonville (Ohio), in Indiana, in Arkansas, on the shores of Lake Erie, and in a kitchen-midding of Long Island. The greater number of them are polished, and some of them have near the top a hole by which they could be fastened to a line or cord. The fish-hooks of California are remarkable for their rounded forms and sharply curved points; the top was covered with a thick layer of asphalt to which the line was probably fastened. They are numerous in all the islands of the Pacific coast. In that of Santa Cruz Schumacker excavated a tomb which must have been that of a fish-hook manufacturer, for care had been taken to place near the deceased, not only the implements of his craft, but also a number of fish-hooks in various stages of advancement. The Californians used the shells of the *Mytilus Californicus* and *Haliotis* to make fish-hooks, and these were even more curved than those made of bone. The shape seems but little suited

---

[1] Captain Edward Johnson, who travelled about in New England from 1628 to 1632, relates that the children there spent their days in shooting at the fish that appeared on the surface of the water, succeeding in catching them with marvellous skill. "A History of New England," London, 1654.

for fishing, but even in our own day the natives of the Samoa Islands use similar tackle with great success. The Indians of the northwest coast make fish-hooks of epicea wood, and those of Arizona utilize for the same purpose the long spikes of the cactus. It is very probable that European as well as American races knew how to use wood in the same manner. During the lapse of centuries, however, these fragile objects have been reduced to dust, and we are unable to make any further conjectures on the subject.

The use of bronze, the first metal to be generally employed, does not seem to have introduced any great modifications in fishing-tackle. Bronze fish-hooks are, however, thinner and lighter than those in other materials, and resemble those in use amongst fishermen at the present day. A certain number have been found in the Lake Stations of Switzerland, in lakes Peschiera and Bourget, as well as in Scotland, Ireland, and the island of Fünen off the coast of Denmark. We must not omit to mention the important foundry of Larnaud, or the *cache* of Saint-Pierre-en-Chatre, both so rich in bronze objects. In America, where the copper mines of Lake Superior were worked at a remote antiquity, a few rare copper fish-hooks have been found, the greater number in the Ancon necropolis.[1] Gold fish-hooks are comparatively more numerous, and have been discovered in New Granada and the Cauca State.[2] One of these was found some forty-nine feet below the surface of the ground, and as there is no trace of disturbance, we cannot assign to it a recent origin. The gold

---

[1] Reiss and Steübel: "The Necropolis of Ancon in Peru," London and Berlin.
[2] *Matériaux*, 1870, p. 348.

fish-hooks are about four inches long, and look like big pins with the lower end bent back upon the upper.

Other fishing implements were also used by our prehistoric ancestors. At Laugerie-Basse a rough drawing shows us a man striking with a harpoon a fish that is trying to escape. These harpoons were generally made of reindeer horn (Figs. 10 and 13). Some had but one barb, others several. One of the largest was found in the Madeleine Cave; it is eight inches long, and has three barbs on one side and five on the other. Most of these weapons have a notch in the handle, with the help of which they could be firmly fastened to a spear or lance. Different fashions prevailed in different localities, and sinews, leather thongs, roughly plaited cords, creepers, and resinous substances were often pressed into the service.

Many harpoons have been found in the caves of the south of France; others come from Belgium, from Keyserloch

FIG. 13.—*A*, a large barbed arrow from one side of the Plantade shelter (Tarn-et-Garonne). *B*, lower part of a barbed harpoon from the Plantade deposit.

in Germany, Kent's Hole in England, from Conches, Wauwyl, and Concise in Switzerland. Excavations in Victoria Cave, near Settle (Yorkshire), yielded amongst other interesting objects a bone harpoon cut to a point and with two barbs on either side. On the banks of the Uswiata, a little Polish river flowing into the Dnieper, two harpoons made out of the horns of some bovine animal were found, both in perfect preservation, and with several barbs.[1] Count Ouvaroff, in an excellent work published a little before his death, mentions a bone spear from the shores of the Oka, and Madsen and Montelius speak of Scandinavian harpoons. These weapons must have been especially useful in the North during the severe frosts of winter. The fisherman made a hole in the ice and struck the fish with his harpoon when the poor creatures came up to the surface to breathe.

From the most remote times the Americans knew how to make and use harpoons. As many as twenty-eight different kinds are known.[2] In some the barbs are bilateral, but most of them have them on one side only. Some, however, are made of stag or elk horn, and one harpoon from Maine is made of whalebone. A harpoon-point found near Detroit (Michigan) is nearly a foot long by one inch thick. Excavations in a rock shelter in Alaska yielded a harpoon which lay side by side with some of the most ancient Quaternary mammals of America. A good many copper harpoon-heads are also mentioned; one of the largest from Wisconsin is ten inches long. Others have been found in the island of Santa Barbara (Cali-

---

[1] *Wiadomosci Archéologiznc*, No. iv., Warsaw, 1882.
[2] Ch. Rau: "Prehistoric Fishing in Europe and America."

fornia) and in Tierra del Fuego, where the natives of the present day still use similar ones. These harpoons with barbs are by no means simple weapons, the idea of which would naturally occur to the human mind, so that it is really extremely strange to find weapons so entirely similar in regions so different and so widely separated from one another. This constant similitude in the working of the genius of man is, as we shall never tire of repeating, one of the most striking facts revealed by prehistoric researches.

Herodotus tells that the Pœni (Carthaginians) plunged baskets into the water and drew them up full of fish. It is probable that the Lake Dwellers of Helvetia employed a similar process, but these ancient Swiss were already more advanced than that. They knew how to cultivate hemp, to spin it, and to make nets of it; the remains of some of these nets have often of late years been taken from the beds of the lakes.

It is almost impossible to class with any certainty the numerous Lake Stations of Switzerland. Some few certainly date from the Stone age, others from the transition period, between it and that of the early use of metals, or even from the Bronze age. As therefore they have been occupied at different times by different people, some of them having even been still in use in the time of the Romans, it is most difficult to fix with any precision the date to which belong the various objects mixed together beneath the deep waters of the lakes. We can only say that the nets differ very much in the size of the meshes, and the thickness of the rope used. Those found at Robenhausen are very like those in use in France at the present day. There has, in fact, been no advance in the art of making fishing-tackle since the remote days of the Lake Dwellers.

We are ignorant of the mode of manufacture of prehistoric nets. Did the Lake Dwellers, as some archæologists are disposed to think, use a loom? Did they use shuttles and rollers such as are employed by the Esquimaux and Californians of the present day? It is impossible to say, but it is supposed that the bears' teeth sharpened to a point, found in some stations, were used to tighten the meshes. These meshes were generally square, and each one was finished off with a knot of the same size at each intersection.

The lead weights so indispensable to fishermen of the present day for sinking the nets, were represented in prehistoric times by stones. These stones, which are drilled or notched, are found in all the Lake Stations. The fragments of pottery pierced with a hole, found at Schussenried, a Lake Station of the Stone age on the Feder-See (Wurtemburg), were probably used for the same purpose. In some of the Swiss Lake Stations have also been found pieces of wood and cork, pierced with one or more holes, which had certainly served as floats.

Numerous stone implements of the most primitive forms, often of rock not native to the country, have been found in some of the islands of Greece, as well as in Corsica, Sardinia, Elba, and Sicily. These discoveries bear witness to the presence of man in these islands at a very remote antiquity, though no other traces of the existence of prehistoric human beings have as yet been found there. These men can only have reached the islands by way of the sea. Boats were the only means of communication between the

Lake Dwellers of Switzerland and the mainland, and, as we have seen, the ancient Scandinavians hunted fish on the deep ocean. We must therefore admit that attempts at navigation were made in the very earliest days of humanity. Man, impelled by necessity, or perhaps only by curiosity, was not afraid to launch his bark, first upon the rivers, and later upon the more formidable waves of the sea :

> Illi robur et æs triplex
> Circa pectus erat, qui fragilem truci
> Commisit pelago ratem
> Primus.[1]

The Latin poet is right, and we cannot but admire those who were the first to brave the terrors of the deep and the horrors of the tempest; for they were gifted alike with the intelligence which conceives, the courage that dares, and the strength that achieves.

Trees torn up by the roots by the force of the waters, and floating on the surface of those waters, naturally attracted the attention of primeval man, and the first boats were doubtless the trunks of such trees roughly squared and then hollowed out with the help of fire. Later experience led to the addition of a prow which would more easily cleave the water, and a stern which would serve as a pivot. These canoes, if such a name may be already given to them, were at first guided by branches stripped of their leaves, or with long poles. Then oars or paddles were introduced, which are better for beating the water, and in later barks traces have been made out of what is supposed to have been a mast, indicating the use of a sail. The art of navigation may now be said to have been

---

[1] Horace: "Odes," book i., ode iii.

inaugurated. In different parts of Europe have been found boats which certainly belong to very remote times, though their exact date cannot be fixed. Their construction greatly resembles that of the pirogues of the Polynesians, or the kayaks of the Greenlanders. One of the most ancient, now in the Berlin Provincial Museum, was taken from a peat-bog of Brandenburg.[1] It is 27 feet long and scarcely 16 inches wide.

Sir W. Wilde describes several boats from the marshes and peat-bogs of Ireland,[2] many of which have handles cut in the wood at the ends, by the help of which they could easily be dragged along overland. Sir W. Wilde adds that the Irish also used *curraghs*, or *coracles*, which were mere wicker frames covered with the skins of oxen. These frail barks introduce us to a new mode of navigation; they are met with not only in the different countries of Europe, but also in America, and were in use there in pre-Columbian times. Even more interesting examples have been found in Scotland.[3] Towards the close of last century a pirogue was taken from the ancient bed of the Clyde at Glasgow. Since then have been discovered, at depths varying from six to twelve feet, more than twenty similar boats. The deposits in which they lay had formerly been beneath the sea, but are now some twenty feet above the level of the ocean. Great changes have therefore taken place since these barks were launched upon the waves.[4] Their mode of con-

---

[1] Friedel: "Führer durch die Fischerei Abtheilung."
[2] "A Catalogue of the Antiquities in the Museum of the Royal Academy."
[3] *Proceedings of the Royal Academy of Scotland*, vol. iii. Dr. R. Munro: "Ancient Scottish Lake Dwellings or Crannoges," Edinburgh, 1882.
[4] Geikie, *Edinburgh New Philosophical Journal*, vol. xv. De Lapparent: "Traité de Géologie," first edition, p. 518.

struction is an excellent indication of the date to which they belong. Some which are hollowed out of the trunks of oaks by the help of fire, or with a blunt tool, are supposed by Lyell to date from the Stone age. Others have clean-cut notches, evidently made with metal implements. Some are made of planks joined together with wooden pegs, and one canoe found in County Galway even contained copper nails. Most of the boats from the bed of the Clyde seem to have foundered in still waters. Some, however, were discovered in a vertical position, others had the keel uppermost, and these latter had evidently sunk in a storm. In one of these boats was a diorite hatchet of the kind characteristic of Neolithic times; another, the wood of which was perfectly black, had become as hard as marble, and in it was a cork plug. Then, as now, the oak which yields cork was foreign to the cold climate of Scotland.

We will quote but one of the discoveries made in England. In 1881 a canoe, hollowed out of the trunk of a tree, was found at Bovey-Tracey in Devonshire. It lay in a deposit of brick-earth more than twenty-nine feet below the highest level reached by the waters of the Bovey.[1] It was more than thirty-five inches wide, and its length could not be exactly determined, the workmen having broken it in getting it out. An eminent archæologist is of opinion that this boat dates from the Glacial epoch, perhaps even from a more remote time. If this hypothesis, the responsibility of which we leave to him, be correct, this is the most ancient witness in existence of pre-

---

[1] "Discoveries in the more Recent Deposits of the Bovey Basin," *Trans. Devonshire Ass.*, 1883.

historic navigation. We must also mention a boat found near Brigg (Lincolnshire), a few feet from a little river that flows into the Humber. It is about forty-five feet long by three and a half feet wide, and is some three feet high. The prow is fluted. There are no traces of a mast, though the size of the boat must have made it difficult to manage with oars alone.

One of the pirogues preserved at the Copenhagen Museum is made of one half of the trunk of a tree, some six feet long, hollowed into the shape of a trough, and cut straight at both ends.[1] It is curious to compare this clumsy structure with a boat recently discovered beneath a tumulus at Gogstadten in Norway (Fig. 14), of which, though it dates from historic times, we give a drawing, as it is a good illustration of the progress made. The dead Viking had been laid in his boat, as the most glorious of tombs; with its prow pointing seawards, for would not the first thoughts of the chief when he awoke in another life be of the sea which had witnessed his triumphs? The sides of the boat, which was more than sixty-six feet long and fifteen across the widest part, were painted, and around it was ranged a series of shields lapping over one another like the scales of a fish, and not unlike the designs seen in the celebrated Bayeux tapestry. A block of oak intended to receive the mast was placed in the centre of the boat, and near the skeleton were oars some fifteen feet long and similar in form to those now in use.

In laying the foundations of the bridge of Les Invalides, Paris, a boat was taken out of the mud which had lain there for many centuries. Like most of those

---

[1] "Nordische Oldsager i der kongelige Museum i Kjobenhawn."

FIG. 14.—Ancient Scandinavian boat found beneath a tumulus at Gogstadten.

already mentioned, it had been made out of a single trunk roughly squared. Everywhere, we must repeat once again, man's original ideas were the same; everywhere the tree floating on the top of the water excited his curiosity, and became the starting-point for one of his most important discoveries. Traces of similar attempts at navigation are met with in other parts of France; a canoe was found in the Loire near Saint Mars, and the Dijon Museum possesses another from the same river, the latter some sixteen feet long, and traces have been made out of what are supposed to have been seats, but may have been mere contrivances for strengthening the boat. A canoe taken last year from the bed of the Cher is of the shape of a trough closed at the end by pieces of wood fixed by means of vertical grooves. The prow had been shaped in the first instance in the trunk itself, and it was probably owing to an accident, a collision perhaps, that it had had to be mended in this way (Fig. 15).

The Lake Dwellers of Switzerland owned boats from the time of their first settlement in their water homes. One of them found at Robenhausen is more than ten feet long, and is very shallow, varying from six to eight inches. Like most of those already mentioned, it was hollowed out of the trunk of a tree, bulging out towards the centre, and rounded at the ends. So far none but stone tools have been found at the station of Robenhausen, so that we must presume that it was with such tools that the boat was made. The lakes of Bienne and Geneva, and the stations of Morges and Estavayer have also yielded boats which are doubtless less ancient than those of which I have just spoken. In nearly all of them the prow is curiously pointed.

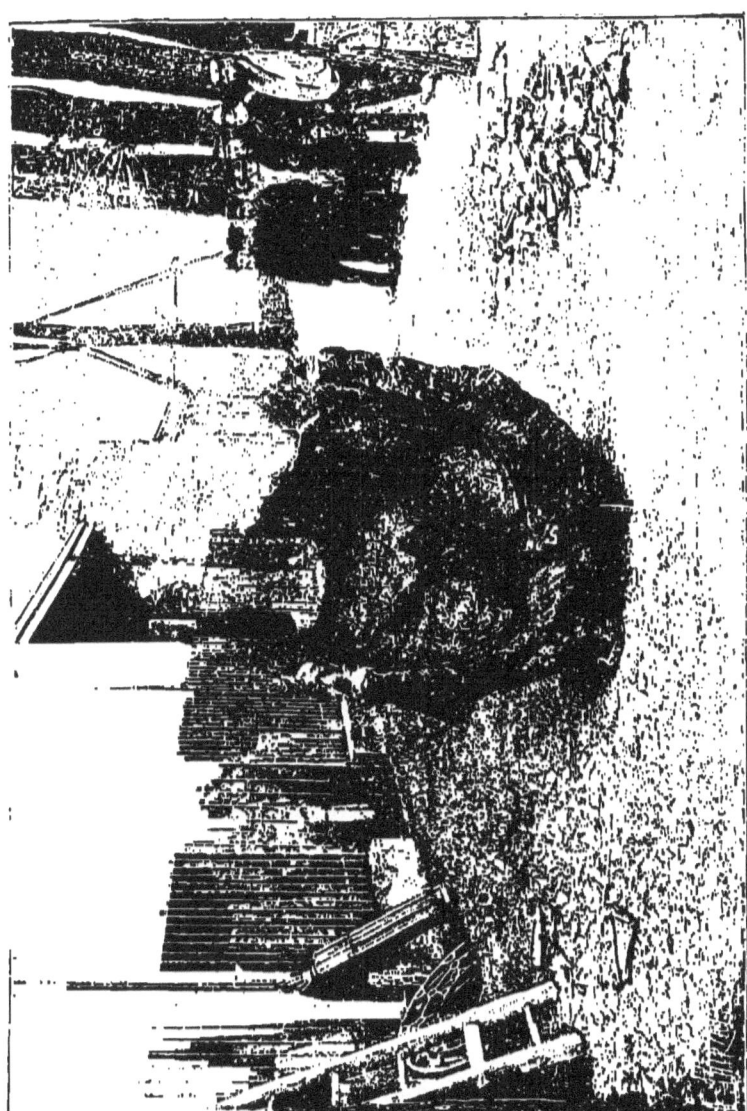

Fig. 15.—Ancient boat discovered in the bed of the Cher.

One of them from the Lake of Neuchâtel, large enough to hold twelve people, has a beak at the stern and a rounded prow; but there is no sign of any contrivance for keeping the oars in place.

Lastly, a boat has been found in Switzerland some 3,900 feet above the valley of the Rhine, but no one can say how it came to be at such a height.

These canoes, whatever their shape or size, can only have been worked by means of oars, yet oars have seldom been found. The Geneva Museum, however, has

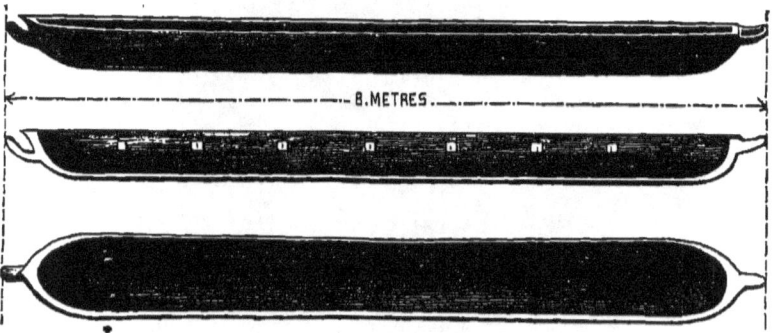

FIG. 16.—A lake pirogue found in the Lake of Neuchâtel. 1. As seen from the outside. 2 and 3. Longitudinal and transverse sections.

one which came from the muddy bed of an Italian lake, and others are preserved in the Royal Museum of Dublin, which have every sign of great antiquity. In default of the actual oars, we have other proofs of their use. Gross[1] mentions a boat (Fig. 16) in which holes had been made in the upper parts of the sides to hold the oars. In 1882 a pirogue was taken out of the bed of the Rhone at Cordon (Ain), which had been half buried in the mud of the river. The wood was black and the upper portions were charred, but the middle part

---

[1] "Les Proto-Helvètes," *Nature*, 1880, 1st week, p. 151.

was still intact and very hard. The holes, pierced in the sides at regular intervals, may have served to keep the oars in place. The position of the rowers at the bottom of the boat was very unsatisfactory. It was not, however, until later that we find seats so placed as to enable the rowers to put out all their strength. At a recent meeting of the Anthropological Society (July 21, 1887) M. Letourneau observed that the rudder came into use very slowly. It was not known to the Egyptians or to the Phœnicians, nor, which is still more strange, to the Greeks and Romans. Their vessels, whatever their size, were guided by two large oars *(gubernaculum)* placed in the stern. The Chinese appear to have been the only people who were acquainted with the use of the rudder from time immemorial. It is probable that from them it passed to the Arabs and even perhaps to the people of Europe.

A discovery made near Abbeville is the most ancient example we have of the use of the mast. Some works being executed at the fortifications of the town, brought to light a boat which must have been some twenty-one feet long. Two projections form part of the planking, leaving between them a rectangular space in which the mast was probably fixed.[1]

Professor Gastaldi speaks of a wooden anchor taken from a peat-bog near Arona, beneath which was a pile dwelling. He dates it from the time when the use of bronze was already beginning to spread in the north of Italy. A stone of peculiar shape found at Niddau is, they say, an *Ankerstein* (anchor stone). This name is also given by Friedel to a good-sized round lump of sandstone with a deep groove near the middle. Lastly,

---

[1] " Mém. Soc. d'Emulation d'Abbeville," 1867.

Kerviler, in crossing a basin of the Bay of Penhouet, near Saint-Nazaire, found several stones which had evidently been used to keep boats at anchor, and with the aid of which we can get an idea of the methods employed by ancient navigators (Fig. 17).

Such are the only details we have on the important subject of prehistoric anchors, but we may add that ancient fishermen probably ventured but a short dis-

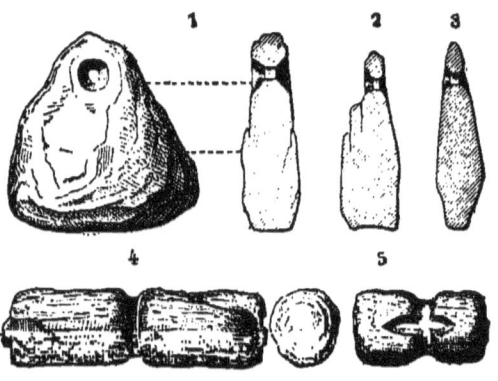

FIG. 17.—Stones used as anchors, found in the Bay of Penhouet. 1, 2, 3, stones weighing about 160 pounds each. 4 and 5, lighter stones, probably used for canoes.

tance from the land, and would not need anchors, as they could easily carry their light boats on shore.

We have now passed in review the conditions of the life of our remote ancestors, noting the animals that were their contemporaries, and the fish that peopled the watercourses near which they lived. We have studied the earliest efforts at navigation, made in the pursuit of fish, and we must now go back to examine the weapons, tools, and ornaments of these ancient peoples, and trace in those objects the dawn of art. This will be the aim of our next chapter.

CHAPTER III.

WEAPONS, TOOLS, POTTERY; ORIGIN OF THE USE OF FIRE, CLOTHING, ORNAMENTS; EARLY ARTISTIC EFFORTS.

THE Vedas show us Indra, armed with a wooden club, seizing a stone with which to pierce Vritra, the genius of evil.[1] Does not this call up a picture of the earliest days of man upon the earth? His first weapon was doubtless a knotty branch torn from a tree as he hurried past, or a stone picked up from amongst those lying at his feet. These were, however, but feeble means with which to contend with formidable feline and pachydermatous enemies. Man had not their great physical strength; he was not so fleet a runner as many of them; his nails and teeth were useless to him, either for attack or defence; his smooth skin was not enough protection even from the rigor of the climate. Such inequality must very quickly have led to the defeat of man, had not God given to him two marvellous instruments: the brain which

---

[1] Indra, the all-seer, to whom it is given to pierce the cloud, personified by Vritra, and "to open the receptacles of the waters with his far-reaching thunder-bolts," is of course the sun, the worship of which was one of the earliest and most natural instincts of humanity; whilst Vritra was in the first instance merely the symbol of the cloud, intervening between heaven and earth, shutting out from men the light of the sun, and keeping back the refreshing rain. The gradual conversion of these natural phenomena into a good and a malignant power, ever struggling for the mastery, is a forcible illustration of the way in which myths are evolved.—TRANS.

conceives, and the hand which executes. To brute force man opposed intelligence, a glorious struggle in which he was sure to come off victorious, for in the words of Victor Hugo, "Ceci devait tuer cela." The huge animals of Quaternary times have disappeared for ever, whilst man has survived, victor over Nature herself. Even before his birth, an immutable decree had ordained that nothing on the earth should check his development.

Man alone amongst the countless creatures around him knew anything of the past, and he alone was able to predict the future. Even apes, however great the intelligence that may be attributed to them, have remained very much what they were from the first. In vain has one generation succeeded another; they still obey the dictates of their brutal instincts, as their ancestors did before them; and if apes continue to propagate their species thousands of years hence they will remain what we see them to be now. Dogs, too, will remain dogs, elephants will continue to be elephants; beavers will make their dams exactly like those of the present day, wasps will never learn to make honey as bees do, and bees will never be able, like ants, to bring up plant-lice to be their servants, or to enslave other families. Their instincts are incapable of progress, and in their earliest efforts they reach the limit assigned to them by the Eternal Wisdom. To man alone has it been given to understand what has been done by his predecessors, to walk more firmly in the path along which they groped, to pronounce clearly the words they stammered. Without a doubt we descend from the men who lived in the midst of primeval forests, or amongst stagnant marshes, dwelling in caves, for the possession of which they often had to fight with the wild beasts around them. These men, however, knew that one result achieved would lead to another, if similar means were used; they saw that a pointed stone would inflict a deeper wound than a blunt one on the animal they hunted, and therefore they learnt to sharpen stones artificially; the skins of beasts, flung over their shoulders, protected them from cold, and they learned to make garments; seeds sprouted around them, and they learned to plant them; they noticed the effect of heat upon metals, and tried to mix them; wild animals wandered around them, and they learned to reduce them to slavery. Every bit of knowledge won, and every progress made, became the starting-point for fresh acquisitions, fresh advances, which thenceforth remained forever the common heritage of the human race.

It was thus that experience early taught our remote ancestors that rock chips more easily under the blows of a hammer when fresh from the quarry; and everywhere men learnt to choose the stone best suited to their purpose. For hatchets, wedges, and hammers, they used jade and kindred substances, such as fibrolite, diorite, and basalt, which were at the same time extremely durable, and very impervious to blows. For spear- and arrow-heads, knives, saws, and all instruments requiring sharp points and cutting edges, they employed quartz, jaspar, agate, and obsidian, according to the situation of the worker; all these materials, though extremely hard, being easily split into thin sharp flakes. The blocks of stone were very methodically cut up; they were, in fact, to use a very appropriate expression of M. Dupont's, scaled *(écaillés)*. We give drawings of a few of these implements (Figs. 18, 19, and 20), which illustrate the earliest efforts of man, efforts which may be looked upon as the starting-point of all those industries which in the course of centuries have developed results which it is impossible to contemplate without astonishment.

The most ancient tools which have come down to us were clumsy and heavy, cut on both sides and pointed

Fig. 18.—Scraper from the Delaware Valley.

Fig. 19.—Implement from the Delaware Valley.

(Fig. 20). They may vary in material, in size, and in finish, but they can always be easily recognized.[1] Were they man's only weapons? We hesitate to believe it, and the careful researches of M. d'Acy add to our incredulity.[2] He tells us that at Saint-Acheul,

---

[1] De Mortillet: "Le Préhistorique," Paris, 1883, p. 133.
[2] "Limon du Plateau du Nord de la France," Paris, 1878. Acheuléen et Moustérien: *Revue des Questions Scientifiques*, October, 1880. *Bul. Soc. Anth.*, 1884, 1887.

which was the very cradle of these strange discoveries, the almond shape is found mixed with the pointed amongst the Moustier flints, so that what is true in one place is not in another, and any general conclusion would certainly be premature.

It would take us a long time to enumerate the countries where tools of the Chelléen[1] type have been found. They are met with in the valleys of the rivers of

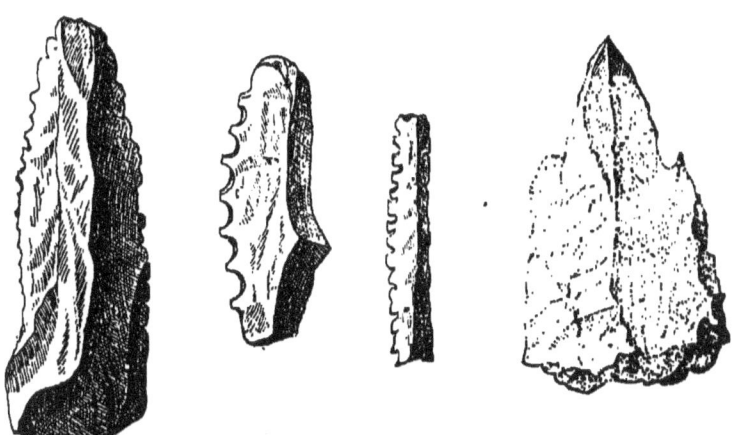

Fig. 20.—Worked flints from the Lafaye and Plantade shelters (Tarn-et-Garonne).

France, now imbedded in the flinty alluvium, now strewn upon the surface of the soil. Though rare in Germany, they are found in abundance in the southeast of England, and it is to this period that must be assigned the discoveries at Hoxne, and in the basins of the Thames, the Ouse, and the Avon. Similar discoveries have been frequent in Italy, Spain, Algeria,

---

[1] *Chelléen*, so called from their having been found at Chelles (Seine-et-Marne), where the remains of the *Elephas antiquus*, the most ancient of the pachyderms now known in Europe, was associated with these tools.

and Hindostan. Dr. Abbott speaks of the finding of such implements in the glacial alluvium of the Delaware (Figs. 18 and 19), Miss Babitt in the alluvial deposits of the Mississippi, Mr. Haynes in New Hampshire, Mr. Holmes in Colombia, and other explorers in the basin of the Bridget and at Guanajuato in Mexico. Everywhere these implements are identical in shape and in mode of construction, and very often they are associated with the bones of animals of extinct species.

Sometimes these Chelléen tools (the French call them *coups de poing*) have retained at the base a projection to enable the user to grasp them better; these certainly never had handles, but it will not do to draw any general conclusions from that fact; and an examination of the collection of M. d'Acy, the most complete we have of relics of the Chelléen period, proves on the contrary that certain tools could not have been used unless they had been fixed into handles.

In the following epoch, to which has been given the name of Moustérien, from the Moustier Cave (Dordogne), we already meet with more varied forms, including scrapers, saws, knife-blades, and spear- or arrow-heads, with the special characteristic of being cut on one side only. These implements are found not only in the alluvium as are the Chelléen *coups de poing*, but also in the cave or rock-shelter deposits. Amongst the mammalian remains with which they are associated are those of the mammoth, the *Rhinoceros tichorhinus*, the elk, the horse, the aurochs, the cave-lion, the cave-hyena, and the cave-bear, remarkable for the constancy of their characteristics. The *Elephas antiquus* and the *Rhinoceros Merckii* that belonged to the preceding period have now completely passed away, and the reindeer, now appearing for the first time, are still far from numerous.

In the Solutréen period, so named after the celebrated Lake Station of Solutré, we find stalked arrow-heads with lateral notches,[1] flint-heads of the form of laurel leaves, which are remarkable for their regularity of shape and delicacy of finish; as compared with those of previous periods, the forms are much more delicate and elegant. Many of the caves of the south of France belong to this period. It is difficult to mention them all, and even more difficult to make out a complete list of contemporary mammalia; the deposits generally actually touch those of another period, and the separation of the objects in them has not always been made with all the care that could be wished. At Solutré, remains of the horse predominate; whilst in other places those of the reindeer are met with in considerable quantities, and with them are found the bones of the cave-bear, the wild cat (a creature considerably larger than the tigers of the present day), and of the mammoth, which lived on in Europe many centuries.

Lastly to the Madeleine period, so named after the Madeleine Cave (Dordogne), and considered one of the most important of the cave epochs, belong tools and weapons of all manner of shapes and materials, including bone, horn, and reindeer antlers; from this time also date barbed arrows and harpoons, bâtons of office, telling of social organization; the engravings and carvings on which bear witness to the development of artistic feeling. On the other hand, the flint arrow-heads and knife-blades are not so finely cut; we see that man had learned to use other materials than stone.

---

[1] De Mortillet: " Musée Préhistorique," pl. xvi. to xix.

The reindeer is the most characteristic animal form of the Madeleine period.

To the times we have just passed in review succeeded others of a very different kind, to which has been given the general name of Neolithic. The fauna, probably under the influence of climatic and orographic changes, underwent a complete transformation; the mammoth, the cave-bear, the megaceros, and the large felidæ died out, the hippopotamus was no longer seen, except in the heart of Africa; the reindeer and other mammals that love to frequent the regions of perpetual snow, retired to the extreme north; and in their place appeared our earliest domestic animals, the ox, the sheep, the goat, and the dog. Man, who witnessed these changes, continued to progress; he abandoned his nomad for a sedentary life; he ceased to be a hunter, and became an agriculturist and a shepherd. Everywhere we meet with traces of new customs, new ideas, and a new mode of life. This progress is especially seen in the industrial arts. Metals it is true are still unknown, but side by side with tools, which are merely chipped or roughly cut, we find for the first time hatchets, celts, small knife-blades, and arrow-heads admirably polished by the long-continued rubbing of one stone on another. Polishers, so much worn as to bear witness to long service, are numerous in all collections, and rocks and erratic blocks retain incisions which must have been used for the same purpose.[1]

It is impossible to enumerate the number of polished hatchets which have been found; their number is simply incalculable. Of all of them, however, those of

---

[1] M. de Mortillet enumerates 127 polishers found at various points in thirty departments of France. "Le Préhistorique," first edition, p. 534.

Scandinavia are the most remarkable for delicacy of
workmanship. With the fine hatchets of Brittany,
may be compared the blades found at Volgu, and preserved in the Museum of Copenhagen, and those in
pink, gray, and brown flint, from the Sordes Cave in
the south of France; but we cannot fix the date of the
production of any of them. One of the great difficulties of prehistoric research, a difficulty not to be got
over in the present state of our knowledge, is to distinguish with any certainty the periods into which an
attempt has been made to divide the life-story of man
from his first appearance upon earth.

Was there any abrupt transition from one period to
another? Must we accept the theory of a long break
caused by geological phenomena, and the temporary
depopulation which was one of the consequences of
these phenomena? Did the new era of civilization
date from the arrival of foreign races, stronger and
better fitted than those they succeeded for the struggle
for existence? Or are these changes merely the result
of the natural progress which is one of the laws of our
being? These questions cannot now be solved, and if
the industries which are at the present moment the object
of our researches, bear witness to the employment of a
new process, that of polishing, we are bound to add
that everywhere Palæolithic forms are still persistent.
Flints, merely chipped, are clumsy tools, but there is
no break in their series till we come to the splendid
specimens from Scandinavia or from Mexico. Of the
seven types of the Solutréen period, six are met with
in the time now under consideration.[1] Five types of
Solutréen javelins have also been found in the Durfort

---

[1] Piette: *Ass. Franç. pour l'Avancement des Sciences*, Nantes, 1875, p. 909.

Cave, and beneath the dolmens of Aveyron and of Lozère. Neolithic weapons, such as those found in the Moustier Cave, are not so numerous, but the type adopted there is not such a fine one nor so carefully finished, which accounts for its having been more rarely copied. If we examine the knives, awls, scrapers, and saws, we come to the same conclusion, although comparison is not so easy. "A knife is always a knife, an awl is always an awl," remarks M. Cartailhac; "they were made at every period, and their resemblance to each other proves nothing with any certainty."

Rounded stones of granite or sandstone seem however to have been weapons peculiar to the Neolithic period. Dr. Pommerol recently spoke at the Anthropological Society of Paris, of two such rounded stones picked up in the Puy-de-Dôme. Similar stones have been discovered at Viry-Noureuil, and M. Massénat has one in his collection from Chez-Pourré. Are not these rounded stones of a similar character to the *bolas* flung by the ancient Gauls, and still in use amongst the inhabitants of the pampas of South America?

As we have already remarked, man from the earliest times must often have held in his hands the stones which served him as weapons or as tools. The marks of hammering on the smooth surfaces, the rounded projections and the grooves worked in these stones, were evidently made to prevent the hand or the thumb from slipping. Soon, however, reflection led man to understand the increase of force he would gain by the addition to the stone of a handle of wood or horn, stag or reindeer antler. This addition of a handle was simple enough: the workman merely bound it to the hatchet with fibrous roots, leather thongs, or ligaments taken from the gut of the animals slain in the chase (Fig. 21). At first sight we are astonished at the results obtained with such wretched materials, but it is impossible to dispute them, for we have seen the same thing done in our own day.

Other hatchets, chiefly those of a small size, were fixed into sheaths made of stag-horn, and two chief types of them have actually been made out.[1] The

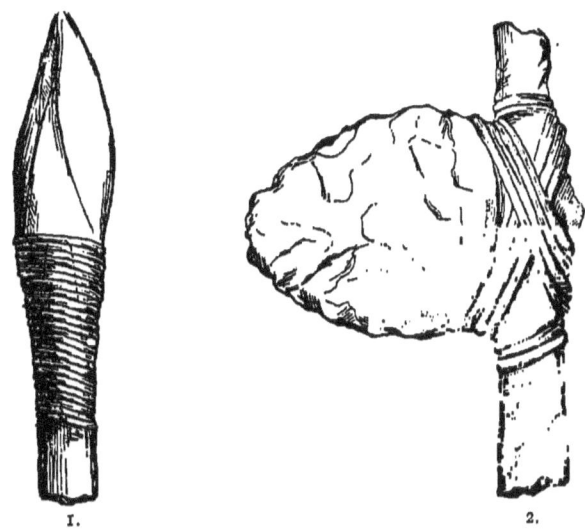

FIG. 21.—1. Stone javelin-head with handle. 2. Stone hatchet with handle.

sheaths of the first type are short and end in quadrangular heads. They are found most frequently in Switzerland, in the basins of the Rhone and of the Saône, and throughout the south of France. Those of the second type are pierced with a hole large enough to pass the handle through. These are found in the northwest of France, in Belgium, and in England.

---

[1] De Mortillet: "Le Préhistorique," p. 544; "Musée Préhistorique," figs. 431 to 434.

Flint arrows of triangular or oval form, notched or stalked, were everywhere used for a considerable length of time. They are found in the numerous caves of France, beneath the *antas* of Portugal, in the tombs of Mykenæ, as well as among the Aïnos of Japan and the Patagonians of South America. Their use necessarily involves that of a bow, yet we do not know of a single weapon such as that, or of one that could take its place, dating from Palæolithic times. Probably the rapid decomposition of the wood of which bows were made has led to their disappearance. De Mortillet[1] mentions a bow found in a pile-dwelling in a bog near Robenhausen, which he ascribes to the Neolithic period. Another is known which was found at Lutz, also in Switzerland. To all appearance the most ancient bows of historic times greatly resemble these two prehistoric examples.

Though flint was the material *par excellence* of Quaternary times for weapons and tools, it could not long suffice for the ever-growing needs of man. Our museums contain a complete series of bone or stag-horn implements such as darts, arrow-heads, barbed arrows, harpoons, fibulæ, and finely cut needles often pierced with eyes (Fig. 22). The invention of barbs is worthy of special notice; the series of points made the blow much more dangerous, as the projectile remained in the flesh of a wounded animal which was not able to get it out. But this was not the only object of the barbs. Arranged symmetrically on either side of the arrow they kept it afloat in the air like the wings of a bird, which may perhaps have suggested their use and increased the effect and precision of the shot.

---

[1] "Musée Préhistorique," fig. 410.

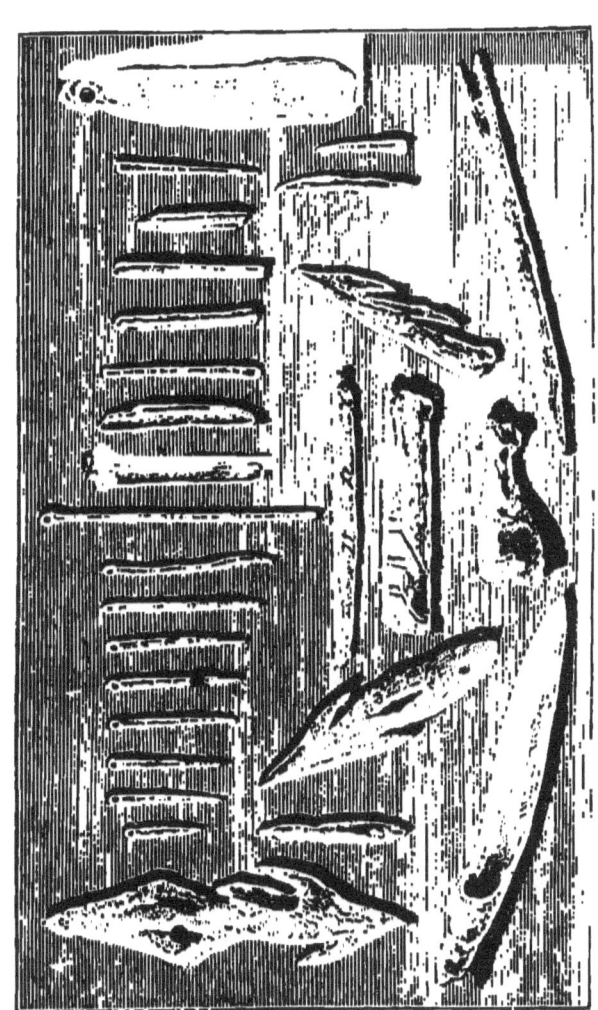

FIG. 22.—1. Fine needles. 2. Coarse needles. 3. Amulet. 4 and 6. Ornaments. 5. Cut flint. 7. Fragment of a harpoon. 8. Fragments of a reindeer antler with signs or drawings. 9. Whistle. 10. One end of a bow (?). 11. Arrow-head. (From the Vache, Massat, and Lourdes caves.)

The Marsoulas Cave has yielded one bevelled arrow shaft, made of reindeer antler, with a deep groove on the surface. A similar arrow-head was found in the Pacard Cave, and in other places arrows have been found with one or more grooves on the surface. Were these grooves or drills intended to hold poison, and was man already acquainted with this melancholy mode of destruction? We know that the use of poison was known at the most remote historic antiquity.[1] The Greeks and Scythians used the venom of the viper, and other peoples employed vegetable poisons. There is nothing to prevent our believing that similar methods were in use in prehistoric times.

FIG. 23—Amulet made of the penien bone of a bear, and found in the Marsoulas Cave.

There is no doubt that it is the caves of the south of France which have yielded the most interesting objects; needles with drilled eyes, and barbed arrows have been picked up in considerable numbers at Eyziès, Laugerie-Basse, at Bruniquel, Massat, and in the Madeleine Cave. Dr. Garrigou mentions some reindeer or roebuck antlers found in Ariège caves, which had been made into regular stilettos. In the deposits at Lafaye were found stilettos or bodkins, varying in length from two to six inches; needles measuring from nineteen to one hundred and five millimetres and provided with eyes; at Marsoulas were found

---

[1] Lagneau: "De l'Uusage des Flèches empoisonnées chez les Anciens Peuples l'Europe," *Ac. des Insc.*, 2d November, 1877.

an amulet made of the penien bone of a bear (Fig. 23), some pendants, and some pointed pieces of bone which astonish us by the delicacy of their workmanship, and the drawings with which they were adorned.

At Paviland, Dr. Buckland discovered a wolf bone cut to a point. Kent's Hole yielded a number of needles resembling those of the Madeleine Cave; at Aggtelek (Hungary) were found some bones of the cave-bear pointed to serve as daggers, cut into scrapers

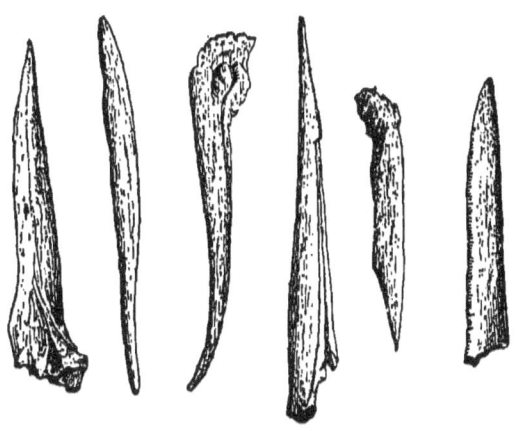

Fig. 24.—Various stone and bone objects from California.

or pierced to serve as amulets or ornaments. In Belgium, objects very similar to these have been found made of reindeer antler and dating from the most remote times. The antlers moulted by the reindeer in the spring were in especial request.

Excavations in the sepulchral mounds near San Francisco (California) have yielded thousands of bone implements (Fig. 24). Others similar to them have been found in the layers of cinders at Madisonville

(Ohio) and beneath the numerous kitchen-middings of the coasts of the Atlantic and Pacific.

The processes employed by the cave-men were very simple. In one of the excavations superintended by him, M. Dupont[1] picked up the radius of a horse bearing symmetrically made incisions executed with a view to getting off splinters of the bone. These splinters were rounded by rubbing either with chips of flint, or on such polishers as are to be seen in any of the museums; then one end was sharpened, and the other, if need were, pierced with a hole. It is astonishing to find some of them as fine as the steel needles of the present day, and with perfectly round eyes made with the help of nothing but a rough flint, and there would still be some doubt on the subject, if M. Lartet[2] had not obtained exactly similar results by working on fragments of bone with the flints he had found in these excavations. Other experiments of a similar kind were no less conclusive, for Merk[3] perforated an ivory plaque with a pointed flint which he used as a gimlet.

Some objects, which are supposed to date from Neolithic times, bear witness to an altogether unexpected degree of civilization. In the heart of Germany, in the peat-bogs of Laybach and Wörbzig on the banks of the Saale, have been found earthenware spoons of the shape of modern spatulæ; at Geraffin on Lake Bienne, a finely shaped spoon made of the wood of a yew tree; and at Lagozza, another in shining black earthenware. Lartet had already brought to light a bone implement covered with ornaments in relief which

---

[1] "Les Temps Préhistoriques en Belgique," p. 151.
[2] "Reliquiæ Aquitanicæ," p. 127.
[3] *Nature*, 1876, second week, p. 5.

POTTERY. 95

he ascribed to the Palæolithic period, and which he imagined had been used for extracting marrow; and another archæologist tells of objects in reindeer antler found in the Gourdan Cave, which he thinks were used for a similar purpose. In the Saint-Germain Museum are preserved the remains of spoons from the bed of the Seine, and in the collections of England are fragments of bone taken from beneath the West-Kennet dolmen, which were all probably employed for extracting marrow. But the most important discovery of all, which leaves no doubt on the subject, is that made by M. Perrault at the Chassey Camp, near Chalon-sur-Saône, beneath a hearth dating from Neolithic times. He collected fourteen earthenware spoons; one of them of a round shape and remarkable for its size, was unfortunately broken (Fig. 25). It is of brown earthenware with a rather rough surface mixed with bits of flint, and is so much worn that it had evidently been in use a long time. Lastly two spoons, also of earthenware, have recently been found

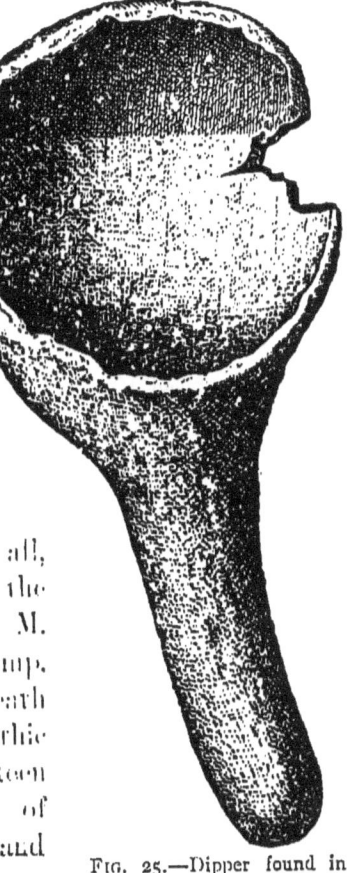

Fig. 25.—Dipper found in the excavations at the the Chassey Camp.

near Dondas (Lot-et-Garonne). The use of spoons, which certainly marked considerable progress, must therefore have spread rapidly.

Long previously, however, pottery of a great variety of form bore witness to the plastic skill of man. Everywhere we find vessels of coarse material mixed with grains of sand or mica to give more consistency to the paste which was baked in the fire, and had often no further ornamentation than the marks of the fingers of the potter. Does this pottery date from Palæolithic times, or were the earthenware vessels later additions at the time of those disturbances of deposits which are the despair of archæologists? A few examples may enable us better to answer this question.

Fraas tells us that fragments of pottery have been found in all the caves of Germany in which excavations have been made. He quotes that of Hohlefels, where he himself picked up such fragments amongst the bones of the mastodon, the mammoth, the rhinoceros, and the cave-lion, when the remains of these animals were for the first time found in Germany. In 1872, the making of the railway from Nuremberg to Ratisbon brought to light a cave of considerable depth. In its lower deposits were found nothing but the bones of hyenas, bears, and lions, of which the cave had been the resort for centuries. Among the most ancient deposits, relics of a similar kind were found in abundance, but now mixed with numerous fragments of pottery, worked flints, and fish bones, including those of the carp and the pike, with the bones of mammals, amongst which predominated those of the rhinoceros, most of them intentionally split open. At Argecilla, twenty leagues from Madrid, Vilanova discovered a regular workshop, in which were knives and flint arrow-heads, together with some very primitive pottery made of clay that had evidently been brought from a distance, as there is none in the district in which the pottery was found. In an upper deposit Vilanova collected more than two hundred implements made of diorite, a rock frequently used in Spain, some very remarkable celts of serpentine dating from the Neolithic period, and numerous fragments of very delicate pottery. Not far off he discovered another workshop, containing some very fine hatchets perfectly polished, and some keramic ware tastily ornamented. The progress made is as marked in the weapons and tools as in the pottery.

We have also seen some fragments of earthenware from the caves of Chiampo and Laglio, near Lake Como, and from that known as the Cave dei Colombi, in the island of Palmaria, which was occupied shortly before the Neolithic period. But it is Belgium which yields the most decisive proof on this subject, and a visit to the Brussels Museum is enough to convince the most incredulous. The excavations made under M. Dupont in the caves of the Meuse and the Lesse have again and again brought to light fragments of pottery, associated with the bones of Palæolithic animals. Schmerling, too, had already found similar fragments in the Engis Cave, mixed with flint weapons of the rudest description; and his discoveries have been strikingly confirmed by those recently made at Spy, near Namur,[1] and by others made by M. Fraipont.[2] In portions of this same Engis Cave not previously explored the

---
[1] In this cave, in the second ossiferous deposit, were found four fragments of pottery. De Puydt and Lohest : " L'Homme Contemporain du Mammouth."
[2] " La poterie en Belgique à l' age du mammouth," *Revue d'Anthropologie*, 1887.

7

learned professor of Liège found, in 1887, fragments of a vase of ovoid form, some flints of the Moustérien type, and some bones of extinct mammals. Most of the pottery in the Brussels Museum is black and of primitive make; some few fragments, however, are of finished workmanship. We may mention especially an ovoid vase, remarkable for its size and for its lateral projections. This vase, which is hand-modelled, came from the Frontal Cave; the clay is of blackish hue mixed with little bits of calcareous spar. M. Ordinaire, Vice-Consul for France at Callao, speaks of the *cayanes* or *macahuas*, which are earthenware basins of great symmetry of form, made by the Combos women, without turning wheels or mills of any kind. Though the elegant shape of the Frontal and other vases at first surprises us, reflection convinces us that men who could cut stones with such rare skill would certainly be able to produce equally good pottery.

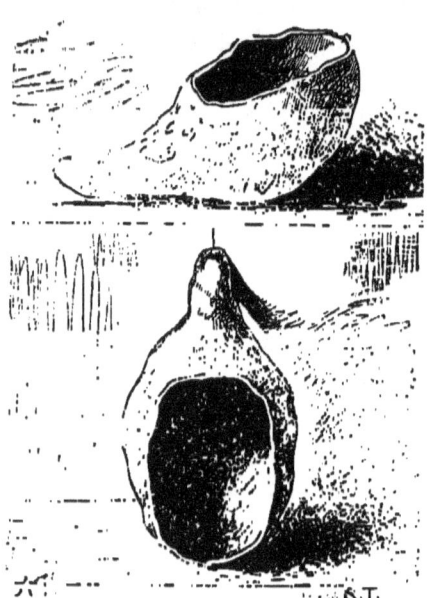
FIG. 26.—Pottery of a so far unclassified type found in the Argent Cave (France).

Similar instances may easily be quoted from France. Excavations at Solutré have yielded several fragments of yellow, hand-made pottery very insufficiently baked; and other pieces have been found in the peat-bogs of

Bastide de Béarn with the bones of reindeer, and worked flints similar to those found in Quaternary deposits. We may add that at Lafaye, Bize, and Pondre (Hainault) discoveries were made of pottery mixed with human remains and with those of animals now extinct; and in the Argent Cave (Basses-Alpes) a new type, shown in Fig. 26, has been found which merits special attention. In the very earliest days of prehistoric research the Nabrigas Cave (Lozère) was excavated by M. Joly, who found in it many fragments of pottery. In a volume published shortly before his death he relates the circumstances of his discovery, and earnestly maintains its authenticity. Later excavations, made under the direction of masters in prehistoric science, would have thrown some doubts on the assertions made by the professor of Toulouse, if MM. Martel and Launay had not brought forward a fresh proof in support of it. "On the 30th August, 1885,"[1] they say, "we picked up at Nabrigas in a deep hole, untouched by previous excavations and not displaced by water, some human bones and a piece of pottery side by side with two skeletons of *Ursus spelæus*. The human bones, of indeterminate race, included an upper left maxillary, still retaining three teeth, an incomplete mastoid apophysis, and seven pieces of crania, belonging to different individuals. The piece of pottery only measured one and a half by two and a quarter inches; the clay is gray and friable, bound together with big bits of quartz, mica, and a few particles of charcoal." There would appear to be no sufficient reason to question the exactness of a discovery so carefully studied.

---

[1] *Ac. des Sciences*, Nov. 9, 1885. We must add that at a later séance M. Cartailhac contested, if not the facts, the conclusions deducted from them.

Many eminent archæologists, however, maintain that pottery was completely unknown in Palæolithic times, and they do not hesitate to attribute to a later period any deposit in which it occurs where its presence cannot be accounted for by later displacements. M. Cartailhac declares that he has never been able to establish either in the south of France or in the central table-land a single fact which justifies us in asserting that the men of the Reindeer period, still less those of earlier epochs, knew how to make pottery. The first explorers, he adds, did not always distinguish with sufficient care the vestiges of different epochs, the relics of diverse origins. How often have bones carried along by water, or brought where they are found by animals, been mixed with those abandoned by men, or the deposits of the Neolithic period with those of the earliest Quaternary times! How often have the contents of a passage giving access to a cave been confounded with those of the cave itself! Hence deplorable errors, which it is impossible to rectify now. Evans and Geikie in their turn assert the absence in England[1] of Palæolithic pottery, and Sir J. Lubbock energetically maintains this opinion.

Doubtless these are great authorities, and yet, in view of the facts now known, it is difficult to believe that man was long a stranger to the art of making pottery. Its invention required no great effort of intelligence, and its fabrication presented no great difficulties. Man had but to knead the soft clay

---

[1] But what is the value of categorical assertions of this kind in presence of the fragments of pottery found at different levels in Kent's Hole? One of these fragments was so rotten that when placed in water it formed a black liquid mud as it decomposed.

which he trod under his foot, and the plasticity of which he could not fail to notice. This clay hardened in the sun, and hollows were formed as it shrunk—the first vessel was discovered! Experience soon taught man to replace the heat of the sun by that of the fire, and to add a few bits of some hard substance to give the clay greater consistency. These first crude and clumsy vases have been preserved to our own day as irrefutable witnesses to the work of our ancestors. Though, therefore, we cannot be sure that pottery was made in Quaternary times by all the races that peopled Europe,[1] it is impossible to deny that a great many of them were in possession of the art. This difference in the degree of civilization attained to by men living but short distances from each other need not surprise us, for all travellers report similar facts amongst contemporary savage races.

The baking of pottery is a proof that the use of fire was known in the most remote times. The existence in various places of masses of cinders, fragments of charred wood, and half-calcined bones, proves it yet more decidedly. At Solutré, at Louverné (Mayenne), at Saint-Florent (Corsica), to give but a few examples, we find large slabs of half-calcined stone, laid flat and covered with heaps of cinders and all sorts of rubbish. These slabs formed the family hearth, where man prepared his food, with the help of the fire he had learnt to ignite and to keep burning.

How did man arrive at a discovery so vital to his

---

[1] I have not space to speak here of the curious pottery found in America. The most ancient specimens, moreover, are of much later date than the Quaternary epoch. I can only refer those interested in the subject to my book on "Prehistoric America," published in French by M. Masson of Paris, and in English in America by Messrs. G. P. Putnam's Sons.

existence? The Vedas assign the origin of fire to the rubbing together in a storm of the dry branches of trees. "The first men," says Vitruvius,[1] "were born, as were other animals, in the forests, caves, and woods. The thick trees violently agitated by the storm took fire, through the rubbing together of their branches; the fury of the flames terrified the men who found themselves near them and made them take to flight. Soon reassured, however, they gradually approached again and realized all the advantages they might gain for their bodies from the gentle warmth of the fire. They added fuel to the flames, they kept the fire up, they fetched other men whom they made understand by signs all the usefulness of this discovery. The men thus assembled articulated a few sounds, which, repeated every day, accidentally formed certain words which served to designate objects, and soon they had a language which enabled them to speak and to understand one another. It was, then, the discovery of fire which led men to come together to form a society, to live together, and to inhabit the same places."

Without pausing to consider the somewhat puerile theories of Vitruvius, or the myths which testify to the importance attached to fire by primeval man, we are at liberty to suppose that a conflagration caused by lightning or by the spontaneous combustion of vegetable materials in a state of fermentation, or other similar phenomena, made known to man the power of fire, and the use it might be to him. The accidental striking together of two flints produced a spark; observation taught men to obtain a similar result by the same process; a great step in advance was made, and

---

[1] "De Architectura," book ii., c. i.

the future of humanity was assured. M. Dupont picked up in the Chaleux Cave a kidney-shaped piece of iron pyrites, hollowed out in a peculiar manner, which had evidently been used to obtain the precious spark. The Christy collection contains a granite pebble with a hole the shape of a cup, which had evidently been used to obtain fire, by rubbing round in it a stick of very dry wood. The two methods employed at the present day were therefore already in use. Lumholz tells us that the Australians of Herbert River get fire by rubbing two pieces of wood together. The Indians of the northwest of Colorado, the Yapais of the Caroline Islands, and the Mincopies of the Andaman Isles, with many other races, know no other process. We must, however, still maintain a certain reserve in dealing with the fire-obtaining implements of so imperfect a nature, and belonging to times so remote as those called prehistoric.

During bad seasons, or in the bitter cold of winter, primeval man contented himself with flinging over his shoulders the skins of the animals he had killed. He prepared these skins with flint scrapers, and sewed them together with bone needles. In hot weather man probably roamed about stark naked. Shame is not a natural instinct; education alone develops it. Writing in 1617, Fynes Morison speaks of having seen at Cork young girls quite naked, engaged in crushing corn with a stone. The Tchoutchi women, says Nordenskiöld, wear no clothes when in their tents, however great the cold. In tropical countries men, women, and children, all completely nude, went to meet the travellers who landed on their shores. Count Ursel, in a recent journey in Bolivia, in going through a little town, saw "near the public fountain some young girls already growing up making their ablutions and playing about in the garb of the earthly paradise." Travellers who visited Japan a few years ago reported that the inhabitants, without distinction of age or sex, came out of the water in a state of complete nudity, presenting a strange spectacle to European eyes. The sight of what is actually going on amongst comparatively civilized people in our own day enables us to understand better what must have been the state of things when the whole world was in a state of barbarism.

It was not until much later, in the times to which the name of Neolithic has been given, that men made stuffs, and replaced the skins of animals by lighter and more flexible garments. The inhabitants of the Lake Stations of Switzerland and of Italy cultivated hemp. At Wangen and at Robenhausen have been found shreds of coarsely woven cloth, and at Lagozza fragments of yet more primitive material. On some of these pieces it is supposed that traces of fringe and attempts at ornamentation have been made out. Even in the Périgord caves Lartet noticed some long slim needles which could not have been used for sewing skins; and he concluded that they were intended for more delicate work, perhaps even for embroidery. A new art, and one which we certainly should not have expected to find is now met with for the first time.

It is probable that our savage ancestors tatooed themselves, or painted their bodies, as did the Britons in the time of Cæsar, and as do modern savages, or, not to go so far afield, as do English sailors and some of the workingmen of France.[1] At Montastruc

---

[1] On the subject of tatooing an excellent work may be consulted by Dr. Magitot ("Ass. Franç. pour l'Avancement des Sciences," Alger, 1881).

have been picked up some fragments of red chalk, and in Mayenne of red iron ore, whilst in the cave of Spy was found a bone filled with a very fine red powder, and in that of Saltpétrière some powder of the same kind was discovered preserved from destruction in a shell. Lartet and Christy have made similar discoveries in the caves of the Dordogne; M. Dupont in a shelter at Chaleux, and M. Rivière at Baoussé-Roussé. The Abbé Bourgeois found at Villehonneur not only a piece of red chalk as big as a nut, but also an oval-shaped pebble, which had been used for grinding it, the interstices of the surface still retaining traces of coloring matter.

Red chalk was not the only substance employed. At Chatelperron, were picked up fragments of manganese; at Cueva de Rocca, near Valentia, pieces of cinnabar; in the Placard Cave, bits of black lead; and in the different stations in the Pyrenees, especially in that of Aurensan, ochre has been found which was doubtless used for the same purpose. At Solutré, ochre, manganese, and graphite were found; the last named had been scraped with a flint, and the scratches made by it are still distinctly visible. From a Westphalian cave, Schaafhausen took some dark yellow ochre; at Castern (Staffordshire), a bit of this same calcareous substance, worn with long service, was picked up; in Cantire (Argyleshire), a piece of red hematite, which had evidently been brought from Westmoreland or Lancashire; and lastly, in Kent's Hole was found some peroxide of manganese.

All these fragments of ochre or manganese, red chalk or black lead, were reduced to powder with the help of pebbles, artificially hollowed out. Everywhere we meet with these primitive mortars, and side by side with them other pebbles in their native condition, which had evidently been used for crushing the coloring matter.

A recent discovery tends to confirm the hypothesis that these colors were used for the decoration of the human body. A curious engraving on a bone represents the head and arm of a man, and on the lower part of the forearm it is easy to make out a four-sided design which evidently indicated tatooing.

In every country, and in every climate, we find men as well as women manifesting a taste for ornament. The progress of civilization has greatly increased this taste, but it existed as a natural instinct in the very earliest days of humanity, and the contemporary of the mammoth and the cave-bear, the cave-man cowering in his miserable den, sought for ornaments with which to deck himself. In the caves near the stations occupied by primeval men we find little bits of fossil coral, beads of hardened clay, the teeth of bears, wolves, and foxes, boars' tusks, and the jawbones of small mammals, fish-bones, and belemnites pierced with holes, and intended to be used as amulets or ornaments to be worn round the neck. At Lafaye, we find the incisors of small rodents serving the same purpose. The dweller in the Sordes Cave owned a precious necklace made of forty bears' and three lions' teeth. The teeth found often have on them ornamental lines, which doubtless indicated the rank or celebrated the deeds of the chief. The Abbé Bourgeois describes some stags' teeth found at Villehonneur (Charente), two of which bore scratches which may have had some signification. At Cro-Magnon were picked up some ivory

ORNAMENTS.

plaques pierced with three holes; at Kent's hole were found some oval disks measuring five by three inches, which in the delicacy of their workmanship presented a curious contrast to the other objects taken from the same cave. In the Belgian caves were picked up some thin slices of jet and some ivory plaques, and in those of the south of France fragments of steatite, cut into rectangular and lozenge shapes, whilst in the Thayngen Cave was found a pendant of lignite (Fig. 27). Men were not content with natural products; fashion demanded new forms and fresh materials.

FIG. 27.—1. Lignite pendant. 2. Bone pendant (Thayngen Cave).

But what most attracted the attention of the ancient inhabitants of France were bright-colored shells. The caves of Roquemaure have yielded nearly a thousand disks and beads made of cockle-shells; at Cro-Magnon more than three hundred shells were picked up which formed a collar or necklace, which was not however so valuable as that of the man of Sordes. M. de Maret discovered at Placard numerous shells; some belonging to ocean species still extant, and others fossils of forms now extinct. Many of them are foreign to the country in which they were found. From the most remote times therefore the inhabitants of the present department of Charente fished in the Gulf of Gascony, crossed Aquitania, visited the shell marl deposits of Anjou and Touraine, and penetrated as far as the present Paris basin. The finding of the *Cyprina Islandica* in one of the French caves proves that the prehistoric men of France even went as far away as the north of England. This is by no means an isolated fact; numerous shells from the department of Champagne had been taken to the shores of the Lesse and the Meuse. At Solutré have been found belemnites, ammonites, and Miocene shells, which were certainly never native to that district, with pieces of rock-crystal from the Alps, and beads made of a jadeite of unknown origin.

In Scotland have been found necklaces of nerites and limpets; at Aurignac, eighteen little plaques of cockle shell pierced with holes in the centre. At Laugerie-Basse, a man overtaken by a landslip had been crushed by the stones which had fallen upon him; time has destroyed his clothes, but the shells with which he had decked himself are still preserved.[1] He had worn four on his forehead, two on each shoulder, four on each knee, and two on each foot. All idea of these shells having formed a necklace must be abandoned; they were all notched, and had been used either to adorn or fasten the clothes.

The most interesting discoveries, however, were those made in the caves of Baoussé-Roussé, of which we have so often spoken. M. Rivière picked up the skeletons of two children, some thousand shells *(Nassa neritea)* artificially pierced, which had been used to deck their garments. Near an adult were other shells forming a

---

[1] *Cyprœa rufa, Cyprœa lurida (Comptes rendus Acad. des Sciences,* vol. lxxxiv., p. 1060).

necklace, a bracelet, an amulet, and a garter worn on the left leg; whilst on the head was a regular *résille* or net, not unlike that of the Spanish national costume, which net was made of small nerita shells and kept in place by bone pins.

We must also mention amongst favorite ornaments beads made of jet and of very fine ochreous clay dried in the sun, of calcareous crystalline rock, and of grayish schist, and in other places of beads of amber or of hyaline quartz, the brightness of which attracted the attention. At the station of Menieux (Charente) with flints of a type to which it is usual to give the names of Moustérien or Solutréen, excavations have yielded numerous carefully polished balls of calx, varying in diameter from one to two inches. If there had been any doubts as to their use, those doubts would have been removed by the discovery at Laugerie-Basse of a fragment of the shoulder-blade of a reindeer on which was engraved the figure of a woman wearing round her neck a necklace of clumsy round balls. Other yet stranger ornaments have been found, for which what we have said about the cannibalism of early man should have prepared the reader. Our ancestors of the Stone age adorned themselves with necklaces of human teeth, and two skeletons have been dug out wearing round their necks this token of their victories. M. de Baye possesses in his collection some round pieces of skull pierced with holes (Fig. 28), and at the meeting of the American Association in 1886, at Ann Arbor (Michigan) were presented some ornaments made of human bones from a mound in Ohio.

In taking from the gangue in which it was imbedded a skull from the megalithic monument of Vauréal,

Pruner Bey noticed a fragment of a human shoulder-blade pierced with an incision in which was fixed a little rounded piece of bone. This style of ornament seems to have remained in use for many centuries, for M. Nicaise has lately discovered at Moulin d'Oyes (Marne) a necklace made of calx balls, shells, and pendants cut out of the scales of unio shells. On this necklace hung a round piece of human cranium, and in the Gallic cemetery at Varille, the exterior lamina of a human lumbar vertebra was fastened to a necklace made of coral beads.

We are also acquainted with facts of another order, which may be mentioned in this connection. The men

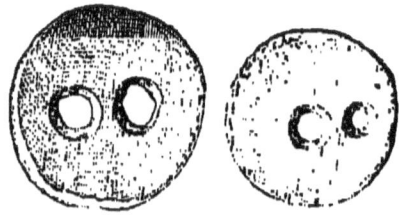

FIG. 28.—Round pieces of skull pierced with holes (M. de Baye's collection).

of Marjevols drank out of human crania; the Grenoble Museum owns a drinking-vessel of this kind; others have been discovered at Billancourt, at Chavannes, at the Chassey Camp, and at Sutz, Æfelé, and Locras in Switzerland, as well as at Brookville in the State of Indiana. Dr. Prunières possesses half a human radius, probably that of a female, carefully polished and converted into a stiletto (Fig. 29). Dr. Garrigou has an arrow-head made of a human bone, Pellegrino a fibula converted into a polisher found in the lower beds of the celebrated Castione *terremare* near Parma. At the meeting of the Prehistoric Congress in Paris in 1869, Pereira da Costa mentioned a femora converted into a sceptre or staff of office, and to conclude this melancholy list, Longpérier mentions a human bone pierced with regular openings, which, by a strange irony of death, served as a flute to delight the ears of the living.

One of the earliest necessities of human nature must have been companionship; for help was absolutely

FIG. 29.—Part of a rounded piece of a human parietal—Stiletto made of the end of a human radius—Disk made of the burr of a stag's antler.

necessary to enable man to cope with the dangers surrounding him. Tribes, formed at first of members of the same family, must have existed from the very dawn of humanity. The reindeer phalanges, pierced to serve as whistles (Fig. 30), found at Eyziés, Schussenreid, Laugerie-Basse, Bruniquel, in the Chaffaud Cave and the Belgian shelters, in a peat-marsh of Scania, in the island of Palmaria, and in many other places, were doubtless used to summon men to war or to the chase. In the Cottes Cave were found some reindeer and aurochs' shanks, which may naturally be supposed to have served the same purpose. The curious objects preserved in the Christy collections must also have been used in war or in the chase. They bear, in addition to the mark of their owner, notches of different shapes commemorating his exploits in battle or in hunting. At Solutré, MM. Ducrost and Arcelin noticed fragments of elephants' tusks, calcareous plaques, and some sandstone disks from the Trias, with notches and equidistant lines evidently having a similar purpose.

FIG. 30.—Whistle from the Massenat Collection.

From whistles to regular musical instruments the transition is simple. Without describing that mentioned by M. de Longpérier, which we cannot confidently assert to be of great antiquity, M. Piette, in one of his numerous excavations, discovered a primitive flute made of two bird bones which, when put together and blown into, produced modulations similar to those of the pipes used by the people of Oceania; the monotonous music of which is alluded to by Cook. Some time afterwards M. Piette noticed similar bones in the Rochebertier collection. So far we know of no other discovery of a similar kind.

EARLY ARTISTIC EFFORTS. 113

The curious objects known under the name of staves of office would, if it were needed, afford yet another proof that the men of the Stone age lived in societies, possessed an organization, and acknowledged a chief. The staves of office consist of large pieces of reindeer or stag antler, artistically worked and presenting a pretty uniform appearance. Their surface is decorated with carvings and engravings representing animals, plants, and hunting scenes. They are thicker than they are wide, and the care often taken to reduce the thickness is a proof that an attempt was made to combine elegance and lightness with solidity (Figs. 31, 32, 33, 34, and 35). Nearly all of them are pierced at one

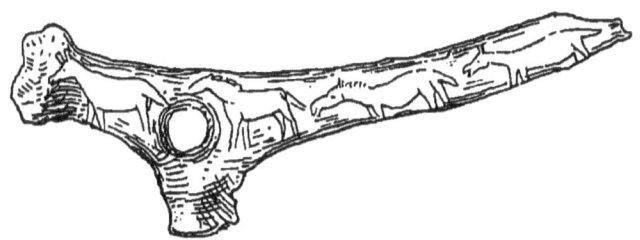

FIG. 31.—Staff of office.

end with large holes, of which the number varies. Some of these holes were later additions. May we perhaps see in them the signs of a priesthood, in which successive ranks were attained, and in which every new achievement was rewarded with a new distinction? This is difficult to prove, but these staves could not have been used as weapons or as tools; the care taken to cover them with ornaments, with the long time required for this decoration, shows the value their owners attached to them. The impossibility of any other hypothesis is the best proof we have of their use.

Amongst the marvellous objects collected by Dr. Schliemann at Hissarlik, were two fragments of reindeer antler pierced with holes presenting a singular resemblance to those we have been describing. We may also compare with them the *pogomagan*, the badge of office of Indian chiefs on the Mackenzie River, the Tartar *kemous*, the sticks on which the Australians mark by conventional signs any event of importance to themselves or their tribe, and the similar objects from Persia, Assam, the Celebes, and New Zealand. But why seek examples so far away? Is not the

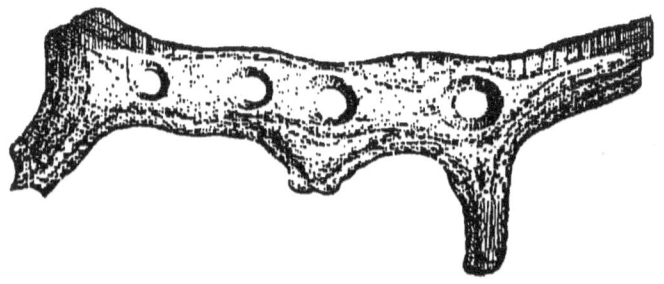

FIG. 32.—Staff of office made of stag-horn pierced with four holes.

memory of these ancient insignia preserved in our own day, and may they not have been the original forms of the sceptres of our kings and the croziers of our bishops?

These staves, of which hundreds have now been found, were picked up in many different places, including the Goyet Cave in Belgium, the caves of Périgord and Charente, and the Veyrier Station in Savoy. At Thayngen, as many as twenty-three were found, all pierced with one hole only.[1] We must not

---

[1] On this point an excellent work may be consulted by S. Reinach: "Le Musée de Saint Germain," p. 232.

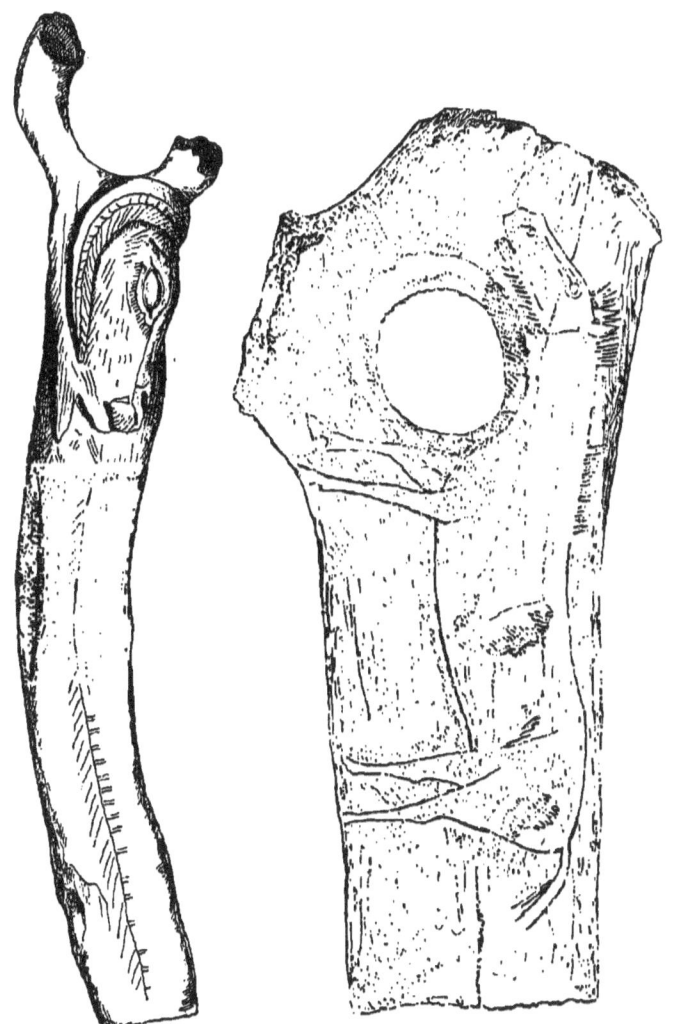

Fig. 33.—Staff of office found at Lafaye.

Fig. 34.—Staff of office in reindeer antler, with a horse engraved on it, found at Thayngen.

omit to mention amongst these relics of ages gone by, one of the most interesting found in 1887 at Montgaudier (Charente) (Fig. 35), which bears on one side a representation of two seals, and on the other of two eels, the former of which especially are executed with a truth to form, boldness of execution, and delicacy of touch which are positively astonishing when we remember that the artist (we cannot refuse him this title) had no tools at his disposal but a few miserable flints or roughly pointed bones. The hinder limbs, so strangely placed in amphibia, are faithfully rendered; each paw has its five toes, the texture of the skin can be made out, the head is delicately modelled; the muzzle with its whiskers, the eye, the orifice of the ear, all testify to real skill. The existence of the seal in the Quaternary epoch in the south of France was not known until quite recently, when Mr. Hardy found in a cave near Périgueux the remains of a seal *(Phoca grœnlandica)*, associated with quite an arctic fauna. In part at least therefore of the Quaternary period, very great cold must have prevailed in Périgord.[1]

With this staff of office were picked up some pieces of ivory covered with geometrical designs, engraved with some sharp implement, stilettos, bone needles, knives, flint scrapers, and, stranger still, the remains of the cave-lion, the cave-hyena, and the *Rhinoceros tichorhinus*, all contemporaries of the most ancient Quaternary fauna.

It was not only on the staves of office that the men of the Stone age exercised their talent. Many and varied are the subjects which have been found engraved on plaques of ivory or on stone, and incised on

---

[1] Vaudry: *Acad. des Sciences*, August 25, 1890.

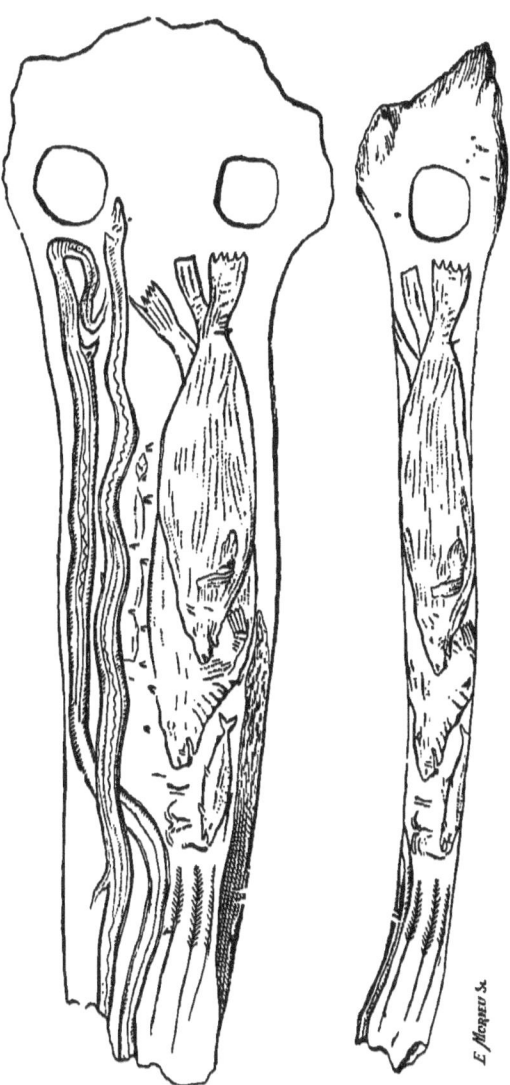

FIG. 35.—Staff of office found at Montgaudier.

bears' teeth or on stag horn. We represent one forming the hilt of a dagger (Fig. 36), and another representing a bear with the convex forehead, characteristic of the species, engraved on a piece of schist (Fig. 37), and a mammoth engraved on an ivory plaque with its

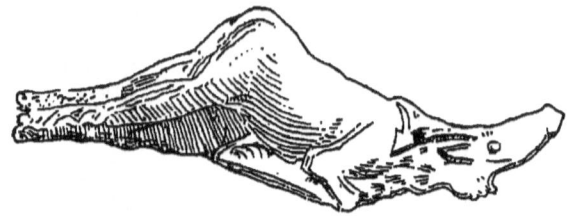

Fig. 36.—Carved dagger-hilt (Laugerie-Basse).

long mane, trunk, and curved tusks (Fig. 38). The artist who depicted these animals with such faithful exactitude evidently lived amongst them. The first discovery of this kind was made by Joly-Leterme in

Fig. 37.—The great cave-bear, drawn on a pebble found in the Massat Cave (Garrigou collection).

the Chaffaud Cave (Vienna); it was a reindeer bone on which two stags were represented.[1]

In the Lortet Cave was found the bone of a stag on

---

[1] A. Bertrand: *Acad. des Inscriptions*, April 29 and May 6, 1887.

which could be made out a representation of fish and reindeer, whilst at Sordes was discovered a bear's tooth with a seal engraved upon it (Fig. 39), at Marsoulas a piece of rib on which is depicted an animal said to be

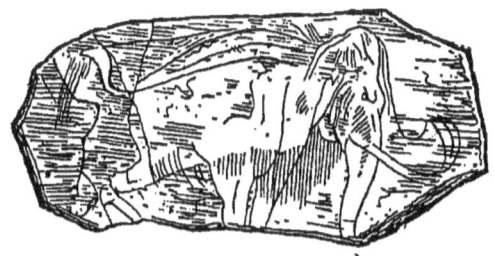

Fig. 38.—Mammoth, or elephant, from the Léna Cave.

a musk-ox (Fig. 40), and at Feyjat (Dordogne) a bird's bone bearing on it a drawing of three horses moving rapidly along. I am obliged to pass over many other most interesting examples, but I must not omit to men-

Fig. 39.—Seal engraved on a bear's tooth found at Sordes.

tion the magnificent examples which form part of the Peccadeau collection at Lisle. Cartailhac mentions some chamois, an ox, and an elephant; some engraved on the bones of deer and others on fragments of ivory, or on reindeer antlers. The art of the cave-men was now at its zenith.

But for one exception to which I shall refer again, it is curious to note that we only find these engravings and carvings, which so justly excite our astonishment in a district of limited extent, bounded on the north by the Charente, on the south by the Pyrenees and extending on the east no farther than the department of the Ariège. It is a pleasant thought that in the

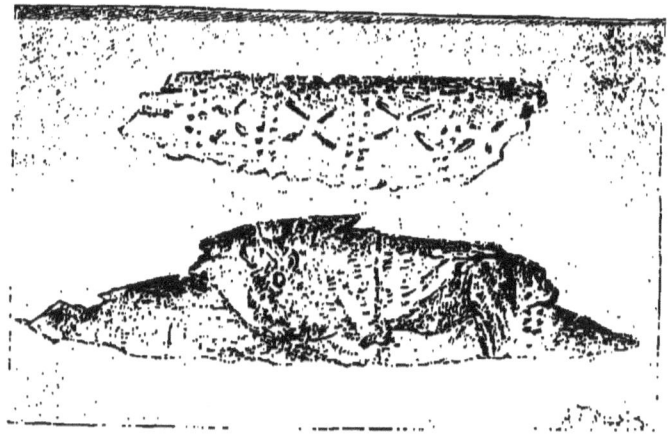

Fig. 40.—Fragment of a bone with regular designs. Fragment of rib on which is engraved a musk-ox, found in the Marsoulas Cave.

midst of their struggle for existence, and when they had to contend with gigantic pachyderms and formidable beasts of prey, our most remote ancestors, the contemporaries of the mammoth and the lion, already developed those artistic tendencies which are the glory of their descendants.

I referred above to an exceptional example of prehistoric art found beyond the borders of France. In excavations in the Thayngen Cave, on the borders of

Switzerland and Wurtemberg, twenty most remarkable examples were found, in which it is easy to recognize the horse (Fig. 41), the bear (Fig. 42), and the reindeer grazing (Fig. 43).[1] All, especially the last named, are rendered with such perfection, that it was at first supposed that they were the work of a forger. A searching inquiry has proved that they are nothing of the sort; a skilful zoölogist would have been needed to represent the *Ovibos moschatus* (Fig. 44), which re-

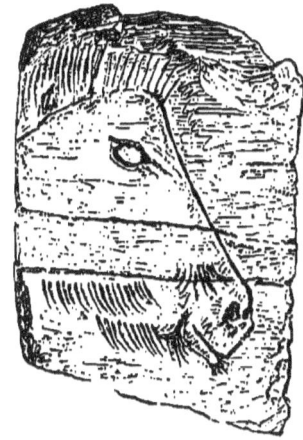 

FIG. 41.—Head of a horse from the Thayngen Cave.

FIG. 42.—Bear engraved on a bone from the Thayngen Cave.

tired many centuries ago towards the extreme north. If we do find a few rare attempts at art in other districts, they are absolutely rudimentary. The staff of office found in the Goyet Cave is of very rude workmanship. The Brussels Museum contains a few other specimens, of which the most important is a fragment of sandstone from the Frontal Cave, on which a few

---

[1] Reinach in his "Catalogue of the Saint-Germain Museum" gives the best description I know of this now celebrated reindeer.

uncertain scratches represent what looks like a stag. Some indistinct traces of engraving have been made out on the bones found in the Altamira Cave, near Santander, and recently a bone on which a kind of horse was engraved, was picked up at Cresswell's Crags, Derbyshire, in a cave known in the district as *Mother Grundy's Parlor*. This specimen, as were those of Thayngen, was associated with numerous bones of Quaternary animals, amongst which those of the hippopotamus were the most curious.

The representation of the human figure is extremely rare. I have already mentioned the young man trying to strike an aurochs which is running away from him; and the woman wearing a necklace. The former (Fig. 45), found at Laugerie, is engraved on a piece of reindeer antler about twenty-five centimetres

FIG. 43.—Reindeer grazing, from the Thayngen Cave.

long. The aurochs with its head down and quantities of bristling hair, widely open nostrils, arched and uplifted tail, presents the appearance of a terrified animal endeavoring to escape the danger threatening it. The man is naked, and has a round head, his hair is stiff and seems to stand up on the top of his skull; on the chin a short beard can clearly be made out; the face expresses the delight and excitement of the chase. The neck is long, the arm short, and the spine of unusual length. In the other example of the representation of the human figure, that of the woman

FIG. 44.—Head of *Ovibos moschatus* engraved on wood, found in the Thayngen Cave.

wearing a necklace, drawn on a piece of a shoulder-blade of a reindeer, she is seen lying by a stag, and would seem to be in an advanced state of pregnancy. The piece of bone however is broken, and the head of the woman is lost, which of course greatly lessens the value of the relic.

On a fragment of a staff of office from the Madeleine Cave is engraved a man between two horses' heads (Fig. 46). On a reindeer antler is represented a woman with flat breasts and very high hips, followed by a

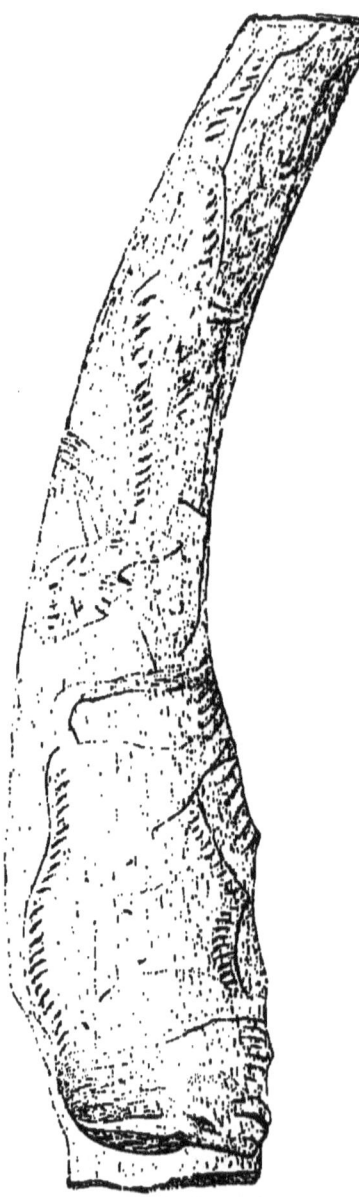

FIG. 45.—Young man chasing the aurochs, from Laugerie.

serpent; a shell from the crag near Walton-on-the-Naze had a human face roughly engraved on one side. The Abbé Bourgeois, in the excavations so fruitful of results at Rochebertier, found a rough carving of a human face (Fig. 47); M. Piette at Mas d'Azil found a little bust of a woman, carved on the root of the tooth of a horse. This statuette had a low forehead, a prominent nose, a retreating chin, and breasts of the negress type of the present day; characteristics quite unlike those of the skeletons taken from this cave or those near it. We wonder whether the artist meant to represent the features of a race other than his own.[1] M. du Bouchet mentions a rough sketch engraved on a flint discovered near Dax; the workman, doubtless daunted by the difficulties of his task, had abandoned it unfinished. It is, however, easy to tell what

---

[1] A. Milne Edwards: *Acad. des Sciences*, May 8, 1888.

it was meant for. The skull is low and flat, the nose but slightly prominent, the eyes are oblique, and neither

FIG. 46.—Fragment of a staff of office, from the Madeleine Cave.

the mouth nor the chin are finished. The magnificent collection of the Marquis de Vibraye contains a little figure from Laugerie, representing a nude woman without arms. Thin and stiff, she is chiefly remarkable for the exaggerated size of the sexual organs, and for some peculiar protuberances on the loins. We dwell upon the former peculiarity, because it is so far extremely rare, whereas certain relics of the Greeks and Romans, in spite of the comparatively advanced civilization of these two great races, are such that they can only be exhibited in private museums. Such depravity as this implies was then quite an exception among the cave-men, and but for the one example I have just mentioned, I have no phallic representa-

FIG. 47.—Human face carved on a reindeer antler, found in the Rochebertier Cave (Charente).

tions to refer to except the few from the Massenat collection, which were shown at the Exhibition of 1889.

We must not close this account of the art efforts of the men of the Stone age without mentioning the remarkable discovery by M. Siette, of flints covered with lines and geometrical designs colored with red chalk. These are the very earliest examples of the art of painting which have hitherto come to our knowledge. They bear witness to a remarkable progress made by our remote ancestors of the valleys of the Pyrenees.

We cannot more appropriately close this chapter than by quoting the magnificent verse of Lucretius, which brings before us, better than could a long description, the condition of these men, and the humble starting-point from which humanity has advanced to achieve its immortal destiny :

> Necdum res igni scibant tractare neque uti
> Pellibus et spoliis corpus vestire ferarum,
> Sed nemora atque caveos monteis sylvasque colebant
> Et frutices inter condebant squalida membra
> Verbera ventorum vitare imbreisque coactei.[1]

---

[1] "De Natura Rerum," book v., v. 951, etc.

CHAPTER IV.

CAVES, KITCHEN-MIDDINGS, LAKE STATIONS, "TERREMARES," CRANNOGES, BURGHS, "NURHAGS," "TALAYOTI," AND "TRUDDHI."

THE earliest races of men lived in a climate less rigorous than ours, on the shores of wide rivers, in the midst of fertile districts, where fishing and the chase easily supplied all their needs. These races were numerous and prolific, and we find traces of them all over Western Europe, from Norfolk to the middle of Spain. What were the homes of these men and their families? Did they crouch in dens, as Tacitus says the German tribes did in his day? In his "Ancient Wiltshire," Sir R. Coalt Hoare says that the earliest human habitations were holes dug in the earth and covered over with the branches of trees. Near Joigny there still remain some circular holes in the ground, about fifty feet in diameter by sixteen to twenty deep, known in the country under the name of *buvards*. The trunk of a tree was fixed at the bottom and rose above the ground, and the branches plastered with clay formed the roof. The floor of these *buvards* consists of a greasy black earth mixed with bones, cinders, charcoal, and worked flints. Amongst the last named, polished hatchets predominate, which proves that these refuges were inhabited in Neolithic times, but there is nothing to prevent our supposing that they were also occupied in the Palæolithic period. Ameghino gives a still more striking example of an earth-dwelling. Near Mercedes, about twenty leagues from Buenos Ayres, he picked up numerous human bones, together with arrow-heads, chisels, flint knives, bone stilettos and polishers, and bones of animals scratched and cut by man. Later, Ameghino discovered the actual dwelling of this primeval man, and his strange home was beneath the carapace of a gigantic armadillo, the now extinct glyptodon seen in Fig. 48.

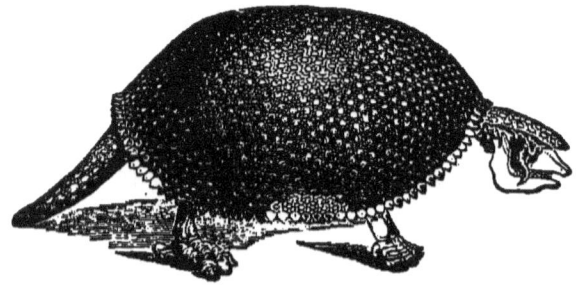

Fig. 48.—The glyptodon.

"All around the carapace," says Ameghino, "in the reddish agglomerate of the original soil lay charcoal cinders, burnt and split bones, and flints. Digging beneath this, a flint implement was found, with some long split llama and stag bones, which had evidently been handled by man, with some toxodon and mylodon teeth." Fig. 49 represents the now extinct mylodon. Some time afterwards, the discovery of another carapace under similar conditions added weight to Ameghino's supposition.[1] In the midst of the pampas,

---

[1] "El hombre seguramente habitaba las corazas de los Glyptodon pero no siempre las colocaba en la posicion que acabo de indicar."—" La Antiguedad del Hombre en el Plata," vol. ii., p. 532.

those vast treeless plains, where no rock or accident of conformation affords shelter from heat or cold or a hiding-place from wild beasts, man was not at a loss; he hollowed out for himself a hole in the earth, roofing it over with the shell of a glyptodon, and securing a retreat where he could be safe at least for a time.

It was not until later, driven to do so by the cold, that man learnt to use the natural caves hollowed out

Fig. 49.—Mylodon robustus.

in limestone rocks, either in geological convulsions or by the quieter action of water. The absence in the caves which have been excavated in America of implements of the Chelléen type, the most ancient known as yet, would point to this conclusion, though it is impossible to fix the earliest date of their occupation. This date, moreover, varies very much in different localities. The earth was but gradually peopled, and our ancestors penetrated into different countries in successive migrations. Some caves have recently been discovered in Wales, in the midst of Glacial deposits.[1] The Boulder Clay and marine drift on neighboring heights are incontrovertible proofs of the submergence of this region, when Great Britain was almost completely covered with ice. Excavations made in 1886 have brought to light a series of deposits, one above the other, the gravel and red earth containing Quaternary bones and worked flints, whilst the stalagmite and ooze are evidently of more recent origin. This is the usual state of things in all the English caves; but in those of the Clyde, the bone beds had been disturbed and mixed with striated pebbles and Glacial drift. From this Hicks, who superintended the excavations, concluded that man and the Quaternary animals had lived in those caves before the Glacial epoch, and before the great submergence, which in some places was no less than some 1,300 feet below the present level of the sea. If this were so, it would be one of the most ancient proofs not only of the presence of man, but also of the kind of habitation he first dwelt in. These conclusions have, however, been hotly disputed. M. Arcelin[2] remarks that there are in England two exceptional geological landmarks, the Forest Bed representing the last Pliocene formations, and the River Gravels, which are the most ancient Quaternary deposits. Between the two, we find the Boulder Clay of Glacial origin. Now the fauna of the caves of the Clyde, far from resembling that of the Forest

---

[1] "On Some Recent Researches in Cone-Caves in Wales," *Proc. Geol., Asso.*, vol. ix. "On the Flynnon, Benno, and Gwyu Caves," *Geol. Mag.*, Dec., 1886.

[2] *Revue des Questions Scientifiques*, April, 1887.

Bed, appears to be more recent than that of the ancient deposits of the River Gravels. Amongst this fauna we find neither the *Elephas antiquus* nor the *Rhinoceros Merckii;* the worked flints are not like those known as belonging to the River-Gravel type, but the relics more nearly resemble those of the Reindeer period of France. It is therefore impossible, in the present state of our knowledge, to assert that man lived in the southwest of England in the Glacial epoch, to the phenomena of which, if he witnessed them, he must eventually have fallen a victim.

Our ancestors must constantly have disputed the possession of their caves of refuge with animals, but there is often a certain distinction between those chiefly occupied by man and the mere dens of wild beasts. The latter are generally more difficult of access, and are only to be entered by long, low, narrow, dark passages. Those permanently inhabited by man are wide, not very deep, and they are well lighted. That at Montgaudier, for instance, has an arched entrance some forty-five feet wide by eighteen high. The cavemen had already learnt to appreciate the advantages of air and light.

The caves are often of considerable height; that of Massat is some 560 feet high, that of Lherm is 655, that of Bouicheta nearly 755, that of Loubens 820, and that of Santhenay is, as much as 1,344 feet high. Those of Eyziès, Moustier, and Aurignac are also very lofty. As the valleys were hollowed out by the rushing torrents of the Quaternary floods, men sought a home near the waters which were indispensable to their existence, and came to dwell on the shores of rivers. The most ancient of the inhabited caves, therefore, are those on the highest levels, but the difference in the nature of the country and the varying force of geological action have led to so many exceptions, that all we can say with any certainty is that the caves were inhabited at different epochs. That of Montgaudier, for instance, was filled with an accumulation of ooze about forty feet thick. Weapons and tools lay one above the other from the bottom to the top, and it is easy to distinguish the succession of hearths by the blackened earth, cinders, charcoal, and crushed bones lying about them.

In the Placard Cave eight different deposits bear witness to the presence of man; and these are separated by others bare of traces of human occupation. The lowest deposit, which is some twenty-five feet below the present level of the soil, contains worked flints of the Moustérien type, above which, but separated by an accumulation of *débris* which has fallen from the roof, comes a layer in which was found a number of arrow-heads of the shape of laurel leaves. The fauna of both these levels includes the reindeer, the horse, and the aurochs. As we go up we find, above another layer of *débris*, the Solutréen type of tools and weapons represented by bone implements and numerous arrow-heads, this time stalked and notched. The four following levels correspond with those belonging to what is known as the Madeleine type, and the arrow-heads are decorated with geometrical designs. The traces of human occupation at different times, doubtless separated by long intervals, are therefore very clearly defined. The Fontabert Cave, in Dauphiné, contained, at a depth of about six feet, traces of fire and roughly worked flints, and about three feet below the surface lay the skeleton of a man, who had perhaps been overtaken by a fall of earth, still holding in his hand a polished dipper of fine workmanship. Yet a third and evidently more recent period is characterized by a jade crescent. We might easily multiply instances of a similar kind, but that we wish to avoid so much repetition.

We soon begin to find evidence of the progress made by man, and though in Neolithic times he still continued to occupy caves he learned to adapt them better to his needs. The rock shelters of the Petit-Morin valley, so well explored by M. de Baye, are the best examples we can give.

These caves are hollowed out of a very thick belt of cretaceous limestone. They date from different epochs, and each presents special characteristics which can easily be recognized. Some were used as burial-places, others as habitations. In the former the entrance is of irregular shape, the walls are roughly cut, and the work is of the most elementary description. The sepulchral caves were simply closed by a large stone rolled into place and covered with rubbish, the better to hide the entrance. The shelters used to live in show much more careful work, and are divided into two unequal parts by a wall cut in the living rock. To get into the second partition one has to go down steps, cut in the limestone, and these steps are worn with long usage. The entrance was cut out of a massive piece of rock, left thick on purpose, and on either side of the opening the edges still show the rabbet which was to receive the door. Two small holes on the right and left were probably used to fix a bar across the front to strengthen the entrance. A good many of these caves are provided with an opening for ventilation, and some skilful contrivances were resorted to for keeping out water. Inside we find different floors, shelves, and crockets cut in the chalk, and on the floors M. de Baye picked up shells, ornaments, and flints, which were lying just where their owners had left them. Very different is all this from the Vezère caves, and everything proves an undeniable improvement in the conditions of life.

The most interesting of all the objects found in these caves are, however, the carvings; but few date from Neolithic times, and some archæologists have argued from their absence in favor of the displacement everywhere of old races by the incursion of new-comers. Some of these carvings represent hafted hatchets, the flint being painted black to make the raised design stand out better. Others represent human figures. In the Coizard Cave, for instance, was found a roughly outlined representation of a woman with a prominent nose, eyes indicated by black dots, highly developed breasts, but no lower limbs. A necklace adorns her throat, and a pendant hanging from this necklace is colored yellow. On the passage leading to the door is engraved another figure which was originally more accurately drawn than the others, but is not in such good preservation. In the Courjonnet Cave we see a woman with a bird's head; she was probably one of the *lares penates*, the protectors of the domestic hearth. We meet with this same goddess at Santorin, and at Troy, and on the shores of the Vistula, which is a very interesting ethnological fact.

The objects found in the sepulchral caves are important, and included a number of arrow-heads with transverse cutting edges. There is no doubt about their use; they have been picked up in black earth, in contact with human bones, the decomposition of the soft parts of which caused them to fall out of the mortal wound they had inflicted. With these arrowheads were found flint knives, large sloped scrapers, polishers, and bone stilettos, the femora of a ruminant with a pig's tooth fixed on to each end, hoes made of stag horn, beads and pendants made of bone, shell, schist, quartz, and aragonite, with the teeth of bears, boars, wolves, and foxes, all pierced with holes. Some of the shell and schist beads were spread upon the surface of the skull, and perhaps formed a net or *résille*, such as that already referred to as found at Baoussé-Roussé.

For centuries this occupation of caves continued, offering as they did a shelter that was dry and warm in winter, and cool in summer. Homer tells us that the Cyclops lived on the heights of the mountains and in the depths of the caves,[1] and Prometheus says that, like the feeble ant, men dwelt in deep subterranean caves, where the sun never penetrated.[2]

Whilst the men of the Petit-Morin valley hollowed out caves, or enlarged those made by nature, others took refuge in huts made of dried clay and interlaced branches, or in tents of the skins of the animals they had slain, and, though these fragile dwellings have disappeared, leaving no trace, there yet remain indelible evidences of the presence of many successive generations. Everywhere throughout the world we find heaps of rubbish, consisting chiefly of the shells of mollusca and crustacea, broken bones, flakes of flint,

---

[1] "Odyssey," book ix., v. 105–124.
[2] Æschylus: "Prometheus Bound."

and fragments of stone and bone implements, covering vast areas and often rising to a considerable height.

Not until our own day did these rubbish heaps attract attention, and it was reserved to our own generation, so interested in all that relates to the past, to recognize their true significance. Steenstrup noticed, in the north of Europe, that these mounds consisted nearly entirely of the shells of edible species, such as the oyster, mussel, and *littorina littorea;* that they were all those of adult specimens, but not all subject to similar conditions of existence or native to the same waters. The kitchen-middings, or heaps of kitchen refuse—such was the name given to these shell-mounds—could not have been the natural deposits left by the waves after storms, for in that case they would have been mixed with quantities of sand and pebbles. The conclusion is inevitable, that man alone could have piled up these accumulations, which were the refuse flung away day by day after his meals. The excavation of the kitchen-middings confirmed in a remarkable manner the opinion of Steenstrup, and everywhere a number of important objects were discovered. In several places the old hearths were brought to light. They consisted of flat stones, on which were piles of cinders, with fragments of wood and charcoal. It was now finally proved that these mounds occupied the site of ancient settlements, the inhabitants of which rarely left the coast, and fed chiefly on the mollusca which abounded in the waters of the North Sea.

These primeval races, however savage they may have been, were not wanting in intelligence. The earliest inhabitants of Russia placed their dwellings near rivers above the highest flood-level known to or foreseen by them. The Scandinavians were most precise in the orientation of their homes, and M. de Quatrefages points out that the kitchen-midding of Sœlager is set against a hill in the best position for protecting those who lived near it from the north winds, which are so trying in these districts on account of their violence. At Havelse, says Sir John Lubbock, the settlement was on rather higher ground, and, though close to the shore, was quite beyond the reach of the waves. The English visitors had an excavation made whilst they were present, and in two or three hours they obtained about a hundred fragments of bone, many rude flakes, sling stones, and fragments of flint, together with some rough axes of the ordinary shell-mound type. The excavations at Meilgaard a little later by the same explorers were even more fruitful in results.

Scandinavia does not appear to have been occupied in the Palæolithic period, and the most ancient facts concerning it only date from the expeditions of the Romans against the Teutons, and our knowledge even of them is very incomplete.[1] We are still ignorant of much which may have been known to the Carthaginians and the Phœnicians. It is possible that in the remote days under notice the Scandinavians were ignorant of the art of tilling the ground, for so far no cereal or agricultural product of any kind has been discovered, nor the bones of any domestic animal, except indeed those of the dog, which may, however, have been still in a wild state. Amongst the bones collected from the kitchen-middings, those of the stag, the kid, and the

[1] A. Maury: "La Vieille Civilisation Scandinave," *Revue des Deux Mondes*, September, 1880.

boar are much the most numerous. The bear, the urus, the wild cat, the otter, the porpoise, the seal, and the small mammals, the marten, the water-rat and the mouse, have also been found. At Havelse were collected more than 3,500 mammal bones, amongst which do not occur those of the musk-ox, the reindeer, the elk, or the marmot; their absence bearing witness to a more temperate climate than that of the present day in the regions under notice. The stag antlers found belong to every season of the year, from which we may conclude that the people of these districts, like the cave-men of the Pyrenees, had given up a nomad life and remained at home all the year round, living in the dwellings they had built upon the shores of the sea.

Amongst the birds found, we may mention the large penguin, now extinct, the moor-fowl, which fed entirely on pine buds, and several species of ducks and geese; whilst amongst the fish were the herring, the cod, the dab, and the eel. The numerous relics of chelonia prove the existence of numbers of the turtle tribe in the North Sea.

A great variety of objects, most of them of a coarse type, have been found beneath the kitchen-middings; metals are however completely absent, and it is probable that they were quite unknown to the Scandinavians for several centuries after their arrival in the country.

It is easy to quote similar facts in other countries. In 1877, Count Ouvarof mentioned, at the Archæological Congress at Kazan, some kitchen-middings near the Oka, a little river flowing into the Volga near Nijni-Novgorod. In excavating some *bougrys*, or little mounds of sand overlooking the valley, he discovered amongst the layers of alluvium, successive deposits of cinders and fragments of charcoal, which appear to have been the remains of a fire. A little lower down in another deposit were fragments of pottery, stone weapons and implements, and an immense number of shells. Judging from these relics of their daily life, this numerous population must have fed exclusively on fish and mollusca, for excavations brought to light but few mammal bones. The mollusca were all of species that only live in salt water. From this we know that the waves washed the shores near this *bougry*, and that a milder climate probably prevailed in these regions, making life more supportable.

Virchow has recognized on the shores of Lake Burtneek in Germany, a kitchen-midding belonging to the earliest Neolithic times, perhaps even to the close of the Palæolithic period. He there picked up some stone and bone implements, and notices on the one hand the absence of the reindeer, and on the other, as in Scandinavia, that of domestic animals. But in this case, the home of the living became the tomb of the dead, and numerous skeletons lay beside the abandoned hearths. Similar discoveries have been made in Portugal; shell-heaps having been found thirty-five to forty miles from the coast, and from sixty-five to eighty feet above the sea-level. Here also excavations have brought to light several different hearths; and in many of the most ancient kitchen-middings in the valley of the Tigris were found crouching skeletons, proving that here too the home had become the tomb.[1]

Similar deposits are by no means rare in France. M. du Chatellier mentions one in Brittany, which he

---
[1] F. de Olivera: "As Raças dos Kjoekkenmoeddings de Mugem," Lisbon, 1881.

estimates as 325 cubic feet in size. From it he has taken spear- and arrow-heads, knives and scrapers, some highly finished, others but roughly cut and often with scarcely any shape at all. The population was evidently ichthyophagous, to judge by the vast accumulations of shells of scallops, oysters, limpets, pectens, and other mollusca. The few animal bones are those of the stag, the bear, and certain wading birds.

At Cauche, near Étaples, has been made out a series of mounds forming a semicircle some eight hundred and fifty feet in extent. These mounds are made up of successive layers of shells and charcoal, the relics of successive occupations. Lastly we must mention a kitchen-midding situated at the mouth of the Somme, which is eight hundred and twenty feet long by about one hundred wide. It consists principally of shells of adult species, with which are mixed fragments of coarse black pottery and numerous goat and sheep bones, the latter bearing witness to a more recent date than that of the kitchen-middings of Scandinavia or of Germany.

Throughout Europe similar facts are coming to light. Evans mentions heaps of shells on the coasts of England. Chantre speaks of others near Lake Gotchai in the Caucasus, and Nordenskiöld of others at Cape North, to which he wishes to restore its true name of Jokaipi. He says these mounds are exactly like those of Denmark.

It is, however, chiefly in America that these heaps attract attention, for there huge shell-mounds stretch along the coast in Newfoundland, Nova Scotia, Massachusetts, Louisiana, California, and Nicaragua. We meet with them again near the Orinoco and the Mississippi, in the Aleutian Islands, and in the Guianas, in

Brazil and in Patagonia, on the coasts of the Pacific as on those of the Atlantic. Owing to the darker color of the vegetation growing on them, the shell-heaps of Tierra del Fuego are seen from afar by the navigator. For a long time the true character of these mounds was not known, and they were attributed to natural causes, such as the emergence of the ancient coast-line from the sea, and it was not until lately that it was discovered that they were the work of men.

Some of these kitchen-middings are of great size. Sir Charles Lyell describes one on St. Simon's Island, at the mouth of the Altamaha (Georgia), which covers ten acres of ground and varies in height from five to ten feet. It consisted almost entirely of oyster shells. In America, as in Europe, excavations brought to light hatchets, flints, arrows, and fragments of pottery. Another of these mounds, near the St. John River, consists, as does that visited by Lyell, of oyster shells, and is of extraordinary dimensions, being three hundred feet long, and though the exact width cannot be made out, is certainly several hundred feet across. Putnam[1] gives an account of the excavation of one of these mounds formed of shells of the *Mya, Venus, Pecten, Buccinum,* and *Natica* genera. It stretched along the sea-coast for a distance of several hundred feet, it was from four to five feet thick, and penetrated some distance below the surface of the ground. The valves had been opened with the aid of heat, and the animal bones found with the shells had been broken with heavy hammers which were found in the kitchen-midding. The bones included those of the stag, the wolf, and the fox. Fishes were also represented by remains of the cod, the plaice,

---

[1] *Report Peabody Museum,* 1882.

and chelonia by turtle shells. Some bird bones were also found, and the knives, arrow- and spear-heads, scrapers, etc., were all of the rudest workmanship. Mr. Phelps has superintended yet more important excavations at Damariscotta[1] and all along the coast to the mouth of the Penobscot. In the lowest layers he made out ancient hearths, and found numerous fragments of pottery which are the most ancient examples of keramic ware found in New England, and were covered with incised ornamentation of considerable refinement.

The kitchen-middings of Florida and Alabama are even more remarkable. There is one on Amelia Island which is a quarter of a mile long with a medium depth of three feet and a breadth of nearly five. That of Bear's Point covers sixty acres of ground, that of Anercerty Point one hundred, and that of Santa Rosa five hundred. Others taper to a great height. Turtle Mound, near Smyrna, is formed of a mass of oyster shells attaining a height of nearly thirty feet, and the height of several others is more than forty feet.[2] In all of them bushels of shells have already been found, although a great part of the sites they occupy are still unexplored; huge trees, roots, and tropical creepers having, in the course of many centuries, covered them with an almost impenetrable thicket.

Whether man did or did not live in the basin of the Delaware at the most remote times of which we have any knowledge, we meet with traces of his occupation in the same latitude at more recent periods. At Long-Nick-Branch is a shell-mound that extends for half a

---

[1] *Report Peabody Museum*, 1882 and 1885.
[2] Brinton: "Notes on the Floridian Peninsula," Philadelphia, 1849.

mile, and in California there is a yet larger kitchen-midding. It measures a mile in length by half a mile in width, and, as in similar accumulations, excavations have yielded thousands of stone hammers and bone implements (Fig. 24).

The shell-mounds of which we have so far been speaking are all near the sea, but there is yet another consisting entirely of marine shells fifty miles beyond Mobile. This fact seems to point to a considerable change in the level of the ground since the time of man's first occupancy, for he is not likely to have taken all the trouble involved in carrying the mollusca necessary for his daily food so far, when he might so easily have settled down near the shore.

I cannot close this account of the kitchen-middings, without calling attention to two very interesting facts. The importance of these mounds bears witness alike to the number of the inhabitants who dwelt near them, and the long duration of their sojourn. Worsaae sets back the initial date of the most ancient of the shell-mounds of the New World more than three thousand years. This is however a delicate question, on which in the present state of our knowledge it is difficult to hazard a serious opinion. It is easier to come to a conclusion on other points: the close resemblance, for instance, between the kitchen-middings of America and those of Europe. In both continents we find the early inhabitants fed almost entirely on fish; their weapons, tools, and pottery were almost identical in character; and in both cases the characteristic animals of Quaternary times had disappeared, and the use of metals still remained unknown. Are these remarkable coincidences the result of chance, or must we not rather suppose that people of the same origin occupied at the same epoch both sides of the Atlantic?

The man of the kitchen-middings evidently had a fixed abode. Long since, the tent, the temporary shelter of the nomad, had given place to the hut. We have already said what this hut may have been like, but the most certain data we have as to human habitations at this still but little known epoch, are those supplied by the Lake Stations of Switzerland, and it is to our own generation that we are indebted for the first discoveries relating to them.

The memory of these Lake Stations had completely passed away, and it was only the long drought which desolated Switzerland in 1853 and 1854, and the extraordinary sinking of Lake Zurich, revealing the piles still standing, that attracted the attention of archæologists. In the space still enclosed by these piles lay scattered pell-mell stones, bones, burnt cinders of ancient hearths, pestles, hammers, pottery, hatchets of various shapes, implements of many kinds, with innumerable objects of daily use. These relics prove that some of the ancient inhabitants of Switzerland had dwelt on the lake where they were found, in a refuge to which they had probably retired to escape from the attacks of their fellow-men or wild beasts. Though they had succeeded in getting away from these enemies, they were to fall victims to a yet more formidable adversary, and the half-burnt piles have preserved to our own day the traces of a conflagration that destroyed the Lake dwelling so laboriously constructed.

The discovery of these piles excited general interest, an interest that was redoubled when similar discoveries revealed that all the lakes of Switzerland were dotted with stations that had been built long centuries before in the midst of the waters. Twenty such stations were made out on Lake Bienne, twenty-four on the Lake of Geneva, thirty on Lake Constance, forty-nine on that of Neuchâtel, and others, though not so many, on Lakes Sempach, Morat, Mooseedorf, and Pfeffikon. In fact more than two hundred Lake Stations are now known in Switzerland; and how many more may have completely disappeared?

There is really nothing to surprise us in the fact of buildings rising from the midst of waters. They are known in historic times; Herodotus relates that the inhabitants of pile dwellings on Lake Prasias successfully repelled the attacks of the Persians commanded by Megabasus. Alonzo de Ojeda, the companion of Amerigo Vespucci, speaks of a village consisting of twenty large houses built on piles in the midst of a lake, to which he gave the name of Venezuela in honor of Venice, his native town. We meet with pile dwellings in our own day in the Celebes, in New Guinea, in Java, at Mindanao, and in the Caroline Islands. Sir Richard Burton saw pile dwellings at Dahomey, Captain Cameron on the lakes of Central Africa, and the Bishop of Labuan tells us that the houses of the Dayaks are built on lofty platforms on the shores of rivers. The accounts of historians and travellers help us to understand alike the mode of construction of the Lake Stations and the kind of life led by their inhabitants.

The Lake dwellings of Switzerland may be assigned to three different periods. That of Chavannes, on Lake Bienne, belongs to the earliest type. The hatchets found are small, scarcely polished, and always of native rock, such as serpentine, diorite, or saussurite; the pottery is coarse, mixed with grains of sand or bits of quartz; the bottoms of the vases are thick, and no traces of ornamentation can be made out. The pile-dwellings of the second period, such as those of Locras and Latringen, show considerable progress; the hatchets, some of which are very large, are well made. Several of them are of nephrite, chloromelanite, and jade; and their number, as compared with those in minerals native to Switzerland, varies from five to eight per cent. Here and there in rare instances we find a few copper or bronze lamellæ amongst the piles. The pottery is now of finer clay, better kneaded; and ornamentation, including chevrons, wolves' teeth, and mammillated designs, is more common. The handle, however, is still a mere projection. The third period, which we may date from the transition from stone to bronze, is largely represented; copper weapons and tools are already numerous, and bronze is beginning to occur. The stone hatchets and hammers are skilfully pierced, and wooden or horn implements are often found. The vases are of various shapes, all provided with handles, and are covered with ornaments, some made with the fingers of the potter, others with the help of a twig or some fine string. On the other hand, there are no hatchets of foreign rock; commerce and intercourse with people at a distance had ceased, or at least become rarer. The tools are fixed into handles of stag horn, which are found in every stage of manufacture. The personal property of the Lake Dwellers included bead necklaces, pendants, buttons, needles, and horn combs. The teeth of animals served as amulets, and the bones that were of denser material than horn were used as javelin- or arrow-heads. The arrows were generally of triangular shape and not barbed.[1]

The distance from the shore of the most ancient of the Lake dwellings varies from 131 to 298 feet. Gradually men began to take greater and greater precautions against danger, and the most recent stations are 656 to 984 feet from the banks of the lake. The piles of the Stone age are from eleven to twelve inches in diameter; those of the later epochs are smaller. They are pointed at the ends, and hardened by fire. When the piles had been driven into the bottom of the lake, a platform was laid on them solid enough to bear the weight of the huts. This platform was made of beams laid down horizontally, and bound together by interlaced branches. Two modes of construction can easily be distinguished. In one the platforms were upheld by numerous piles, ten yards long, firmly driven into the mud. This is how the *Pfahlbauten*, *Palafittes*, or pile dwellings situated in shallow waters were generally put together. In other cases it seemed easier to raise the soil round the piles, than to drive them into the hard rock which formed the bed of the lake. Care was then taken to consolidate them, and keep them in position with blocks of stone, clay, and tiers of piles. Keller gives to these latter the name of *Packwerbauten*, and other German archæologists call them *Steinbergen*.

The mean depth of the waters in those parts of the lakes formerly occupied by the pile dwellings is from thirteen to sixteen feet, and we can still make out the piles when the water is calm and clear. Worn though

---

[1] We take many of these details from Dr. Gross' excellent work on the "Pile Dwellings of Switzerland."

they may be, their tops still emerge at a height varying from one to three feet above the mud at the bottom of the lake. Their number was originally considerable, and it is estimated that there were forty thousand at Wangen, and a hundred thousand at Robenhausen. The area occupied by the stations varies considerably; according to Troyon, that at Wangen was seven hundred paces long by one hundred and twenty broad. Baron von Mayenfisch explored seventeen sites in the Lake of Constance, the area of which varies from three to four acres. At Inkwyl is a little artificial island about forty-eight feet in diameter. The Lake dwelling of Morges, which was still inhabited in the Bronze age, covers an area of twelve hundred feet long by a mean width of one hundred and fifty. It is, however, useless to enumerate the various calculations that have been made, as they are founded on nothing but more or less probable guesswork.

Excavations show that the huts that rose from the platforms were made of wattle and hurdle-work. In different places calcined and agglutinated fragments have been picked up, and pieces of clay which had served as facing. The house to which they had belonged had been destroyed by fire, and the clay, hardened in the flames, had resisted the disintegrating action of the water. On one side this clay is smooth, and on the other it still retains the marks of the interlaced branches, which had helped to form the inner walls. Some of these marks are so clear and regular that Troyon, noticing the way they curve, was able to assert that the huts were circular, and that they varied in diameter from ten to fifteen feet.

A recent discovery at Schussenreid (Wurtemberg) gives completeness to our knowledge of the Swiss

Lake dwellings. In the midst of a peat-bog rises a hut known as a *Knüppelbau*, which is supposed to date from the Stone age. It is of rectangular form, and is divided into two compartments communicating with each other by a foot-bridge consisting of three beams laid side by side. The floors of this hut are made of rounded wood, and the walls of piles split in half. Excavations have brought to light several floors, one above the other, and divided by thick layers of clay. The rising of the level of the peat doubtless compelled the Lake Dweller to add by degrees to the height of his house.

The Proto-Helvetian race were well-developed men, and the bones that have been collected show that they were not at all wanting in symmetry of form or in cranial capacity. The crania found are distinctly dolichocephalous, and their owners had evidently attained to no small degree of culture and of technical skill. Judging from the length of the femora found, though it must be added that they are mostly those of women, the ancient Lake Dwellers were not so tall as the present inhabitants of Europe. The smallness of the handles of their weapons and tools points to the same conclusion.[1]

Though the importance and number of the discoveries made in Switzerland render it the classic land of Lake Stations, it is not the only country in which they have been found. They have been made out in the Lago Maggiore and in the lakes of Varèse, Peschiera, and Garda in Lombardy; in Lake Salpi in the Capitanata, and in other parts of Italy. Judging from the objects recovered from these stations, they belonged partly to the Stone and partly to the Bronze age.

---

[1] Virchow: "Drei Schädel aus der Schweiz."

The pile dwelling of Lagozza is one of the most interesting known to us. It forms a long square, facing due east, and covers an area of two thousand six hundred yards, now completely overgrown with peat six and a half feet thick. Amongst the posts still standing can be made out a number of half-burnt planks, which are probably the remains of the platform. One of the posts was still covered with bark, and it was easy to recognize the silver birch *(Betula alba)*. Other posts consisted of the trunks of resinous trees, such as the *Pinus picea*, the *Pinus sylvestris*, and the larch, which now only grow in the lofty Alpine valleys. Amongst the industrial objects found in the Lagozza pile dwelling were polished stone hatchets, hammers, polishers of hard stone, knife-blades, flint scrapers, and seven or eight arrows with transverse cutting edges, a form rare in Italy.

Castelfranco,[1] from whom we borrow these details, has also, in the excavations he superintended, picked up a number of earthenware spindle-whorls with a hole in the middle, amulets, and numerous pieces of pottery, some fine and some coarse, according to the purpose for which they were intended. The first mould had in most cases been covered over with a layer of very fine clay spread upon it with the aid of a kind of boasting-chisel. We may also mention a bone comb. The combs found in Swiss Lake dwellings are of horn, with the exception of one from Locras of yew wood.

What chiefly distinguishes the Lagozza pile dwelling, however, is the absence of the bones, teeth, or horns of animals, and also of fish-hooks, harpoons, or nets, so that we must conclude that the inhabitants did not

---

[1] *Revue d'Anthropologie*, 1887, p. 607.

hunt or fish, that they did not breed domestic animals, and were probably vegetarians. The researches of Professor Sordelli confirm this hypothesis; from amongst the objects taken from the peat he recognized two kinds of corn *(Triticum vulgare antiquorum* and *Triticum vulgare hibernum)*, six-rowed barley *(Hordeum hexastichum)*, mosses, ferns, flax, the Indian poppy *(Papaver somniferum)*, acorns, and an immense number of nuts and apples.

The acorns are those of the common oak, and their cups and outer rind had been removed, so that they had evidently been prepared to serve as food for man; the apples were small and coriaceous, resembling the modern crab-apple; the Indian poppy cannot have grown without cultivation; but this was perhaps but an example of the same species already recognized in the Lake dwellings of Switzerland. It is difficult to say whether it was used for food or whether oil was extracted from it.

We have already spoken of the discoveries made in Austria and Hungary. Count Wurmbrand has described the difficulties with which explorers had to contend. The lakes have in many cases become inaccessible swamps, and in others, the waters having been artificially dammed to regulate their overflow, the sites of the pile dwellings are so far below the level of the lakes that any excavations are impossible. Long and arduous researches have, however, been rewarded with some success, and the numerous objects recovered bear witness, as in Switzerland, to the gradual progress made by the successive generations who occupied these pile dwellings.

A lake near Laybach had been converted in drying

up into an immense peat-bog, nearly thirty-eight miles in circumference, bounded on the right and left by lofty mountains.[1] When this bog was under water it had been the site of several Lake Stations. One, for instance, has been made out over three hundred and twenty yards from the bank. The piles, which

FIG. 50.—Objects discovered in the peat-bogs of Laybach. A. Earthenware vase. B. Fragment of ornamented pottery. C. Bone needle. D. Earthenware weight for fishing-net. E. Fragment of jawbone.

consisted of the trunks of oaks, beeches, and poplars, varying from eight to ten inches in diameter, were placed at regular intervals. The objects taken from the peat-bog are simply innumerable (Fig. 50), and in-

---

[1] G. Cotteau: *Nature*, 1877, first week, p. 161.

clude hundreds of needles of different sizes, stilettos, dagger-blades, arrows, and hatchets, with stag-horn handles. Coarse black earthenware vases are equally numerous and are of a great variety of form, but their ornamentation is of the most primitive description, and was done sometimes with the nail of the potter, and sometimes with a pointed bone. Little earthenware figures (Figs. 51 and 52) were also found, some of which were sent from the Laybach Museum to the

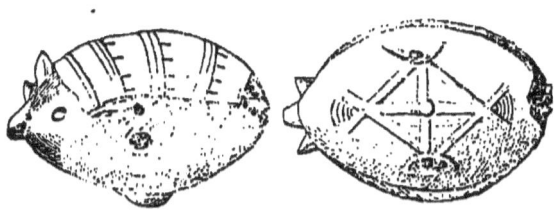

FIG. 51.—Small terra-cotta figures, found in the Laybach pile dwellings.

French Exhibition of 1878. One of them is said to represent a woman, probably an idol. This is one of the first known examples of the representation of the human figure from a Lake dwelling. At Nimlau, near Olmutz, the drying up of a little lake brought to light a Lake Station surrounded by the trunks of oak trees of a large size. They were piled up, one above the other, and strongly bound together with osiers. These trunks were evidently intended to fortify the station.

The mode of construction of the Lake Stations of the marshes of Pomerania is very different from that employed in Switzerland or in Austria. The foundations rest on horizontal beams, kept in place either by great blocks of rock or by piles driven in vertically. In many cases notches had evidently been made, the better to place the cross-beams; whilst in others forked branches had been selected, so that a second branch could be fitted into the fork. Primeval man soon learnt to appreciate the solidity of such a combination. Do these stations, however, really date from prehistoric times? Virchow, returning to his first opinion, now thinks that the pile dwellings of Germany belong to the same epoch as the intrenchments known as *Burgwallen*, when metals and even iron were already in general use. They were inhabited until the thirteenth century, and it is easy to trace in them, as in those of Switzerland, the signs of the successive occupations, the dwellings having evidently been abandoned and restored later by fresh comers.

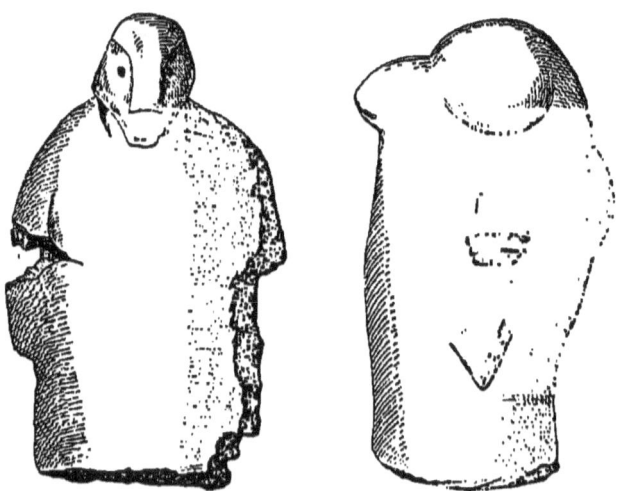

FIG. 52.—Small terra-cotta figures, from the Laybach pile dwellings.

At the meeting of the British Association at Newcastle in 1863, Lord Lovaine described a Lake Station in the south of Scotland, and Sir J. Lubbock mentions one in the north of England. Others are known at Holderness (Yorkshire), at Thetford, on Barton Mere, near Bury St. Edmunds; but judging from the description of them they are not of earlier date than the Bronze age.

Other stations are more ancient. A few years ago a number of piles were found a little above Kew, beneath a layer of alluvium, and embedded in the gravel which formed the ancient bed of the Thames. All around these piles were scattered the bones of animals, of which those of the *Bos longifrons* were the most remarkable. The long bones had been split to get out the marrow, an evident proof of the intelligent action of man. In London two similar examples were found on the site of the present Mansion House, and beneath the ancient walls of the city. They are supposed to date from times earlier, not only than the cutting out of the present course of the Thames, but before that invasion of the sea which preceded the formation of the Thames valley, now the home of more than four million men and women.

The Lake Stations of France are less important than those of the neighboring countries. It is supposed that Vatan, a little town of Berry, was built on the site of a Lake city. It is situated in the midst of a dried-up marsh, and at different points piles have been removed which were driven deep into the mud. We also hear of pile dwellings in the Jura Mountains, in the Pyrenean valleys of Haute-Garonne, Ariège, and Aude, as well as in those of the Eastern Pyrenees. In the department of Landes, which on one side joins the plateau of Lannemezan, and on the other the lofty plains of Béarn, are many marshy depressions, where have been found numbers of piles, with charred wood and fragments of pottery.

Discoveries no less curious have been made in the Bourget Lake, but the dwellings rising from its surface date from a comparatively recent epoch. The numerous fragments of pottery found prove that terracotta ware had attained to a beauty of form and color unknown to primitive times. Indeed some of the vases actually bear the name of the Roman potter who made them. We must also assign to an epoch later than the Stone age the buildings, remains of which have been found in the peat-bogs of Saint-Dos near Salies (Basses-Pyrénées). At a depth of about thirty-two inches has been found a regular floor formed of trunks of trees resting on piles and bound together in a primitive fashion with the filaments of roots. These piles bear a number of deep clean-cut notches, such as could only have been made with an iron implement. In other parts of France there are Lake Stations, which were occupied until the time of the Carlovingians. To this time belong the pile dwellings of Lake Paladru (Isère), which were abandoned, so far as we can tell, by their owners when they were swamped by the rising of the water.

When the Lake Stations of Europe were inhabited, the characteristic animals of the Quaternary epoch, such as the elephant, the rhinoceros, the lion, and the hippopotamus had disappeared from that continent, and their place was taken by the earliest domestic animals. The Lake fauna of Switzerland includes about seventy species, thirty mammals, twenty-six birds, ten kinds of fish, and four reptiles.[1] The mammals were the stag, the dog, the pig, the goat, the sheep, and two kinds of oxen. These animals were

---

[1] Rutimeyer : " Fauna der Pfahlbauten in der Schweiz."

already domesticated; there can be absolutely no doubt on this point, for in many *Pfahlbauten* their very dung has been found, a conclusive proof that they lived side by side with man.

The remains of the stag and of the ox are more numerous than those of any other animal, and it is easy to see that every day the importance of a pastoral life became more clearly recognized. In the most ancient Lake Stations, those of Mooseedorf, Wangen, and Meilen, for instance, the stag predominates; in those of the western lakes, which are comparatively more recent, relics of the ox are more numerous. In the Lake village of Nidau, which dates from the Bronze age, a greatly increased number of bones of domestic animals have been found, whilst those of wild creatures become rarer and rarer. The progress of domestication is evident, and it is no less certain that the lapse of centuries must have been required for the formation of the herds which evidently existed in certain localities. It is possible that these animals may have first entered Europe in the wake of foreign invaders, and before being reduced to servitude, they may have roamed about in a wild state, and even have been contemporaries with species now extinct. However that may be, there can be no doubt on one point, they could not domesticate themselves; one race of creatures after another must have fallen under the subjection of man, who gradually became the master of all the animals that are still about us.

We do not meet in the pile dwellings with the common mouse, the rat, or the cat, and the horse is very rare. It is the same with the kitchen-middings and the caves occupied in Neolithic times. The disappearance of the horse, so numerous in earlier epochs, is general, and this would be inexplicable if history did not solve the mystery. The Bible, which gives us such complete details of the pastoral life of the Hebrews, speaks for the first time of the horse after the exodus from Egypt of the children of Israel, and in Egypt itself the horse is not represented in any monument of earlier date than the Seventeenth Dynasty. It is the same in America, animals of the equine race, that were so numerous in early geological times, had long since disappeared on the arrival of the Spaniards, and the horses they brought with them inspired the Mexicans and Peruvians with unutterable terror.

Domestic animals require regular food through the long winter months; so that their presence alone is enough to prove that their owners were tillers of the soil. The discovery in many of the Helvetian Lake Stations of calcined cereals confirms this hypothesis. Amongst the cereals found, corn is the most abundant, and several bushels of it have been collected. In the department of the Gironde, regular silos or subterranean storing-places for grain have been found in which the calcined corn was stowed away. In the Lake Stations have also been found millet, peas, poppy-heads, nuts, plums, raspberries, and even dried apples and pears, doubtless set aside as a provision for the winter. From the water at Cortaillod, have been taken, with a few ears of barley, cherry-stones, acorns, and beech-nuts[1]; and at Laybach, some water-chestnuts *(trapa natans)* of a kind that has long since disappeared from Carniola. Sometimes the cereals were roughly roasted, crushed, and put away in large earthenware vessels;

---

[1] *Anzeiger für Schweizerische Alterthums Künde*, April, 1884.

but in some places, regular flat round loaves of bread have been found about one or two inches thick, which were baked without leaven. We may well assert that great changes had taken place since the first arrival of man upon the earth.

The so-called *terremares* of Italy date from the same period as the Danish kitchen-middings and the Swiss pile dwellings. They are met with chiefly in Lombardy and in the ancient duchies of Parma and Piacenza, and consist of low mounds rising from thirteen to sixteen feet above the surface of the soil. In some cases a number of *terremares*, close to one another, form regular villages covering an area of from five to six miles square. Excavations of the *terremare* have brought to light rows of piles from seven to ten feet long, connected by transverse beams, forming a regular floor, from which rose huts built in a similar way to those of the Swiss pile dwellings, of interlaced branches or of clay and straw, for no trace has been made out of the use of bricks or of stones. The refuse of the kitchen and rubbish of all kinds rapidly accumulated round about these huts, and formed the first nucleus of the mound, which soon grew to a considerable height as one occupant of the house succeeded another. When the refuse became too much of a nuisance, the owner of the hut set up fresh piles at a greater height on the same site, laid down another platform, and built a new hut. In some places three such platforms have been found one above another.

As in the Lake Stations, excavations of the *terremares* have brought to light numerous bones of domestic animals; but those of wild creatures, such as bears, stags, roedeer, and boars, are even rarer than in Switzerland. The inhabitants evidently had other resources than hunting at their command, and though the processes they employed were but elementary, they cultivated corn, beans, vines, and various fruits. Though iron was still unknown, some bronze objects have been found in certain *terremares*, but these were only roughly melted pieces of metal, showing no traces of having been either hammered or soldered. Amongst the pottery found in the *terremares*, we must mention a number of small objects not unlike acorns in form, pierced lengthwise, and decorated with incised lines, some straight, others curved. Italian archæologists call them *fusaïoles*, and Swiss savants, who have found a great many in the lakes of their native country, give them the name of *pesons de fuseau*. Both these names connect them with the process of spinning; but their number renders this hypothesis inadmissible, and when we give an account of the excavations carried on at Hissarlik, under Dr. Schliemann, we shall be able to determine their character (see Chapter VII.).

At Castione, near the town of Parma, and in several other parts of the provinces of Parma and Reggio, *terremares* have been discovered rising from the midst of vast rectangular basins artificially hollowed out. Some have concluded from this that the *terremare-colli*, as the inhabitants of the *terremares* have been called, were descended from the people who built the pile dwellings of Switzerland, and that, faithful to the traditions of their race, they hollowed out ponds in default of natural lakes. If this were so, Italy must have been peopled with a race that came over the Alps.[1] Who or what this race was can only be matter

---

[1] Comte Conestabile: "Sur les Anciennes Immigrations en Italie." Heilbig: "Beitrage zur Altitalischen Kultur und Kund Geschichte," i. Band. G. Boissier: *Révue des Deux-Mondes*, October, 1879.

of conjecture. It cannot, however, have been the Ligures, a branch of the great Iberian family, who were totally ignorant of culture, and to whom the builders of the most ancient of the *terremares* were certainly superior ; nor can it have been the Etruscans, for all relics of that race, which are moreover easily recognizable, were found quite apart from the deep deposits containing the *terremares*. Many indications point to the conclusion that when the Celts came down into Italy their knowledge of metallurgy was already more advanced than that of the builders of the *terremares*. We are therefore disposed to think with Heilbig, that the *terremarecolli* were the Itali, of Arian race, who were the ancestors of the Sabini, Umbri, Osci, and Latins. In the great migrations of races, the Itali had separated themselves from their brethren the Pelasgi, who had remained in Epirus, and, continuing their march, they peopled Switzerland and crossed the Alps, settling down in the fertile plains watered by the Po, where it is easy even now to prove their presence.

In superintending the excavation of a *terremare* at Toszig, in Hungary, Pigorini,[1] was greatly struck by the resemblance between it and similar erections in Italy, especially that of Casarolo. This is very much in favor of the Itali having been the builders. But the objects collected in some of the *terremares*, those of Varano and Chierici for instance, prove that they were inhabited from Neolithic times, so that the Itali of Italy, if Itali they were, did but follow the traditions of their predecessors. In spite, however, of zealous study, all that relates to the origin of tribes

---

[1] *Bul. di Palethnologia Ital.*, 1879. The *terpens* of Holland, though of much more modern date, greatly resemble the *terremares*.

and races remains involved in the greatest obscurity, and we can but look to the future to supply what the present altogether fails to give.

We have yet other tokens of the presence of the ancient races who peopled Italy. Dr. Concezio Rosa[1] noticed in the Abruzzi extensive black patches on the ground, which bore witness to the former residence of men. The excavation of these *Fonli di Cabane*, as they are called, led to the finding of a great many stone knives and scrapers with numerous bone stilettos and the bones of various animals, all of them of species still living. Later, similar *fondi* were found between the Eastern Alps and Mount Gargano. In Reggio, at Rivaltella, at Castelnuovo de Sotto, and at Calerno, they formed regular groups, and from one of these stations more than one thousand worked flints were collected. We mention them especially because they were of lozenge *(selci romboidali)* and half-lozenge *(semi-rombi)* shapes, which are forms unknown in other districts.

With these flints were hand-made vases with handles, the clay unmixed with sand or quartz and ornamented with lines, grooves, and raised knobs. These vases differ greatly from those found in the *terremares;* are they then, as has been said, of earlier date? It is impossible to come to any decision on the point.

Before closing our account of prehistoric buildings surrounded by water, we must say a few words on crannoges though there is the greatest difference of opinion as to their date.

Crannoges are artificial islets raised above the level of certain lakes in Ireland and Scotland[2] by means of a

---

[1] "Ricerce di Archeologia Preistorica nella Valle della Vibrata."
[2] Wylie, *Arch. Brit.*, vol. xxxviii. Wylde, *Proc. Royal Irish Acad.*, vol. i., p. 420.

series of layers of earth and stone, and strengthened by piles, some upright, others laid down lengthwise. Wylde counted forty-six in Ireland in his time, some of them of considerable extent. That of Ardkellin Lough (Roscommon) is surrounded by a wall of dry stones resting on piles. In other places have been found the remains of stockades very intelligently set up in such a manner as to break the force of the shock of the water.

To add to the difficulties of dealing with the subject of crannoges, they were successively occupied for many centuries. They are mentioned in the most ancient Irish legends, and even in the sixteenth century they served as refuges for the kings of the country in the constant rebellions that took place. The objects taken from the lakes belong to very different epochs, and it is impossible to say anything positive as to the time of their construction.

A hut found in Donegal may, however, date from an extremely remote age.[1] It rested on a thick layer of sand brought from the neighboring shore, and was covered over by a bed of peat not less than sixteen feet thick. Since the hut was deserted by man the peat had gradually accumulated till it had at last invaded the dwelling itself. The hut included a ground-floor, and one story about twelve feet long by nine wide and four high. The walls consisted of beams scarcely squared, joined together with wooden mortices and pegs. The roof, which was probably flat, consisted of oak planks, the spaces between which had been filled in with mortar made of sand and grease. On the ground-floor lay several flint

---

[1] *Arch. Brit.*, vol. xxvi., p. 361. *Proc. Royal Irish Academy*, vol. vii., p. 155.

implements, showing no signs of having been polished, a quartz wedge, and a stone chisel, which had evidently seen long service. This chisel, the discoverers say, corresponded exactly with the notches around the mortices. A regular paved way, formed of sea-beach pebbles placed on a foundation of interlaced branches, led up to a hearth made of flat stones measuring some three feet every way. All about lay fragments of charcoal and broken nuts, the latter partly burnt. Another hut, with an oak floor resting on four posts, has recently been discovered in County Fermanagh, beneath a deposit of peat about twenty feet thick. No trace of metal has been found in either of these Irish huts, and the thickness of the peat beneath which they lay is another proof of their great antiquity. One serious objection, however, is this: Were the Irish sufficiently advanced in prehistoric times to be able to erect dwellings implying so considerable an amount of civilization?

Crannoges are met with in Scotland as well as in Ireland, and excavations in Loch Lee have enabled explorers to make out their mode of construction. The Lake Dwellers began by piling up a number of trunks of trees in the shallower waters of a lake. They then strengthened these trunks with branches or beams about which the mud collected till the whole formed an islet. All about this islet, beneath the waters of the lake, were found various objects in stone, wood, and horn, as well as some canoes several feet long. Similar crannoges are to be seen on the lakes of Kincardine and Forfar, which Troyon thinks date from the Stone age.[1] If he be right, and we should not like to

---

[1] 'Habitations Lacustres des Temps Anciens et Modernes," p. 170.

make any assertion one way or the other, the bronze objects and the enamelled glass bowls found near these dwellings prove that they were occupied by several successive generations.

It is probable that Lake dwellings were also used in Asia and in Africa from prehistoric times. History tells us that the inhabitants of Phasis, the Mingrelians of the present day, lived in reed huts on the water, and that they went from one islet to another in canoes hollowed out of the trunks of oak-trees. A bas-relief from the palace of Sennacherib, preserved in the British Museum, represents warriors fighting on artificial islands made of large reeds. But here we enter the domain of history, and we must return to Neolithic times, and speak of the habitations built of more durable materials and the ruins of which are still standing.

It is impossible to say with any certainty to what period the most ancient of these structures belong. It is probable that man early learned to pile up stones, binding them together at first with clay, and then with some stronger cements. The *burghs* of Scotland, the *nurhags* of the island of Sardinia, the *talayoti* of the Balearic Isles, the *castellieri* of Istria, are all ancient witnesses of the modes of building employed in the most remote ages.

Burghs, brocks, or *broughs* are numerous in Scotland,[1] and also in the islands of the Atlantic. For a long time they were supposed to be of Scandinavian origin, but Sir J. Lubbock[2] remarks with reason that no

---

[1] R. Munro: "Ancient Scottish Lake Dwellings or Crannoges, with a Supplementary Chapter on Remains of Lake Dwellings in England," Edinburgh, 1882.
[2] "Prehistoric Times." Wilson: "Prehistoric Scotland."

building at all like them exists in Norway or in Denmark, and it is difficult to admit the idea that the Scandinavians set up in the islands tributary to them buildings which were unknown to their own mainland. We are therefore disposed to think that these curious structures, which were inhabited until the twelfth and thirteenth centuries of the Christian era, are of much earlier date than the first invasion by the Northmen, and that the burgh still standing on the little island of Moussa, one of the Shetlands, is one of the best examples that we can quote. A tower, forty-one feet high, rises on the borders of the sea. The walls are of unhewn stones, piled up without cement, and they form two circles, separated by a passage four feet wide. In each story are a series of very small openings, intended to admit air and light to the cell-like rooms inside, and to a staircase that leads to the top of the tower. The only way into this burgh is through a door only seven feet high, and so narrow that it is impossible for two people to go in abreast.

The regularity of the building of this burgh, and the architectural knowledge it implies, prevent our ascribing it either to the Stone or even to the Bronze age; but we find in Scotland itself more ancient examples, if we may so express ourselves, of domestic architecture. These examples are subterranean dwellings, made of rough-hewn stones of considerable size, laid down in regular courses, to which the names of *earth-houses*, *Picts' houses*, and *weems* have been given. The walls converge towards the centre, leaving an opening at the top, which was covered in with large flat stones. These dwellings are certainly of earlier date than the burghs, and the discovery of a *Picts' house* actually beneath the ruins of a burgh enables us to speak with certainty on this point.

In Ireland similar proofs have been found of the great antiquity of man. More than one hundred towers have been found in that country, all built of large stones, and varying in height from seventy to one hundred and thirty feet, with a diameter of from eight to fifteen feet. The most diverse origins have been attributed to these towers, from prehistoric times to the centuries immediately preceding the Christian era; from the time of the Druids to that of the Friars. According to the point of view of different archæologists, they have been called temples of the sun, hermitages, phallic monuments, or signal towers.

We meet with a similar problem in considering the *nurhags*, as in considering the burghs. They have been justly called a page of history, written all over the surface of Sardinia by an unknown people. Count Albert de la Marmora counted three thousand of them a few years ago, and more recent explorers tell us that this number is greatly exceeded. Like the burghs, which they strangely resemble, the *nurhags* are conical towers with very thick walls made of huge stones, some hewn, others in their natural state, arranged in regular courses without mortar. On entering one of them we find ourselves in a vaulted room, which looks exactly like one half of an egg in shape. In the upper stories are two, and sometimes three rooms, one above the other, to which access is gained by steps cut in the walls. The whole structure is crowned by a terrace (Fig. 53). We must add that the entrance to the *nurhag* is through an opening on a level with the ground, and so low that one can only go in by crawling on the stomach.

Many conjectures have been made as to the use of these towers. Were they temples in which to worship, or trophies of victory? Their number is against either of these hypotheses. Were they then habitations or towers of observation? Not the former certainly, for no one could live between walls sixteen or twenty-two feet thick, shut out from air and light. Some travellers think they were tombs, but excavations have brought to light no bones or sepulchral relics. We can com-

Fig. 53.—Nurhag at Santa Barbara (Sardinia).

pare them to nothing but the Towers of Silence, on which the Parsees expose their dead to the birds of heaven, which are ever ready rapidly to acquit themselves of their melancholy functions.

The origin of the *nurhags* is as uncertain as their use. Diodorus Siculus considered them very ancient, and one fact has come to light in our day which enables us to arrive at a somewhat more exact decision. The island of Sardinia was taken by the Romans from the Carthaginians in 238 B.C., and an aqueduct, the ruins of which can still be seen, was built by the conquerors on the foundations of an ancient *nurhag*, so that the latter must belong to an earlier date than the third century before our era. Fergusson, who speaks with authority on everything relating to the monuments of the Stone age, assigns the *nurhags* to the mystic times of the Trojan War. In all probability they were built by an invading people. La Marmora thinks these invaders were the Libyans; M. de Rougemont, in his history of the Bronze age, says that the curved vault is the characteristic feature of Pelasgian architecture, which is often confounded with that of the Phœnicians. Although any final conclusion would be premature, we ourselves think that the builders of the *nurhags* belonged to the great stream of emigration from the East, the course of which is marked by megalithic monuments in so many parts of the world. In some instances, *nurhags* were surrounded by cromlechs, of which most of the stones have now been thrown down. Some of these stones bore prominences resembling the breasts of a woman.

The accumulations of earth and rubbish about the *nurhags* are, some of them, from six to ten feet high. In the lower deposits have been found coarse pottery, with no attempt at ornamentation, fragments of flint, and obsidian hatchets of black basalt, or porphyry of the Palæolithic type, arrow-heads, flint knives, stones used in slings, and numerous shells; whilst in the upper deposits were picked up black pottery and fragments of bronze belonging to the transition period between the Stone and Metal ages.

All over the island of Sardinia, side by side with

the *nurhags*, rise tombs to which have been given the name of *Sepolture dei Giganti*. They are from thirty-two to thirty-nine feet long by a nearly equal width, and are built, some of huge slabs of stone, some of stones of smaller size. They are in every case surmounted by a pediment, formed of a single block, and often covered with sculptures dating from different epochs. These sepulchres are certainly of later date than the *nurhags*, and in them have been found numerous implements of bronze, but none of stone.

Fig. 54.—"Talayoti" at Trepuco (Minorca).

The *talayoti*, of which one hundred and fifty are still standing in the island of Minorca, are circular or elliptical truncated cones, built of huge unhewn stones, laid one on the other without cement (Fig. 54). The most remarkable of all of them, that at Torello, near Mahon, is thirty-three feet high. In many cases there are two stones, one placed upright, the other across it, in front of the *talayoti*. The meaning of these biliths is unknown.

Yet another series of cyclopean monuments are known under the name of *nanetas*, and are not unlike overturned boats. Seven such *nanetas* are still to be seen in the Balearic Isles. The one which is best preserved consists of large unhewn stones of rectangular shape, enclosing an inner chamber about six feet in width. The roof having fallen in, its height cannot be exactly determined; we only know that the lateral walls are some forty-five feet high.

In Algeria also have been preserved some towers built of stones without cement. Some of them are square *(basina)* and surmounted by a small dolmen, others are round *(chouchet)* and closed at the top by a large slab of stone, as in the *nurhags* we have just described.

It is difficult to bring this account to a close without mentioning the *truddhi* and the *specchie* of Otranto.[1] A *truddhi* is a massive conical tower consisting of a heap of scarcely hewn stones piled up without cement and with an exterior facing. Inside is a round room, the roof of which is formed by a series of circular courses of stone projecting one beyond the other. Sometimes a second chamber rises above the first, which is reached by steps cut in the facing, which steps also lead to the platform on the top of the tower. Thousands of *truddhi* are to be seen in Italy; they date from every epoch, and the people of Lecce and Bari continue to erect them as did their fathers before them. Side by side with the *truddhi* rise the *specchie*, which are conical masses of stone, of greater height and probably of more ancient date than the towers. Lenormant thinks they were used to live in; but his opinion has

---

[1] Nicolucci: "Scelse Lavorate, Bronzi e Monumenti di Terra d'Otranto." Lenormant, *Revue d'Ethnographie*, February, 1882 (*Bul. Soc. Anth.*, 1882 and 1884). S. Reinach: "Esquises Archéologiques."

been much questioned, and it is necessary to speak on this point with great reserve.

The *castellieri* of Istria, which the Slavonian peasants call *starigrad*, are as yet but little known. Doubtless an examination of them will bring out their resemblance to the *nurhags* and *talayoti*. They are, however, more than mere towers, forming regular *enceintes* between walls formed of two facings of dry stones, the space between which is filled in with smaller stones. There are fifteen of these *castellieri* in the district of Albona, a little town on the southeast of Trieste. They were at first attributed to the Roman epoch, but later researches relegate them rather to prehistoric times, and the discovery near them of numerous stone implements rather tends to support this latter opinion, but it must not be considered conclusive.

Perhaps we ought also to connect with the earliest ages of humanity the stations recently discovered in Spain by MM. Siret.[1] These were evidently centres of population, surrounded by walls of a very primitive description. We shall have to refer again to these discoveries; we will only add now that in the black earth forming the soil were found worked flints, polished diorite hatchets, pierced shells, with various pieces of pottery, and mills for grinding corn. So far, however, though many of the stations have been explored, no trace has been found of the use of metals.

A vast period of time, countless centuries, indeed, have passed away since the close of the Palæolithic epoch. The burghs, *nurhags*, and *castellieri* show the progress of civilization, and at the same time prove that this progress extended throughout Europe, and that at

---

[1] "Les Premiers Âges du Métal dans le Sud-Est de l'Espagne," Brussels, 1887.

a time not so very far removed from our own. The close resemblance between buildings of different dates enables us to speak with certainty of the connection between the races which succeeded each other in Europe. The importance of these conclusions is very great, and will be brought out still more in our study of megalithic monuments.

CHAPTER V.

MEGALITHIC MONUMENTS.

MEGALITHIC monuments are perhaps the most interesting of all the witnesses of the remote past, into the history of which we are now inquiring, and of which so little is known. From the shores of the Atlantic to the Ural Mountains, from the frontiers of Russia to the Pacific Ocean, from the steppes of Siberia to the plains of Hindustan, we see rising before us monuments of the same characteristic form, built in the same manner. This is a very important fact in the history of humanity, and of which it is difficult to exaggerate the importance.

What is the age of all these monuments? Were they all erected by one race, which has thus carried on its traditions from one generation to another? Were they the temples of the gods of this race, or the tombs of their ancestors? Did the people who set them up come from the East, or did they come from the North, on their way to the warmer regions of the South? These and many other questions are eagerly discussed, but in the present state of our knowledge not one of them can be answered in a perfectly satisfactory manner. *Scire ignorare magna scientia*, said an ancient philosopher, and this is a truth which we must often repeat when we are dealing with prehistoric times.

Under the name of megalithic monuments we include *tumuli, dolmens, cromlechs, menhirs*, and *covered avenues*. It may at first sight appear strange to include tumuli amongst stone monuments, but they almost always enclose a dolmen, a cist, or a crypt communicating with the outside by a covered passage. The excavation of more than four hundred tumuli in England has brought to light now a stone coffer made of a number of stones set edgeways and called a *kistvaen;* now of a tomb

FIG. 55.—Dolmen of Castle Wellan (Ireland).

hollowed out beneath the surface of the ground, and enclosed by huge blocks of stone.[1] Mounds are as numerous in Portugal as tumuli in England, and the fact that they are of low height has led to their being called *mamous* or *maminhas*, which signifies little mounds. In Poland, tumuli consist of piles of massive stones; beneath each is a cist made of four large slabs, and containing as many as eight or ten urns full of

---

[1] Bateman: "Ten Years' Diggings," Preface, p. 11.

calcined bones. The excavation of a tumulus in the plain of Tarbes brought to light an enormous block of granite resting on blocks of quartz. The spaces between these blocks were filled in with rubble made of small stones cemented into one mass with clay. Edwin-Harness Mound, near Liberty (Ohio), is 160 feet long by eighty or ninety wide, and thirteen to eighteen

Fig. 56.—The large dolmen of Coreoro, near Plouharnel.

high in the middle. It contained a dozen sepulchral chambers.

More rarely tumuli are merely artificial mounds of earth, sometimes rising to a great height. Those of North America are the most remarkable known. That of Cahokia is now ninety-one feet high,[1] and was for-

---

[1] W. MacAdams: "The Great Mound of Cahokia." Am. Ass., Minneapolis, 1883.

merly surmounted by a low pyramid, now destroyed. Its base measures 560 feet by 720, the platform at the top is 146 feet by 310 feet wide, and it has been estimated that twenty-five million cubic feet of earth were used in its construction. Major Pearse mentions a tumulus near Nagpore, which is 3,900 feet in circumference, and 174 feet high. Another between Tyre and Sarepta, is 130 feet high by 650 in diameter. It has never been excavated.[1]

FIG. 57.—Dolmen of Arrayolos (Portugal).

The dolmen type of monument is a rectangle of unhewn upright stones covered over with a slab laid across them; this slab being the largest block of stone that could be found in the neighborhood or obtained by the builders.

Dolmens are generally found either on the top of a natural or an artificial mound, in the middle of a plain, or on the banks of a watercourse. We must mention, amongst others, those in Persia, which are some 7,000

---

[1] Pelagaud: "Préhistoire en Syrie."

feet high and from twenty-one to twenty-six feet long by six wide; that near Mykenæ, that of Aumède-Bas, excavated by Dr. Prunières; that of New Grange, in Ireland, surmounted by a cromlech of stones of considerable size, many of them brought from a distance; that of Hellstone, near Dorchester, consisting of nine upright stones supporting a table more than twenty-seven and a half feet in circumference, seven feet wide and two and a half thick. The dolmens near Saturnia, one of the most ancient Etruscan towns, include a quadrangular room, sunk some feet into the earth, and having walls

FIG. 58.—Megalithic sepulchre at Acora (Peru).

made of blocks of stone and a roof of a couple of large slabs, sloped slightly to let the rain run off. We give illustrations of the dolmens of Castle Wellan in Ireland (Fig. 55), of Coreoro near Plouharnel (Morbihan) (Fig. 56), of Arrayolos in Portugal (Fig. 57), and Acora in Peru (Fig. 58), which will enable the reader to judge of the different modes of construction employed in building these megalithic monuments.

In some cases the dolmen, which alone is visible from without, is placed upon a mound, covering a hidden sepulchral chamber, whilst in others the crypt is replaced by a simple stone cist, generally of rectangular shape. We may mention in this connection the dolmen of Bekour-Noz at St. Pierre Quiberon, which is remarkable for its great size, and rises from the midst of a cemetery in which a great many coffins have been found. The bones they contained were unfortunately dispersed at the time of their discovery.

Dolmens are scattered about in great numbers in the Kouban basin and all along the coasts of the Black Sea occupied by the Tcherkesses. These curious vestiges of an unknown civilization are still an unsolved enigma to us, as are those of Western Europe; they are generally formed of four upright slabs surmounted by a fifth laid horizontally, and one of the supporting slabs is nearly always pierced with a small round or oval opening. Excavations have brought to light arrow-heads, rings, and bronze spirals, but Chantre, an authority of considerable weight, and who has moreover had the advantage of actually seeing these megalithic monuments of the south of Russia, attributes the objects found beneath them to secondary interments, and does not hesitate in assigning the more ancient monuments themselves to the Stone age. We must not omit to mention the dolmens found in the southern portion of the island of Yezo (Japan),[1] nor that described by Darwin at Puerto Deseado (Patagonia). They are both very similar to those of Europe.

To resume, dolmens, called *Hünengräber* in Germany, *stazzona* in Corsica, *antas* in Portugal, and *stendos* in Sweden, have all alike one large flat horizontal slab

---

[1] Moore, *Popular Science Monthly*, New York, March, 1880; *Zeitschrift für Ethnologie*: Berlin, 1887.

placed on two or more upright unhewn stones. This is the one fixed rule; local circumstances, perhaps even the caprice of the builders, decided the position and the mode of erection. Often, as I have already remarked, dolmens are buried beneath tumuli, but exceptions to this are numerous. General Faidherbe, after having examined more than six thousand dolmens in Algeria, affirms that the greater number have never been covered with earth.[1] In the Orkney Islands there are more than one hundred dolmens without tumuli, and Martinet failed to find any trace of mounds in Berry. In Scotland and Brittany we find dolmens buried, not beneath mounds of earth, but under accumulations of pebbles, called *cairns* in Scotland and *galgals* in Brittany. However minor details may vary, and they do vary infinitely, one main idea everywhere dominated the builders, and that was the desire to protect from all profanation the resting-place of what had once been a human being.

Cromlechs are circles of upright stones often surrounding dolmens or tumuli. Sometimes they form single circles, and at others two, three, or even seven separate enclosures. They are common in Algeria, Sweden, and Denmark, and in the last-named country two kinds are distinguished: the *langdyssers*, which form an ellipse, and the *rundyssers* which form a perfect circle. In other countries cromlechs are not so numerous; there are but few in France, of which we may name those of Kergoman (Morbihan), Lestridion in Plomeur, and Landaondec in Crozon (Finistère). The last-named, known as *le temple des faux dieux*, is closed by a double row of small menhirs. In Italy, the only

---

[1] "Monuments de Roknia," p. 18.

cromlechs known are those of Sesto-Calende and those of the plateau of Mallevalle near Ticino. One of the latter still retains in their original position fifty-nine huge granite blocks, forming a circular enceinte, a semicircle, and an entrance avenue. A few leagues from the ancient Tyre can still be seen a circle of upright stones. Ouseley describes another at Darab, in Persia; a missionary speaks of three large circles at Khabb, in Arabia, which circles he compares with those at Stonehenge; and Dr. Barth tells us of a cromlech between Mourzouk and Ghât.

A kurgan, or tumulus, having been opened in the Kherson district, three or four concentric circles were discovered beneath it, surrounding a structure of considerable size.[1] The cromlech of Anajapoura in Ceylon, probably, however, erected comparatively recently, consists of fifty-two granite pillars, about thirteen feet high, encircling a Buddhist temple. At Peshawur is another circle, fourteen of the stones of which are still upright, whilst traces can be made out of an outer enceinte of smaller stones; in Peru there are several cromlechs, whilst others have been found at the foot of Elephant Mount, in the desert plains of Australia. The last-named vary from ten to one thousand feet in diameter, but excavations beneath them have brought to light only a few human bones.

At Mzora, in Morocco, the traveller will notice a mound of elliptical shape, some 21 or 22½ feet high, flanked on the west by a group of menhirs, and surrounded by an enceinte of upright stones which now

---

[1] Haxtausen: "Mém. sur la Russie," vol. ii., p. 204; A. Bogdanow: "Mat. pour Servir à l'Histoire des Kourganes," Moscow, 1879; Margaret Stokes: "La Disposition des Principaux Dolmens de l'Irlande," *Rev. Arch.*, July, 1882.

number about forty. In 1831, there were still ninety, and on the south side were noticed two round pillars parallel with each other, which probably formed an entrance.[1] This group evidently originally formed the centre of a series of megalithic monuments, for on the north and southwest some fifty monoliths can still be made out, some still erect, others fallen.[2]

It was in Great Britain, however, that cromlechs appear to have reached their highest development. That of Salkeld in Cumberland includes sixty-seven menhirs; that near Loch Stemster in Caithness, thirty-three, whilst in Westmoreland, *Long Meg and her daughters* are still the objects of superstitious reverence. The remains at Avebury are among the most remarkable prehistoric monuments still extant, and evidently originally formed part of a most important group. This group had an outer rampart of earth, with a ditch on the inner side, within which was a circle of upright stones, probably numbering as many as one hundred. Within this circle were two others of smaller size, each in its turn enclosing yet another circle of upright stones. In the middle of one of these inner circles, that on the north, was a dolmen, whilst that on the south enclosed in the centre but a single upright menhir. The stones used in constructing these various groups were all such as are still to be found on the Wiltshire downs. From the southeastern portion of the extensive earthen rampart, a stone avenue extended for a considerable distance in a perfectly straight line, and is still known as Kennet's Avenue,

---

[1] Sir A. de Capell Brooke: "Sketches in Spain and Morocco."
[2] Tissot: "Récherches sur la Géographie Comparée de la Mauritanie Tingitane."

on account of its leading to the village of Kennet. The remains on Hakpen Hill and on Silbury Hill are all supposed to have been originally connected with those at Avebury. The remains at Hakpen consist of relics of two circles, one about 140 feet in diameter, the other not more than forty. About eighty yards from the inner circle was found a double row of skeletons, all with the feet pointing towards the centre. Silbury Hill is itself an artificial conical mound, the largest in England, 170 feet high, on which were originally no less than 650 upright stones, of which only twenty are still standing, surrounded by a trench. In the centre of the circle of stones a single menhir of great height still remains with three others sloped so as to form a kind of crypt.

The megalithic monuments of Stonehenge, which are probably better known than any others in the world, are perhaps also the most curious. The group is supposed to have originally consisted of an outer stone concentric circle some one hundred feet in diameter, formed by thirty piers of solid masonry, of which about twenty can still be made out, some few standing, others lying broken upon the ground. This outer circle enclosed a second of similar shape but lesser diameter, within which again were two elliptic circles, the outer consisting of ten or twelve sandstone blocks some twenty-two feet high, standing in pairs, each pair united by a slab laid horizontally across, so as to form a trilithon. The inner ellipse was formed by nineteen upright masses of granite, within which was the famous slab of blue marble, by many supposed to have been an altar. The pillars and lintels of the outer portico, and those of the trilithons, are fitted together with the greatest skill, with tenons and mortices, a remarkable exception to the general rule with megalithic monuments. Everywhere in the neighborhood of Stonehenge, as far as the eye can reach, are tumuli, all nearly equidistant from the principal group of monuments, a fact which has led many archæologists, including Henry Martin, to look upon Stonehenge as a temple surrounded by a necropolis. Excavations at Stonehenge have yielded a few human bones which have escaped the flames, with some stone and bronze weapons.

The megalithic monuments of Ireland are not less important, and a recent survey has reported no less than 276 still standing.[1] The cromlechs of Moytura[2] are supposed to commemorate the fearful combats which took place between the *Firbolgs*, or Belgæ as they are called by Irish antiquaries, and the Tuatha de Danauns, when the plains of Sligo and Meath were dyed with blood, before the former were vanquished and retired to Arran. There are still no less than fourteen dolmens and thirty-nine cromlechs. The bones picked up beneath the stone circles, which keep alive the memory of these sanguinary conflicts, are those of the warriors who fell on the battle-field, but the story of how they met their fate belongs rather to history than to the subject we are considering. It is the same with the two huge monoliths of Cornwall. which commemorate a battle between the Welsh King Howel Dha and the Saxon Athelstane, as well as with the cromlechs of Ostrogothland, where, in 736, took

---

[1] Margaret Stokes: "La Distribution des Principaux Dolmens de l'Irlande." *Revue Arch.*, July, 1882.

[2] Sir W. Wilde: "Ireland, Past and Present." Miss Buckland: "Cornish and Irish Prehistoric Monuments." *Anth. Inst.*, Nov., 1879. O'Curry: "Lectures on the Manuscript Materials of Irish History."

place the battle in which the old King Harold Hildebrand was overcome and killed by his nephew, Sigurd-Ring. A group of forty-four circles also marks the site of the celebrated combat of 1030, in which Knut the Great defied Olaf the patron saint of Norway. We may also name in this connection the twenty circles of stone erected at Upland in memory of the massacre of the Danish prince, Magnus Henricksson, in 1161. Yet another group of circles marks the spot where, about 1150, the Swedish heroine, Blenda, overcame King Sweyne Grate. We might easily multiply instances of the erection in historic times of similar monuments, but we have said enough to show that the megalithic form was by no means confined to prehistoric days.

Menhirs properly so called, also known as *lechs* in Brittany, are in reality isolated monoliths or single upright stones, often of considerable size. One of the best known is that of Locmariaker (Fig. 59) which was nearly seventy feet high.[1] It was still standing in 1659, but is now overturned and broken into four pieces. The flat stone resting on one portion of it is known as Cæsar's table. On some menhirs, notably on Sweno's pillar in Scotland, a cross has been cut on one side, showing either that this form of monument was early adopted by Christians, or more probably, that it was adapted to their use after having long previously been a relic of prehistoric times. On the other side of Sweno's pillar is a bas-relief of fairly good execution.

In some cases menhirs mark the site of a tomb, and sometimes, as is the case with the obelisks of Egypt, they commemorate some happy event. A standing stone in Scotland preserves the memory of

---
[1] *Bul. Soc. Pol. du Morbihan*, April, 1885.

FIG. 59.—The great broken menhir of Locmariaker, with Cæsar's table.

the battle of Largs, which took place in the thirteenth century, and a piously preserved legend tells how the menhir of Aberlemno was set up in honor of a victory over the Danes in the tenth century.

Some archæologists, in view of the shape of certain menhirs and the superstitions connected with them, think they must be phallic monuments. Menhirs in France are quoted in this connection, cut into the form of the phallus; and the same form occurs in some menhirs near Saphos, in the island of Cyprus,[1] and in others found amongst the ruins of Uxmal, in Yucatan. Herodotus relates that Sesostris caused to be set up, in countries he conquered, monoliths bearing in relief representations of the female sexual organs. These are, however, but exceptions, isolated facts, and it would certainly never do to argue from them that menhirs were connected with the worship of the generative powers of nature.

It is extremely difficult to get at the statistics of menhirs. A great many have been overthrown, and yet more have disappeared altogether. Probably, besides the alignments or stone avenues, there are not more than twenty still standing.[2] One thing is certain, the monolithic form of monument has always had a great attraction for the human race, and we meet with it in Egypt, Assyria, Persia, and Mexico, as well as in England and Brittany. The historian speaks of such monuments in the earliest of existing records; Homer refers to them in the Iliad,[3] and in the

---
[1] S. Reinach, *Rev. Arch.*, 1888. Wilson: "Megalithic Monuments of Brittany." Cartailhac: "La France Préhistorique," in which the measurements are given of the principal monuments of Brittany.

[2] A. Bertrand: "Archéologie Celtique et Gauloise," p. 105.

[3] Iliad, book xxiii., v. 380.

Bible we find it related that the Lord ordered Joshua to set up twelve stones in memory of the crossing of the Jordan by the Israelites.[1]

Alignments are groups of menhirs set up in one or more rows. Sometimes large slabs are laid across them, when they are called covered avenues. One such alignment at Saint Pantaléon (Saône et Loire) consists of twenty menhirs. The menhirs of El Wad, in Algeria, form long avenues, running from west to east. The Arabs call them *essenam*, and according to tradition they were erected in fulfilment of a vow made in the hope of arresting the march of an enemy. The tumulus of Run-Aour (Finistère) has two avenues running at right angles to one another.[2] This disposition, which is very rare, also occurs at Karleby, in Sweden, and by a remarkable coincidence the length of the avenues (about thirty-nine and fifty-five feet), is the same in both cases. Sometimes such avenues form communications between several dolmens, leading us to suppose that near the chief slept the members of his family or his favorite companions.

The covered avenues are often built beneath masses of earth, and the inner rooms became regular hypogea, These hypogea, or subterranean chambers, are very common near Paris, and we may mention amongst many others those of Meudon, Argenteuil, Conflans-Sainte-Honorine, Marly, Chamant, La Justice, and Compans. The tombs of Denmark, the *Gang Graben* of Nilsson, show an arrangement somewhat similar, a vast subterranean chamber being reached by a passage ending in a small stone cist. The tumulus of Dissignac,

---
[1] Joshua, chap. iv., v. 13 *et seq.*
[2] P. du Chatellier, *Mém. Soc. d'Émulation des Côtes-du-Nord*, vol. xix.

near Saint-Nazaire (Fig. 60), shows this strange arrangement of two galleries running parallel with each other at a distance of about eighteen feet. The walls and ceilings are made of slabs, and the interstices are filled in with flints. These galleries are some thirty feet long, and their height insensibly increases from about three to nine feet.

Fig. 60.—Covered avenue of Dissignac (Loire-Inférieur); view of the chamber at the end of the north gallery.

We must also mention the Cueva de Mengal, near the village of Antequera, in the province of Malaga (Fig. 61.) Twenty stones form the walls of the crypt, five blocks of remarkable size serve as a roof, and to ensure solidity three pillars are set upright inside of the junction of the roof blocks. The crypt is some seventy-nine feet long, its greatest width is about nineteen feet, and its height varies from about eight to nine feet. The length of the Pastora room, near Seville is about eighty-seven feet, but its height is not to be compared with that of the one at Antequera. The square crypt at Pastora is very interesting. One of the roof stones having been broken, it has been strengthened by the addition of an inside pillar.[1]

At Gavr'innis, the length of the passage leading to the crypt exceeds forty-two feet (Fig. 62), and the Long

FIG. 61.—Covered avenue near Antequera.

Barrow of West Kennet is more than seventy-three feet long by a width in some parts exceeding thirty-two feet. In the Long Barrows of Littleton, Nempnitt, and Uley, the crypt is reached by an avenue, the entrance of which is closed by a trilithon, and a similar arrangement is met with in many megalithic monuments of Scania. The sepulchral chambers of oval shape, such as that met with in the island of Moen, were surmounted by

---

[1] Cartailhac : "Les Âges Préhistoriques en Espagne et en Portugal."

a tumulus some 100 yds. in circumference; twelve unhewn stones formed the walls, and five large blocks the roof. In removing the earth from the Moen tomb, the bones of several human individuals were found; and a skeleton, doubtless that of the chief, lay stretched out in the middle of the chamber, whilst the bones of the others had evidently been ranged against the walls either in a sitting or crouching position. With the bones were found a flint hatchet, which appeared never to have been used, a number of balls of amber, and several vases of different shapes.

FIG. 62.—Ground plan of the Gavr'innis monument.

The megalithic monuments of Mecklenburg are supposed to date from Neolithic times, and are constructed in two very different ways. The *Hünengräber*, formed of huge blocks of granite set up at right angles to each other, resemble the covered avenues of France and elsewhere; in the so-called *Riesenbetten*, or giant's beds, on the contrary, the sepulchral chamber is merely sunk in the ground.

We must also mention the so-called *Grotte des Fées*, or fairy grotto, forming part of so many of the megalithic monuments of Provence. This fairy grotto includes an open-air gallery cut in the mountain limestone and roofed in with huge flat stones. This gallery leads to a sepulchral chamber not less than seventy-nine feet long.

The stones used for the covered avenue of Mureaux (Seine et Oise) came from the other side of the Seine, so that the builders must have crossed the river in a raft. Excavations have brought to light several skeletons that had been buried without any attempt at orientation, the bones of which were still in their natural position. The objects found in this tomb were very numerous and belonged to the Neolithic period.[1]

We have now specified the chief forms and modes of arrangement of megalithic monuments, and must add that they are often found in juxtaposition. At Mané-Lud, for instance, on a rocky platform which had been artificially smoothed, and which is some 246 feet long by 162 in area, we find at the eastern extremity an avenue of upright stones, on the west a dolmen, and in the centre a crypt surmounted by a conical pile of stones. Between the cone and the avenue the ground is covered with an artificial paving of small stones cemented together, and known in France as a *nappe pierreuse*, and amongst the stones forming this paving were found quantities of charcoal and bones of animals. The megalith was completely buried beneath a mound of earth, or rather of dried mud, the amount of which was estimated at more than 37,986 cubic feet. At Lestridiou (Finistère), a cromlech forms the starting-point of an alignment formed of seven rows of small menhirs, the mean height of which above the ground does not exceed three feet; and these alignments lead up to two covered avenues and a central dolmen. In other cases, in England and the land of

---

[1] Verreaux, *L'Anthropologie*, 1890, p. 157.

Moab for instance, alignments simply lead to cromlechs; whilst in some few cases, as at Stennis (Fig. 63), the menhirs are scattered about a plain in great numbers, with nothing either in their form or their position, or in the traditions relating to them, to throw the slightest light on their origin.

FIG. 63.—Monoliths at Stennis, in the Orkney Islands.

One of the most important monuments that have come down to us is that of Carnac. The alignments of Menec, Kermario, and Kerlescant include 1,771 menhirs, of which 675 are still standing. The alignments of Erdeven, which succeed those of Carnac, extend for a length of more than a mile and a half. They originally included 1,030 menhirs, of which 288 are still extant.

The archæologists of Brittany, carried away perhaps by their patriotic enthusiasm, claim that when these monuments were intact they included two thousand menhirs. What is really certain, however, is that a definite plan was evidently followed, the distances between the alignments tallying exactly; the menhirs being set up in straight parallel lines gradually decreasing in size towards the east. Excavations near them have brought to light fragments of charcoal, masses of cinders, chips of silicate of flint, with numerous fragments of pottery, and tools made of quartzite, granite, schist, and diorite, similar to those met with under all the other megaliths of Morbihan. This is yet another proof, if such were needed, that they were all the work of the same race and all probably date from the same period.

The number of megalithic monuments in the world is simply incalculable. M. A. Bertrand estimates the total number in France as 2,582, distributed in 66 departments and 1,200 communes. They are most numerous of all in Brittany; there are 491 in the Côtes-du-Nord, 530 in Ille-et-Vilaine. I am not sure of the number in Morbihan, but I know it is very considerable. The commission appointed at the instigation of Henry Martin decided that there were as many as 6,310 megaliths in France, but then amongst these were included polishing stones and cup-shaped stones, with other similar relics of the remote past. Lastly, a report recently presented to the Chamber of Deputies by M. A. Proust estimates at 419 the number of groups classed by government. In other countries these numbers are greatly exceeded. There are 2,000 megaliths in the Orkney Islands and a great many in the extreme north of Scania, and in Otranto in the southern extremity of Europe, where they resemble the *pedras fittas* of Sardinia. Pallas, and after him, Haxthausen, tells us that there are thousands of kurganes in the steppes of Central and Southern Russia.¹ These kurganes are cromlechs, tombs surmounted by upright stones, square or conical hypogea, all scattered about without any apparent system, surmounted by roughly sculptured female busts, known amongst the common people as *kamena baba*, or stone women. Tumuli, too, abound on the shores of the Irtisch and of the Yenisei, mute witnesses to the former presence of a vanished race of which we know neither the ancestors nor the descendants. These monuments are, however, by some attributed to the Tchoudes, a people who came from the Altai Mountains. The Esthonians, the Ogris or Ulgres, the Finns, and perhaps even the Celts, are supposed to be branches of the same ethnological tree. This is however quite a recent idea, and at best but a mere hypothesis.²

Algeria presents a vast field for research, and it is easy to find dolmens and cromlechs, such as that shown in Fig. 64, which are sepulchres with a central dolmen surrounded by a double or triple enceinte of monoliths

---

[1] Haxthausen : " Mém. sur la Russie Mér., vol. ii., p. 204. " Fouilles des Kourganes," par M. Samokoasof, *Revue Arch.*, 1879. Much : *Mittheilungen der Anth. Gesell. in Wien*, 1878.

[2] On this point see the excellent work by Maury, " Les Monuments de la Russie et les Tumulus Tchoudes," and Meynier and Eichtal's "'Tumulus des Anciens Habitants de la Sibérie."

driven into the ground. These monuments, much as they differ in form and arrangement, are undoubtedly the work of one strong and powerful race that dominated the whole of the north of Africa; and are represented in historic times by the Berbers, and at the present day by the Kabyles.

FIG. 64.—Cromlech near Bône (Algeria).

Although a very great many of them have been destroyed, the French possessions in Algeria are still as rich in monuments of this kind as any of the countries of Europe. On Mount Redgel-Safia six hundred dolmens have been made out, with stone tables resting on walls of dry stones and frequently surrounded by cromlechs. Dr. Weisgerber has recently announced the discovery in the valley of Ain-Massin, on the west of Mzab, of a cromlech consisting of a number of concentric circles of large stones set upon an elliptical tumulus, more than fifty-four square yards in area. Quite close is a workshop of flint weapons, probably in use at the time of the erection of the megaliths.[1] In Midjana, the number of megaliths exceeds 10,000, and General Faidherbe counted more than 2,000 in the necropolis of Mazela, and a yet larger number in that of Roknia. "At Bou-Merzoug," says M. Feraud,[2] "in a radius of three leagues, on the mountain as well as on the plain, the whole country about the springs is covered with monuments of the Celtic form, such as dolmens, demi-dolmens, menhirs, avenues, and tumuli. In a word, there are to be found examples of nearly every type known in Europe. For fear of being taxed with exaggeration, I will not fix the number, but I can certify that I saw and examined more than a thousand in the three days of exploration, on the mountain itself, and on the declivities wherever it was possible to place them. All the monuments are surrounded with a more or less complete enceinte of large stones, sometimes set up in a circle, sometimes in a square, In some cases the living rock forms part of the enceinte, which has been completed with the help of other blocks from elsewhere. It is often difficult to decide where the monument ends and the rock begins. When the escarpment was too abrupt, it was levelled with the aid of a kind of retaining wall,

---

[1] *Revue d'Anth.*, 1880, p. 655.
[2] *Mém. de la Soc. Arch. de la Province de Constantine*, 1863.

which forms a terrace round the dolmen. The dolmens in the plain seem to have been constructed with even greater care. The enceintes are wider and the slabs of the tables larger." Megalithic monuments are met with even in the desert. A pyramid built of stones without mortar rises up in the districts inhabited by the Touaregs; and quite near to it are four or five tombs surrounded by standing stones.

In Algeria, we also meet with quadrangular pyramids called *djedas*, which measure as much as ninety feet on each face, but do not rise more than three feet above the ground. The dead were buried beneath them in a crouching position. We know nothing either of the origin of these djedas or of the date to which they belong.

The monuments of Tunisia were probably as numerous as those of Algeria. We may note especially the vast area in Enfida, completely covered with dolmens, one hundred of which are still standing, and in excellent preservation, whilst the ruins of others strew the soil, bringing up their original number to at least three thousand. Those described by M. Girard de Rialle[1] are yet more interesting. Near the village of Ellez, on the road from Kef to Kerouan, are some fifteen covered avenues distributed without apparent order, and rising from the midst of Roman ruins. The upright stones vary from about ten to thirteen feet, and are surmounted by huge slabs. The chief dolmen has within it as many as ten chambers.

There are also numerous tumuli in Syria. We have already alluded to that of Sarepta; and there are

---

[1] "Monuments Mégalithiques de la Tunisie," *Ant. Afric.*, July, 1884. Dr. Rouire: "Les Dolmens de l'Enfida," *Bull. Geog. Hist.*, 1886.

others near Antioch and in the plain of Beka, between Lebanon and Anti-Lebanon. Major Conder, who as captain conducted the interesting campaign organized by the Palestine Exploration Society in 1881 and 1882, speaks of the exploration of the rude stone monuments as one of the most interesting features of the surveys, and says: "The distribution of the centres where these monuments occur in Syria, is a matter of no little importance . . . no dolmens, menhirs, or ancient circles have been discovered in Judaea, and only one doubtful circle in Samaria. In Lower Galilee a single dolmen has been found; in Upper Galilee four of moderate dimensions are known. West of Tiberias is a circle, and between Tyre and Sidon an enclosure of menhirs. At Tell el Kady, one of the Jordan sources, a centre of basalt dolmens exists, and at Kefr Wal . . . there is another large centre. At Amman several fine dolmens and large menhirs are known to exist . . . it is doubtful, however, if all these examples added together would equal the great fields of rude stone monuments to be found in Moab, for it is calculated that seven hundred examples were found by the surveyors in 1881.[1] There is one group of dolmens at Ali Safat, in Palestine, in which the supports of the table are pierced with an opening. This is a very interesting fact, to which I have already alluded, and to which I shall have to refer again. Another group of some twenty dolmens was discovered by M. de Saulcy on the plateau of El Azemieh, one of which rises in the centre of a belt of roughly sculptured upright stones; and yet a third group is to be seen near Mount Nebo, which Major Conder thus describes: "Here a well-

---

[1] "Heth and Moab," pp. 191 and 192.

defined dolmen was found northwest of the flat, ruined cairn, which marks the summit of the ridge. The cap-stone was very thick, and its top is some five feet from the ground. The side-stones were rudely piled, and none of the blocks were cut or shaped . . . In subsequent visits it was ascertained that on the south slope of the mountain there is a circle about 250 feet in diameter, with a wall of twelve feet thick, consisting of small stones piled up in a sort of vellum." [1]

With regard to the megalithic monuments of India, we can only repeat what we have already said. Colonel Meadows Taylor has counted 2,129 in the district of Bellary (Deccan) alone. Many legends are connected with them which remind us of those of Europe, some attributing their erection to dwarfs or giants, to fairies or to genii, whilst others think they were the work of the Kauranas and Pandavas, the celebrated families whose long struggle is described in the Mahabharata, and were probably aboriginal races of the continent. The plain of Jellalabad and of Nagpore, and the valley of Cabul are literally strewn with these monuments. They are not less numerous in the Presidency of Madras, where they chiefly consist of subterranean chambers made of huge unhewn stones or of dolmens above ground surrounded by one or more circles of upright stones, such as are shown in Fig. 65. Major Biddulph, when he ascended the valleys of the Hindoo Koosh Mountains, was astonished to see on every side megalithic monuments resembling those of his own country, and, like them, the work of an unknown race.[2]

---
[1] "Heth and Moab," p. 249.
[2] "Tribes of the Hindoo Koosh," Calcutta, 1881.

This is, of course, but a very rapid survey of the megalithic monuments of our globe. They are most of them either tombs intended to hold the bodies of the dead, or memorials set up in their honor. New facts are constantly coming to light in this connection, and we may add to what we have already said, that beneath the tumulus of Mugen, as in the Cabeço d'Aruda (Portugal), there are numerous skeletons;

FIG. 65.—Dolmen at Pallicondah, near Madras (India).

sixty-two repose in the sepulchral chamber of Monastier (Lozère); the dolmen known as the Mas de l'Aveugle (Gard) covers a circular cavity in which fifteen corpses had been placed; that of La Mouline (Charente) also enclosed a number of skeletons, all in a crouching position, whilst above them were placed two clumsy vases, a pious offering to the unknown dead. The prehistoric cemetery of Maupas contains several crypts of irregular form, built of rubble stone, and surmounted by a huge stone which had become corroded by age. In these crypts, too, the dead were piled up on each other, and the relics found with them justify us in assigning them to the Neolithic age. Beneath the dolmens of Port-Blanc (Morbihan) were two upper layers of dead, stretched out horizontally and separated by flat stones. In the Isle de Thinic (Morbihan) excavations have brought to light twenty-seven stone cists or coffins of different sizes, all intended to be used for burial. Beneath the menhirs of Finistère, cinders and stones charred by fire bear eloquent witness to the cremation of the dead. "Whenever a dolmen has been opened in Finistère," says Dr. Floquet, "cinders or bones have been picked up; why, then, should we not admit that all dolmens are tombs?" This is really a conclusion to which we are almost compelled to come, and the names handed down by popular tradition are, if need be, yet another proof of the same thing. One dolmen at Locmariaker, for instance, is known as *le tombeau du vieillard*, a covered avenue at Saint Gildas is *le champ du tombeau*, and farther on a pathway leading to a ruined megalith is known as the *chemin du tombeau*. The Abbé Hamard speaks of a remarkable monolith known as *la pierre du champ dolent*, and another *champ dolent* is met with near Rheims, whilst a group of monuments near Tréhontereuc is called the *jardin des tombes*, and the upright stones of Auvergne are known by the characteristic name of the *plourouses*.

Whether we examine the megaliths of Germany or of Poland, the mounds of Ohio or of Kentucky, of Missouri or of Arkansas, it is ever the same thing;

excavations bring to light striking proofs of their destination, and everywhere we are led to the same conclusions.

Archaeologists would certainly appear to have been justified in hoping that the tombs thus scattered about all over the world would yield such useful information as to lead to some final conclusions. Unfortunately, however, this has not been the case. Often all trace of burial has disappeared in successive displacements, and more often still, the home of the dead has been violated in the hope, which turned out to be imaginary, of finding treasures; whilst in other cases the earliest inhabitants of the tombs have been removed to make way for their successors, who in their turn were soon afterwards expelled. Victory and defeat were not over with life, but were met with yet again in the grave.

It has been well pointed out by Fergusson, in his "Rude Stone Monuments," that the megalithic architecture of the remote past is a thing altogether apart; its special form indicating now the tendencies of a race or group of races of mankind, now the particular degree of civilization attained by a race at a certain period of its development. A cursory view of these monuments as a whole would lead us to class them all together as masses of rough, scarcely hewn stones piled up without cement, and almost always without ornamentation. In studying them one by one, however, we find, in spite of their undeniable family likeness, if we may use such a term, that it is quite easy to make out certain differences, the result of the peculiar genius of the race by whom they were erected, or of the nature of the materials the builders had at their disposal. To take a case in point: Cromlechs are most numerous in England, and dolmens in France, and in both these countries we meet with a form of dolmen (Fig. 66) such as is rarely set up in other districts; one of the extremities of the table resting on the ground, and the other on two supporting stones. In Scandinavia the supports are erratic blocks, in India fragments of the rocks in the neighborhood; in

FIG. 66.—Dolmen at Maintenon, with a table about 19¼ feet long.

Algeria and the south of France buildings in courses are often met with; in Brittany the monuments of Mané-er-H'roek and Mané-Lud are paved with large stones. The ground from which rises the dolmen of Caranda, near Fère in Tardenois (Aisne), is covered with slabs, and the opening is closed with a flat stone resting on two lintels. We cannot speak of Caranda without referring to the discoveries and magnificent publications of M. F. Moreau, thanks to whom the daily life of the Gauls, Gallo-Romans, and Merovingians is brought vividly before us. To return, however to our monuments: As we have seen, the crypt was in many cases divided into two or more sepulchral chambers by walls made of stones. We find this arrangement at Gavr'innis, at Gamat (Lot), at Alt-Sammit in Mecklenburg, in Wayland Smith's cave in Berkshire, and in a great many monuments in Scandinavia. M. du Chatellier speaks of several megalithic monuments in Finistère, including a central dolmen and several lateral chambers. The chambered graves at Park Cwn in Wales, and at Uley in Gloucestershire, contain side chambers, those of the former with a covered passage between them, whilst in the latter the side chambers are grouped round a central apartment. At New Grange, in Ireland, a passage more than ninety-two feet long leads to a double chamber of cruciform shape, with a roof of converging stones. Yet another fine example of a similar kind is that of Maeshow in the Orkney Islands. The tomb of Vauréal (Seine-et-Oise) contains three crypts of different sizes. The long barrow of Moustoir-Carnac contained four separate chambers, the western one of which is a dolmen of the kind known as *Grottes des Fées*, and is supposed to be much older than the rest of the group. A central circular chamber, with walls of upright stones, has a roof in which an attempt has been made to form a kind of dome, the stones of which project and overlap each other, marking, clumsy as is the construction, a considerable advance on anything previously accomplished, and adding considerably to the solidity of the monument.

An examination of the megalithic monuments still

standing enables us to judge of the difficulties with
which their builders had to contend, bearing in mind
the primitive nature of their tools. We have already
given the dimensions of the stones forming the alignments at Carnac. Those at Avebury vary in height
from about fourteen to sixteen feet, and in the Deccan
is a tumulus surrounded by fifty-six blocks of granite
of an even greater size. One of the slabs of the Pedra-
dos-Muros (Portugal) is remarkable for its size; and
the length of the table of a dolmen on the road from
Loudun to Fontevrault is more than seventy-two feet
long; that of the dolmen of Tiaret (Algeria) is some
seventy-five feet long by a width of nearly twenty-six
feet and a thickness of nine and a half feet. This
extremely heavy block rests on supports rising more
than thirty-nine feet from the ground.[1]

Stone as well as wood can be much more easily cut
in one direction than in any other. Men early learnt
to recognize this peculiarity, and to take advantage of
it in attacking rock. With their stone hammers they
struck in straight lines, always aiming at the same
points, and then, probably with the help of a fierce
fire, they succeeded in breaking off fragments. They
also employed wedges of wood, which they drove into
natural or artificial fissures, pouring water on to this
wedge again and again. The wood became swollen
with the damp, and in course of time a block of stone
would be detached. Neither time nor sinewy arms
were wanting, and Fergusson has remarked that any one
who has seen the ease with which Chinese coolies

---

[1] *Matériaux*, 1887, p. 458. M. Pallart ("Mon. Meg. de Mascaro"), thinks that this dolmen was not erected by man, but that a long slab of stone has slipped down the slopes of the mountain and rested on two natural supports. It is not easy to accept this view.

transport the largest monoliths for considerable distances, will not look upon the difficulties of transport as insurmountable. A more serious difficulty would be the placing of the table of the dolmen on the supports, which are often raised to a great height above the ground. It is supposed that earth was piled up against the jambs so as to form an inclined plane, up which the table was slid into place with levers and rollers of the most primitive form, such as were in use in the most remote antiquity. Sometimes the way in which these stones are balanced is perfectly marvellous. The Martine stone, near Livernon (Lot), for instance, is the shape of a boat, and the slightest touch is enough to make it rock on its two supports. That of Castle Wellan (Fig. 55) rests on three stones pointed at the top, and some of the trilithons of India are of even more remarkable construction.

Although, as a general rule, megalithic monuments are without ornamentation, there are a good many exceptions in the case of dolmens made of very hard granite, on which numerous carvings and engravings have been made. It is, however, impossible to decipher any but a very few of these signs, whether circles, disks, dots, tooth or leaf mouldings, spirals, serpentine lines, lozenges, or striæ.

M. du Chatellier describes at Commana (Finistère) an entrance gallery loaded with carvings, and the walls of one of the Deux-Sèvres monuments have on them some very rough representations of the human figure cut in *intaglio*, whilst various megaliths of Ireland are adorned with circles, spirals, stars, etc. One of the supports of the dolmen of Petit-Mont-en-Arzon has on it a representation of two human feet in relief; that of

Couedic in Lockmikel-Baden is paved with flat stones covered with engravings. On the granite ceiling of the crypt beneath the dolmen of the Merchants, or as it is called in Brittany the *Dol Varchant*, is engraved the figure of a large animal supposed to have been a

FIG. 67.—Part of the Mané-Lud dolmen.

horse, but the head of which was unfortunately broken off at some remote date.[1] We often meet with representations of hammers, sometimes with and sometimes without handles. We give an illustration of one of

---

[1] Dr. de Closmadeuc, agreeing, I think, with Henry Martin, derives the name of *Dol Varchant* from *Dol March'-Hent*, the table of the horse of the avenue.

the walls of the Mané-Lud monument (Fig. 67), which will enable the reader to judge of the general character of these engravings.

The monument of the Isle of Gavr'innis, of which we have already spoken, is the most remarkable of any for the richness of its decoration. It includes a gallery, consisting of forty-nine blocks of granite and two of quartz, leading to a spacious apartment. These blocks were brought from a distance, and the fact that the little arm of the sea separating the island from the mainland was crossed, proves that the men who built the monument owned boats strong enough to carry heavy loads. Excavations carried on in 1884 brought to light a pavement consisting of ten large slabs of granite, and beneath this pavement was found a kind of crypt at least three feet deep, the lower part of the lateral menhirs forming the walls. We must add, however, that Dr. de Closmadeuc, and his opinion should carry weight, thinks that when the Gavr'innis monument was erected the island was connected with the mainland. Three of the supports, forming the walls of the crypt, and all those of the gallery are covered with chevrons or zig-zag ornaments, circles, lozenges, and scrolls of which Fig. 68 will give some idea, and which Mérimée compares to the tatooing of the inhabitants of New Zealand. Megalithic monuments of Ireland and certain stones in Northumberland are ornamented in a manner resembling the Gavr'innis engraving, similar designs being produced by similar means, and although the engravings of Morbihan are generally more clearly cut and distinct, we note in all alike the same absence of regularity, the same roughness of execution, the same strange types, the same disorder in the arrangement of the signs, and the same care to preserve the surface of the block in its natural condition.

There has been a good deal of discussion about the orientation of megalithic monuments, and the truth on that point once ascertained, some light might be thrown on the aim of the builders. It is evident, however, that there never was any general system of orientation. The dolmens of Morbihan, it is true, nearly all face the east, doubtless in homage to the sun rising in its splendor; but this is not the case in Finistère, and the dolmens of Kervinion and Kervardel, for instance, are set due north and south.

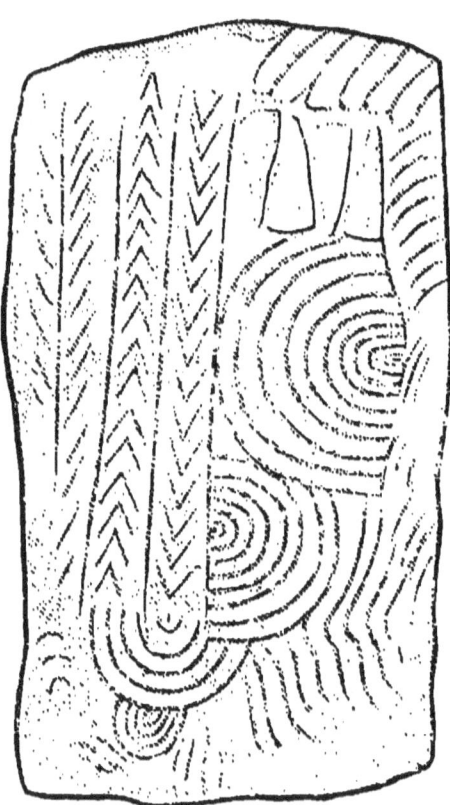

Fig. 68.—Sculptures on the menhirs of the covered avenue of Gavr'innis.

Leaving Brittany, we are told by the Rev. W. Lukis that the position of the megalithic monuments of England varies considerably: most of the dolmens of Berry, Poitou, Aveyron, and the island of Bornholm, face west; and those of Algeria are set southwest, and northeast, so that it is really impossible to come to any final conclusion.

Some of the megalithic monuments already noticed have a peculiarity to which we must refer here on account of its importance. One of the supports, in nearly every case that which closes the entrance, is pierced with a circular opening. Sometimes, however, the opening is elliptical or square.

Fig. 69.—Dolmen with opening (India).

We meet with dolmens thus distinguished in India (Fig. 69), in Sweden, in Algeria, in France, and in Palestine, where they are often associated with sepulchral niches hewn out of the rock and also pierced with an opening corresponding with that of the entrance. In Alemtejo (Spain), square openings occur. West of Karleby in Sweden, is a sepulchral chamber about twenty-nine feet long, made of slabs set upright, all those facing south being pierced with a nearly circular opening; and on the shores of the Black Sea dolmens made of four upright stones surmounted by a slab, have, in every case, one of the uprights pierced with an artificial opening about six inches in diameter. These dolmens are said by the country people to have been set up by a race of giants who built them as shelters for a dwarf people on whom they had compassion.

FIG. 70.—Dolmen near Trie (Oise).

In France, dolmens with openings are so numerous that it is difficult to make a selection. That known as La Justice, near Beaumont-sur-Oise, consists of a small vestibule and a very long mortuary chamber, separated by a slab pierced with a round opening. We must also mention the megalithic monument of Villers-Saint-Sépulchre at Trie (Oise) (Fig. 70), that of Grand-Mont, with many of those of Morbihan, of which that of Kerlescant has an oval opening; the covered avenue of Conflans-Sainte-Honorine, originally erected at the confluence of the Seine and Oise, and now set up exactly as it was found at Saint Germain, has an oval opening, and presents the exceptional feature, of which I know no other instance, of having a stone for closing the opening if necessary; the covered avenue of Bellehaye in Normandy, reproduced with precision at the Paris Exhibition of 1889, which was closed by a transverse stone with an opening some inches in diameter.

Of English examples we may mention the dolmens of Rodmarten and Avening; Mérimée quotes several megalithic monuments in Wiltshire; and Sir J. Simpson, the well-known and oft-described *Kit's Cotty House*, which is nothing more than a dolmen with an opening. *Holed Stones*, as they are called, are numerous in Cornwall, the size of the opening varying considerably; that at Men-an-Tol, for instance, is more than a foot in diameter, whilst others are but a few inches long. At Orry's Grave, in the Isle of Man, two large stones are so placed as to leave a circular space between them, which was evidently intended to serve the same purpose, or at least was in accordance with the same superstition, as were similar characteristics elsewhere. Setting aside the interminable legends connected with dolmens having openings, there is no doubt that this peculiarity of structure, which we meet with in India as in Scandinavia, in the Caucasus as in France, shows that the builders of all of them were impelled by a similar idea. These openings are too small to allow of the introduction of other corpses, or to afford to the living a refuge in the home of the dead; they could but have served for the passing in of food, of which a supply was so often left for the departed; or yet another interpretation is possible: they may have been left for the soul or the spirit to leave its earthly prison and take flight for those happy regions in which all races more or less believe, and to which belief these openings may be witnessed to the present day. M. Cartailhac, however, hazards yet another explanation, and suggests that the megalithic monuments were intended for the interment of whole families, and that the bodies were not introduced into the tombs until all the flesh was gone, when the skeletons might have been slipped through the openings left for that purpose. The repeated disturbances of the remains in the graves have unfortunately often entirely dispersed all the human bones.

It was in Brittany that the art of erecting dolmens reached its fullest development, and it is there that the relics found in the tombs are of the most important character. Nowhere do we find weapons more carefully preserved, more delicately finished ornaments of a more remarkable kind. The Museum of Vannes, where most of the valuable objects found in the excavations are preserved, possesses quartzite, fibrolite, diorite, and even nephrite and jadeite hatchets, some of which materials are not native to Europe; as well as amber beads and a necklace of calaïte, that precious stone described by Pliny, and which long remained unknown after his time.

Hatchets or celts are more numerous than any other objects found beneath dolmens of Brittany. A report, read by M. R. Galles to the Société Polymathique of Morbihan, enumerates the objects found with the dead beneath the dolmen of Saint-Michel. This report is a regular inventory, in which figure eleven jade celts of great elegance of form and varying from about three and a half to sixteen inches, two larger celts of coarse

workmanship both broken, twenty-six small fibrolite
celts with sharp edges, nine pendants, more than one
hundred jasper beads which had been part of a necklace, and lastly an ivory ring. Other megalithic monuments were not less rich in relics. Thirty hatchets
were picked up at Tumiac; more than a hundred,
nearly all of tremolite, at Mané-er-H'roek; which were
remarkable for their regularity of form, their polish,
and the variety of their colors. They seldom bear any
traces of having been used, and in many cases they
appear to have been intentionally broken, probably in
conformity with some funereal rite. Finistère, though
not so rich as Morbihan, furnished an important con-
tingent. The excavations of the Kerhué-Bras tumulus
brought to light a sepulchral chamber which contained
thirty-three arrow-heads. Beneath other dolmens
were picked up a number of little plaques of slate, all
pierced with holes; one of these pieces of slate, which
was oblong in form, bore on it a representation of a
sun with rays surrounded by ornaments not easy to
make out. The Breton megalithic monuments also contained numerous fragments of pottery, some of which
had formed part of vases without stands, such as those
found at Santorin and at Troy.

In other parts of France, similar discoveries have
been made; shells often brought from distant shores,
glass beads, amber bowls, hatchets and celts made
of stone foreign to the country. Dr. Prunières presented to the French Association, when it met at Bordeaux, a collection of weapons and ornaments which
came from the megalithic monuments of Lozère. M. Cartailhac described at the Prehistoric Congress of Copenhagen the dolmen of Grailhe (Gard). A skeleton

was found beneath it crouching in a corner; whilst round about it lay a knife, a flint arrow-head, a vase of coarse pottery, and in the earth forming the tumulus were picked up twenty arrow-heads, a hatchet of chloromelanite, with numerous beads and fragments of pottery. Were these offerings to the dead, or to the infernal deities, given to them in the hope of propitiating them in favor of the deceased? Beneath the megalith of Saint Jean d'Alcas were found beads of blue glass and of enamel which Dr. Prunières, having compared with those in the Campana collection in the Louvre, thinks are of Phœnician origin. The tumuli of the Pyrenees have yielded calaïte beads of the shape of small cylinders pierced with holes; and the dolmen of Breton (Tarn-et-Garonne) eight hundred and thirty-two necklace beads, some of the shape of a heart. Beneath the Vauréal dolmen were found five skulls in a row, and near one of them, that of a woman, lay a necklace made of round bits of bone and slate, on which hung a little jadeite hatchet as an amulet. These human relics were also accompanied by a fibrolite celt, numerous little worked flints, and some fragments of pottery. This arrangement of skulls in a tomb is very rare, and the only thing I can compare it to is the row of five horses' heads placed at the end of the entrance gallery of Mané-Lud.

At Alt-Sammit (Mecklenburg), were round stone hatchets, flint knives, fragments of pottery covered with striæ and ornaments; at Tenarlo (Holland), urns and amber beads. At Ancress in the island of Jersey, we find a regular necropolis dating from Neolithic times, and one hundred vases or urns of different forms were collected. In the Long Barrow of West Kennet, too, were found numerous fragments of pottery, and with these fragments boars' tusks longer than those of the boar of the present day, the bones of sheep, goats, roe-deer, pigs, and of a large species of ox, all of which are probably relics of a funeral feast. At a little distance from West Kennet the Rev. Doyen Merewether found several flint implements. Here too, then, as elsewhere, the home of the living was side by side with the resting-place of the dead.

Beneath the dolmens of West Gothland have been found polished stone weapons and tools associated with the bones of domestic animals, in many cases bearing traces of the work of the hand of man. At Olleria, in the kingdom of Valencia, at Xeres de la Frontera, we find diorite hatchets, and in Algeria vases filled with the shells of land mollusca. In every clime we meet with tokens of the respect in which the dead were held.

This respect is really very remarkable. The builders of the dolmens did not hesitate to sacrifice their most precious objects, their richest ornaments, their hatchets and precious stones brought from a distance by their tribe in their long migrations. No one would dream of robbing the sacred collection. Our own contemporaries, however civilized we may flatter ourselves by considering them, would not prove themselves as disinterested.

Hatchets, pottery, and personal ornaments of stone, bone, etc., are not the only artificial objects found beneath the megalithic monuments. Metals, too, have been discovered, and M. Piette in one of his excavations, came across a plate formed of very thin layers of gold leaf welded together by hammering; and in several parts of the south of France have been found olives made of gold and pierced lengthwise. The dolmen of

Carnouet in Brittany, insignificant as it appears and containing but one small sepulchral chamber with no gallery of access or lateral crypts, beneath a tumulus about thirteen feet high by some eighty-five in diameter, and which was left untouched until our own day, actually contained a golden necklace weighing over seven ounces; in the crypt of the Castellet monument was found a golden plaque and a golden bead; whilst the Ors dolmen in the isle of Oleron concealed a nugget which had been rolled into the shape of a bead probably after having been beaten thin with a hammer. At Plouharnel, two golden amulets were found beneath a triple dolmen, and M. du Chatellier, in excavating beneath a megalithic monument in Finistère, found a magnificent chain of gold. A somewhat similar chain was taken from the Leys dolmen near Inverness, and in 1842 Lord Albert Cunningham picked up at New Grange (Ireland) two necklaces, a brooch, and a ring, all of gold.

More than a hundred megalithic monuments of France have been found to contain bronze, and this number would be more than doubled if we counted the finds in tombs not connected with megaliths, such as those of Aveyron and Lozère, where a few bits of bronze were found mixed with numerous stone objects. One fifth of the weapons, especially the swords and daggers found beneath the dolmens, are of bronze. At Kerhué in Finistère, a number of bronze swords were arranged in a circle round a little heap of cinders and black earth, relics, probably, of the cremation of the dead, in honor of whom the tumulus had been erected.

Beneath the dolmens of Roknia (Algeria) were found thirteen bronze ornaments, and two in silver gilt of very superior workmanship, and under those of the Caucasus were picked up blue-glass beads, arrow-heads, and bronze rings; but M. Chantre, who is an authority in the matter, thinks these objects date from interments subsequent to the erection of the dolmens.

Iron was much more rarely used than bronze in the greater part of Europe. It was not even known in Scandinavia before the Christian era. In Germany, Pannonia, and Noricum its use dates from the sixth or seventh century B.C. Beneath the mounds of Central America we find but a few fragments of meteoric iron, the rarity of which made them extremely valuable; on the other hand iron was known to the Hellenes as long ago as the fourteenth century B.C., and it had been employed in Egypt for many centuries prior to that time. The most ancient sepulchres of Malabar contain iron tridents, and Genesius dates their use from before the deluge. It is therefore surprising to find that some races remained for an illimitable time ignorant of the way to procure a metal of such great utility.

Iron was not used in Brittany until towards the close of the period during which megalithic monuments were erected. Stone, bronze, and iron were found together in the Nignol tomb at Carnac, which dates from the time when cremation was already practised. We find the same association of different materials in the Rocher dolmen.

In the British Isles, especially in Scotland and in Ireland, bronze and iron objects are more numerous than in France. At Aspatria, near St. Bees in Cumberland, a cist was discovered containing the skeleton of a man measuring seven feet from the crown of the head to the feet. Near the giant lay numerous valuable objects, including an iron sword inlaid with silver, a gold buckle, the fragments of a shield and of a battle-axe, and the iron bit of a snaffle bridle. The great cairn of Dowth, in Ireland, contained iron knives and rings mixed with bone needles, copper pins, and glass and amber beads, all showing rapid progress in the industrial arts. The remarkable cairns near Lough Crew (Ireland), which were untouched and indeed unknown to archæologists until 1868, were found to contain, amongst many other interesting objects, numerous human bones, fragments of pottery, shells of marine mollusca, 4,884 bone implements, and seven pieces of iron very much oxidized. The tumuli of the Grand Duchy of Posen and those of Prussia cover kistvaens containing funeral vases, weapons, and silver and gold ornaments.

We are altogether in the dark as to the date or the use of the various objects found in these tombs, and the coins bearing dates which are often associated with them, do not seem to help us much, belonging as they doubtless do to a much later period than the erection of the monuments. We may, however, mention that near the surface of the mound of Mané-er-H'roek eleven medals of Roman emperors from Tiberius to Trajan were found; whilst under the tumulus of Rosmeur, on the Penmarch Point (Finistère), were various Roman coins; at Bergous in Lockmariaker, at Mané-Rutual, and at other places in Brittany, coins of the earliest Christian emperors; at Uley, in Gloucestershire, some coins of the time of the sons of Constantine; at Mining-Low (Derbyshire), beneath a kistvaen surrounded by a cromlech, some medals of Valentinianus; at Galley-Low, with a magnificent gold necklace set with garnets, a coin of Honorius, but as these last were found at the outer edge of the mound there are doubts as to the time of their deposition; these doubts were, however, to some extent set at rest by the finding of a coin of Geta beneath the monument itself. We might multiply instances of similar finds, but I will only mention one more, the discovery under some Scotch barrows of silver necklaces and coins of the Caliphs of Bagdad, bearing date from 887 to 945 A.D.

This last discovery confirms what I have already said, that the introduction of the coins was of much later date than the erection of the monument. Another fact adds weight to this decision. The most ancient Gallic coins date from about three centuries before our era, and the earliest British from a century earlier than that. How is it that excavations have brought to light no specimens of either? The Romans successively occupied all the countries of which we have just spoken; the tombs themselves bear witness to their conquests; and it is to the violation of the tombs, the displacements, and secondary interments that we owe the introduction of coins, pottery, and bricks that undoubtedly date from the Roman period, and were probably placed beside their dead by the Roman legionaries.

Whatever may be the difficulties, however, we are already able to come to certain definite conclusions. We cannot connect the megalithic monuments with any one of the ancient religions known. They were certainly not set up in honor of Odin or of Osiris, of Astarte or of Athene, the Phœnician or the Egyptian, the Greek or the Roman gods; their erection seems to

Erdeven, which were, of course, much more complete in her day than in ours. In fact, they are mentioned for the first time by Sauvagère, in his " Recueil des Antiquites de la Gaule," in which he attributes them to the Romans. We may therefore, perhaps, conclude that these decayed and clumsy-looking monuments were despised for generations, no one realizing their importance or caring to penetrate their secrets.

If need were, we have yet other proofs of their extreme antiquity. In excavating an alignment in the district occupied by the Kermario group, a Roman encampment was discovered. The enceinte is represented by a long wall about six feet thick, and propped up against this wall were found a number of flat stones blackened with smoke, on which the legionaries doubtless cooked their food. In some instances these hearths were made on an overturned menhir, and other menhirs, which had belonged to the alignment, were fitted into the walls. A Roman road passes near Avebury, and, contrary to their general custom, the haughty conquerors had turned aside to avoid the tumulus. These are decisive proofs that in France and England at least the megalithic monuments were erected before the advent of the Romans.

Difficult as it is to come to any definite conclusion as to the age of the monuments, it is yet more difficult to ascertain to what race their builders belonged. In the first place we ask : Are they all the work of one race? The contrary, earnestly maintained by M. de Mortillet, has long been the general opinion. M. Worsaae declared, at the Brussels Congress,[1] that the dolmens were erected by different peoples; M. Cazalis de Fon-

---

[1] *Compte rendu*, p. 421.

douce,[1] M. Broca,[2] and M. Cartailhac,[3] share this belief. "Are not the monuments of huge stones," says M. Fondouce, "the product of a progressive civilization growing by degrees, rather than the work of a single people maintaining their own manners and customs in the midst of the old primitive populations they visited, without borrowing anything from their hosts?" To Broca, the resemblance between the dolmens of Europe, Africa, and even of America proves but one thing: the similarity of the aspirations and powers of all men. Everywhere, and at every time, men have aimed, in their monuments, not only at durability, but at the expression of force and of power. It was with this end in view that they erected menhirs and selected enormous stones for their megalithic monuments. The dolmen, which looks like an architectural building, is but a modification of primitive tombs. The cave-man first turned to account natural or artificial rock shelters, and when they were not to be had, he imitated them in such materials as he had at his disposal. Hence we have crypts, kistvaens, and dolmens; and the resemblance between them proves nothing as to the parentage of their builders.

We may add that the distances between what we may call megalithic zones is considerable. We meet, for instance, with dolmens in Circassia and in the Crimea, but there are no others nearer than the Baltic. There are none in the districts peopled by the Belgæ, from the Drenthe to the borders of Normandy, nor are there any in the valleys of the Rhine or of the Scheldt.

---

[1] *Mat.*, 1877, p. 470.
[2] *Ass. Française*, Bordeaux, 1872, p. 725.
[3] *Rev. d'Anth.*, 1881, p. 283.

There are but a few in Italy or in Greece, where Pelasgic buildings were early erected, and bore witness to a more advanced civilization. We meet with them again, however, in Palestine, but we must traverse many miles before we find other examples at Peshawur and in the valley of Cabul. It is difficult to overrate the importance of these facts, or to explain these gaps. Are they, however, so complete as has been supposed? The few travellers who have crossed Afghanistan and Daghestan have seen tumuli which may have served as points of union between the monuments of India and those of the Caucasus. The megalithic monuments of Palestine and of Arabia may yet be found to be linked with those of Algeria, by examples in the little known regions between the Nile and the Regency of Tripoli. If our ignorance forbids us to assert anything on this point, it equally forbids our denying anything with any confidence. We may also add one general remark: the countries where megalithic monuments are found, abound in granite, in sandstone, and in flint, whilst other districts have only very friable limestones; and their monuments, if they were ever erected, would have been more easily destroyed, the very ruins disappearing and leaving no trace.

It has been said, moreover, that the mode of construction of the dolmens, and we have ourselves made the same remark, is far from being the same everywhere. The dolmens of Brittany have sepulchral chambers with long passages leading to them; those of the neighborhood of Paris have wide covered avenues with a very short entrance lobby. In the south of France we see nothing but rectangular compartments formed of four or five colossal stones. All this is true enough; but if we examine our old cathedrals of comparatively modern date, the common origin of which is never disputed, we note differences no less remarkable. On the other hand it is urged that if megalithic monuments were all erected by one race, the objects they contain would certainly resemble each other to a great extent. But even this is not the case. The hatchets so numerous in the west of France are rare in the south; those from the Algerian monuments are always of coarse workmanship, whilst those of Denmark are highly finished. We might multiply instances, but as a matter of fact do we not see the same kind of thing in the present day, in spite of our railways and other modes of rapid communication, and the perpetual intermarrying of modern peoples? Compare the ornaments of Normandy with those of the Basque provinces, those of Brittany with those of Burgundy, and surely the differences between them will be found to be as great as we note in the weapons and ornaments of the builders of the megalithic monuments.

To sum up: according to the opinion of many eminent savants, numerous races have been in the habit of raising megalithic monuments, the form of which varies *ad infinitum* according to the genius or the circumstances of each race, and according to the nature of the soil or of the material at the disposal of the builders. All, however, belong to one general type, and bear witness to one general influence, which extended throughout the whole world at a certain epoch. M. Cazalis de Fondouce, from whom I borrow these last observations, would probably find it as difficult to say how a general influence was extended to races of which he denies the common parentage, and the relations and contemporaneity he can but guess at, as I myself should—granting the contrary hypothesis—to explain how a people could wander about the world in incessant migrations without modifying its own habits or communicating to others its rites and its mode of erecting monuments.

We cannot, however, fail to recognize the evidence of facts. We can understand how men were everywhere impelled to raise mounds above the bodies of their ancestors, to perpetuate their memory or to enclose their mortal remains between flat stones to save them from being crushed by the weight of earth above them. We may even, by straining a point, admit the idea that a large cist developed into a dolmen, but when in districts separated by enormous distances we see monuments with the wall pierced with a circular opening or combining an interior crypt with an external mound and dolmen, it is impossible to look upon these close resemblances as the result of an accidental coincidence, and equally impossible to fail to conclude that the men whose funeral rites were remarkable for such close similarity belonged to the same race.

What then was this race? Are these monuments witnesses of the great Aryan immigration which was for so long supposed to have spread from India over the continents of Asia and Europe, and of which the Indo-European languages were said to preserve the memory? Or is it really the fact that a relationship of language does not imply a relationship of race? Were the builders of the dolmens Celts or Gauls, Ligures or Cymri? was Henry Martin right in ascribing to the Cimerii of Scandinavia the erection in the Bronze age of the megaliths of Ireland? Was it the Turanians, with their worship of ancestors, their respect for the tombs of their forefathers, and their desire to perpetuate their memory to eternity, who set up the dolmens of Brittany? Was it not perhaps rather the Iberians, whose descendants still people Spain and the north of Africa? According to Maury, the distribution of the megalithic monuments of Europe marks the last refuge of vanquished Neolithic races, fleeing before their conquerors. All these hypotheses are plausible, all can be defended by arguments, the weight of which it is impossible to deny, but none are capable of conclusive proof, none can finally convince the student.[1]

An old Welsh poet, referring to the long barrows of his native land, says that they are altogether inexplicable, and that it is impossible to decide who set them up or who is buried beneath them. And surely this ancient bard [2] is right even now. Vainly do we question these silent witnesses of the remote past. They give us no answer, and we can but repeat

---

[1] By permission of the author, the translator adds the following quotation from Taylor's "Origin of the Aryans," p. 17, which is referred to by Professor Huxley in his paper on the Aryan question in the *Nineteenth Century* for November, 1890. Taylor says: "It is now contended that there is no such thing as an Aryan race in the same sense that there is an Aryan language, and the question of late so frequently discussed as to the origin of the Aryans can only mean, if it means anything, a discussion of the ethnic affinities of those numerous races which have acquired Aryan speech; with the further question, which is perhaps insoluble, among which of these races did Aryan speech arise and where was the cradle of that race?"

[2] This poet is one of those whose work is to be found in the so-called "Black Book of Caermarthen." See also "The Four Ancient Books of Wales, Containing the Cymric Poems Attributed to the Bards of the Sixth Century." Edinburgh, 1868.

here what we said at the beginning of this inquiry: Human science is powerless to lift the veil hiding the early history of humanity. Will it ever be so? Or will the day yet dawn when the veil will be rent asunder at last? Time alone can solve this question, which is one of those secrets of the future as difficult to fathom as those of the past.

CHAPTER VI.

INDUSTRY, COMMERCE, AND SOCIAL ORGANIZATION; FIGHTS, WOUNDS AND TREPANATION.

When we consider the discoveries connected with the Stone age as a whole, we are struck with the immense numbers of weapons of every kind and of every variety of form found in different regions of the globe. The Roman domination extended over a great part of the Old World, and it lasted for many centuries. Everywhere this people, illustrious amongst the nations, has left tokens of its power and of its industry. Roman weapons, jewelry, and coins occupy considerable spaces in our museums; but numerous as are these relics of the Romans, they are far inferior in number to the objects dating from prehistoric times, and flints worked by the hand of man have been picked up by thousands in the last few years, forming incontestable witnesses of the rapid growth of a large population.

One important point remains obscure. Schmerling has excavated fifty caves in Belgium, and only found human relics in two or three of them; and of six hundred explored by Lund in Brazil, only six contained human bones. Similar results were obtained in the excavations of the mounds of North America, as well as in the caves of France. M. Hamy, in a book published a few years ago, only mentions twelve finds of human bones, which could, without any doubt, be dated from Palæolithic times. True, this number has been added to by recent discoveries, but it is still quite insignificant. It is the same thing with the kitchen-middings and the Lake settlements. This paucity of actual human remains forms a gap in the evidence relating to prehistoric man, which disturbances and displacements do not sufficiently account for, and to which we shall refer again when speaking of prehistoric tombs.

Worked flints are generally found in numbers in one place, probably formerly a station or centre of human habitation. Men were beginning to form themselves into societies, and the dwellings, first of the family and then of the tribe, rapidly gathered together near some river rich in fish, or some forest stocked with game affording plenty of food easily obtained. The caves also afford proofs of the number of men who inhabited them. In one alone, near Cracow, Ossowski discovered 876 bone implements, more than 8,000 flint objects, and thousands of fragments of pottery. From the Veyrier cave, near Mount Salève, were taken nearly 1,000 stone implements; from those of Petit Morin, 2,000 arrow-heads; from that of Côttes, on the banks of the Gartampe, more than 264 pounds' weight of flints, some of the Moustérien and others of the Madeleine type, mixed with the bones of the rhinoceros, and of several large beasts of prey of indeterminate species. The Abbé Ducrost picked up 4,000 flints in one dwelling alone at Solutré, where the soil is calcareous and flint is not native, so that it must have been brought from a distance. More than 8,000 different objects were taken from the fine Neolithic station of Ors in the isle of Oleron; 12,000 chips of stone, bearing marks of human workmanship, were picked up in the Thayngen Cave, and more than 80,000 in the different caves of Belgium. The shelter of Chaleux alone yielded 30,000 pieces of stone, at every stage of workmanship, from the waste of the manufactory to the highly finished implement. Other explorers have been no less fortunate. The Marquis of Wavrin found in the environs of Grez no less than 60,000 worked stones belonging to no less than thirty different types, chiefly arrow-heads, some triangular, others almond-shaped, others again cutting transversely, some with and some without feathers, some stalked, others not; in a word, arrows of every known type. Nothing but an actual visit to the Royal Museum of Brussels can give any idea of the importance of the discoveries made in Belgium.

The environs of Paris are, however, no less rich. As early as Palæolithic times the valleys of the Seine and its tributaries were evidently inhabited by a numerous population. M. Rivière mentions a station near Clamart, where, in a limited space, he picked up more than 900 flints, some worked, others mere chips, many of which had been subjected to heat. A sand-pit of Levallois-Perret yielded 4,000 stone objects, and on the plateau of Champigny, full of such terrible memories for the people of France, were found nearly 1,200 flints, knives, polished hatchets, lance heads and scrapers, mixed with numerous fragments of handmade pottery without ornamentation.

Are yet other examples needed? M. de Mortillet estimates at more than 25,000 the number of specimens found on the plateau of Saint Acheul, the scene of the earliest discoveries that revealed the existence of man in Quaternary times; and the station of Concise, on Lake Neuchâtel, which is one of the most ancient in Switzerland, yielded a yet more considerable number. Many have, however, been lost or destroyed; the ballast of the railway skirting the lake contains thousands of worked stones and of pieces of the waste left in making them, all of which were taken from the bed of the lake. It must not be forgotten that it is only of late years that the importance of these relics of the past has been recognized and that any one has dreamt of preserving or of studying them.

The excavation of a gravel pit at Dundrum (County Down, Ireland) yielded 1,100 flint implements, and M. Belluci himself picked up in the province of Pérouse more than 17,000 pieces, chiefly spear-, lance-, or arrow-heads, belonging to six different types. The Broholm Museum contains 72,409 weapons and implements, all found in Denmark.

We can quote similar facts in other countries. Prehistoric stations are numerous in the Sahara and throughout the Wady el Mya, in Algeria, and we have already spoken of the numerous specimens found near Wargla. The workshops in this district are generally surrounded by immense numbers of ostrich eggs, which seem to indicate that that bird was already domesticated.[1]

In America, Dr. Abbott has sent to the Peabody Museum more than 20,000 stones, which were collected by him at Trenton, on the banks of the Delaware, and quite recently I was told that in sinking a well in Illinois the workmen came upon a deposit of more than 1,000 worked flints, all of oval form. Every one knows the importance of the recent discoveries at

---

[1] Foureau, *Bul. Soc. Géog.*, June 1, 1883.

Washington, and we might multiply examples *ad infinitum*, for everywhere explorers come upon undoubted traces of the active work and intelligence of comparatively dense populations, all of whom had attained to about the same degree of development.

These numerous deposits often mark the site of regular workshops, tokens of the earliest attempt at social organization. In no other way can we explain the piles of flints in every stage of workmanship lying beside the lumps from which they were detached. One of the most celebrated of these workshops is that of Grand-Pressigny, chief town of the canton of the department of Indre-et-Loire, which is admirably situated between two picturesque rivers, the Claise and the Creuse.

The flint implements of Grand-Pressigny, of which specimens can be seen in all the museums of Europe, are some sixteen inches long, of light color, pointed at one end and square at the other. One face is rough, the other chipped into three oblong pieces, whilst the sides are roughly hewn into saw-like teeth. If we examine these flints closely we can easily make out the exact point, the *eye*, as workmen call it, where the stone was struck. At Charbonnière, on the banks of the Saône, to quote other examples, in a radius of less than a mile, were found weapons, tools, and nuclei, which may be compared with those of Grand-Pressigny. In some places the collections of flints still remaining look as if they had been used for road-making. In some cases hatchets, knives, and scrapers seem to have been buried in pits. Were these the reserve stores of the tribe, or the so-called *caches* of the merchants?

It is difficult merely to name the different workshops or manufactories discovered in the last few years. We must, however, endeavor to mention the most important, for these workshops, we must repeat, are an important proof of the existence of a society of organized working communities. We meet with them on the shores of the bay of Kiel, in the island of Anholt, in the midst of the Kattegat, and on the borders of the Petchoura, and of the Soula, among the Samoieds. Virchow discovered an arrow-head manufactory on the shores of Lake Burtneck, and in 1884 the Moscow Society of Natural Sciences made known the existence of important workshops near the Vethuga River, in the province of Kostroma, so that we know that in remote prehistoric times men lived and fought in a rigorous climate in districts but sparsely populated in our own day.

There is nothing to surprise us in all these facts. Recently near the Yenesei River, in the heart of Siberia, were found bronze daggers, hatchets and bridle bits (Fig. 71), all bearing witness in the beauty of their workmanship to a more advanced state of civilization than the Lake Dwellings or megalithic monuments farther south. Many of them are ornamented with figures of animals, so that at an epoch less remote, it is true, than the one we have been considering, but still far removed from our own, we find that there was an intelligent race, with artistic tastes, living in a country now so intensely cold as to be uninhabitable to all but a few miserable nomad Tartars.

At Spiennes, near Mons, a field was discovered, known as the *camp des cayaux*, strewn with flints, some uncut, others hewn, together with knives and hatchets innumerable. There were also centres of manufacture at Hoxne and Brandon, in England, at Bellaria in Bologna, and at Rome on the Tiburtine Way. At Ponte-Molle, where worked flints were discovered for the first time in Italy a few years ago, a workshop was found, remarkable for the great number of stags' antlers, from which the middle part had been removed, doubtless to be used as handles for tools. M. de Rossi, who gives us these details, thinks that

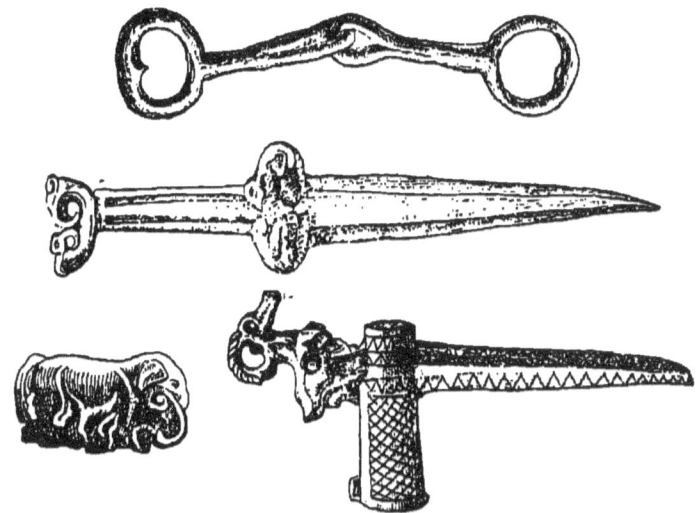

Fig. 71.—Bronze objects found at Krasnojarsk (Siberia).

this station was inhabited in the Palæolithic period. In the settlement of Concise have been found not only stone implements, but a great many articles made of bone, so that this place was evidently an important manufacturing centre. Knives, stilettos, and arrowheads were turned out here, and in the hands of skilful workmen the tusks of the boars, which abounded at this time in Switzerland, were converted into excellent chisels.

To name the districts where tools were manufactured in prehistoric times in France would be to give a list of all the departments. In the commune of Saint-Julien du Sant we find a large manufactory where every division of the Stone age is fully represented, from the time of the simply chipped hatchet to that of the polished implement of rare perfection. Everything bears witness to the prolonged residence of man in a neighborhood which offered the attraction of vast deposits of chalk with bands of flint that supplied alike weapons and tools. Amongst others, we must name the so-called *atelier de la Treiche*, near Toul, which extends for an area of about a hundred acres, that of Bonaruc, near Dax; surrounded by waste lands covered with a scanty vegetation; that of Rochebertier (Charente), which probably dates from the Madeleine period; and that of Ecorche-Bœuf, near Périgueux. The Abbé Cochet tells us of an atelier in the Aulne valley, and Maurice Sand of another near La Châtre, where we meet with the most ancient traces of man in Berry. In the fields, near an alignment not far from Autun, were picked up numbers of hatchets of hard rock, barbed arrows, flakes of flint worked into scrapers or chisels, whilst near them were the very polishers on which they had been pointed.

We have just spoken of polishers, and we said some time ago that it was by prolonged rubbing that the remarkable weapons of Neolithic times were produced. We must add now that a whole series of the polishers used are to be seen on the right bank of the Loing, near Nemours; one of which is a regular table (Fig. 72), on which can be made out no less than fifty grooves and twenty-five cup-like depressions.

FIG. 72.—Prehistoric polisher, near the ford of Beaumoulin, Nemours.

One would have expected to find the ground near these polishers covered with flakes of flint and pieces of tools of all kinds, but nothing of the kind has been discovered; a fact which leads us to suppose that the workmen only came down into the valley to finish off their weapons by polishing them.

At the period we are considering all the continents were peopled, and we must repeat, for it is the most important point of our present study, that the civilization attained to by the inhabitants was everywhere almost identical. Thus we find centres of manufacture similar to those of Europe at the foot of the mountains of Tunis and of Algeria. In one of the latter, at Hassi al Rhatmaia, the knives were piled up in one place, the scrapers in another, and the arrow-heads in a third. In this disposition M. Rabourdin thinks he sees a sign of the division of labor, one of the most important features of modern progress. M. Arcelin mentions a similar deposit on the summit of the Jebel Kalabshee, near Esneh in Egypt, and a few years ago another was found in Palestine, near the ancient Berytus, containing great numbers of hatchets, saws, scrapers, and all the implements characteristic of the Stone age; whilst amongst them lay the blocks from which they had been cut. Asia Minor was evidently an important manufacturing centre during the Stone age, and, as a matter of course, it must have had a considerable population; and even in America discoveries of similar extent have been made. At Kinosha, in Wisconsin, Lapham made out a manufactory of flint and quartzite arrow-heads, which dates from prehistoric times, and quite recently a yet more important centre of industry has been discovered at St. Andrew (Winnipeg).

The manufactories of Spiennes and Brandon deserve special notice, as they show us how our ancestors got the flint they used instead of metal. At Spiennes,[1] the excavations were begun in the open air, then the chalk containing the flint was reached by the sinking of vertical shafts, many of which were as much as forty feet in depth. These shafts were connected with each other by galleries running in every direction, but always following the belts of flints. Cuttings have brought to light the very implements of the ancient miners. They were of the simplest description, such as picks made of stag-horn and heavy stone hammers, all alike bearing marks of long service.[2]

Similar results were obtained in England. Canon Greenwell explored near Brandon, in Suffolk, a series of 254 shafts, known in the neighborhood as Grime's Graves. As at Spiennes, the shafts were connected by galleries from three to five feet high, and one of them was twenty-seven feet long. The shafts and galleries had been hollowed out with the help of picks exactly like those found in Belgium; seventy-nine were picked up that had been thrown away by the workmen.[3]

Some few years ago MM. Cartailhac and Boule discovered one of these primitive quarries at Mur de Barrez, the chief town of the department of Aveyron.[4] They made out eight shafts in the face of a layer of limestone some eighty-one feet long, and at every turn of their excavations they came to fresh shafts. These

---

[1] Munck has just discovered a similar station at Oburg (Hainault), where similar implements, produced by similar processes as those at Spiennes, were discovered.

[2] Briart, Cornet, and Houzeau: *Rapport sur les découvertes faites à Spiennes en 1867.* Malise: *Bul. Acad. royale de Belgique.*

[3] *Journal, Ethnological Society*, 1878, p. 419.

[4] *Académie des Sciences*, Nov., 1883. *Mat.* Jan., 1884. *Nature*, June 18, 1887.

shafts opened out towards the top like funnels, and they were not more than three feet three inches below the surface, the flint having been struck at that depth (Fig. 73). These shafts were, in many cases, continued by galleries, as seen in our illustration (Fig. 74), or by trenches, where the light is, however, more or less shut out by small landslips. It is still easy, in spite of this, to make out the floor of the mine, for it is trodden hard by the feet of the ancient miners.

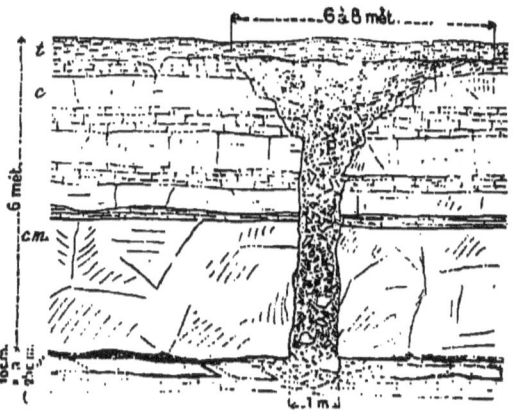

Fig. 73.—Section of a flint mine; *t* vegetable earth, *c* pure limestone, *c m* Marly limestone, *s* flint.

Traces of charcoal, too, reveal the path they took, and we learn at the same time that they used fire to help them in their work.

M. Boule,[1] from whom we borrow these details, cannot restrain his astonishment at the practical knowledge shown by these prehistoric miners. He tells us that they sometimes left the flint standing as pillars at pretty short intervals, or they propped up the galleries with even more resistant material, cementing them with

---

[1] *Nature*, June 16, 1887.

INDUSTRY. 243

clay or with calcareous earth taken from the detritus. In spite of these precautions, landslips frequently occurred, and implements of stag-horn (Fig. 75) have often been flattened by the fall of the roof of the gallery. It is really curious to find implements of an exactly similar kind used for exactly similar purposes at Spiennes, Brandon, Mur de Barrez, and at Cissbury, to which, however, we shall have to refer again. In the shafts of Aveyron, as in those of England, the marks

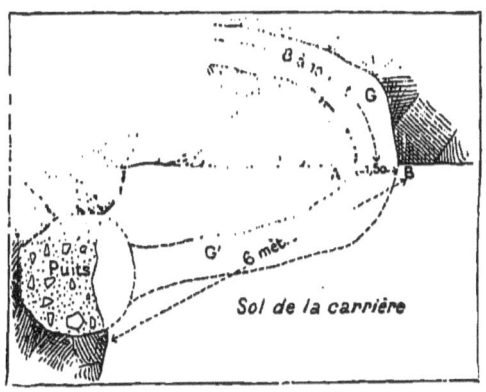

FIG. 74.—Plan of a gallery, half destroyed in making the excavation which revealed its existence. G gallery still visible; G' gallery destroyed by the excavation.

of blows of the picks are still to be seen, and in many cases a flint or horn-pick point is still imbedded in the rock or limestone, as if the miner had but just left his work.

In this last example of what has been done in France, we must also add that of the shafts of Nointel (Oise) and those discovered in Maine by M. de Baye, in both of which were found nodules of flint in different stages of preparation, together with some stag-horn picks. In none of these excavations was any metal implement found, or any trace of the use of metal, so that we must conclude that the mines date from Neolithic times.

We have seen how man gradually brought to perfection the tools and weapons which were at first so clumsy. The growth of industry led to the birth of commerce, or, to speak more accurately, to that of barter. From the time of the earliest migrations intercourse was begun, or rather was carried on, between the tribes, as they gradually dispersed, often travelling considerable distances from each other, and fresh proofs of these relations are continually brought to light as we become better acquainted with prehistoric times. The flints worked by the cave-men of Belgium, the fossil shells so numerous at Chaleux, in the Frontal and Nuton caves, at Thayngen on the frontier between Switzerland and Germany, in Italy, in the stations of anterior date to the *terremare* beds, have been found the shells of the pearl oyster of the Indian Ocean, whilst in the caves of the south of France, such as the Madeleine, that of Cro-Magnon, Bize in Hérault, and Solutré on the banks of the Saône have been picked up the shells of Arctic marine mollusca. The cave-man of Gourdan was decked with shells from the Mediterranean, and the man of Mentone in his turn wore a head-dress made of Atlantic shells. Fossil shells were also much sought after; we have alluded to those from Champagne found in Belgium; others from the shell-marl of Touraine and Anjou had been taken into the caves of Périgord, whilst sea-urchins from the cretaceous strata of the south of France were found in a prehistoric station of Auvergne, and M. Massenat picked up at Laugerie-Basse two specimens of a species

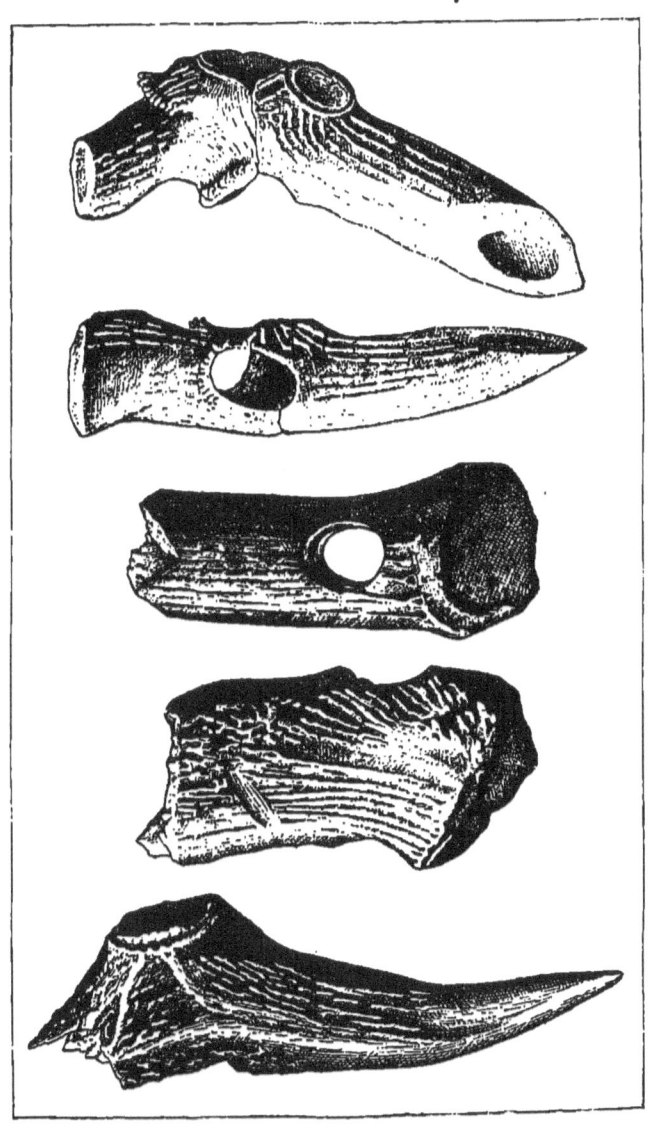

FIG. 75.—Picks, hammers, and mattocks made of stag-horn.

not met with anywhere but in the Eocene deposits of the isle of Wight. The Neolithic station of Champigny, near Paris, has yielded some objects from the Alps, and from Belgium, from the Vosges Mountains, and the Puy de Dôme.

In the caves of Périgord were also found fragments of hyaline quartz, which must have been brought from the Alps or the Pyrenees. In Brittany and in Marne flints foreign to these granite districts are numerous; and Dr. Prunières tells us that similar discoveries were made under the megalithic monuments of France, and that neither in the eroded limestone districts of Lozère, known locally as *les causses*, nor under the dolmens of Haute-Vienne, were found any but implements made of rock not native to the country.

Hatchets, daggers, and nuclei, or as they are characteristically called by the country peope *livres de beurre*, from Grand-Pressigny, have been picked up in the bed of the Seine, at Limagne in Auvergne, in Brittany, at Saint Médard near Bordeaux, on the banks of the Meuse, and even as far north as the Shetland Islands. At Concise was found red coral from the Mediterranean, whilst the yellow amber of the Baltic was picked up in the Lake Dwellings of Switzerland, beneath the dolmens of Brittany, in sepulchral caves, such as those of Oyes (Marne) or Lombrives (Ariège), beneath the megalithic tomb of La Roquette, at Saint Pargoue (Hérault) beneath the dolmen of Grailhe (Gard), at Malpas, and at Baume (Ardèche).[1] These

---

[1] Heilbig: "Osservazioni sopra il Commercio del l'Ambra" (*Acad. dei Lincei*).. We must not confound the yellow amber of the Baltic with the red amber found in Italy, in the mountains of Lebanon, and even in some lignites in the south of France. Sadowski: "Le Commerce de l'Ambre chez les Anciens."

are nearly all Neolithic tombs, though some few of them may date from the beginning of the Bronze age; but the cave-men of France owned amber even earlier than this, for five fragments have been found in the Aurensan Cave near Bagnères-de-Bigorre, which was inhabited in Palæolithic times. Jadeite and nephrite [1] are met with in the Lake Dwellings of Switzerland and Bavaria, as in the caves of Liguria and Sardinia; chloromelanite [2] in France, and obsidian [3] in Lorraine, in the island of Pianosa and in the Cyclades. We have already spoken of the calaïte [4] found beneath the dolmens of Brittany, and we may add now that it has also been found in the caves of Portugal and beneath the megalithic monuments of the south of France.

Commerce developed rapidly during Neolithic times, and, as far as we can make out from traces left, its course was from the southeast to the northwest. Streams and rivers were followed by merchants as by emigrants, and at an extremely remote date the sea no longer arrested the journeys of men. At a recent meeting of the British Anthropological Insti-

---

[1] Nephrite is found in Turkestan, in Siberia, and in New Zealand. Deposits of jadeite are known in Burmah, Jeannetay, and Michel.—"Note sur la Néphrite ou Jade de Sibérie" (*Bul. Soc. Minéralogique de France*, 1881). Meyer: "Die Nephritfrage kein ethnologische Problem," Berlin, 1882.

[2] Objects made of chloromelanite have been picked up in thirty-eight of the departments of France. No deposit of it is known now.—Fischer and Damour: *Rev. Arch.*, 1877.

[3] Obsidian is chiefly found in the mines and quarries of Terro de las Navajas (Mexico), known in the time of the Aztecs. Deposits have also lately been discovered in Hungary and the island of Melos.

[4] Calaïte differs from the turquoise by an equivalent of aluminium; it was described by M. Damour in 1864. It is said that traces of it have been found in the tin mines of Montebras, which appear to have been worked from prehistoric times.—*Mat.*, 1881, p. 166, etc. Cartailhac: *Bul. Soc. Anth.*, 1881, p. 295.

tute, Miss Buckland dwelt on the resemblance in the material, shape, and ornamentation of a golden cup found in Cornwall, to other cups found at Mykenæ and at Tarquinii, and maintained that the Cornish cup must have been the work of the same artisans, and have been brought by commerce from what was then the extremity of the known world.

It is not only in Europe that we can trace the relations established between men separated by vast distances, by oceans, and by apparently impassable deserts. The shells of the Atlantic and those of the Pacific, the copper of Lake Superior, the mica of the Alleghanies, and the obsidian of Mexico lie together beneath the tumuli of Ohio, and quite recently Mr. Putnam exhibited to the Society of Antiquaries a collection of jade celts and ornaments, some from Nicaragua, others from Costa Rica, and a hatchet with both edges sharpened from Michigan. No deposit of jade has so far been discovered on the American continent, so that we can only suppose these objects to have been brought from Asia at an unknown date. The marks they retain of having been rubbed up, and the holes made in them to hang them up, show what store was set by them.

Monuments of many kinds scattered over different countries, weapons and implements, relics as they are of a remote past, enable us to gain a closer insight into the manners, customs, and mode of life of our ancestors of the Stone age. We can picture their daily life, which we know to have been one long struggle, without break or truce, for they had to contend, not only with wild animals but with each other, to fight for the use of their caves of refuge, for their hunting fields, and for their watercourses; and later, the first shepherds had to do battle for the pasturage necessary for their flocks. It is only too certain that, from the earliest dawn of humanity, men gave way, without any effort at self-control, to their brutal passions. The right of the strongest was the only law, and wherever man penetrated his course was marked by violence and by death. One of the femora of an old man was found in the celebrated Cro-Magnon Cave, bearing a deep depression caused by a blow of a projectile, and on the forehead of the woman that lay beside him is a large wound made by a small flint hatchet (Fig. 76). This gash on the frontal bone penetrated the skull, and was probably the cause of death, but not of sudden death, for round about the wound are marks of an attempt at healing it.[1] According to Dr. Hamy, many of the bones found in the Sordes Cave have very curious wounds. A gaping hole on the right parietal of a woman must have been a terrible wound (Fig. 77). The woman of Sordes, like that of Cro-Magnon, must have survived for some time; the marks of the removal of splinters of bone, which can quite easily be made out, leave no doubt on that point.[2]

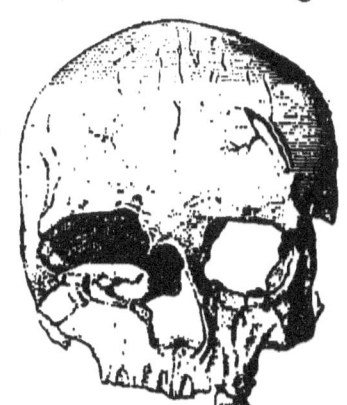

FIG. 76.—Cranium of a woman, from Cro-Magnon, seen full face.

In the Baumes-Chaudes caves, situated in that part

---

[1] Broca: "Les Ossements des Eyziès," Paris, 1868.

[2] Lartet and Chaplain-Duparc: "Une Sepulture des Anciens Troglodytes des Pyrénées."

of the valley of the Tarn which belongs to the department of Lozère, Dr. Prunières picked up numerous bones bearing scars, characteristic of wounds produced by stone weapons.[1] Some fifteen of these bones, such as the right and left hip bones, tibiæ, and vertebræ, still contain flint points flung with sufficient force to penetrate deeply the bony tissue. Always indefatigable in his researches, Dr. Prunières also mentions having found in the cave known as that of *L'Homme Mort* bones bearing traces of cicatrized wounds, and he presented to the Scientific Congress at Clermont a human vertebra found beneath the Aumède dolmen pierced with an arrow-head, which is, so to speak, encased in the wound by the formation of bony tissue.

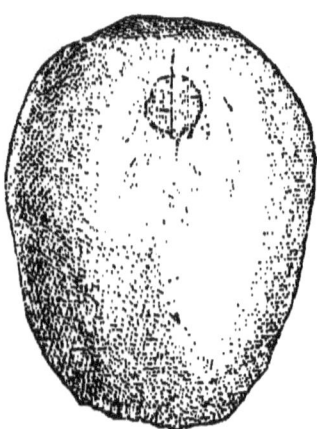

FIG. 77.—Skull of a woman found at Sordes, showing a severe wound from which she recovered.

Of the nineteen crania found in the Neolithic sepulchre of Vauréal two show traces of old wounds. One of them, that of a woman, has three different scars, two of which were of wounds that had healed, whilst the third in the occiput was a gaping hole, which had evidently caused death.

A sepulchral cave at Nogent-les-Vierges (Oise) contains the skeleton of a man with a wound on the forehead, no less than four and a half inches long by

---

[1] *Bull. Soc. Anth.*, 1878, p. 215. The Baumes-Chaudes caves are the most complete charnel houses of Neolithic times yet discovered. Dr. Prunières collected in them as many as three hundred skeletons.

three broad. This man, who was quite young, the sutures being still very apparent, survived this serious wound for some time.

The Gourdan Cave has yielded crania and jaws broken by blunt weapons, whilst on other crania have been made out scratches and stripes which could only have been produced after the hair and skin had been removed. In the caves of the Petit-Morin valley, M. de Baye picked up some human vertebræ pierced with flints, the points of which were still imbedded in the bones. In the Villevenard Cave one skull was found containing three arrow-heads with transverse points imbedded in the skull, the bone of which had closed upon them. Another arrow was lodged between the dorsal vertebræ. It is probable that these arrows had remained in the wounds; certainly that is the simplest way to account for their position. About two miles from the caves of which we have been speaking, M. de Baye discovered a sepulchre containing thirty skeletons, all of adult and strongly built individuals. The bodies were laid one above the other, and separated by large flat stones and a thin layer of earth. This sepulchral cave contained seventy-three flint points. As in the case of Villevenard, their position leads us to suppose that these points had been sticking in the flesh of the bodies when they were interred, and had fallen out when decomposition set in. Probably the bodies were those of men who had fallen victims in a bloody conflict that had taken place in the valley. In a cave at the station of Oyes, was found stretched upon a bed of stones a skeleton with a piece of flint, which had been flung with great force, imbedded in the upper part of the humerus. Round about the wound are the marks of many attempts at healing it.

Many of the human bones found in the Vivarais Cave bear traces of having been violently fractured by stone weapons with tapering points. In the Challes Cave (Savoy) lies the skeleton of a woman whose skull was fractured by a flint weapon, but in this case death was evidently immediate, at least if we may judge from the fact that there are no signs of the wound having received any treatment. In the Castellet Cave, a human vertebra contained the weapon which had pierced it, but when the bone was touched

FIG. 78.—Fragment of human tibia with exostosis enclosing the end of a flint arrow.

the arrow-head broke off. It had, however, been flung with such a sure hand that it had been driven ten inches deep into the bony tissue. Here, too, the absence of any exostosis proves that death quickly followed the wound.

In other cases the victims seem to have lived for some time. We have already spoken of wounds in crania that had healed, and we may add that a few years ago a human bone was presented to the Archæological Society of Bordeaux which still retained a flint arrow-head in the wound it had made. Traces could clearly be made out of the inflammation caused by the presence of the foreign body, and the bony tissue secreted by the periosteum had, so to speak, taken the mould of the arrow (Fig. 78).

In the cave known as the Trou d'Argent (Basses-Alpes) amongst the bones of ruminants and carnivora, fragments of pottery and rubbish of all kinds, was found a piece of humerus (Fig. 79) pierced at the elbow joint and very neatly cut at the lower end, no doubt with the help of some of the implements of hard rock scattered about the cave. The position of this human bone

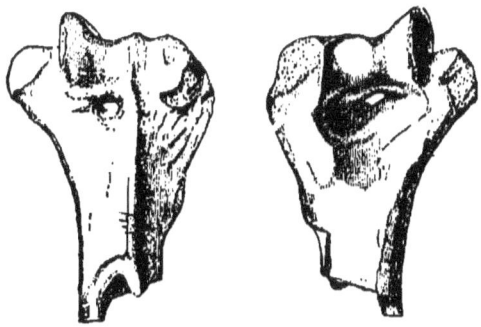

Fig. 79.—Fragment of human humerus pierced at the elbow joint, found in the Trou d'Argent.

amongst the remains of animals and fragments of a meal, points to its being a relic of a scene of cannibalism; adding yet another proof to what I said at the beginning of this work.

Similar facts are reported from England and Germany. Dr. Wankel mentions an interesting prehistoric deposit at Prerau, near Olmutz, amongst the bones of animals belonging to the most ancient Quaternary fauna, such as the mammoth, the cave-bear, the cave-lion, the glutton, and the arctic fox; and amongst clumsy bone and ivory weapons and ornaments he found a human jaw and a femur covered with striæ produced by flint hatchets. In 1801 Mr. Cunnington took several skeletons from a barrow near Heytesbury, the skull of one of which had been broken with a blunt implement; and Sir R. Hoare speaks of a skull from the neighborhood of Stonehenge split open by a blow from one of these formidable weapons. Several crania taken from a long barrow at West Kennet have similar wounds.

Similar facts were noticed at Littleton-Drew, at Uley, at Cotswold, and at Rodmarten, and from this Dr. Thurmam concluded that nearly all those who were buried in long barrows had met with a violent death.[1] He speaks, however, of one skull pierced with a large hole, the edges of which had become rounded smooth, showing the action of a recuperative process, and proving that the injured man had long survived his serious wound. In 1809, a farmer of Kirkcudbrightshire set to work to demolish a large cairn that interfered with his tilling of the soil, and which, according to popular tradition, was the tomb of a Scotch king. In taking away the earth the workmen found a large stone coffin, in which lay the skeleton of a man of great stature. The arm had been almost separated from the trunk by the blow of a diorite hatchet, a broken bit of which remained imbedded in the bone.[2]

One of the few crania that can with certainty be said to have belonged to Lake Dwellers of Switzerland was

---

[1] "In a large proportion of the long barrows I have opened, the skulls exhumed have been found to be cleft apparently with a blunt weapon, such as a club or stone axe."—*Archæologia*, vol. xlii., p. 161, etc.

[2] Wilson: "Prehistoric Annals of Scotland," 2d ed., vol. i., p. 187.

found at Sutz, near Zurich; this skull was fractured at the back. The roundness of the wound, which had been serious enough to cause death, has led authorities to conclude that it was made with one of the formidable pick-hammers, so many of which were found in the lake of Bienne.[1] Nilsson speaks of a human cranium pierced with a flint arrow, and of another, both found at Tygelso (Scandinavia), containing a dart made out of the antler of an eland.[2] At Chauvaux, at Cesareda, and Gibraltar other crania have been found bearing the marks of mortal wounds, and if we cross the Atlantic we meet with similar instances. Lund tells us that at Lagoa do Sumidouro crania were found pierced with circular tools, whilst near them lay the implements that had caused death.[3] At Comox, in Vancouver Island, a skeleton was found with a flint knife imbedded in one of the bones, and at Madisonville (Ohio) another, one of the bones of which was pierced by a triangular stone arrow; whilst beneath a mound in Indiana was picked up a skull pierced by a flint arrow more than six inches long. Excavations at Copiapo (Chili) brought to light the skeleton of a man who had sustained no less than eight wounds from arrows. The force with which they must have been shot is really astonishing; one had broken the upper jaw and knocked out several teeth, penetrating to the brain; and others were still sticking in the vertebræ and ribs.[4]

In the New as in the Old World man survived many of these horrible wounds, and a skull found

---

[1] Keller: "Pfahlbauten," *Siebenter Bericht*, p. 27, Zurich, 1876.
[2] "Habitants Primitifs de la Scandinavie," pp. 212 and 213.
[3] "On the Occurrence of Fossil Bones in South America."
[4] *Journal Anthropological Society*, May, 1882.

under a mound near Devil's River shows a serious wound inflicted many years before death, and one of the Peruvian crania in the Peabody Museum bears a long frontal fracture, doubtless produced by the violent blow of a club; the five or six fragments still to be made out are, so to speak, solidified, and the wounded man had evidently lived on for many years, thanks apparently to his good constitution alone, for there are no signs of the performing of any surgical operation, such as the removal of the splinters of bone, for instance.[1]

In 1884 a human vertebra, with an arrow-head imbedded in it, was picked up on the island of Santa Cruz. The apophysis was broken, and the extent of the fracture shows the great force of the blow. The victim evidently died of the wound, for there is no sign of its having been healed.

I have dwelt upon these deaths and wounds in spite of the inevitable monotony of such a list, not because I wish to bring into prominence the fact that from the earliest times the struggle for existence was fierce and bloody, but because I am anxious to prove that in these remote days an organized and intelligent society had grown up. No one could have survived such wounds as we have described, but for the care and nursing of those around him, such as the other members of his family or of his tribe. The wounded one must have been fed by others for months; nay more, he must have been carried in migrations, and his food and resting-place must have been prepared for him. Moreover, and this is of even yet more importance to our argument, they must have been men able to treat wounds and to set bones.

---

[1] Wyman: *Report Peabody Museum*, 1874, p. 40.

This last fact has been proved beyond a doubt by the discovery of numerous bones with the old wounds completely cicatrized. "In several examples," says Dr. Prunières, speaking in this connection, "we can make out the fractures set with a neatness which gives us a very high opinion of the skill of the Neolithic bone setters. The setting of one fracture at the lower end of the tibia and of another at the neck of the femur, are not inferior to what we should expect from the most skilful surgeons of the globe."[1] A remarkable fact truly, but one often met with in the most widely separated regions of the earth, the importance of which cannot be overrated, and justifies the giving of a few more details.

In 1873 Dr. Prunières, to whom science has reason to be very grateful for his singular discovery, presented to the members of the French Association, in session at Lyons, a human parietal with a rounded piece of bone let into it. This piece of bone was rather larger than a five-franc piece, and the skull into which it had been fixed was found beneath the Lozère dolmen. A large opening, some three inches in diameter, the edges of which were worn smooth, had been made in this skull, and the piece of bone let into it was thicker than the skull itself, as well as different in color, the cranium being dark and the foreign piece of bone pale yellow. It was evident therefore that the two pieces did not belong in life to one person, and that the rounded piece had been cut out of some other skull. The following year Dr. Prunières added fresh details about other rounded

---

[1] This skill was not always shown, for Dr. Topinard speaks of a femur found at Feigneux which had been so clumsily set that one part greatly overlapped the other.—*Bul. Soc. Anth.*, p. 534.

pieces of skull that he had discovered let into crania, some of which pieces had evidently been introduced during the life of the patient, who had died under the operation of trepanation, whilst others had been put in after death. Dr. Prunières in every case speaks of *rondelles* or rounded pieces of skulls, and we prefer to quote him exactly, but as a matter of fact the trepanation was sometimes done with elliptical, triangular, or even pyramidal pieces of bone.

Later no less than sixty fresh examples, corroborating Dr. Prunières' discoveries, were found in the Baumes-Chaudes caves, and Broca in his turn reported the finding of three crania in the cave of *L'Homme Mort*, from which great pieces had been taken which had evidently not been lost by accident.

From this time excavations and discoveries made under Dr. Prunières succeeded each other rapidly. In 1887 his collection contained 167 crania or fragments of crania, all perforated, 115 of which were picked up in the caves of Lozère, which are probably of more recent date, beneath the dolmens of the *devèzes*, as those vast plains given up to pasturage are called. These dolmens, which were doubtless reserved for the burial of chiefs, often contain many valuable objects. Beneath one, for instance, were found fifteen beautiful darts of variegated flint, four polished boars' tusks, some schist pendants, some shells cut into the shape of teeth, some bone and stone necklace beads, and, lastly, two small bronze beads. These last-named objects justify us in dating the dolmen from the Bronze epoch, when the use of bronze began to spread over the district, though it was still not generally employed.

Attention once awakened, similar facts began to be

announced from many different quarters. In the
Neolithic caves of Marne were found skulls with
rounded holes in them, pieces of skull such as are
shown in Fig. 28, which were probably worn as amulets.
M. de Baye has in his fine collection more than twenty
examples of trepanation, one of which is shown in
Fig. 80. In nearly every case the operation had been
performed after death; three examples alone show it to
have been done during life, and that the patient certainly survived, for the wound shows very evident
signs of having healed,
and the edges of the
openings no longer
bear the marks of the
tool of the operator.
On one of the three
crania there were two
wounds near each
other, but they were
quite separate, and
were evidently not
treated at the same
time.

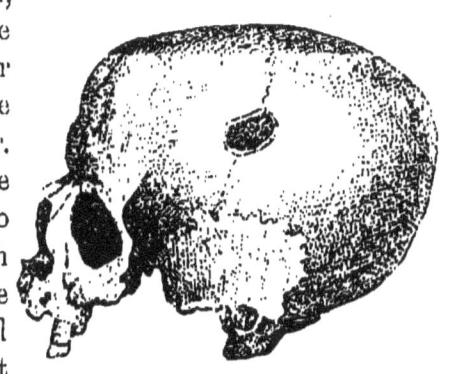

FIG. 80.—Mesaticephalic skull, with wound which has been trepanned.

A tumulus in the Guisseny commune (Finistère),
excavated about two years ago, covered over a sepulchral crypt. At the southeastern extremity was
picked up a badly baked hand-made earthenware
vase with four handles. Beside the vase lay a skull,
on which could be made out traces of oxidation,
which had probably been caused by the wearing of
a metal band, which has not been found. This
skull bears on the right side a little oval hole with
cicatrized edges about an inch long by two fifths

of an inch broad. The discovery of a bronze dagger and two bronze plaques leaves no doubt as to the age of this tumulus. This example of trepanation is the only well authenticated one of which I know in Brittany. It is true one skull has been mentioned as found beneath the megalithic monument of Saint-Picoux de Quiberon (Morbihan), which is even said to bear marks of sawing and scraping made in attempting trepanation, but this fact has been very much questioned, and the date at which the trepanation was performed, if performed it were, is very doubtful.[1] The proof we are seeking of the antiquity of the operation of trepanation is not therefore to be found here.

On a plain amongst the hills of the right bank of the Seine, above Paris, rises a mound resembling a promontory which is known as the Guérin mound, and consists of a vast deposit of chalk which was excavated long ago. Successive operations have brought to light eight caves, most of which contained a number of human remains, which were unfortunately dispersed without having been scientifically examined. One alone, opened in 1874, contained numerous bones belonging to individuals of every age and of both sexes, with polished flints, fragments of pottery, and implements of stag-horn. Amongst these relics was found the skull of an old man showing a very curious example of trepanation. It was unfortunately broken by the workmen in the very moment of discovery, and could only be very insufficiently examined. Other examples, however, which

---

[1] *Bul. Soc. Anth.*, 1883, pp. 258–301; 1885, p. 412. *Bul. Soc. Polymatique du Morbihan*, 1883, p. 12.

could be properly authenticated, are not wanting from the banks of the Seine and Marne; two fragments of skull were found in the canton of Moret, one of which had been trepanned during the life of its owner, and the other after death. We must also mention the crania presented to the learned societies at the Sorbonne, one of which came from the plateau of Avrigny, near Mousseaux-lès-Bray (Seine-et-Marne). Side by side with the skeleton lay polished hatchets, scrapers, and arrow-heads, fragments of pottery blackened by smoke, and lastly a solitary bone of an ox, pierced with three holes at regular distances, which had probably been used as a flute. Of nine crania found in this excavation three were pierced, two after death and one during life, the edges of the last named bearing very evident traces of treatment.

A trepanned skull was also discovered in a Neolithic sepulchre near Crécy-sur-Morin, where lay no less than thirty skeletons, remarkable for the strongly defined section of the tibiæ, whilst around were strewn hatchets, flint knives, bones, stilettos and picks of siliceous limestone with handles made of pieces of stag-horn. The tomb, built of stones without mortar, contained two contiguous chambers separated by a wall, and covered over by a stone weighing more than 1,200 tons. It seems likely that this huge stone had not been moved—it must have been beyond the strength of the makers of the tomb to lift it,—but that the spaces beneath, in which the dead had been placed, had been merely hollowed out. In the covered *Avenue des Mureaux*, of which I have already spoken, were picked up several trepanned crania. The tools, scrapers, and piercers, which had probably been used for the operation, lay near the crania.

A Neolithic sepulchre containing three trepanned crania was opened at Dampont, near Dieppe. The operation had been as neatly executed as if it had been performed by one of our most distinguished surgeons. As at Crécy, the sepulchral crypt was divided into two chambers, and the slab between them was pierced with a square opening,[1]—a fresh example of the curious practice of making openings, of which we have spoken in treating of so many different regions, often apparently completely cut off from communication with each other.

Beneath the Bougon dolmen (Deux-Sèvres), in the west of France, was found a skull, and at Lizières in the same department, the skeleton of a tall old man with a dolichocephalic skull and platycnemic tibiæ bearing traces of old wounds badly healed. The bony tissue of the skull was in an unhealthy state and the trepanation had evidently been part of medical treatment. At Saint-Martin-la-Rivière (Vienna), a tomb dating from Neolithic times contained five trepanned crania, on one of which the perforation had been made by scraping. In this tomb was also found a round piece of skull with a hole in it, which had doubtless been used as a pendant. The other objects found in this sepulchre were of a remarkable character, and included hatchets made of coralline limestone, jade, fibrolite, and serpentine, the blades of flint knives, arrows, some feathered, others stalked, some necklace beads, and a number of vases, some apodal, others with flat stands, and nearly all without any attempt at orna-

---

[1] *Nature*, January 2, 1886.

mentation. Beneath a dolmen near St. Affrique, M. Cartailhac discovered a skull with two holes in it; one near the bregma, which had been made during life, and the other on a level with the lambda, which had not been made until after death.[1] We cannot now note the important conclusions founded on these two perforations, we must be content with adding here that the tomb contained four other skeletons with crania showing no trace of trepanation; the tibiæ were platycnemic and the humeri had the so-called perforation of the olecranon fasces, which certain anthropologists, as I think without sufficient reason, consider characteristic of inferior races. We must mention yet one more discovery which it will not do to omit. A human parietal with a piece missing that had evidently been taken out, was found beneath the rock-shelter of Entre-Roches near Angoulême. The skull bore very evident traces of the performance of an operation which may or may not have been executed during life. Was it done to remove the diseased bone—for it was diseased—in the hope of prolonging life? Did the patient die under the hands of the surgeon, or was the piece of bone taken out after death to be used as an ornament or an amulet? Any one of these hypotheses is possible, and all we can say for certain is that there is no sign of the wound having been healed in any way. This is a common thing enough, and the interest of the discovery arises from a different cause. The rock-shelter of Entre-Roches is supposed to date from Palæolithic times, and if it were certain that there has been no displacement of the soil on which the parietal was found, it is to be concluded that trepanation was practised in the Quaternary

---

[1] *Bul. Soc. Anth. de Lyon*, 1883-1884.

period when man was living amongst the large extinct pachydermata and felidae. But it will be difficult to admit this unless other discoveries confirming it are made. If, however, we cannot prove that trepanation was practised in France in Palæolithic times, we can assert that it was continued down to the earliest centuries of the Christian era. One remarkable case of trepanation was found, for instance, in the Merovingian cemetery near St. Quentin; and a trepanned skull was recently exhibited at a meeting of the Anthropological Society in Paris, which had been found beneath a Merovingian tomb at Jeuilly. The patient had long survived his wound. The skeleton was found in a stone trough, narrower at the foot than at the head. The skeleton of a man between forty and fifty years of age was found in a Frank cemetery at Limet, near Liège. On the left parietal of the skull was an oval hole as big as a pigeon's egg, bearing traces of having been medically treated. The patient, like the man of Jeuilly, certainly survived the operation. His tomb, as were the resting-places of his neighbors in death, was covered over with a huge unhewn stone, and beside him lay another skeleton. A few nails and bits of wood were the only things found in the tomb. We may also mention the skeleton of a Frank of between fifty-five and sixty-five years of age with a trepanned skull, found by M. Pilloy, in a cemetery of the St. Quentin *arrondissement*, which also contained numerous objects dating from the sixth century A.D.

So far we have only spoken of France, but similar facts are reported all over Europe, and the difficulty really is to make a selection. Some round pieces of skull, like those of Lozère, have been picked up in

Umbria[1]; and a skull, bearing traces of an operation, the aim of which was to remove a portion of the left parietal, was found in the Casa da Mouva (Portugal), which dates, as do so many in France, from Neolithic times.

Goss mentions a discovery in one of the pile-dwellings of Lake Bienne, of a skull with a large hole in it with bevelled edges. There is no trace of this wound having healed, and the patient had evidently died soon after the operation.

The Prague Museum possesses two crania found at Bilin in Bohemia; one, of a pronounced dolichocephalic type, has near the middle of the right parietal an opening measuring one and a half by two and a third inches; the cicatrization is complete, and trepanation was evidently performed long before death. The other is mesaticephalic, and bears a round opening about one and a half inches in diameter. Dr. Wankel, to whom we owe these details, is well known through other discoveries; his excavations in the Bytchiskala Cave brought to light the skeleton of a young girl of ten or twelve years old, who had undergone the operation of trepanation. The wound, which was on the right side of the forehead, was half healed. The child still wore the ornaments she had been fond of in life—bronze bracelets and a necklace of large glass beads.

Discoveries of a similar character succeeded each other in Bohemia, and in nearly every case the operation of trepanation had been performed on the upper part of the forehead. Not very long ago it was reported to the Anthropological Society of Berlin that in excavating two tombs containing the remains of burnt bodies at Trüpschutz, on the west of Brux, some

---

[1] Belluci: *Congrès Préhistorique de Lisbonne*, 1880, p. 471.

fragments of skull were picked up, showing traces of trepanation. The edges of the wound in this case had been healed, and the patient had lived on after the operation. Professor Virchow came to the same conclusion with regard to a skull from a Neolithic tomb which bore on the right parietal traces of an ancient cicatrized wound. He also tells us of the finding in Poland of a round piece of skull which had evidently been worn as an amulet.[1]

In the north of Europe similar discoveries have been made. At Borreby, in Denmark, a skull was found from which large pieces had been taken; and another from beneath a dolmen at Nœs, in the island of Falster, had a hole in it no less than two and a quarter by one and three quarter inches in size. In the one case the holes were parts of a wound to which the victim had succumbed; in the other the edges were too regular to have been caused by traumatism. A Russian skull, a cast of which has recently been presented to the Italian Anthropological Society, bears traces of two trepanations; one performed during life, the other after death. The former had evidently been caused neither by illness nor by a wound.

General Faidherbe discovered at Roknia, in Algeria, two trepanned skulls, dating from a remote antiquity, in one of which the wound is half an inch in diameter, and shows no sign of cicatrization; and travellers speak of evident traces of similar operations on skulls dating from the time of the Ainos, the ancestors or predecessors of the Japanese at the present day; and if we cross the Atlantic, we shall meet with in-

---

[1] "Uber trepanirte Schädel von Giebiechenstein" (*Verh. der Berliner Gesellschaft für Anth.*, 1879, p. 64).

stances of trepanations executed in a similar manner, and probably for similar reasons.

We meet with numerous examples of trepanation in America, and fresh discoveries are daily made by the energetic men of science in that country. Dr. Mantegazza[1] mentions three examples of trepanation from Peru, which are of very great interest. One skull, still bound up in many cloths, was found in the Sanja-Huara Cave (province of Anta), which had been twice trepanned, and on which yet two more attempts at trepanation had been made. The latter seem to have taken place at different times, and death seems to have succeeded the last operation. Another skull which had belonged to an adult of Huarocondo has two frontal openings close to each other; the upper, of elliptical shape, is of large size and was evidently made after death. Yet another skull from the province of Ollantay-tambo bears a double trepanation, evidently made during life. The healing of the parietal opening proves that it was made before the wound in the forehead, in which the edges have remained rough. Dr. Mantegazza thinks that in the two first cases the operations took place after the patient had been wounded, but that in the third, the patient operated upon had been epileptic or perhaps even insane. We find it difficult to follow the learned professor here, as we are ignorant of the grounds for his conclusions.

We give an illustration (Fig. 81) of a trepanned skull found in a cemetery in the Yucay valley. A square piece has been cut out by making four regular incisions. The bone shows traces of an ancient inflammation, and many eminent surgeons, including

---

[1] *Matériaux pour l'Histoire de l'Homme*, Aout, 1886.

Nélaton and Broca, have not hesitated to attribute the opening, large as it is (seven by six inches), to a surgical operation. If the incisions are carefully examined it is easy to see that they were made with the help of a pointed instrument, such as a clumsily made drill, for instance. Each incision must have taken a long time to make, and we note with ever-increasing astonishment that the ancient Peruvians were not acquainted with the use of iron or steel, and that the hardest metal they employed was bronze.

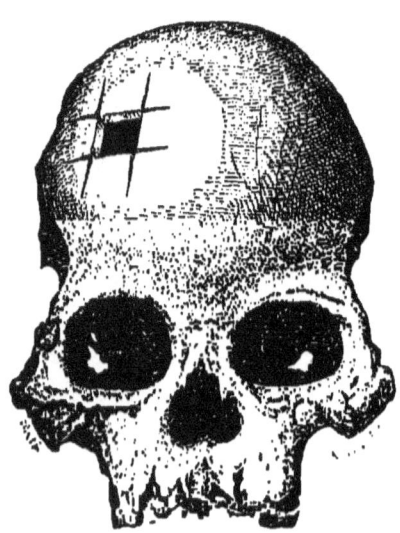

Fig. 81.—Trepanned Peruvian skull.

A few years ago a sepulchre was opened at Chaclacayo, at the foot of Mount Chosica, not far from Lima. In this tomb lay three mummies, of a man, a woman, and a child. Near them lay a human skull, having about the middle of the forehead an opening, measuring some two and a half by two inches. It is of polygonal form, and eight different incisions can easily be made out, which appear to have been made with some notched stone implement. On raising a strip of skin, still adhering to the skull, there was seen on the front part of the sagittal suture a very small perforation, the result either of a wound or of an operation which had taken place during life. It has been suggested that the piece of bone taken from the skull had been used to make a lance or arrow-head, which was superstitiously supposed by the owner to ensure his victory. This is, however, a mere suggestion, of which no proof can be given.

In other parts of America discoveries have been made of trepanned skulls, supposed to date from even more remote times than those we have just been considering. A few years ago Professor Putnam found, in the State of Ohio, some old wells filled with cinders and rubbish of all kinds. From one of them, which was deeper than the others, he took several crania, some of which bore evident traces of trepanation. From a mound near Dallas (Illinois) were taken more than one hundred skeletons, all of adults, placed side by side in a crouching attitude. Every one of them had a round opening on the left temple, and in some of these wounds the flint implement which had produced them was still imbedded. It is very evident that we have here tokens of some funereal rite, the meaning of which is uncertain, though it was evidently practised also in districts very remote from Illinois. To mention yet other examples, the excavation of a tumulus of irregular form near Devil's River (Michigan) has brought to light five skeletons buried upright, whilst a sixth lay in the centre of the tumulus, which was evidently, if we may so express it, the place of honor. On each of the six crania a perforation had been made after death.

A number of crania and parts of crania on which trepanation had been performed have also been taken from several mounds on Chamber's Island, from beneath the mound in the neighborhood of the Sable River, near Lake Huron, and near the Red

River.[1] Gillman thinks that the Michigan trepanations, which had been made with clumsy tools, were simply holes for hanging up skulls as trophies, as is still customary amongst the Dyaks of Borneo; but this seems scarcely a tenable hypothesis, for as a rule the skeletons lying in their last home are complete. Quite recently were discovered, beneath a tumulus near Rock River, eight skeletons, the skull of one of which bore a circular perforation made during life, which rather upsets Gillman's theory.

But to resume our narrative. The trepanations reported from North America are generally posthumous, and we can prove nothing as to their origin. Were they marks of honor made in some religious rite? Were they openings to allow the spirit of the departed to revisit the body it had abandoned? or, to suggest a far more worldly and revolting motive, were they merely holes through which to pick out the brains of the dead. A missionary, in a letter dated from Fort Pitt (Canada) in 1880, describes the mode of scalping practised by the Redskins, and says that they often take a round piece of skull as well as the scalp. May not this be a case of atavism, or the transmission of a custom from one generation to another, for the origin of which we must go back to the most remote ages? In the present state of our knowledge, insufficient as it is, this explanation is the most plausible.

It is even more difficult to come to a satisfactory conclusion with regard to European examples of the practice we have been describing. Trepanation was

---

[1] American Ass., Detroit, 1875, Nashville, 1877; "Ancient Men of the Great Lakes"; "Additional Facts Concerning Artificial Perforation of the Cranium in Ancient Mounds in Michigan." See also on this question generally Fletcher "On Prehistoric Trepanning and Cranial Amulets," Washington, 1882.

certainly practised in the treatment of certain diseases of the bone, such as osteitis or caries. Professor Parrot mentions a case worth quoting.[1] A few years ago several skeletons were found at Bray-sur-Seine (Seine-et-Marne) with numerous objects, such as polished stone hatchets, bone stilettos, shell necklaces and ornaments, all undoubtedly Neolithic. One of the crania had been trepanned, the position of the operation showing that its object had been to treat an osteitis. The operation had succeeded, and the cicatrization of the bones, both about the wound and in the parts originally affected, shows that recovery was complete. This is the only example we have of an operation executed with a view to curing a disease that can actually be seen, and it enables us to conclude that these men, of whom we know so little, had some notion of surgery. Were trepanations also practised to cure epilepsy or to heal mental affections? From the earliest times the seat of these troubles was always supposed to be the brain, and an ancient book of medicine recommends as a remedy the scraping of the outside of the skull.[2] In a recent book ("De la Trépanation dans l'Épilepsie par le Traumatisme du Crâne"), Echeverria mentions several cases of cure by trepanation when epilepsy had been the result of an injury. Observation may have led our prehistoric ancestors to discover this. May we date this custom then from prehistoric times? It is very difficult to decide with certainty either for or against it.

Of one thing, however, we may be quite certain.

---

[1] *Bul. Soc. Anth.*, February 17, 1881.
[2] Jehan Taxil: "Traité de l'Épilepsie, Maladie Appelée Vulgairement la Gouttète aux Petits Enfants."

The cranial perforations so much like one another reported from districts so remote and different in character, cannot be accidental. It is impossible to attribute to chance the occurrence of injuries of exactly the same size in crania of totally different origins. Setting aside the Entre-Roches skull, the antiquity of which does not seem to us sufficiently established, we find this custom maintained throughout the period characterized by the use of polished stone weapons and implements, the erection of megalithic monuments, and the domestication of animals. It was practised by the men of the cave of *L'Homme Mort* at the beginning of the Neolithic period, and was still in use at Moret when metals began to be known. The discoveries of Dr. Wankel, the excavations of the tumulus of Guisseny, prove that trepanation was continued throughout the Bronze age, whilst the Jeuilly and Limet tombs show that it was not discontinued even in Merovingian times.

The long continuance of such a practice is a very interesting fact, and we may mention a yet more curious one. How are we to explain trepanations that had no apparent motive on crania showing no symptoms of disease? How account for the repetition at different times of this operation, first on the living subject and then on the corpse, as at St. Affrique, Bougon (Fig. 82), at Feigneux (Oise), where Dr. Topinard has recently made excavations in a Neolithic cave and reports that a dolichocephalic skull of the same type as the crania of the cave of *L'Homme Mort*, belonging to a man of about thirty years of age, bore two perforations, one made during life, the other after death? The first measured two and a third by two and a half inches, and was surrounded by scratches, showing how clumsy the operator had been.[1]

In nearly every case the subjects operated on were young, and long survived the operation. The knowledge of this fact was from the first a very useful guide in the study of the subject of trepanation, and eagerly pursued researches constantly confirm it. One skull, for instance, from the cave of *L'Homme Mort* (Fig. 83),

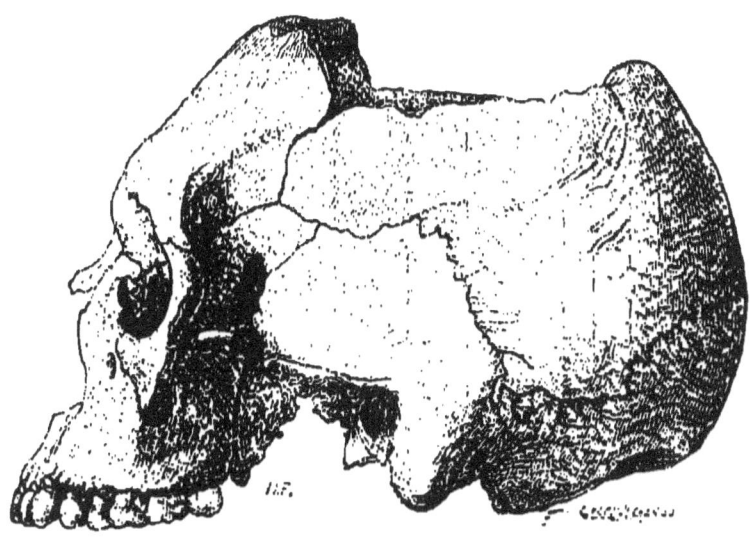

FIG. 82.—Skull from the Bougon dolmen (Deux-Sèvres), seen in profile.

had a large opening produced partly by an old operation and partly by two posthumous trepanations. The subject had been trepanned in childhood or early youth. There could be no doubt on that point; cicatrization had been complete, the bony tissue having

---

[1] *Bul. Soc. Anth.*, 1887, p. 527.

returned to its original condition. Then after death, at an adult age, the relations or friends of the deceased had cut out further round portions of the skull as near as possible to the old wound, probably with a view to keeping these pieces as amulets.

This was to Broca a flash of illuminating light, and according to him was in some cases a religious rite, a

Fig. 83.—Trepanned prehistoric skull.

ceremony of initiation, perhaps even a custom inculcated by an established religion. The child who had been subjected to it and had survived—as probably most of the victims did survive,—attained to a certain position and celebrity in his life, and after his death the fragments of his skull, especially those portions near the old wound, became treasured relics, and were in the end buried with their fortunate possessor on his death.

This superstition appears to have long survived even in historic times, and a Gallic chain is quoted[1] on which hung a round piece of skull with three holes in it. Indeed, these ornaments were so much sought after that counterfeits of them were made; at least, we cannot in any other way account for the occurrence of objects exactly resembling round pieces of human crania, but in reality made out of pieces of a stag's antler found in the Baumes-Chaudes Cave.

Yet another point deserves mention. It was evidently considered undesirable that the crania from which pieces had been taken should be left in a mutilated condition, and therefore pieces from other crania were taken to fill up the gap, so that, says Broca,[2] a new life was evidently supposed to await the dead, for otherwise what object can the restitution have served?

Dr. Prunières is also of opinion[3] that the introduction into the crania of certain deceased persons of round pieces from other skulls implies the belief in another life. This explanation, hypothetical as it is, is really very plausible, and it is a pleasant thought that our remote ancestors had faith in a future life; which faith is alike the greatest honor and the greatest comfort of humanity. Is not yet another more striking proof of the belief in a second existence to be found in the number of objects placed in tombs at all periods of time and in every part of the world? It is this belief, raising man as it does above the material needs of his

---

[1] De Baye: "Trépanations Préhistoriques," p. 28, fig. 11.

[2] *Bul. Soc. Anth.*, 1877, p. 42. Broca constantly dwells on this idea. "This funeral rite," he said, addressing the Anthropological Society, "implies belief in another life."

[3] *Ass. Française*, Lille, 1874, p. 631.

daily life, which forms the true grandeur of the human race, and if a nation once loses it it is sure to relapse into barbarism.

When trepanning was the fashion there is no doubt that the operation was performed in many different ways. Posthumous trepanations were accomplished with the aid of a flint implement used as a chisel or a saw. There was greater difficulty about an operation on a living subject. Broca is of opinion that it was done with a drill turned round and round in the skull in the way the French shepherds still treat diseases of the crania in their sheep. The elliptical form of the wound seemed to him to prove this, and he was further of opinion that when an opening had been drilled in the skull at the point chosen, the trepanation was completed by scraping the bone with a small flint blade.[1] Discoveries made since the death of the great French anthropologist, however, compel us to modify this opinion. The inflammation of the bone noticed along the edges of the trepanation proves that a notched implement was used to saw out the piece of skull.[2]

However the operation may have been performed, it is not one of great danger to the patient or of great difficulty to the operator. Experiments on animals with Quaternary flint implements have always been successful, and have had no tragic results, which is the best proof we can possibly give.

The size of the perforations made varies *ad infinitum*. One, the largest known, is described which is no less than sixteen inches in diameter.[3] Examples are

---

[1] *Bul. Soc. Anth.*, 1864, p. 199.
[2] *Bul. Soc. Anth.*, 1882, pp. 143, 535.
[3] *Ass. Française*, Blois, 1884, p. 417.

known of the trepanation of every part of the skull, even of the forehead, which at one time was supposed to have escaped. We have ourselves given instances of frontal trepanation, and Dr. Prunières mentions eleven cases in which the forehead had been operated on.

To conclude, we must repeat that trepanation is not really a dangerous operation, and the reason it is nearly always followed by the death of the subject in our own time is because it is never attempted except in desperate cases, and the fatal result is really caused by the cerebral disease, on account of which the operation was performed. History tells us of its practice in very ancient times; Hippocrates speaks of it as often resorted to by Greek physicians. It is performed in the present day by the Negritos of Papua and the natives of Australia and of some of the South Sea Islands, where it is considered efficacious in many maladies. We also find it practised by the rough miners of Cornwall and the wild mountaineers of Montenegro.[1] An army doctor who travelled in Montenegro a few years ago said that it was no rare thing to meet men who had been subjected to trepanation seven, eight, or even nine times. It is an interesting question, though we must not enter into it here, whether many races could stand such a number of operations as this.

The only instance we know in the present day of trepanation practised as a religious rite, is met with among the Kabyles, who are established at the foot of Mount Aurès on the south of the Atlas. The opera-

---

[1] Boulogne: *Mém. de Médecine et de Chirurgie Militaires*, 3d series, Paris, 1868. Védrènes: "Le Trépanation du Crâne" (*Rev. Anth.*, October, 1886).

tion is performed among them by the *thébibe*, one of their priests, by the aid of a simple gimlet which he turns rapidly round between his fingers. Among the Kabyles are men who have submitted to an operation of this kind several times.

We have now passed in review the weapons of prehistoric peoples, the wounds they caused, and the modes of healing them known to our ancestors; we have still to study the modes of defence resorted to by them in face of the many dangers by which they were surrounded; but the importance of this subject is such as to deserve separate consideration.

CHAPTER VII.

CAMPS, FORTIFICATIONS, VITRIFIED FORTS; SANTORIN; THE TOWNS UPON THE HILL OF HISSARLIK.

Combativeness, to use the language of phrenology, is one of the most lively instincts of humanity. The Bible tells us of the struggle between the sons of Adam, and shows us might making right ever since the days of primeval man. History is but one long account of wars and conquests, victories or defeats, and progress is chiefly marked in inventions which made battles more sanguinary and added to the number of victims slaughtered. At the very dawn of humanity man learned to make weapons; very soon, however, weapons ceased to appear sufficient. The first fortification was doubtless the cave, which its owner strengthened by closing the entrance with blocks of stone and piles of broken rock, or by digging deep trenches about it.

Population rapidly increased and war was declared between tribe and tribe, nation and nation, race and race. Terrible must have been the struggles between invaders and the original possessors of the soil. Means of defence were multiplied to keep pace with new modes of attack, and our ancestors of the Stone age were intelligent enough to make places of refuge in which on necessity they could shelter their wives and children, and later, when they became sedentary, their flocks and their stores of grain. In many different localities we find the remains of camps and fortifications, which, to avoid using a more ambitious term, we may characterize generally as enclosures.[1]

These primitive enclosures, says Bertrand in his "Archéologie Celtique et Gauloise," may have been very much more numerous than is supposed, if we include amongst them, as it appears we ought, many ruins long thought to date from the Roman era.

There is no doubt as to the purpose served by the camps, but we are not prepared to speak as positively as does Bertrand as to their origin, and the difficulty of deciding is very greatly increased on account of these camps having been successively occupied at different epochs by different peoples. Bearing in mind this reservation, we will now sum up to the best of our ability all that is so far known about the most important remains hitherto examined.

The residence of prehistoric man in the rich districts between the Sambre and the Meuse is proved by worked flints, fragments of pottery, and human bones dating from most remote times. The stations successively occupied were situated near watercourses or copious springs, and, where possible, on isolated escarped plateaux surrounded by ravines. Hastedon, about a mile and a quarter from Namur, is one of the best examples we

---

[1] On this point an admirable book should be consulted, by De la Noë: "Enceintes Préhistoriques," *Mat.*, 1888, p. 324, in which the author says that positions protected by escarpments bordering the greater part of the circumference of the *enceinte* were at all times chosen for the erection of fortifications. The absence of water, however, often makes him hesitate in coming to a decision, and leads him to think that the remains where it is absent must have been temples for the worship of deities.

can quote.¹ The camp, first made out in 1865, formed a long square, covering some thirteen hectares, or about thirty-two acres. It is situated on an isolated mound connected with the main plateau by an isthmus 227 feet long, and is protected on the south and west by a deep ravine. To these natural defences men had added important works to those parts that were accessible. The cutting of trenches a few years ago brought to light walls of a mean thickness of more than nine feet, formed of masses of rock and sand and round pieces of wood parallel with a *revêtement* of dry stones surmounted by a palisade consisting of three pieces of wood parallel with the walls, and seven perpendicular traverses. All the wood was charred; the besieged had evidently been driven out by fire. Excavations led to the finding of Roman coins; this and the resemblance of the palisades to those described by Caesar,² the very name of Hastedon, and the tradition everywhere prevalent in the district, that this had been the site of a Gallic Roman camp, led to the general adoption of that opinion. In fact, Napoleon III. actually ordered excavations to be made in the hope of finding traces of the Atuatuques, one of the most warlike of the tribes of northern Gaul; but side by side with historic relics were no less than ten thousand flints. These are chiefly merely chips or nuclei which had served as hammers, or long thin slices, with some few arrow- and lance-heads often skilfully cut, some polished hatchets, and saws with fine teeth. Nearly all are notched and worn with use, which does away with the idea that the place where they were

---

¹ *Congrès Préhistoriques*, Brussels, 1872, p. 318.
² "De Bello Gallico," book vii., chap. xxiii.

found was the site of a workshop such as I have already described. With these worked flints were found some fragments of coarse pottery, which could not possibly be confounded with Roman or Gallic work. The flints and pottery, and the walls put together without cement, point to the conclusion that if the camp of Hastedon was occupied by the Roman legions, it was long previous to their day inhabited by some Neolithic race, ignorant of the use of any but stone weapons and implements.

The camp of Pont-de-Bonn in the commune of Modave (Namur) very much resembles in its arrangement that of Hastedon.[1] A mound stands out upon the plain protected on the north and west by rocks difficult of access and connected with the main plateau by a very narrow tongue of land. Outside we can make out regular trenches parallel with each other, and connected by a wall of masonry, at the foot of which wall were picked up a good many iron nails. Inside the *enceinte* itself worked flints were associated with Roman coins. Are not these proofs in the first place of a long Neolithic occupation, then of the residence of Gallic Romans, and yet later of even more modern people of whom the masonry walls and iron nails are relics?

Limburg also contains some defensive works, many centuries old, which are as yet but little known. We may mention amongst them the so-called dyke of Zeedyck, near Tongres, a formidable intrenchment some 2,186 yards long by more than 325 feet wide at the base, and of a height varying from 49 to 65 feet; the earthen ramparts of Willem on the Geule, the not

---

[1] Dupont: "Les Temps Préhistoriques en Belgique," p. 235.

less important ones of Houlem, with many others far away from the great highways of communication, but within the limits of the two provinces of Liège and Limburg.[1]

A few years ago Bertrand said that there are in France some four hundred earthen *enceintes*, only sixty of which contain relics connecting them with the Gallic Romans. Since Bertrand's announcement this number has been greatly increased, thanks to eagerly prosecuted local researches. De Pulligny mentions a hundred in Upper Normandy[2]; Martinet says they are very numerous in Berry; one of the most remarkable, the quadrilateral of Haute-Brenne, covered an area of nearly three thousand acres.[3] Amongst the forests on the Vosges Mountains were discovered long single and double walls, the course of which follows the crest of the ramparts overlooking the valley of the Zorn, between Lutzelbourg and Saverne.[4] At Rosmeur, on Penmarch Point (Finistère), Du Chatellier excavated two tumuli which appear to have been connected with a series of defensive works encircling the whole promontory.[5] It would be merely fastidious to multiply instances, we will content ourselves with describing a few of the most interesting of these antique fortifications.[6]

The camp of Chassey (Saône-et-Loire) may be compared with those of Belgium. It is situated on a

---

[1] H. Bauduin: *Bul. Soc. Belge de Géographie*, 1879.

[2] *Recueil des Travaux de la Société de l'Eure*, Évreux, 1879.

[3] *Rev. d'Anth.*, 1880, p. 469.

[4] "Notice sur Quelques Monuments Trouvés sur le Sommet des Vosges" (*Soc. des Monuments Historiques de l'Alsace*, vol. i.).

[5] *Rev. d'Anth.*, 1880, p. 295.

[6] We may also mention the *Pen Richard* in Charente Inférieure, so well described by Cartailhac in his "France Préhistorique," p. 131.

plateau 2,440 feet long by a width varying from 360 to 672 feet. A huge natural rocky barrier rises on the south and east, whilst on the northeast and southwest we find two important intrenchments made of huge blocks of stone with a *revêtement* of earth. One of these intrenchments is 45, the other only 29 feet high. There is no trace inside of springs, and the inhabitants must always have had to obtain their water-supply by artificial means. The cisterns now in this camp appear to have been dug out with iron implements, and are certainly of later date than the first occupation of the plateau. Numerous objects picked up in the Chassey Camp belong to Neolithic times, but the people who have occupied it since those remote days, the men of the Bronze and Iron ages, the Gauls, the Romans, and the Merovingians, have so turned over the ground that products of industries, completely strange to each other, are everywhere mixed together in inextricable confusion.[1]

There were originally a good many hearths about the camp, and it was near to one of them that the spoon was found, figured in an earlier chapter of this book (Fig. 25). With it were picked up polished fibrolite, basalt, chloromelanite, serpentine, and diorite hatchets; evidently made in the neighborhood, as is proved beyond a doubt by the numerous chips and partly worked pieces lying about, as well as the discovery of no less than thirty polishers, many of them showing signs of long service. Bone implements

---

[1] Arcelin: "L'Âge de Pierre et la Classification Préhistorique," Paris, 1873. Flouest: "Notice sur le Camp de Chassey." Perrault: "Un Foyer de l'Âge de la Pierre Polie au Camp de Chassey" (*Mat.*, 1870). Coynart: "Fouilles au Camp de Chassey" (*Rev. Arch.*, 1866 and 1867).

of all kinds and whistles made of the phalanges of
oxen are also constantly found. Even if the presence
of these objects does not enable us to come to any final
conclusion, they are at least most useful and interesting
in enabling us to put together little by little a picture
of the life of the most ancient inhabitants of France.

The camp of Catenoy, near Liancourt (Oise) is
arranged very much in the same manner as that of
Chassey.[1] *Cæsar's Camp*, as it is called by the people
of the neighborhood, forms a long triangle, the apex of
which rests on the eastern extremity of the plateau.
Excavations have yielded a number of Gallic-Roman
objects, with some polished hatchets, some broken,
others intact, with stone and bone weapons, resembling
but for a few slight differences those we have described
so often. Numerous fragments of pottery were also
picked up, which pottery, hand-made and mixed with
crushed shells, seldom has either handles or any attempt
at ornamentation. Weapons, implements, and pottery
are all alike totally different from any Roman or Gallic
work known. It is impossible to study the relics at
Catenoy without coming to the conclusion that the
camp was occupied at periods prior to Gallic and
Roman times, and that there, as in many other districts,
the Latin conquerors had succeeded an unknown vanquished race.

De Quatrefages has accurately made out a series of
works extending along the left bank of the Nive, as
far as Itsassou, and of which the Pas-de-Roland marks
the extreme limit. A merely superficial examination
is enough to show that these defences existed only on
the side to which access would otherwise have been

---

[1] Ponthieux, "Le Camp de Catenoy" (Oise).

easy, while the height overlooking the river on the other side, which is impregnable by nature, has been left untouched. Here too we find the name Cæsar's Camp given to the relics, a fact of common occurrence all over France, where the great captain was long held in honor. Quatrefages is, however, of opinion that the works are neither Roman, Gallic nor Celtic, and he even arrives by a process of elimination at the conclusion that they were erected by the Iberians, who preceded the Aryans, and have left so deep an impress on all the countries they successively occupied. We do not feel able to accept entirely this hypothesis; but no suggestion of the eminent professor must be overlooked by those who earnestly seek with unbiassed minds to ascertain the truth.

Gregory of Tours relates that at the time of the invasion of the Vandals, the Gabali took refuge with their families in the *Castrum Gredonense*, and there, for two years, energetically resisted the invaders.[1] Grèze, now a little market town of the department of Lozère, is the *castrum* of which the old French chronicler speaks, and Dr. Prunières there collected forty stone hatchets, differing in no material respect from others found in such numbers elsewhere, with flint knives and scrapers, bone stilettos, and millstones, doubtless used for grinding grain, all of which are to the learned French professor proofs of the existence there of a Neolithic station before the historic period.

In the department of Alpes-Maritimes a series of defensive works crown the circle of mountains which rise from the shores of the Mediterranean. These intrenchments certainly date from a remote period, though

---

[1] "Hist. Francorum," book i., chap. xxxii.

CAMPS, FORTIFICATIONS. 287

we cannot assign them to any definite time, and the fact that they have been repaired at different epochs proves that they were successively occupied.[1] They consist principally of circular or elliptical *enceintes* surrounded by walls of stones without mortar, and they vary in diameter from some 30 to 328 feet. One of the largest is that on the Colline des Mulets, above Monte Carlo.

Although the pile-dwellings of Switzerland and of the *terremares* of Italy would appear to have been in themselves protection enough, their inhabitants did not neglect other means of defence, from which we may

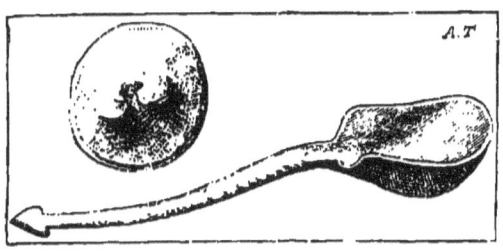

FIG. 84.—Prehistoric spoon and button found in a lake station at Sutz (Switzerland).

gather that they were engaged in constant and terrible struggles. The *terremares* were generally surrounded by a talus or rampart of earth, with an external fosse which protected the approaches to the dwellings. The rampart of Castione (Parma), which dates from the Bronze age, was even strengthened inside with large timber caissons.[2] In Switzerland, some works recently

[1] De Rosemont: "Étude sur les Antiquités antérieures aux Romains." Desjardins: "Les Camps Retranchés des Environs de Nice." Rivière: *Ass. Française*, Rheims, 1880, p. 628.
[2] Pigorini: "Terramara dell'Eta del Bronzo Situata in Castione de' Marchesi."

undertaken to deflect the course of the Aar, on its exit from Lake Bienne, have led to the discovery of a village of the Stone age, with the bridges leading to it and the little forts intended to protect it.[1] As have the neighboring settlements, this station has yielded a great many arrows, hatchets, scrapers, and harpoons. We give an illustration of a curious marrow spoon, and of a round object which seems to have been a button (Fig. 84), as they mark the progress made.

Great Britain is intersected by lines of fortifications of unknown origin, but certainly of extreme antiquity. We may mention Dane's Dyke, Wandyke, the Devil's Dyke at Newmarket, and Offa's Dyke, running from the Bristol Channel to the Dee, and dividing England from Wales. Ancient camps and intrenchments, Sir John Lubbock tells us, crown the greater number of the hills of England. General Pitt-Rivers explored several of these camps in the county of Sussex. Many extend over considerable areas, and all contain numerous worked flints and other relics of prehistoric industry. These relics are met with in great numbers at the base of the intrenchments, so that we may justly conclude that they date from the same epoch.

The most celebrated of these camps is that of Cissbury, three miles north of Worthing. We may also mention that of Hod-Hill in Dorsetshire, which greatly resembles the one at Cissbury, but we will describe the latter in some detail.[2] It is situated on a somewhat lofty plateau of irregular form, its site having been chosen with great skill as one offering great facilities for de-

---

[1] *Nature*, 1887, second week, p. 62.

[2] Memoranda read to the Royal Society of Antiquaries in London (*Archæologia*, vol. xlii., pp. 27–76). Lane Fox: *British Association*, Bristol, 1875. Evans: "Stone Age."

fence. The earthen ramparts and the fosses protecting them cover an area of sixty acres, and their importance varies according to the relief of the ground; thus the thickness of the walls is very much greater on the eastern side where an attack would have been most fraught with danger; four doors give access to the interior, and on each side of these doors are ruins of rectangular structures strengthening their defence. Archæologists, however, are of opinion that these redoubts, though their construction is exactly similar to the rest of the fortifications, are of more recent date. In fact Roman tiles have been found amongst the ruins, but these really prove nothing, as every one is agreed that Cissbury was occupied by the Romans after the subjugation of England by them; and the only point at issue is really whether the walls of which the ruins still remain date from the Roman period, or from times prior to their arrival. We ourselves lean to the latter opinion, as drinking-water is absolutely wanting; a very important point, as the Roman generals always made it their first care to pitch their camps near a good water-supply. On the western slope at Cissbury on each side of the ramparts are fifty funnel-shaped depressions, some of which are as much as seventy feet in diameter and twelve feet deep. These holes may have served as refuges, and the larger ones were certainly lived in, as is proved by the charred stones of the hearths and the pieces of charcoal found near them; moreover, Tacitus[1] tells us that the Germans lived in similar habitations. Whatever,

---

[1] " Solent et subterraneos specus aperire, eosque multo insuper fimo onerant, suffugium hiemi et receptaculum frugibus " (" De Moribus Germanorum," chap. xvi.).

however, may have been their ultimate use, these hollows were in the first place dug out with a view to obtaining flints in the marly chalk forming the hill; and recent excavations have revealed the existence of galleries connecting the depressions. When they became later human habitations some of the inside openings were blocked up with lumps of chalk, carefully piled up so as to make entrance extremely difficult, greatly adding to the security of the inmates.

Thirty of these shafts were excavated in succession; and amongst the rubbish of all kinds with which they were filled were found some well cut celts, showing no trace of polish, and some weapons or tools of the Moustérien type. The number of half-finished implements, and the even greater quantity of chips, points to these shafts having formed a centre of manufacture. Many of the implements were made of stag-horn, and amongst them we must mention some picks which, curiously enough, exactly resemble those of Belgium and the south of France.[1] Similar wooden picks are found in the copper mines of the Asturias, in the salt mines of Salzburg, and in a petroleum well recently opened on the frontier between the United States and Canada. In all these localities traces can be made out of ancient mining operations. But to return to Cissbury: from amongst the prehistoric ruins there were also taken, numerous fragments of pottery, not at all like Roman ware, with the bones of the horse, goat, boar, and ox, all still represented in the fauna of England; with oyster-shells, and the shells of both land and sea mollusca, of species still to be found in Great Britain. But no trace has so far been discovered of metals, and neither the

---

[1] *American Journal of Archæology.*

flint implements nor the bones of animals have any of the marks of rust so characteristic of the Bronze and Iron ages. Must we not then conclude that these shafts were sunk at a time long prior to the earliest historic period?

The walls of the subterranean galleries of Cissbury bore not only cup-shaped ornaments, striæ, and curved or broken lines, recalling those on the megalithic monuments of Scotland and Ireland; but Park Harrison has made out some regular *runes*, or written characters, of which a reproduction was shown at the Paris Exhibition in 1878. This last fact is the more curious, as Sayce discovered in a passage giving access to a cave near Syracuse some characters somewhat similar in form, to which he assigns a proto-Phœnician origin. We may add that certain characters made out at Cissbury, differing but little from the modern letter *b* or the figure 6, are also found in the most ancient Palmyrian, Copt, and Syrian alphabets. Were this fact completely established, still more, if it were corroborated by other analogous facts, we should in it have a very valuable indication of the relations of England with the most ancient known navigators.

Germany also contains some ancient fortifications, of which the most remarkable are the *Heidenmauer* of Saint Odila, near Hermeskiel, between the Moselle and the Rhine. Huge stones, piled up without cement, form a triple *enceinte*, but there is nothing to connect these remains with prehistoric times. It is the same with the intrenchments in the Grand Duchy of Posen, the existence of which was announced at a meeting of the Anthropological Society of Berlin.[1] Many

---
[1] *Zeitschrift für Anthropologie*, 1874, p. 115; 1875, p. 127.

of these defensive works, notably those of Potzrow and of Zahnow, had been erected on piles. In the district between Thorn and the Baltic are numerous mounds of the shape of a truncated cone, the platform of which is surrounded by an embankment some 590 feet in diameter.[1] Near many of these were picked up many broken human bones, mixed together in the greatest confusion with weapons, hatchets, and hammers, resembling Neolithic types. Everything bears witness to the struggles of which these mounds were the scene.

Similar relics of a past still obscure are met with in the south of Europe. Cartailhac has brought into notice the *citanias*, which are strange fortified towns in Portugal. On the plateau of Mouinho-da-Moura, southwest of Lisbon, were found numerous polished hatchets, associated with shells of marine mollusca and the bones of mammals belonging to species still extant.[2] This station was protected by intrenchments of so great an extent that it has been impossible to examine the whole of them. There are also near the same place several caves, now nearly choked up. One of them was originally a regular tunnel; the cutting leading to the entrance was made of earth and small stones; it contained the bones of animals, some cinders, and four large vases of coarse workmanship. It is difficult to make out what this cave was used for, the great confusion in which the bones lay excluding all idea of its having been a tomb. Ribeiro had already made out at Lycea an intrenched camp pro-

---

[1] Zaborowski: "Monuments Préhistoriques de la Basse Vistule."
[2] Ribeiro: "Notice sur Quelques Monuments Préhistoriques du Portugal," Lisbon, 1878.

FIG. 85.—General view of the station of Fuente-Alamo.

tected by clumsily constructed walls. Inside the *enceinte* he picked up numerous fragments of ornamented pottery, with polished hatchets, shells, and a good many bones of animals. He also made out several sepulchres.[1]

The prehistoric station of *La Muela de Chert* in Maeztrago reminds us of those of Portugal. It is situated on a little eminence, protected on the north and east by the natural escarpment of the plateau, and on other sides by a wall of some height made of stones without mortar. Some foundations of an oval shape, on which doubtless were built the homes of the inhabitants, can be made out in the middle of the *enceinte*. We can, however, but repeat here what we have said so often elsewhere, that it is impossible to fix the exact date at which these intrenchments were made. The discovery, however, of polished flint hatchets, diorite lance-heads, and a few bones of ruminants and cervidæ unknown in Spain in prehistoric times, would appear to point to a very considerable antiquity. Lastly, two young Belgian engineers[2] have lately made out between Almeria and Carthagena a considerable number of prehistoric stations in which can be traced successively the different Stone ages and those of Copper and of Bronze. Several of these stations (Fig. 85) are regular fortified camps, protected by thick stone walls cemented with a thin layer of clay. The fire which destroyed the habitations has left behind, beneath the ashes and cinders, numerous objects, with the aid of which we are able to form a picture of the life led by the men who built the fortifications, and we know that

---

[1] "Noticia de Algunas Estarves e Monumentos Prehistoricos."
[2] H. and L. Siret: "Les Premiers Âges du Métal dans le Sud-est de l'Espagne."

they were agriculturists, for the very stores of grain have been found charred and agglutinated by fire. In the more recent stations flint, which was in the earliest time the one material used, has disappeared and is replaced by the copper, of which a plentiful supply was found in the rich mines riddling the mountains. Excavations have even brought to light the workshop of the metallurgist, with its moulds and vases converted into crucibles, its essays at new forms, its scoriæ, and lastly its finished weapons, showing real skill in their production.

Although it is impossible to assign to them a definite date, we must, to make this part of our work complete, say a few words on the earthworks met with in Roumania. A former minister of that principality, M. Odobesco,[1] classes them as *valla*, *tumuli*, and *cetati de pamentu* or citadels.

The *valla* include important works. One of them cuts across Valachie parallel with the Danube and loses itself in Southern Russia. Another crosses the north of Moldavia and Bessarabia, following a direction convergent with the former. These *valla*, although they are known in the country in which they occur as *Fossés de Trajan*, are certainly of earlier date than the Roman occupation, and in fact Roman roads cut across the intrenchments or fosses which have been levelled or covered over to make way for them. Excavations of the large tumuli are not yet sufficiently advanced for us to hazard an opinion about them. The smaller ones, however, are seldom of Roman origin. The funeral vases of calcareous stone which they contain bear witness clearly enough

---

[1] *Congrès Préhistorique de Copenhague*, p. 118.

to their destination, and also to the rite with which they were connected.

The *cetati de pamentu* are regular earthen fortifications set up within short distances of each other on all the heights overlooking the torrential rivers of Roumania. These intrenchments, generally of round or oval form, are protected by deep fosses, parapets, and palisades. Masses of cinders and burnt earth bear unmistakable evidence to the cause of their destruction. All about, excavations have brought to light coarse pottery, grindstones for crushing grain, stores of millet which had been damaged by the flames, and a few primitively constructed bronze idols. When the vanquished Roumanians were driven from their intrenchments, they had evidently learned to use bronze, but were still, as we have already remarked, unacquainted with iron, as no object in that material has been found, nor does anything bear any trace of rust.

Thus, throughout Europe, man, in the presence of the many dangers surrounding him, endeavored in the very earliest times to protect by similar means his family, his flocks, and his wealth. In America we are able to quote facts of even more importance. The vast territory comprised between the Alleghanies and the Rocky Mountains, between the great lakes of Canada and the Gulf of Mexico, is intersected with truly colossal fortifications, almost all of them made entirely of earth. The ancient Americans knew how to protect every height and every delta formed by the junction of two rivers with redoubts, walls, parapets, fosses, and circumvallations. Not without astonishment we make out a regular system of fortresses connected with each other by deep trenches and secret passages, some of them hewn out beneath the beds of rivers, observatories on the heights, and concentric walls, some actually strengthened with casemates protecting the entrances. All these works were constructed by the so-called Mound-Builders, of whose ancestors or of whose descendants absolutely nothing is known.

All the strongholds of the Mound-Builders rise near abundant watercourses, and the best proof that can be given of the intelligence which guided their constructors in their choice of sites, is the fact of the number of flourishing cities such as Newark, Portsmouth, Cincinnati, Saint Louis, Frankfort, and New-Madrid, etc., which were built upon the ruins of various earthworks.

It would take us too long merely to enumerate all the ancient fortifications still existing in North America. Moreover they all resemble each other so much that the description of a few of them is really all that is needed to prove their importance.

Fort Hill (Fig. 5, p. 39) rises from an eminence overlooking a little river called Paint Creek; the walls vary in height from eight to fifteen feet, and exceed thirty feet in thickness.[1] Several doors facilitate entrance, and one of them leads to a square *enceinte*, the walls of which have been almost entirely destroyed. This enclosure probably contained the homes of the people, which may have been mere cabins of adobes or sun-burnt bricks, or huts covered with rushes, interlaced branches, or the skins of animals; on this point we are reduced to guesswork. In the centre of the principal enclosure can be made out, in almost every

---

[1] Putnam: "Report Peabody Museum," vol. iii., p. 348.

case, several much smaller enclosures, each containing in their turn one or more mounds. Some think these were consecrated to religious rites, but this is a mere conjecture, for nothing is really known of the form of government or of the religion of the Mound-Builders.

Forest trees have grown up on these abandoned ruins, succeeding other vegetable growths; the huge girth of the decaying trunks proving their longevity. Man, impelled by motives we cannot fathom, had abandoned the districts where everything bears witness to his power and intelligence, and the vigorous vegetation of nature once more has it all its own way.

The most remarkable group of prehistoric fortifications in North America is perhaps that near Newark, in the valley of the Scioto. It includes an octagonal *enceinte* eighty acres in area, a square *enceinte* of twenty acres, with two others, one twenty the other thirty acres in extent. The walls of the great circle are still twelve feet high by fifty feet wide at the base. They are protected by an interior fosse seven feet deep by thirty-five feet wide. According to measurements carefully made by Colonel Whittlesey,[1] the total area covered by these intrenchments is no less than twelve square miles, and the length of the mounds exceeds two miles. The large entrances protected by mounds thirty-five feet high, the avenues leading to them which are regular labyrinths, the quaintly shaped mounds— one, for instance, represents the foot of a gigantic bird— all combine to strike the visitor with astonishment. We give a representation (Fig. 86) of a group, not unlike that we have just described, which is situated at Liberty (Ohio), and includes two circles and one

---

[1] "Ancient Monuments of the Mississippi Valley."

square. The diameter of the great circle is 1,700 feet, and it encloses an area of forty acres, whilst that of the smaller *enceinte* is 500 feet; the area of the square, each side of which measures 1,080 feet, is twenty-seven acres. The walls are not strengthened by any ditch, and, contrary to general usage, the earth of which they are made was dug out from the inside of the *enceinte* itself. We may also mention Old Fort (Greenup

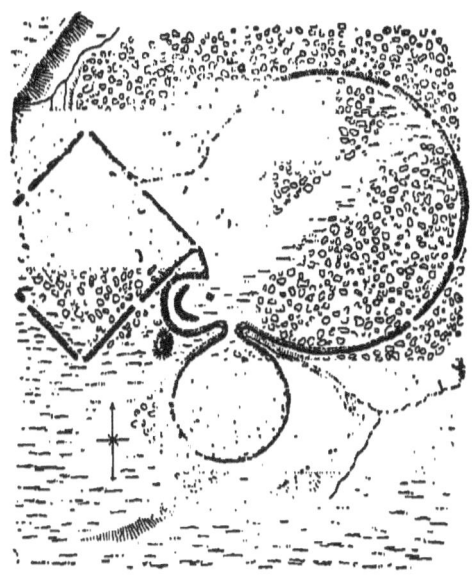

FIG. 86.—Group at Liberty (Ohio).

County, Kentucky), successively described by Caleb Atwater, Squier, and J. H. Lewis. It is situated forty feet above the river, and the total length of the walls exceeds 3,175 feet. Six entrances give access to it, and in the centre rises a mound representing some animal, a bear probably, measuring more than 105 feet. Several small mounds, beneath which were found human bones, cluster about the larger one.

We must not omit to name an extraordinary system of intrenchments at Juigalpa, in Nicaragua, which so far as I know is quite unique. This is a series of trenches extending for several miles (Fig. 87), varying in width from nine and a half to thirteen feet; at equal distances are oval reservoirs, the longest axis of which measures as much as seventy-eight feet. In each

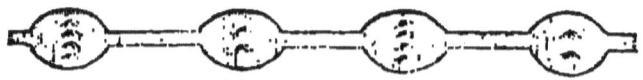

FIG. 87.—Trenches at Juigalpa (Nicaragua).

reservoir are two or four mounds, probably serving as watch-towers. We know nothing either of the people who erected these singular structures or of the enemy from whom they formed a protection. Nor can anything be guessed as to the way in which the defence was conducted. All is involved in obscurity, and at every turn we are compelled to repeat that prehistoric studies are weighted with uncertainty, long and arduous study being necessary to bring ever so little order into the chaos in which everything connected with them is involved.

We must cursorily refer to some other fortifications which really scarcely belong to our subject, though certain archæologists claim for them a prehistoric origin. We refer to the vitrified forts, which are strange structures in which stones, such as granite and gneiss, quartzite and basalt, have been subjected to a heat so intense as to produce vitrification.

These vitrified forts are *enceintes*, generally of round or elliptical form, carefully erected where they were most needed for defence, and protected by one or more ramparts.[1] The ramparts all bear traces of vitrification, more or less complete, which has, so to speak, cemented them together. The vitrification is very unequal, being complete in some parts and scarcely noticeable in others. It is evident that the builders did not know how to direct their fire uniformly.

Ever since 1777 vitrified forts have been known in Scotland, and until 1837 they were supposed to exist nowhere else. About that time, however, Professor Zippe called attention to similar ruins in Bohemia, and later it was announced that discoveries of the same kind had been made in various parts of France, Denmark, and Norway. Virchow speaks of the *Schlaken Wälle*, or ramparts of vitrified scoria, near Kern[2] and Schaafhausen, and gave an account of them at a meeting of German naturalists at Ratisbon. It would be easy to multiply instances. Vitrified walls are known in the Puy-de-Dôme, in which the facing is of clay, and draught flues, for regulating and fanning the flames, have been made out. At Castel-Sarrazin is a camp refuge with similar dispositions,[3] and recently Daubrée presented to the Académie des Sciences a piece of porphyry artificially vitrified from the prehistoric *enceinte* of Hartmannswiller Kopf in Upper Alsace.[4]

It is in Scotland, however, that are situated the most remarkable vitrified forts. A few years ago no less than forty-four were counted. The most celebrated are those of Barry Hill and Castle Spynie in

---

[1] See Dr. Hibbert in the *Transactions of the Society of Antiquaries of Scotland*, vol. iv., Appendix, p. 181.

[2] *Zeitschrift für Ethnographie*, 1870, p. 270.

[3] Pomerol: " Murailles Vitrifiées de Châteauneuf," *Ass. Franç.*, Blois, 1884.

[4] *Congrès Soc. Sav.*, Sorbonne, 1882.

Invernesshire, Top-O-Noth in Aberdeen, and a small fort which rises from a lofty rock in the midst of the Strait of Bute. Vitrified cairns also occur in the Orkney Islands, notably on the little isle of Sanday, but the most interesting structures of the kind are Craig Phœdrick and Ord Hill of Kissock, which rise up like huge pillars on the hills at the entrance of Moray Firth, at a distance of three miles from each other.[1]

Craig Phœdrick is now covered with a luxuriant vegetation of broom, furze, and fern, with groves of firs and larches, amongst which the explorer makes his way with difficulty to the fortifications, or rather to the piles of massive blocks to which that name has been given. These blocks form an acropolis of oval form, the upper part of which is a flat terrace encircling a central basin some six and a half to nine and a half feet deep, which may be compared to the craters of the extinct volcanoes of Auvergne. The sides of the mound are strewn with cyclopean blocks of vitrified granite, which evidently originally formed part of the fortifications. It is on the eastern side, overlooking the valley of the Ness, that the buildings are of the greatest importance; two terraces can be made out, the lower projecting beyond the upper, forming a double series of almost perpendicular fortifications, constructed of vitrified blocks cemented together with thin layers of mortar, spread without any attempt at regularity. The blocks form, with the mortar, a conglomerate so compact that when struck with a hammer they break without separating. Examination of fragments under the microscope prove that they have gone

---

[1] J. Marion: *Bul. des Soc. Savantes*, 4th series, vol. iv. Daubrée: *Rev. Arch.*, July, 1881.

through important mineralogical transformations, under the influence of what must have been an extremely high temperature. The heat must have been indeed intense which could cause mica to disappear entirely, and feldspar to melt almost completely.

The hill known as Ord Hill of Kissock is crowned, as is Craig Phœdrick, with ruins still standing, but the vegetation about them is so dense and thorny that it is difficult to make out the condition of the remains. The ruins, which can only be seen from one side, appear however to have formed part of fortifications, dating from the same time and serving the same purpose as those of Craig Phœdrick. Were they forts? There is certainly no sign of their having been used as habitations. Or were they, as some archæologists are disposed to think, beacon houses used for warning the people of the approach of the Norman pirates or Scandinavian vikings, whose depredations were not discontinued until the eighth century of the Christian era? Hypotheses are always easy, but proofs of these hypotheses are difficult to find, and we confess we have none to bring forward.[1]

Passing to France, we find the greater number of vitrified forts in the Département de la Creuse. At Châteauvieux is an *enceinte* of oval form, 416 feet wide at its broadest part.[2] An earthwork, 22 feet

---

[1] Sir J. Lubbock compares the ruins of Aztalan, in America, with the vitrified forts of Scotland; but we think this is a mistake, for the walls of Aztalan consisted of irregularly shaped masses of hard, reddish clay, full of hollows, retaining the impression of the straw or dried grass with which the clay was mixed before it was subjected to the action of heat, whether the application of that heat was intentional or accidental. There is nothing about this at all resembling the melted granite of the vitrified forts.

[2] De Cassac: "Notes sur les Forts Vitrifiés de la Creuse." Thuot: "La Forteresse Vitrifiée du Pay de Gaudy," p. 102.

wide at the base, serves as foundation to a wall, the outer and inner portions of which consist of small granite stones, arranged in regular layers. The space between the two series of small stones is filled in with a sheet of melted granite, some twenty-four inches wide, resting on calcareous tufa. The whole mass is completely vitrified, and regular geodes or nodules lined with crystals and draped with pendent drops of melted rock have been produced.

The ancient fortress of Ribandelle, of circular form, rises above the Creuse, opposite Châteauvieux. It was successively occupied by the Celts, the Romans, and the Visigoths, but we are unable to fix the date of its erection or the name of the people who built it. There remain but a few ruins at the present day, but we can make out in them the same mode of construction as that followed at Châteauvieux. The walls are faced with unhewn stones, the outer side of which still retains a natural appearance, while the inner is corroded and disintegrated. In the wall itself, separated from the facings by beds of peat mould, are great blocks of vitrified granite. The traces of the action of fire are specially noticeable in the upper part of the walls, so that they were evidently finished when the fusion took place.

The site of the furnace in these forts is difficult to determine. It was evidently not situated under any of the blocks, for the earthworks on which they rest retain no traces of the action of fire. Nor was it situated at the side, for the outer facings have retained alike their original form and consistency. Nor can the furnace have been lit on the blocks, as heat exercises its action by radiating in every direction. We are therefore forced to the conclusion that the fire was spread with the aid of spaces left in the inside of the construction at various points, for the vitrified mass is divided into blocks, about nine and three fourths feet long, at very short distances from each other.

These few examples will be enough to give some idea of the strange vitrified forts. Many of them retain traces of Roman occupation. The Guéret Museum possesses a fragment from the Ribandelle walls in which a Roman tile is completely imbedded; and M. Thuot picked up other tiles in a similar condition amongst the ruins. This is a very decided proof that the vitrification took place after the arrival of the conquerors of Gaul. The weapons and tools discovered would appear to confirm this idea, and to suggest similar explanations of vitrification elsewhere. If so, we shall have to admit that vitrified forts date from the earliest centuries of the Christian era, and are not prehistoric at all. We have, however, noticed them here on account of the grave doubts in the matter, and because they furnish a striking and valuable illustration of the relations existing from the most remote times between widely separated races, and maintained until the present time. In no other way can we account for the practice of the extremely difficult and complicated operation of the vitrification of hard rocks in districts so far apart as Norway and Scotland, Germany and the midlands of France.

The more we think of the difficulties vitrification presents, the greater is our astonishment. How was the fusion achieved of elements so refractory alike in their structure and in the resistance offered by accumulated masses of material? By what processes was heat brought up to the 1300 degrees necessary for the fusion of granite? The incineration and fusion of the materials of which the vitrified forts are made, especially the granite ones of La Creuse and the Côtes du Nord, bear witness, says Daubrée, to a surprising skill and knowledge of the management of fire in those who burned them, but these qualities were manifested also in extremely ancient metallurgical operations. It is quite impossible to suppose the vitrification to have been the result of a conflagration. No fire, whether accidental or the work of an incendiary, could be powerful enough to produce such results. The use of petroleum in the most terrible conflagrations of our own time—those of the Commune in 1871, for instance—did calcine and disintegrate stone, but I know of no case of vitrification.

The Keramic Museum of Sèvres contains several specimens which present very notable differences to each other. Those from Château-Gontier are formed of very close-grained quartzite granite of a greenish color streaked with black. The conglomerate welding them together is a vitrified scoria full of very small bubbles made by the escape of gas which had not had sufficient strength to get out. The block from Sainte-Suzanne (Mayenne) consists of quartz mixed with half calcined grains of feldspar, bleached by the action of fused glass, which once introduced filled up as it congealed all the vacant spaces with a vitreous substance of light greenish-white color. The fractures are green and bright, and are dotted with white points, which are all that is left of the stones after their disintegration in the grip of a heat that was alike intense and rapid in its action. The fragments brought from

Scotland differ from those just described. They consist of small pieces of granite completely merged in a thick paste with which they form the mass, the whole breaking together when it does break ; and the melted matter seldom has any bubbles in it.[1]

The process employed in cementing the materials of the vitrified forts was then perfectly unique. The processes employed to obtain the necessary heat varied according to circumstances and according to the nature of the materials used. At Sainte-Suzanne and at La Courbe marine salt was used as a flux. Captain Prévot[2] thinks that the walls were smeared with a coating of clay, and that as in the baking of bricks spaces were left between so as to produce more intense heat. M. de Montaiglon is of opinion that the buildings were in the first instance erected without the use of any calcareous or argillaceous material, and that glass in a state of fusion was poured over them afterwards, this glass consolidating them and forming with them one indestructible mass. M. Thuot seems much disposed to share this last opinion, but he thinks that some chemical materials such as soda or potash were also used. Yet one other possible solution may be mentioned, a solution which is becoming more and more generally accepted, namely that the granite was not after all really melted, but that the vitrification should either be attributed to the fusion of the argillaceous mass, which has been subjected to an igneous transformation, such as that which often takes place in furnaces for baking bricks and in lime-kilns.[3]

---

[1] We take most of these details from a note by M. A. de Montaiglon published in the *Bulletin des Sociétés Savantes.*

[2] *Mat.*, 1881, p. 371.

[3] *Bul. Soc. Anth.*, 1884, p. 816, etc.

Whatever explanation we may accept, however, the processes employed certainly bear witness to a much more advanced state of civilization than was acquired in the earliest ages of humanity. We have been led by the great interest and mystery of the subject to dwell longer on it than we intended, and we must hasten to return to prehistoric times with a determination not to transgress again.

Fortifications are a proof of combined action leading to a common end; they imply social organization, chiefs to command, workmen to obey. A recent discovery enables us to form a very accurate picture of prehistoric men gathered together not only for purposes of defence, but in a society already rich, industrious, and, if we may so speak, learning to cultivate the arts of peace.

The Ægean Sea has ever been the theatre of igneous phenomena, and the three little islands of Thera, Therasia, and Aspronisi, which shut in the Bay of Santorin, are built up chiefly of volcanic materials.[1] In 1573 an eruptive cone suddenly appeared; in 1707 the inhabitants of Santorin saw rise up a short distance from their shores a rock that increased in size for several days and then suddenly split up. This splitting up was succeeded by a great eruption of incandescent materials; an eruption which lasted for no less than five years, forming at the end of that time an island some 400 feet high by 3,279 feet in circumference. In 1866, after many violent shocks of earthquake, the ground was rent asunder on this island and masses of volcanic matter were belched forth, whilst on the other side of the island the soil sank to such a degree that canoes were used to get to

---

[1] Fouqué, *Nature*, 1876, second week, p. 65.

houses which but the day before were nine feet above the sea-level. This eruption went on until 1870, and the quantity of scoriæ vomited forth during its continuance welded three islets, which had hitherto been separate, to the principal island, of which they now form part. On entering the Bay of Santorin we see on every side banks of lava, beds of scoriæ, and piles of cinders of a purplish-gray color rising in cliffs to a height of more than 1,312 feet. All these materials are the result of innumerable eruptions, and the central crater of the volcano is probably situated about the middle of the bay. It is supposed that at one time a conical mountain, from 1,958 to 2,600 feet high, rose where soundings now give a depth of water of over 1,300 feet. A sudden break up of the mountain probably produced this abyss, and formidable eruptions have led to the pouring forth of immense quantities of pumice-stone. The three islets mentioned above would be the remains of the old central cone, and a bed of pumice-stone from 98 to 131 feet thick is spread over the whole of their surface, telling of a violent cataclysm of which neither history nor tradition has preserved the memory.

The letters of Pliny the Younger[1] say that the eruption of Vesuvius which caused the destruction of Portici lasted five days, and we know that the houses are covered with a uniformly distributed bed of pumice-stone some thirteen feet thick, and of cinders about three feet thick. Everything points to the conclusion that a very similar catastrophe overtook Santorin; there too whole villages were buried beneath cinders, stones,

---

[1] Book vi., chap. xvi. and xx.—Pliny the Elder, uncle and father by adoption of Pliny the Younger, lost his life in this catastrophe, which took place in 79 A.D.

and molten lava, belched forth by a volcano in action; there too men were the witnesses and the victims of the eruption, as is proved by an accidental circumstance which took place some twenty-three years after.[1]

The removal of the *pouzzolana*, so called after the volcanic ashes of Pozzuoli in Italy for the works on the Isthmus of Suez, necessitated important excavations, and the cuttings revealed the existence of dwellings which had been hidden away from the light of day for many centuries. The masses of rubbish hiding these prehistoric ruins were some sixty-five feet high, and consisted chiefly of volcanic ashes piled up, for some accidental reason, in comparatively modern times. Beneath the *pouzzolana* a thin layer of humus contains fragments of pottery of Hellenic origin; which marks the close of the historic period, and covers over the mass of pumiceous tufa vomited out by the volcano. It was in this tufa, which is eight feet thick, that the first signs of buildings were discovered. Further excavation brought to light two houses with doors, windows, and bearing walls. In one of these houses there were five different rooms. Other discoveries rapidly succeeded each other, alike in the island of Therasia and at Acrotiri, the principal island, which has given its name to the group. The plan of these houses is an irregular parallelogram, the angles of which are rounded and the sides more or less curved. This arrangement differs greatly from that adopted in Greece as well as from that in use at Therasia after the time of the volcanic eruptions. The

---

[1] Cigalla: *Acad. des Sciences*, November 12, 1866. Fouqué: *Acad. des Sciences*, March 25, 1867. "Un Pompéi Préhistorique," *Revue des Deux-Mondes*, October 15, 1869.

houses too are quite different in their mode of construction. The walls consist of great blocks of lava placed one above the other, without any trace of cement or of lime, and are merely kept in place by a reddish earth mixed with chopped straw or marine algæ. Large branches of olive or cypress trees, still with the bark on, are imbedded in the masonry. These pieces of wood, the size of which varies considerably, were probably added to give the necessary solidity to the walls in the numerous earthquakes, the disastrous effects of which were only too well known to the ancient inhabitants of Santorin. It is curious and interesting to note the use of the same expedient among the inhabitants of the islands of the Archipelago who are still exposed to the same danger. The doors and windows are clumsily arched, and the roof seems to have been a low vault. It was made of stones and coated with clay and supported by the trunks of olive trees, the charred remains of which lay upon the floors of the crushed homes. These trunks show no sign of having been touched with metal tools; not a metal nail or clamp has been found, and we cannot but conclude that the remains belong to the age when stone alone was employed.

The inside walls were not glazed or decorated in any way, except in one instance, that of a house at Acrotiri, from which the rubbish has been cleared away, revealing on the walls a layer of lime on which was some colored ornamentation which still retained an extraordinary brilliancy when it was discovered.

In all the houses and in every room of each were found beneath the tufa burying them masses of lava and volcanic scoriæ, forming a most eloquent witness of the cause of their destruction. Near one of the houses of Therasia is a little cylindrical structure, about three feet high; which cannot have been a well, as it rests directly on impermeable lava, and was certainly not a cistern, as it is too small for that. May it, as some think, have been an altar? We cannot tell, and though the religious sentiment was probably no more absent among these primitive races than it is among the barbarous peoples of our own day, it does not do to express an opinion in the absence of positive proof.

Successive excavations have yielded a number of objects which throw a new light upon the manners and customs of the inhabitants. Terra-cotta vases are more numerous than anything else (Fig. 88), and among them preponderate large yellow vessels capable of holding about one hundred quarts. Most of them have a clumsy brim, and a rough attempt has been made at ornamentation by the potter with his fingers on the damp clay. Other vases of finer clay, colored red or yellow, are covered with ornaments and graceful arabesques; the garlands of fruit and flowers are often of remarkably beautiful workmanship. Cups with well-shaped rounded handles, made of some kind of red ferruginous earth, others of gray material, were picked up in all the houses. These various vessels were used for many different purposes; some to cook food, the marks of the hearth being still on them, whilst others retained some of the chopped straw with which the domestic animals had evidently been fed. The most curious of all are those which are supposed to represent a woman; the front part projecting and surmounted by a narrow neck bent backwards, with two brown prominences supposed to stand for breasts,

FIG. 88.—Vases found at Santorin.

and dots round the upper part representing a necklace, while ear-rings are indicated by elliptical bands of different colors. We shall have to refer again to these curious vases when we speak of the discoveries made at Troy; we need only add now that the pottery found at Santorin differs completely, alike in form and ornamentation, from the Greek, Phœnician, and Etruscan specimens, of which the museums of Europe contain so many. They are evidently therefore not of foreign origin, but of native manufacture. The absence of clay in the island of Santorin has thrown some doubt on this, however, but the researches of M. Fouqué have revealed the former existence of a large valley, at the base of the principal cone, which valley ran down to the sea-shore near the island of Aspronisi; and in which probably was found the clay which the potters of the district soon learned to turn to account.

With these vases were found some troughs for holding crushed grain, and lava discs very much like those still in use among the weavers of the Archipelago to stretch the woof of their tissues; skilfully graduated lava weights, the correlation of which is very evident, as they weigh 8, 24, and 96 ounces; a flint arrow-head and a saw of the same material with regular teeth; together with a great variety of other objects, including many obsidian arrows and knives, reminding us in their shape of those characteristic of the Stone age in North Europe.

Two rings of gold beaten very thin, and a little copper saw with no trace of any alloy, are, so far, the only metal objects found in the excavations. The origin of the former, moreover, is very uncertain, and there has been much discussion as to where the rings came from. In spite, however, of all the gaps in the evidence about them, there remains no doubt that the inhabitants of Santorin were farther advanced in civilization than the Lake dwellers of Switzerland, the builders of the *terremare* of Italy, or the Iberians of the south of Spain, who were very probably their contemporaries; and we cannot refrain from expressing our admiration of the wonderful progress made by the inhabitants of the little group of volcanic islands under notice.

Before the catastrophe which overwhelmed them, Santorin was covered with comfortable and solidly built houses. Men knew how to till the ground, and gathered in crops of cereals, among which barley was the most abundant, then millet, lentils, peas, coriander, and anise; they had learned to domesticate animals, as is proved beyond a doubt by the number of bones of sheep and goats; they kept dogs to guard their flocks, and horses to aid in agricultural work; they knew how to weave stuffs, to grind grain, to extract the oil from olives, and even to make cheese, if we may give that name to the pasty white stuff found at the bottom of a vase by Dr. Nomicos. They were acquainted with the arch, and they used durable and brilliant colors. The copper saw is an example of the first efforts of the natives at metallurgy; the gold and obsidian which were foreign to the island bear witness to commercial relations with people at a distance. They loved art, as proved by the shape of their vases and the ornamentation on many of them, which is really often worthy of the best days of Greece. All around we see signs appearing as it were suddenly of a civilization, the origin and tendencies of which are alike still unknown.

But one human skeleton has so far been found in Santorin, and that is of an inhabitant who had evidently been overtaken in his flight and crushed beneath the burning scoriæ from the volcano. This man was of medium height, and is supposed to have been between forty and forty-eight years old. The bones of the pelvis are firmly consolidated, and the teeth are worn with mastication.

Let us endeavor to guess at the period when the people of Santorin lived. De Longpérier tells us that vases similar to those left by them are represented on the tomb of Rekmara amongst the presents offered to Thothmes III., who lived in the eighth century B.C., but if so the people of Santorin appear to have borrowed nothing in their intercourse with Egypt. The first invasion of Greece by the Phœnicians is supposed to have been in the fifteenth century B.C., but the buildings, the pottery, and the various implements of Therasia and Acrotiri differ essentially from those of the Phœnicians, who, moreover, from the earliest times, used metals. Must we not therefore conclude that the catastrophe which overwhelmed Santorin took place before the fifteenth century B.C.? Conjectures as to the date of the fatal eruption, however plausible, are of no use in anything relating to the origin of the people, or the time of their first occupation of the island. On these points all is still hopeless confusion, and we must wait for further discoveries before we can hope to come to any conclusions in the matter.

We have gone back to the very earliest days of man upon the earth; we have shown that he was the contemporary of the mammoth and the rhinoceros, of the cave-lion and the cave-bear; we have seen him crouching in the deep recesses of his cave and fighting the battle of life with no weapon but a few scarcely sharpened flints, leading an existence infinitely more wretched than the animals about him. Not without emotion have we watched our remote ancestors in their ceaseless struggle for existence; not without emotion have we seen them gradually growing in intelligence and energy, and attaining by slow degrees to a certain amount of civilization. Santorin is a striking and brilliant proof of their progress, and we shall appreciate this progress yet more when we have examined the ruins piled up on the hill of Hissarlik. There we shall close this portion of our work, for from the time when the buildings of which these remains were the relics met their doom, the use of metals, copper, bronze, gold, silver, and iron became general. History began to be written, and it is her task to tell us of the migrations of races, the early efforts of historic races, the foundation of empires. In a word, the prehistoric age was over; that of self-conscious portraiture was now to begin.

A few years ago I was on the ancient Hellespont and my fellow-travellers, grouped about the deck of our vessel, were trying to make out on the receding coast of Asia the sites of Troy and of the tumuli which were then still supposed to have been the tombs of Achilles, Patrokles, and Hector, but which are now, thanks to the able researches of Dr. Schliemann, known to belong to a comparatively modern epoch. The streams, bearing the ever memorable names of Simoïs and Scamander, were also eagerly pointed out by the watchers, recalling the words of Lamartine:

Le nautonnier voguant sur les flots du Bosphore
Des yeux cherchait encore
Le palais de Priam et les tours d'Ilium.

Great indeed is the privilege of genius, immortalizing all that it touches; for it must be pointed out that Troy was never an important town, and the war in which it disappeared was in reality but one of the incessant struggles between the petty princes of Greece and Asia.

When I visited the East, scholars were not at all agreed as to the site of the town which was so long besieged by the Greeks; and certain sceptical spirits even went so far as to deny that there ever was such a person as Homer at all, or that if there were, he wrote the epic poem which has borne his name so long. Tradition, however, was pretty constant in pointing to the hill of Hissarlik as the site on which Troy was built. Strabo was quite an exception in relegating the town to the lower end of the bay, where the miserable little village of Akshi-koi now stands. In 1788 a new idea was started; Lechevalier in his account of his journey in Troas claims to have recognized the site of Troy at Bunarbashi. At that time erudition was not very profound, and Lechevalier's site was accepted; indeed it was long maintained, and quite recently it has been defended by Perrot. But the nineteenth century is more exacting; the most plausible hypotheses are not enough without facts to support them, and excavations at Akshi-koi and at Bunarbashi show that there never was a town on either of these sites.

Excavations on the hill of Hissarlik, begun by Dr. Schliemann in 1871, and carried on under his superintendence for more than ten years, have, on the contrary, yielded most definite, satisfactory, and conclusive results. At a depth of fifty-two feet the diggers came to the virgin soil, a very hard conchiferous limestone. The immense masses of *débris* of which the embankment is made up date from different epochs; we have before us, if we may use such an expression, a perpendicular Pentapolis or series of five ancient cities one above the other. One town was destroyed by assault and by fire; another rapidly rose from its ruins, built with stones taken from the midst of those very remains. The study of the piled-up rubbish enables us to build up again a picture of the remote past with all its vicissitudes, and Virchow may well say that the hill of Hissarlik will for ever be considered one of the best authenticated witnesses of the progress of civilization.[1]

The first layer of rubbish rests on the rock itself, and may very well have belonged to the town built by Dardanus, of which Tlepolemus relates the destruction by his grandfather Hercules.[2] According to the Homeric story six generations, and according to generally accepted modern calculations two centuries, separate Dardanus from Priam. If therefore we accept 1200 B.C. as the date of the Trojan war, the town built by Dardanus would date from 1400 B.C., and we should possess data, if not absolutely certain, at least approximately so.[3]

---

[1] Schliemann: " Troy and its Remains," translated by Philip Smith, London, Murray, 1875; " Ilios Ville et Pays des Troyens," translated by Mme. E. Egger, Paris, Hachette, 1885; E. Burnouf: *Revue des Deux-Mondes*, January 1, 1874; Virchow: " Alt Trojanische Gräber und Schädel."

[2] Iliad, canto v., v., 692.

[3] Egyptologists tell us that in the fourth year of the reign of Ramses II., or about 1406 B.C., the Hittites placed themselves at the head of a coalition against the Egyptian Pharaoh. With these Hittites, or Khittas, whose descendants still dwell in the north of Syria, were the Mysians, the Lycians, the Dardanians, and other tribes.

There remain but a few relics of the buildings erected by the first inhabitants of the hill of Hissarlik, which relics consist of great blocks of irregular size, with remains of bearing walls composed of small stones cemented together with clay and faced with a glaze which has withstood the wear and tear of centuries.

The second town, which would appear to have been that described in the Iliad, was probably built by a race foreign to those who erected the first. The hill, which was to become the Acropolis of the new town, was surrounded by the new-comers with a wall several feet thick, of which the foundations consisted of unhewn stones; whilst the upper part was made of artificially baked bricks, the baking having been done after they were put in place, by large fires lit in vacant places left at regular intervals; an arrangement recalling what we have said in speaking of vitrified forts.[1] It is also interesting to note a similar mode of construction at Aztalan in Wisconsin in structures which probably date from the time of the Mound Builders. The walls at Hissarlik were protected by re-entering angles and projecting forts. The interior of the *enceinte* was reached by three doors, and it is still easy to make out the ruins of the different buildings. A room sixty-five feet long by thirty-two wide is surrounded by very thick walls, and towards the southeast is a square vestibule, opening into the room by a large door.[2] These, Dr. Schliemann thinks, were the *naos* and *pro-*

---

[1] "Amérique Préhistorique" (Masson), translated by Nancy Bell (N. D'Anvers), and published by Murray, London; Putnam, New York.

[2] "Troy and its Remains," plate ix. See also excellent essay on the same subject by S. Reinach, which appeared in the *Revue Archéologique* in 1885. Later investigations by Dr. Schliemann also brought to light a remarkable resemblance between the buildings at Hissarlik and those of Tiryns.

naos of a temple dedicated to the tutelary gods of the town. Quite close to them is another building with similar dispositions; a square vestibule giving access to a large room, which in its turn leads to a smaller apartment. These two buildings, which are reached through a *propylæum*, are the only ones of which the explorers have been able to make out the measurements with any exactitude.

Other ruins are evidently remains of the royal residence. The homes of the people were clustered on the sides and at the foot of the hill. After the destruction of the town by the Greeks, the Acropolis formed one vast mass of ruins, from which bits of walls stood out here and there as mute witnesses of the catastrophe. The thin layer of black earth covering the ruins seems to point to the speedy rebuilding of the town. The houses of the third settlement are very irregularly grouped, and consisted mostly of one story only, containing a number of very small rooms. Some of the walls are of bricks with glazed facings, others of very small stones cemented together with clay. In one house of rather larger size than the others was found some cement made of cinders, mixed with fragments of charcoal, broken bones, and the remains of shells and pottery. On the northwest the new colonists erected walls in place of those which had fallen down, but they were of very inferior masonry, coarse bricks baked on the spot, in the way customary among the Trojans, having formed the material.

The destruction of the third town was more complete than that of Troy. The walls of the houses can still be made out rising to a certain height, and it was upon them as foundations that the fourth colony set up their abodes. These dwellings are smaller still, with flat roofs formed of beams on which was laid a coating of rushes and clay. Every generation appears to have been poorer than the last, alike in material wealth and in fertility of resource.

The fifth colony spread northwards and eastwards. Their homes were built very much in the same style as those of their predecessors. The resemblance does not end there, and Dr. Schliemann notes that among the ruins of the three towns, which successively rose from the site of Troy, are found similar strange-looking idols, hatchets in jade, porphyry, diorite, and bronze, goblets with two handles, clumsy stone hammers, trachyte grindstones, and fusaïoles or perforated whorls bearing symbolic signs of a similar form. Evidently the men who succeeded each other after the great siege of Troy on the now celebrated hill of Hissarlik belonged to the same race, perhaps even to the same tribe. There are, however, certain notable differences which must not be passed over. The later pottery is not of such fine clay or so well moulded as the earlier specimens, nor are the stone hammers, which appear to have been the chief implements used, of such good workmanship. The piles of shells left to accumulate about the houses of the fourth and fifth towns can only be compared to the kitchen-middings so often referred to, and there is no doubt that those who left such heaps of rubbish about their dwellings could not have been so civilized as were the celebrated Trojans.

Beneath the ruins of the Greek town, which strictly speaking belongs to history, Schliemann found a quantity of pottery of curious shapes and very different to anything he had previously discovered. He ascribes them to a Lydian colony which dwelt for a short time upon the hill. This pottery resembles that known as proto-Etruscan, of which so many specimens have been found in Italy. Probably the makers of both were contemporaries.

By numerous and careful measurements Dr. Schliemann has been able to determine exactly the thickness of the layers, which correspond with the different periods during which Hissarlik was inhabited. The remains of the Greek and Lydian towns extend to a depth of 7½ feet beneath the actual level of the soil; the fourth layer, from 7½ to 15 feet; the third, from 15 to 22½ feet; Troy itself, from 22½ to 32 feet; and lastly Dardania, from 32 to 52 feet. The last layer carries us back to the golden age of Greek art, where all doubt is finally at an end. The bas-reliefs of remarkable workmanship bear witness to the Ilium, founded in memory of Troy. This is the town visited by Xerxes, Alexander the Great, and Julian the Apostate.[1] That the town still existed about the middle of the fourth century is proved by medals taken from the ruins, but it evidently fell into decadence soon after that time, for its very name was forgotten by history, and it was reserved for our own time to resuscitate the ancient city of Priam and its successors from the ruins which had been piled up by the destructive hand of man and by the lapse of time. But this task has been nobly achieved by the enthusiasm, scientific

---

[1] The British Museum contains a manuscript of the fourteenth century, in which is a letter from Julian, written when he was emperor, between 361 and 363 A.D., and relating to his visit to Ilium.

acumen, and we may perhaps add good-fortune of an archæologist who cherished a positive passion for everything relating to Homeric times.

The number of objects picked up at different stages of the excavations was very considerable. Dr. Schliemann neglected absolutely nothing that appeared to him at all worthy of his collection, which now belongs to the Royal Museum of Berlin and contains some twenty thousand objects, including weapons and implements, some of stone, others of bronze, and thousands of vases and fusaïoles, gazing upon which we see rise before our eyes a picture of a civilization unknown before but through the Iliad and a few meagre historical allusions.

Before we note in detail the most remarkable of the objects in Dr. Schliemann's collection, we must add that recent researches have also brought to light the remains of a little temple dedicated to Pallas Athene and referred to in history, as well as those of a large Doric temple erected by Lysimachus, and of a magnificent theatre capable of holding six thousand spectators, and which probably dates from the end of the Roman Republic. The human bones picked up among the ruins of the different towns may be attributed to the practice, already general, of cremation. Virchow has examined the skull of a woman found at Troy, which is of a pronounced brachycephalic type (82.5). The crania from the third town, on the other hand, are dolichocephalic, the mean cranial capacity being sixty-seven. If we could reason with any certainty from cranial capacity, this would appear to point to a different race, but it would not do to come to any positive conclusion with only one Trojan cranium to judge by.

But to return to Dr. Schliemann's fine collection. The pottery from the first town, found at a depth of from thirty-two to fifty-two feet (Fig. 89), is superior alike in color, form, and construction, to the keramic ware of the following periods. The potter's wheel was unknown, or at least very rarely used,[1] and pottery was hand-made and polished with bone or wood polishers, the marks of which can still be made out. The forms are varied and often graceful, many of them, as do those

FIG. 89.—Vase ending in the snout of an animal. Found on the hill of Hissarlik at a depth of 45½ feet.

found in the mounds of North America imitating those of the animals among which the potters lived. The usual color of the keramic ware is black, sometimes decorated with white lozenge-shaped ornaments. Some vases have also been found colored red, yellow,

---

[1] The potter's wheel was, however, in use at a very remote antiquity. In China its invention is attributed to the legendary Emperor Hwang-Ti, who is supposed to have lived about 2697 B.C. The wheel was also known from the very earliest times in Egypt, and Homer (Iliad, c. xviii., v. 599) compares the light motions of the dancers represented on the shield of Achilles to the rapid rotation of the potter's wheel.

and brown, and even decked with garlands of flowers and fruit, as are some of those of Santorin. We must also mention some apodal vases, and others with three feet, used for funeral purposes, containing human ashes (Fig. 90). The terra-cotta fusaïoles, found in such numbers among the ruins of the towns that rose successively from the hill of Hissarlik, are, on the other hand, rare at Dardánia, if we may retain that name.[1]

FIG. 90.—Funeral vase containing human ashes Found at a depth of 50 feet.

Excavations have brought to light more than six hundred celts or knives, generally of smaller size than those found in Denmark or France. Rock of many kinds, including serpentine, schist, felsite, jadeite, diorite, and nephrite, were used; and saws of flint or chalcedony, some toothed on one side only, others on both, are of frequent occurrence. They were fixed into handles of wood or horn, and kept in place with some agglutinative substance, such as pitch, several of them still retaining traces of this primitive glue. We must also mention awls, pins of bone and ivory, and

---

[1] Rivett-Carnac: "Memorandum on Clay Discs Called Spindle Whorls and Votive Seals Found at Sankisa" (Behar), *Journal Asiatic Society of Bengal*, vol. xlix., p. 1.

FIG. 91.—Large terra-cotta vases found at Troy.

ossicles or knuckle bones, in every stage of manufacture, confirming the accounts of Greek historians, who tell us of the great antiquity of the game played with them. The Dardanians used wooden and bone implements and weapons almost exclusively. It is impossible to say whether they were acquainted with the use of metals, but we might assert that they were if we could

 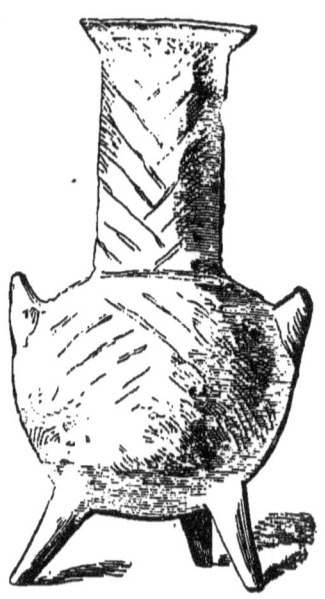

Fig. 92.—Earthenware pitcher found at a depth of 19½ feet.

Fig. 93.—Vase found beneath the ruins of Troy.

quite certainly attribute to them a certain mould of mica schist, found at a depth of 45½ feet, which had been used in the process of casting spits and pins, which are supposed to be of more ancient date than the fibulæ.

The most valuable objects of the collection come from the deposits representing the town of Troy; they are all twisted, broken, and charred, bearing witness to the fierceness of the flames in which the town perished. These discoveries reveal to us the daily life of the people of Troy. Judging from the number of boars' tusks found, hunting must have been a favorite pastime with them. The bones of oxen, sheep, and goats, of smaller species than those of the present day, have also been found. Horses and dogs were rare, and cats unknown. The domestic poultry of the present day was also wanting, no remains of birds having been found except a few bones of the wild swan and the wild goose. Fish and mollusca, as proved by the immense numbers of bones and shells, formed an important part of the diet of the Trojans. They also fed largely on cereals, which they cultivated with success; and wheat, the grains of which were very small, was known to them. The preservation of these vegetable relics was due to carbonization.

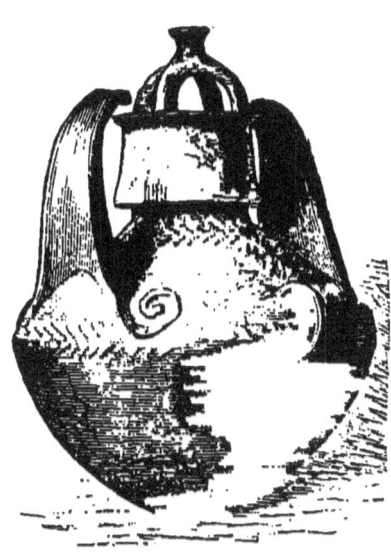

FIG. 94.—Terra-cotta vase found with the treasure of Priam.

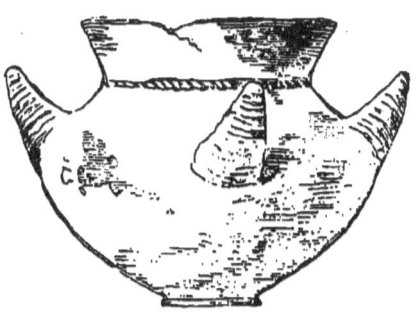

FIG. 95.—Vase found beneath the ruins of Troy.

The pottery discovered is of an infinite variety, and includes jars from 4¾ feet to 7¾ feet high (Fig. 91), of which Schliemann found more than six hundred, nearly all of them empty. Their size need not surprise us, for Ciampini[1] speaks of a pottery *dolium* of such vast size and height that a ladder of ten or twelve rungs was needed to reach the opening.[2] With these jars were found some large goblets, some long-necked vessels (Fig. 92), some amphoræ, and vases with three feet (Fig. 93). Some of the vases had lids the shape of a bell (Fig. 94), others were provided with flaps or

FIG. 96.—Earthenware pig found at a depth of 13 feet.

horns by which to lift them (Fig. 95). The potter gave free vent to his imagination, but the decorations representing fish-bones, palm branches, zigzags, circles, and dots, are all of very inferior execution.

Two series of terra-cotta objects deserve special

---

[1] "De Sacris Ædificiis," ch. ix., p. 128.
[2] It is interesting to note the discovery of urns closely resembling those of Troy, and containing human remains, in Persia (Sir W. Ouseley: "Travels in Persia"), and at Travancore, in the south of Malabar, where, according to tradition, they were intended to receive the remains of young virgins sacrificed in honor of the gods.—"Some Vestiges of Girl Sacrifices," *Journ. Anth. Inst.*, May, 1882.

mention, one representing animals, generally pigs (Fig. 96), though an example has been found of a hippopotamus; a fact of very great interest, as this animal does not live at the present day anywhere but in the heart of Africa. We know from this terra-cotta representation that it lived in Greece in the days of Troy. Pliny speaks of it in Upper Egypt in his day, and according to Mariette it lived thirty-five centuries before the Christian era in the delta formed by the mouth

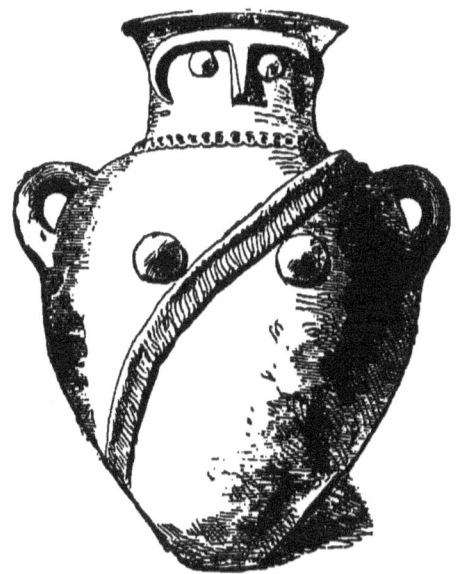

FIG. 97.—Vase surmounted by an owl's head. Found beneath the ruins of Troy.

of the Nile. The second series of objects referred to above as of special interest are vases representing the heads of owls with the busts of women (Fig. 97). It is easy to make out the beak, eyes, and ears of the bird, and the breasts and navel of the woman. In some instances the face, breasts, and sexual organs of a woman are represented by a series of dots forming a triangle with the point downwards.[1] Other dots represent a necklace, and very similar designs are to be seen on the Chaldean cylinders. Can we then connect them in any way with the relics of Troy, and is it possible that the Trojans and Chaldeans were of common origin? However that may be, the constant repetition of these signs proves that they were of hieratic character. Terra-cotta was also used for a very great number of other purposes, as was the case everywhere before the introduction of metals. Some deep and some flat plates made of very common clay have been found, together with buttons, funnels, bells, children's toys, and seals on which, some authorities think, Hittite characters can be made out. No lamps, or anything that could serve their purpose, have been found. The Trojans probably used torches of resinous wood or braziers, when they required artificial light.

It would be impossible to give a list of the objects of every variety found among the ruins of Troy, with the aid of which we can form a very definite idea of the private life of its people. Some fragments of an ivory lyre, and some pipes pierced with three holes at equal distances, bear witness to their taste for music; a distaff, still full of charred wool, deserted by the spinner when she fled before the conflagration, tells of domestic industry and manual dexterity, while marble

---

[1] The vulva was sometimes represented by a large triangle. The same peculiarity occurs on some black marble statuettes, found in the tombs of the Cyclades and Attica. Three such statuettes from the island of Paros are in the Louvre, and the British Museum owns a rich collection. Dr. Schliemann also mentions a female idol made in lead of very coarse workmanship, in which the sexual organs are represented by a double cross.

and stone *phalli* prove that the generative forces of nature were worshipped.[1]

The weapons and implements found included hæmatite and diorite projectiles used in slings, stone hatchets, and hammers pierced to receive handles, flint saws and obsidian knives. Metallurgy began to play an important part, and stone with its minor resisting power was quickly superseded by bronze. In fact, Virchow

FIG. 98.—Copper vases found at Troy.

---

[1] The *phallus* was, as we have already stated, the symbol of generative force. Its worship extended throughout India and Syria; a gigantic *phallus* adorned the temple of the mother of the gods at Hierapolis, and it was carried in triumph in processions through Egypt and Greece. It is still worshipped in some places at the present day. Near Niombo, in Africa, there is a temple

was certainly justified in saying that the whole town belonged to the Bronze age. Iron was still unknown, at least so far no trace of it has been found, either among the ruins of Troy or of the towns which succeeded it. Several crucibles and moulds of mica, schist, or clay have been found with one of granite of

FIG. 99.—Vases of gold and electrum, with two ingots, found beneath the ruins of Troy.

rectangular shape bearing on each face the hollows intended to receive the fused metal. The Schliemann

containing several *phallic* statues; at Stanley-Pool the fête of the *phallus* is celebrated with obscene rites. The Kroomen observe similar ceremonies at the time of the new moon, and in Japan on certain fête days young girls flourish gigantic *phalli* at the end of long poles. The *phallus* is also often represented on the monuments of Central America—on the stones of the temples of Izamal and the island of Zapatero, for instance. Possibly the worship of the productive and generative forces of nature was the earliest religion of many primitive peoples, but all that is said on the subject must be sifted with considerable care.

museum possesses numerous battle-axes [1] of bronze, some double-bladed daggers with crooked ends, lances similar to those discovered at Koban,[2] and thousands of spits, some with spherically shaped heads, others of spiral form. Some of these spits are made of copper, as are some large nails weighing thirty ounces,

FIG. 100.—Gold and silver objects from the treasure of Priam.

so that this metal was evidently still often used in a pure state.

At the foot of the palace, the ruins of which rise from the Acropolis at a depth of $27\frac{1}{2}$ feet, the pick-

---

[1] Similar hatchets of pure copper (Fig. 2) have been found in Hungary, and Butler ("Prehistoric Wisconsin") speaks of them also as being found in North America.

[2] The tin used in making bronze probably came from Spain or Cornwall, perhaps also from the Caucasus, where small quantities of it are still found. It was doubtless imported by the Phœnicians, the great navigators of antiquity. See Rudolf Virchow's "Das Gräberfeld von Koban im Lande der Osseten," Berlin, 1883.

axes of the explorers brought to light metal shields, vases (Fig. 98), and dishes mixed together in the greatest confusion, often soldered together by the intense heat to which they had been subjected. They

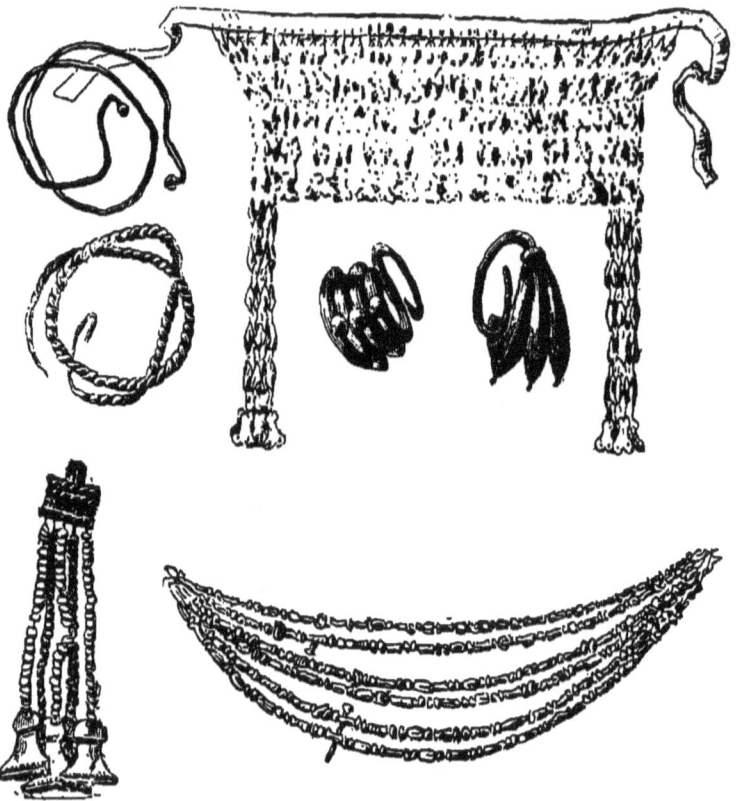

Fig. 101.—Gold ear-rings, head-dress, and necklace of golden beads from the treasure of Priam.

had probably been enclosed in a wooden chest that was destroyed in the conflagration.[1] We are aston-

[1] This idea gains probability from the fact that the remains of a key were picked up near the treasure, which we have reason to suppose belonged to Priam.

ished at the wealth revealed to us. Cups, goblets, and bottles of gold (Figs. 99 and 100) lay side by side with golden necklaces[1] and ear-rings of electrum.[2] The ornaments that had belonged to women are especially curious. At one place alone several diadems (Fig. 101) were picked up, with fifty-six ear-rings, six bracelets, and nine thousand minor objects, such as rings, buckles, buttons, dice, pins, beads, and ornaments of a great variety.[3] All these treasures were piled up in a great silver vase, into which they had doubtless been hastily thrown in the confusion of a precipitate flight. They are all of characteristic forms, quite unlike anything in Assyrian or Egyptian art. Were they made in Troy itself? Dr. Schliemann doubts it; he thinks that the makers of such clumsy pottery are not likely to have been able to produce jewelry of such delicate and remarkable workmanship. I should not like to be so positive, for even amongst the most advanced peoples we find very common objects mixed with others showing artistic skill. Why should it not have been the same at Troy? I think that in future Trojan art must take its place in the history of the progress of humanity. The nineteenth century has brought that art to light, and by a strange caprice of chance the treasures of Priam adorn the museum of Berlin, and we have seen the diadem of fair Helen exhibited in the South Kensington Museum of London.[4]

---

[1] The gold may have come from the mines of Astyra, not far from Troy.

[2] Electrum was the ancient name for amber, but was also given to an alloy of gold and silver, the yellow color of which resembles that of amber.

[3] Dr. Schliemann gives a very careful description of all these objects. See "Troy and its Remains," Figs. 174 to 497, pp. 260 to 353.

[4] The χρήδεμνον or diadem of the wife of Menelaus is a narrow fillet from which hang several little chains formed of links alternating with small leaves,

Treasures nearly as valuable as those we have been describing were found in earthenware vases in several other parts of the ruins. Unfortunately, many of the objects found were stolen and melted down by the workmen, whilst others were taken to the Imperial Palace at Constantinople, whence they are doomed to be dispersed. In 1873, however, Dr. Schliemann was fortunate enough to hit upon a deposit containing twenty gold ear-rings, and four golden ornaments which had formed part of a necklace.[1] Similar ornaments were found at Mykenæ, near Bologna, in the Caucasus, in the Lake dwellings, and, stranger still, on the banks of the Rio Suarez in Colombia.[2]

I will not add more to what I have already said about the towns which succeeded each other on the ruins of Troy, and of which the successive stages of rubbish on the hill of Hissarlik are the only witnesses left. The flames spared none who settled on that doomed spot, and new arrivals disappeared as rapidly as they came. The Ilium of the Greeks and Romans alone enjoyed any prosperity, but it too was in its turn swept away; and at the present day a few wandering shepherds and their flocks are the sole dwellers upon the hill immortalized by Homer.

Before concluding this chapter I must refer once

---

and ending in rather larger leaves, these leaves all representing the woman with the owl's head, so characteristic of Trojan art. The golden objects are all soldered with the same metals, which modern goldsmiths seem unable to do. At Tiryns, which we believe to have been contemporary with Troy, the art of soldering was unknown, and ornaments were merely screwed together.

[1] Bastian, *Zeitschrift der Berliner Gesellschaft für Erdkünde*, vol. xiii., plates 1 and 2.

[2] If we accept 1200 B.C as the date of the Trojan war and the eighth century as that of the foundation of Ilium, the towns that succeeded each other on the hill of Hissarlik only lasted four centuries altogether.

more to a fact of considerable interest. In that part of the deposits of Hissarlik which represents Troy, Dr. Schliemann picked up the perforated whorls to which the name of fusaïoles has been given (Fig. 102), and of which we spoke in our account of the Lake Dwellings of Switzerland. These fusaïoles are generally of common clay mixed with bits of mica, quartz, or silica, though some few have been found at Mykenæ and Tiryns of steatite. The clay whorls before being baked were plunged into a bath of a very fine clay of gray, yellow, or black color, and then carefully polished. They nearly all bear ornaments of very primitive execution, such as stars, the sun, flowers, or animals, and more rarely representations of the human figure.

Fig. 102.—Terra-cotta fusaïoles.

We ourselves think these fusaïoles are amulets which were taken to Troy by the Trojans, and piously preserved by their successors. One important fact tends to confirm this hypothesis. A great number of them bear the sign of the *swastika*[1] (Fig. 103), the cross with the four arms, the sacred symbol of the great Aryan race so long supposed to be the source of all the Indo-European races. The *swastika* is engraved, not only on the fusaïoles, but also on the diadems of the daughters of Priam, on the idols the Trojans worshipped, and on numerous objects from the Lydian and Greco-Roman towns. We meet with the double cross among the prehistoric races of the basin of the

---

[1] In the Vedas the word *swasti* is often used in the sense of happiness or good-fortune.

Danube, who colonized the shores of the Troad and the north of Italy, and it was introduced with the products of that antique civilization on the one side to the Greeks, the Etruscans, the Latins, the Gauls, the Germanic races, the Scandinavians, and the Bretons; and on the other to the people of Asia Minor, Persia, India, China, and Japan.[1]

This sign of the *swastika* meets us at every turn; we find it on many ancient Persian books, on the temples of India, on Celtic funeral stones, and on a Hittite cylinder. It is seen on vases of elegant form from Athens and Melos; on others from Ceres, Chiusi, and Cumae, as well as on the clumsy pottery recently discovered at Königswald on the Oder and on the borders of Hungary; on bronze objects from the Caucasus, and the celebrated Albano urn; on a medal from Gaza in Palestine and on an Iberian medal from Asido. We see it on the Gallo-Roman rings of the Museum of Namur, and on the plaques of the belt, dating from the same epoch, which form part of the magnificent collection of M. Moreau. Schliemann tells us of it at Mykenæ and at Tiryns. Chantre found it on the necropoles of the Caucasus. It is engraved on the walls of the catacombs of Rome, on the chair of Saint Ambrose at Milan, on the crumbling walls of Portici, and on the

FIG. 103.—Cover of a vase with the symbol of the *swastika*. Found at Troy.

---

[1] Comte Goblet d'Auriella, *Bul. Acad. Royale de Belgique*, 1889.

most ancient monuments of Ireland, where it is often associated with inscriptions in the ogham character.[1]

The *swastika* occurs twice on a large piece of copper found at Corneto, which now belongs to the Museum of Berlin. Cartailhac noticed it in the *citania* of Portugal, some of which date from Neolithic times.[2] The English in the Ashantee war noticed it on the bronzes they took at Coomassie on the coast of Guinea, and it has also been found on objects discovered in the English county of Norfolk.

Moreover, if we cross the Atlantic we find the same symbol engraved on the temples of Yucatan, the origin of which is unknown, on a hatchet found at Pemberton, in New Jersey (Fig. 104), on vases from a Peruvian sepulchre near Lima, and on vessels from the *pueblos* of New Mexico. Dr. Hamy, in his "American Decades," represents it on a flattened gourd belonging to the Wolpi Indians, and the sacred tambours of the Esquimaux of the present day bear the same symbol, which was probably transmitted to them by their ancestors. The universality of this one sign amongst the Hindoos, Persians, Hittites, Pelasgians, Celts, and Germanic races, the Chinese, Japanese, and the primitive inhabitants of America is infinitely strange, and seems to prove the identity of races so different to each other, alike in appearance

FIG. 104.—Stone hammer from New Jersey bearing an undeciphered inscription.

---
[1] G. Atkinson, *Congrès Préhistorique*, Lisbon, 1880, p. 466.
[2] "Ages Préhistoriques en Espagne et Portugal," figs. 410, 411, 412, p. 286.

and in customs, and is a very important factor in dealing with the great problem of the origin of the human species.

We have dwelt much on the discoveries of Dr. Schliemann, but we must add that, like all great discoveries, they have been very vigorously contested.[1] Boetticher, for instance, considers the ruins of Hissarlik to be nothing more than the remains of a necropolis where cremation was practised according to the Assyrio-Babylonian custom.[2] A distinguished and very honest savant, S. Reinach, constituted himself the champion of this theory at the meeting of the Congress in Paris in 1889. Schliemann replied very forcibly, and the meeting appeared to be with him in the matter, as were also a number of men of science who visited Hissarlik in 1888, and we think that in the end history will adopt the opinion of the great Danish antiquarian.

We have now passed in review the chief of the works left behind him by man from the earliest days of his existence to the dawn of historic times. We must still show prehistoric man in the presence of death, the universal destroyer, and learn from the evidence of the tombs of the remote past how our ancestors met the common doom.

---

[1] Aussland, 1883. *Zeitschrift für Muscologie und Antequaten Kunde*, 1884. Musœon, 1888 and 1889.

[2] Virchow, who visited the remains at Hissarlik, treats this idea as *furchtbaren Unsinn* (ridiculous nonsense).

CHAPTER VIII.

TOMBS.

The true history of man will be found in his tombs, says Thucydides; and as a matter of fact the sepulchre has ever occupied much of the thoughts of man, the result of a religious sentiment, a conviction that all does not end with the life which so quickly passes by.

From the very earliest times we meet with tokens of the hopes and fears connected with a future existence; but, as I have already stated, the human bones that can with certainty be said to date from Palæolithic times are very rare. We know but very few facts justifying us in asserting that the contemporary of the mammoth and of the cave bear had already learnt to respect the remains of what had once been a man like himself. One of these few facts deserves, I think, to be noticed with some detail.

In 1886, excavations in the cave of Spy[1] (Namur),

---

[1] The true name of this cave is the *Betche aux Roches*. A very excellent essay on the subject was read by the explorers, MM. de Puydt and Lohest, in August, 1886, to the Historic Society of Belgium, and "Les Fouilles de Spy," by Dr. Collignon, published in the *Revue d'Anthropologie*, 1887, may also be consulted. Excavations were also carried on in the same cave in 1879 by M. Bucquoy (*Bul. Soc. Anth. de Belgique*, 1887). He distinguished five ossiferous levels and picked up some flints of the Moustérien type, and even some Chelléen hatchets, to which he gave the name of *coups de poing*.—Fraipont and Lohest; "Recherches sur les Ossements Humains Decouvertes dans les Dépôts Quaternaires d'un grotte à Spy."

or rather in a terrace some thirty-six feet long by nineteen and a half wide giving access to it, brought to light two human skeletons. One was that of an individual already advanced in life, probably of the feminine sex, the other of a man in the prime of life. These skeletons were imbedded in a very hard breccia containing also fragments of ivory and numerous flints of very small size. Some of them had very fine scratches on both sides. From what I could learn on the spot, the skeletons when found were in a recumbent position. The bones, few of which were missing, were still in their natural position, and near to one of them were picked up several arrow- or lance-heads, one of which, of phtanite, some two and a half inches long, was of the purest Moustérien type. The bones were those of short, squat individuals, and the skulls were of the type of the Canstadt race, the most ancient of which anything is known; the thickness of the crania was about one third of an inch. The forehead is low and retreating, the eyebrows are prominent, and the lower jaws strong and well developed.

At the same level and in that immediately above it were picked up the remains of the mammoth, the *Rhinoceros tichorhinus*, the cave bear, and the large cave hyena, the reindeer, and numerous other mammals belonging to the Quaternary fauna. Everything points to the conclusion that the man and woman whose remains have so opportunely come to light were contemporary with these animals, and that their bodies were placed after death in the cave in which they were found.

Belgium has furnished numerous examples of sepulchral caves, of a date, however, less ancient than that we have been considering. Recent excavations in the Chauvaux Cave revealed two skeletons leaning against the walls in a crouching position, the legs tucked under the body. In the Gendron Cave M. Dupont discovered seventeen skeletons lying in a low, narrow passage, stretched out at full length with the feet toward the wall, and arranged in twos and threes, one above the other. In the middle of all these dead was the skeleton of one man placed upright, as if to watch over the other bodies.

The Duruthy Cave at Sordes opens near the point of junction of the waters of the Pau and Oloron, whence their united waters flow into the Adour. At the northern extremity of this cave is a natural niche in which lay more than thirty skeletons, some of men, some of women, and some of children, mixed together in the greatest confusion. Worked flints, bone stilettos, and ornaments lay around, all of the forms characteristic of Palæolithic times.

It would seem that we have here evidence of the practice of a funeral rite, which consisted in first stripping the bodies of flesh, and then laying the bones in caves, where they were often left unnoticed by the living occupants of the same refuge.[1]

The caves of Baoussé-Roussé, near Mentone, give fresh proof of the extension of this rite, if we may so call it. The skeletons lay upon a bed of powdered iron ore, in some cases as much as two fifths of an inch

---

[1] We borrow these details from a valuable work by Cartailhac (*Mat.*, 1886, p. 441 ; *Rev. d'Anth.*, 1886, p. 448). The conclusions of our learned colleague are that we really know nothing of the funeral rites of the men of Chelles and Moustier, and that it is to the Solutréen period that we must assign the first really authenticated tombs. Cartailhac's admirable book, "La France Préhistorique," p. 302, should also be consulted.

thick, and this accumulation could not have taken place if the skeleton had not been deprived of its flesh before inhumation. The flesh must have been taken off by some rapid process, for the bones remain, as a general rule, in their natural positions, united by their tendons and ligaments. In Italy, says Issel, the cave men buried their dead in the caves they lived in, a thin layer of earth alone separating them from the living; the bodies, adds Pigorini,[1] generally lay on the left side, the head rested on the left hand, and the knees were bent. Beside the skeleton was placed a vase containing red chalk, to be used for painting the body in the new world it was supposed to be about to enter.

We could quote similar discoveries in Sicily, Belgium, and the southern Pyrenees. Beneath the tumulus of Plouhennec, in Brittany, bones were strewn about in the greatest disorder. Some archaeologists are of opinion that the openings in certain dolmens were used for throwing in the bones of the dead who successively went to join their ancestors. In many of the Long Barrows of England the bones appear to have been flung in pell-mell; the space was too narrow to hold the complete body, so that before inhumation the flesh must have been separated from the bones. In no other way can we explain the confusion in which the human remains lay when they were discovered.[2] Pigorini thinks this is a proof that primitive races worshipped their dead, and held their bodies in veneration.[3] Perhaps they even carried them about in their migrations. However that may be, the custom

---

[1] "Ipui Antichi Sepolcri dell Italia."
[2] *Archæological Journal*, vol. xxii.
[3] *Matériaux*, 1885, p. 299.

of separating the flesh from the bones was continued until cremation became general. This would explain the huge ossuaries found in regions so widely separated.

Although, however, the mode of sepulture we have just described was practised for a long time in certain places, we cannot admit it to have been general. In certain megalithic tombs we find dispositions similar to those described in speaking of the Gendron Cave. Excavations beneath the Port-Blanc dolmen (Morbihan) brought to light a rough pavement on which lay numbers of skeletons, closely packed one against another, which skeletons were probably those of men who had been held in honor, and to commemorate whom the dolmen was set up. Separated from them by a layer of stones and earth rested another series of skeletons, not so closely packed as the first. The new-comers had respected their predecessors, and no one had violated the sanctuary of the dead. Similar facts were noted at Grand Compans, near Luzarches,[1] and it is evident that successive inhumations beneath dolmens often took place, and instances might, if necessary, be multiplied.

Another singular funeral rite was practised in remote antiquity. Many of the bones found in the various caves of Mentone were colored with red hematite.[2] As this was only the case with the bones of adults, those of children retaining their natural whiteness, it evidently had some special significance. In 1880, the opening of a cave of the Stone age in the district of Anagni, a short distance from Rome, brought

---
[1] This dolmen was carefully excavated by MM. Hahn and Millescamps, *Bul. Soc. Anth.*, 1883, p. 312.
[2] Rivière: *Congrès des Sciences Géographiques*, Paris, 1878.

to light the facial portion of a human cranium, colored bright red with cinnabar. Nor are these by any means exceptional cases, · for similar coloration was noticed on bones picked up at Finalmarina and several other places in Liguria and Sicily. The custom had therefore become general in the Neolithic period in the whole of the Italian peninsula.[1] We also meet with it in other countries; at the Prehistoric Congress, when in session at Lisbon, Dolgado added to what was said about the discoveries in Italy the fact that the cave men of Furninha practised a similar rite. In the *kurganes* of the department of Kiew crania were found colored with a mineral substance, fragments of which were strewn about near the skeletons. The most ancient of the *kurganes* appear to date from the Stone age, for in them were found implements made of flint and reindeer-horn, mixed with the bones of rodents[2] long since extinct in that district. A similar practice is met with in the tombs of Poland, many bones being covered with a coating of red color, in some instances one fifth of an inch thick. Excavations in the Kitor valley (province of Irkutsk, Siberia) have brought to light several tombs which appear to date from the same period as the *kurganes* of Kiew. The dead were buried with the weapons and ornaments they would like to use in the new life which had begun for them. The tomb was then filled in with sand, with which care was taken to mix plenty of red ochre. It is difficult not to conclude that this was a relic of a rite fallen into desuetude.

---

[1] *Atti della R. Acad. dei Lincei*, 1879-1880. Pigorini: *Bul. de Pal. Italiana*, 1880, p. 33.
[2] *Soc. Anth. de Munich*, 1886.

At the present day certain tribes of North America expose their dead on the tops of trees, and before burying the bones, when stripped of their flesh, cover them with a coating of a bright red color. In the island of Espiritu Santo many human bones have also been picked up painted with an oxide of argillaceous iron. These customs, strange as they may appear, were evidently practised in honor of ancestors; atavism is as clearly shown in customs and traditions as in physical structure.

At Solutré is a sepulchre formed of unhewn slabs of stone. The body of the dead rested on a thick bed of the broken and crushed bones of horses. The remains of reindeer were mixed with the human bones. Were these too relics of funeral rites, and were the animal bones those of the horses and reindeer that had belonged to their hunter? It is impossible to say. Solutré, situated as it was on an admirable site on a hill overlooking the valley of the Seine, protected from the north winds and close to a plentiful stream, has also been a favorite resort of man. In the tombs all ages are mixed together, and if some do indeed date from Neolithic times, others are Roman, Burgundian, Merovingian. There may be among them a certain number dating from the Reindeer period; that is about all we can assert with any certainty in the present state of our knowledge. The Abbé Ducrost, however, in an important essay[1] asserts that he has found incontrovertible proofs of the interment of Solutréens on the hearths of their homes in Palæolithic times. If this be so, the custom is one of frequent occurrence, and has been continued for centuries; for

---

[1] *Soc. Anth. de Lyon*, 1889.

De Colanges, in his fine work on ancient cities, shows that at Rome the earliest tombs were on the hearth itself of the dwelling. De Mortillet, on the other hand, dwells very earnestly on the mode of inhumation at Solutré, and sees in the juxtaposition of human remains and the *débris* of hearths but the result of displacement, and of the regular turning upside down of which the hill of Solutré has been the scene. To this Reinach replied, to the effect that, whereas a few years ago De Mortillet's authority led many archæologists to suppose that the men of the Reindeer period did not bury their dead, facts, ever more important than theories, have now proved beyond a doubt that this very decided opinion is a mistake. Not only did the men of remote antiquity bury their dead; they laid them, as at Solutré, on the hearths near which they had lived.[1]

The dead were often buried seated or bent forward, and it is interesting to note the same custom beneath the mounds of America and the tumuli of Europe. It is touching to see how in death men wished to recall their life on earth; the cradle was, so to speak, reproduced in the tomb, and man lay on the bosom of earth, the common mother of humanity, like the child on the bosom of his own mother. Perhaps, too, the seated position was meant to indicate that man, who had never known rest during his hard struggle for existence, had found it at last in his new life. The men of the rough and barbarous times of the remote past were unable to conceive the idea of a future different to the present, or of a life which was not in every respect the same as that on earth had been.

---

[1] "Histoire du Travail en Gaule," p. 24.

Whatever may have been the motive, this mode of burial was practised from the Madeleine period.[1] At Bruniquel, in Aveyron, the dead were found crouching in their last home. This position is, however, peculiarly characteristic of Neolithic times, and is met with throughout Europe. Eight skeletons were recently discovered bending forward in the sepulchral cave of Schwaan (Mecklenburg). In Scandinavia there are so many similar cases that it is difficult to make a selection. In the sepulchral cave of Oxevalla (East Gothland) the dead are all in crouching attitudes, and tumuli dating from the most remote antiquity cover over a passage, formed of immense blocks of stone, leading to a central chamber, in which are numerous seated skeletons resting against the walls.

On the shores of the Mediterranean, excavations of the Vence Cave (Alpes-Maritimes) brought to light a number of dead arranged in a circle as if about to take a meal in common. The bodies were crouching in the position of men sitting on their heels; the spinal column was bent forward and the head nearly touched the knees. In the centre of this strange group were noticed some fragments of pottery and the remains of a large bird, a buzzard probably. Perhaps its death among the corpses was a mere accident.[2] The dolmens of Aveyron yielded some flint-flakes and arrow-heads, pieces of pottery, pendants, and bone, stone, shell, and slate-colored schist beads. Beneath one of these dolmens was found one small bronze object, quite an ex-

---

[1] Troyon: "De l' Attitude Repliée dans la Sépulture Antique," *Revue Arch.*, 1864.
[2] *Matériaux*, 1875, p. 327.

ceptional instance of the occurrence of that metal. The skeletons rested against the walls. In one of the tombs some human bones, which had been originally placed at the entrance to the cave, had been moved to the back; the vanquished had here, as in life, to give way before the conquerors. Excavations in the Mane-Lud tomb have led explorers to suppose that here too the corpses were buried in a crouching position. It is the same at Luzarches and in the Varennes cemetery near Dormans.[1] In the last named were found traces of a fire that had been lit above the tomb, and some pottery was picked up ornamented with hollow lines, filled with some white matter not unlike barbotine. M. de Baye says this mode of interment is confined to the district of Marne; but for all that he himself gives an example of its practice elsewhere.[2]

In the prehistoric tombs discovered at Cape Blanc-Nez, near Escalles (Pas-de-Calais), the position in which the body had been interred could be made out in four instances. The ends of the tibiæ, humeri, and radii were united, the bones of the hands were found near the clavicles, so that the bodies had evidently been bending forward with the arms crossed and the fingers pointing toward the shoulders.[3] Similar facts are quoted from a cave at Equehen on the plateau which stretches along the seashore on the east of Boulogne. The bodies, to the number of nine, were crouching with the face turned toward the entrance of the cave, which was closed with great blocks of sandstone. Two polished stone hatchets, broken doubtless in

---

[1] A. Nicaise: *Matériaux*, 1880, p. 186.
[2] *Arch. Préhistorique*, p. 178.
[3] *Congrès Préhistorique de Bruxelles*, p. 299.

accordance with some sepulchral rite, had been placed near the skeletons.

Numerous human bones were found in the Cravanche Cave near Belfort, which probably dates from the close of the Neolithic period, judging from the total absence of metal and the shape of the flint and bone implements picked up. Here too the bodies were bent almost double, the head drooping forward and the knees drawn up nearly to the chin. Several of these skeletons were completely imbedded in the stalagmite which had formed in the cave, the head and knees alone emerging from the solid mass. The position in which they were originally placed had thus of necessity been maintained.[1]

A similar rite, for rite we must call this mode of burial, was practised in Italy, and the Chevalier de Rossi speaks of a tomb of the Neolithic period at Cantalupo, near Rome, in which one of the bodies was placed in the crouching attitude, which he says is familiar to all who have studied ancient tombs.[2] This practice was still continued in protohistoric times; Schliemann noticed it in the excavations he superintended at Mykenæ, and Homer says that amongst the Lybians the dead were buried seated.

The necropolis near Constantine contains numerous megalithic monuments. These are either round or square cromlechs surrounding sarcophagi, or circular *enceintes*, in which the dead were laid in a trench. In the former there are always a great many funeral

---

[1] *Bul. Soc. Anth.*, 1876, p. 191. Grad: *Nature*, 1877, 1st week, p. 314.
[2] *Memorie sulle scoperte paleoethnologiche della campagna romana.* Pigorini adds in his turn: "*I cadaveri erano abitualmente adagiati sul fianco sinistro, col cranio appogiato sulla mano sinistre e le ginocchia alquanto piegate in guisa che tavolta si trovarono le tibie assai prossime alla cassa toracica.*"

objects in the tomb, and the body of the dead is in a crouching posture; in the latter there are few things beside the corpse itself, and that is in a recumbent position. Do these peculiarities denote different races? Do the tombs all date from the same period, or are these arrangements but fresh indications of the difference everywhere maintained between social classes? It is difficult to decide, and we must be content with enumerating facts. We may add, however, that the crouching position of corpses is constantly met with in Africa[1] and in North and South America, from Canada to Patagonia.[2]

The funeral rites of which we have spoken necessarily imply burial; man did not abandon to wild beasts or birds of prey the bodies of those who had once been like himself. At Aurignac, at Bruniquel, and in the Frontal Cave, the cave man had taken the precaution of closing with the largest stones he could find the entrances to the last resting-places of those belonging to him. The caves of *L'Homme Mort*, and of Petit-Morin which date from Neolithitic times, retain traces of similar blocking up. There were five entrances to the cave of Garenne de Verneuil (Marne) in which was a regular ossuary; the floor was paved and the roof kept up with eleven upright stones. The objects in the tomb with the dead were a clumsy earthenware vase, a few flint knives, and some shell necklace beads.

The sides of the almost inaccessible mountains of Peru are pierced, at a height of several hundred feet, with numerous caves which have nearly all been arti-

---

[1] Pallery: " Mon. Mégalithiques de Mascara," *Bul. Soc. Ethn.*, 1887.
[2] Bancroft: "The Native Races of the Pacific," vol. i., pp. 365, etc. Moreno: "Les Paraderos de la Patagonie," *Rev. d'Anth.*, 1874.

ficially enlarged. It was in them that the Peruvians placed their dead, and the people of the country still call them *Tantama Marca* or abodes of desolation. The entrances were concealed with extreme care, but this care did not save the tombs from violation; the greed for the treasures supposed to be concealed in the tombs was too great for respect to the unknown dead to hold curiosity in check.

In other cases, the dead was laid near the hearth which had been that of his home when living, and his abode during life became his tomb. The dolmens, *cella*, and *Gangraben* in Germany, and the barrows in England, appear to bear witness to the prevalence of a similar custom in those countries; and we find the same idea perpetuated even when cremation became general. At Alba, in Latium, at Marino, near Albano, at Vetulonia and Corneto-Tarquinia were discovered urns with doors, windows, and a roof imitating human dwellings.[1]

Later, other modes of sepulture came into use. In Marne M. Nicaise made out seven funeral pits[2] resembling in shape, he tells us, long-necked bottles with flat bottoms. One of these pits at Tours-sur-Marne contained at least forty skeletons, and among the bones were found thirty-four polished stone hatchets, fifty knives, two flint lance-heads and a great many arrows with transverse edges, a necklace of little round bits of limestone, several fragments of coarse pottery which had been mixed with grains of silica and baked in the fire, and lastly three little flasks made of staghorn

---

[1] "Nécropole de Colonna, prov. de Grosseto," *R. Acad. dei Lincei*, Roma, 1885.
[2] *Bul. Soc. Anth.*, 1880, p. 895.

hollowed out in a curious manner and with stoppers of the same material. These quaint little flasks doubtless contained the coloring matter with which the dead had painted their bodies when alive. All the objects of which we have spoken belonged to the Neolithic period; but a flat bronze necklace bead made by folding a thin slice of metal, a radius, and a bit of rib bearing green marks resulting from long contact with metal, appear to fix the date of this pit at the transition period between the Stone and Bronze ages. If this be so it is quite an exceptional case of a sepulchral pit dating from this time, for most of those known are of much later origin. Those for instance of Mont-Beuvray, Bernard (La Vendée), and Beaugency are not older than Gallo-Roman times.[1] According to Count Gozzadini, those of Manzabotto in Italy, which are twenty-seven in number, date from the IVth century after the foundation of Rome, and are of Etruscan origin. They are constructed with small pointed pebbles, with no trace of cement, and resemble in shape a long amphora vase, or perhaps, to be more accurate, the clapper of a bell. They are from six and a half to thirty-two and a half feet deep, with an opening varying in diameter from one foot to nearly two and a half feet.[1]

We have said so much in preceding chapters on monuments erected in memory of the dead, that but little remains to be added here. Doubtless there are many distinctions to be noted at different times and in different countries, but everywhere the aim remains

---

[1] Abbé Baudry et Ballereau : " Les Puits Funéraires du Bernard," La Roche-sur-Yon, 1873.

[2] " Renseignements sur une Ancienne Nécropole Manzabotta, près de Bologna," Bologna, 1871.

the same, and the means used for attaining that end are radically the same all the world over. Take for example the Aymaras, the most ancient race of Bolivia and Callao; they laid their dead sometimes beneath megalithic monuments (Fig. 58, p. 178) resembling the dolmens of Europe, sometimes beneath towers or *chulpas*, which are however probably of more recent date.

Chulpas, generally of square or rectangular form, consist of a mass of unhewn stones faced outside with blocks of trachyte or basalt, painted red, yellow, or white. A very low door, always facing east, as if in honor of the rising sun, gives access to a cist in which the dead was laid. The *chulpa* of our illustration (Fig. 105) is situated near the village of Palca; it rises from an excavation four feet deep; its height is about sixteen feet, and the cornice consists of *ichu*, a coarse grass which grows in abundance on the mountains, and which after being firmly compressed was cut with the help of sharp instruments. The human bones, which were mixed together in the greatest confusion, made a heap in the sepulchral chamber more than a foot high.

FIG. 105.—Chulpa near Palca.

The mounds of Ohio also cover over sepulchral

chambers of a peculiar construction, being often formed of round pieces of wood, five to seven feet long by five to six inches in diameter; near the bodies were placed a few ornaments, chiefly copper ear-rings, shell beads, and large flint knives. Most of the skeletons lay on the bare earth; but one exception is mentioned in which the ground was paved with mussel shells. A remarkable discovery has quite recently been made at Floyd (Iowa), the account of which in *Nature* for January 1, 1891, we will give in the words of Clement Webster: "In making a thorough exploration of the larger mound . . . the remains of five human bodies were found, the bones even those of the fingers, toes, etc., being, for the most part in a good state of preservation. First, a saucer or bowl-shaped excavation has been made, extending down three and three-quarter feet below the surface of the ground around the mound, and the bottom of this macadamized with gravel and fragments of limestone. In the centre of this floor five bodies were placed in a sitting posture with the feet drawn under them, and apparently facing the north. First above the bodies was a thin layer of earth and ashes, among which were found two or three small pieces of fine-grained charcoal. Nearly all the remaining four feet of earth had been changed to a red color by the long-continued action of fire." Mr. Webster goes on to describe the various skeletons and says of one of them, that of a woman: "The bones in their detail of structure indicated a person of low grade, the evidence of unusual muscular development being strongly marked. The skull of this personage was a wonder to behold, it equalling if not rivalling in some respects and in inferiority of grade, the famous Neanderthal skull. The forehead, if forehead it could be called, is very low, lower and more animal-like than in the Neanderthal specimen. . . .

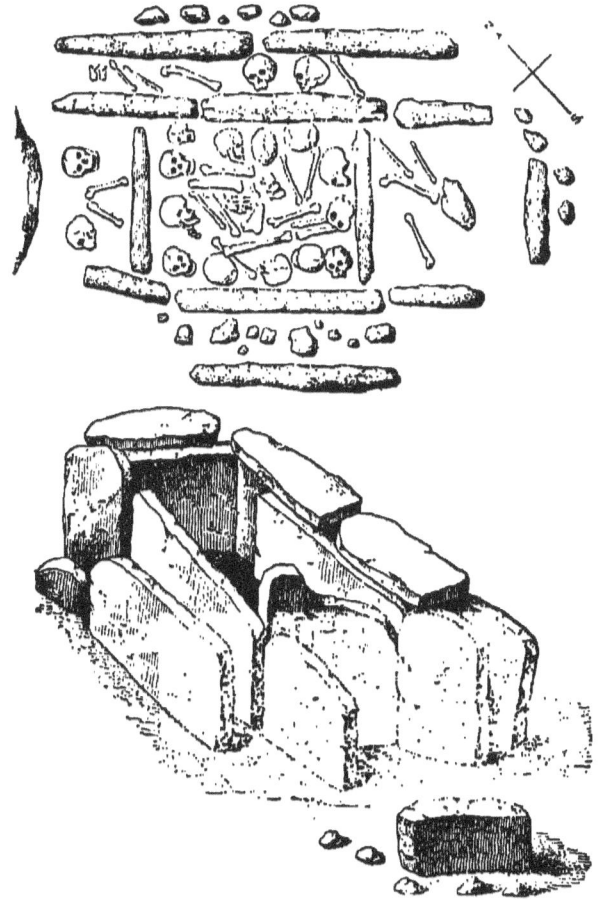

FIG. 106.—Dolmen at Auvernier near the Lake of Neuchâtel.

The question has been raised how was it that these five bodies were all buried here at the same time, their bodies being still in the flesh." . . . Webster adds that the probability is that all but one of the had been sacrificed at the death of that one, who had most likely been a chief.

We have seen that men began by placing the bodies of their dead in caves, and only later took to burying them underground when caves were not to be had. Very often the corpse was placed between large unhewn stones to keep off from it the weight of the tumulus above. Such were the last resting-places alike of the men of Solutré and of those of Merovingian times. In the necropolis of Vilanova, which is supposed to date from times prior to the foundation of Rome, the tombs enclosed a chest, the walls of which consisted of slabs of sandstone set on edge and connected by a conglomerate of small stones. At Marzabotto, the chests are made of bricks, and placed beneath a heap of pebbles. We reproduce a chest discovered near the Lake Dwellings of Auvernier in Switzerland (Fig. 106)[1] and another (Fig. 107) brought to light by MM. Siret in the south of Spain. These drawings will help us better than long descriptions to form an idea of this mode of burial.

In other cases the dead body was enclosed in earthenware jars. At Biskra in Algeria, two of these jars were found together; the one containing the head, the other the feet of the departed. In some instances the jar was replaced by a large clumsy earthenware basin, some six and a half feet long by three feet wide. Such basins are mentioned as having been found near Athens, but there is nothing to help us to determine their date.

---

[1] Gross: "Les Proto-Helvètes." Morel-Fatio: "Sépultures des Populations Lacustres de Chamblandes." As at Auvernier, a great many bears' tusks were found lying near the dead, which may possibly also have had something to do with a funeral rite.

The ancient Iberians used one large jar only (Fig. 108) in which the dead was placed in a crouching position, still wearing his favorite ornaments. The vase was closed with a stone cover and placed in the tomb. We meet with the practice of a similar mode of interment in historic times. The Chaldeans placed their dead in earthenware vases; two jars connected at the neck serving as a coffin. Excavations in Nebuchadnezzar's

Fig. 107.—A stone chest used as a sepulchre.

palace brought to light bodies bent nearly double and enclosed in urns not more than three feet in height by about two feet in width. On the western coast of Malabar, as far as Cape Comorin, we find near megalithic tombs large jars four feet high by three feet in diameter filled with human bones. This mode of sepulture was practised at Sfax, in the Chersonesus of Thracia, and at the foot of the hill on which Troy was built. The tumulus of Hanaï-Tepeh covered over a huge amphora in which crouched a skeleton, and the wealthy Japanese loved to know they would rest in huge artistically decorated vases, masterpieces of native pottery. If we cross the Atlantic, we meet with the same custom in Peru, Mexico, and on the shores of the Mississippi. At Teotihuacan, the bodies of children were placed head downwards in funeral urns,[1] and excavations in the alluvial deposits of the Mississippi yielded, among immense quantities of pottery, two huge rectangular basins glued together with clay and containing the body of a young child. It is indeed interesting to meet with the same practice in so many different places and to find the genius of many races expressing itself in the same way in so many diverse inventions, produced at times so widely separated.

It is probable that early man also turned to account the trees he saw growing around him, using them as coffins for his dead. But the rapid decay of this fragile case led to its total disappearance. A few exceptions must, however, be mentioned. In 1840 some dredgers took from the bed of the Saône, at Apremont, from beneath a bed of gravel five feet thick, the trunk of a tree which still contained the bones that had been placed in it. Similar discoveries were made in the Cher, and in the celebrated cemetery of Hallstadt, near Salzburg. The cairns of Scania covered over split trunks of oak and birch trees, which had been hollowed out to receive the dead. At Gristhorpe, near Scarborough, in England, a coffin was found made of scarcely squared planks roughly put together; and another very like it was discovered at

---

[1] D. Charnay: *North American Review*, January, 1881.

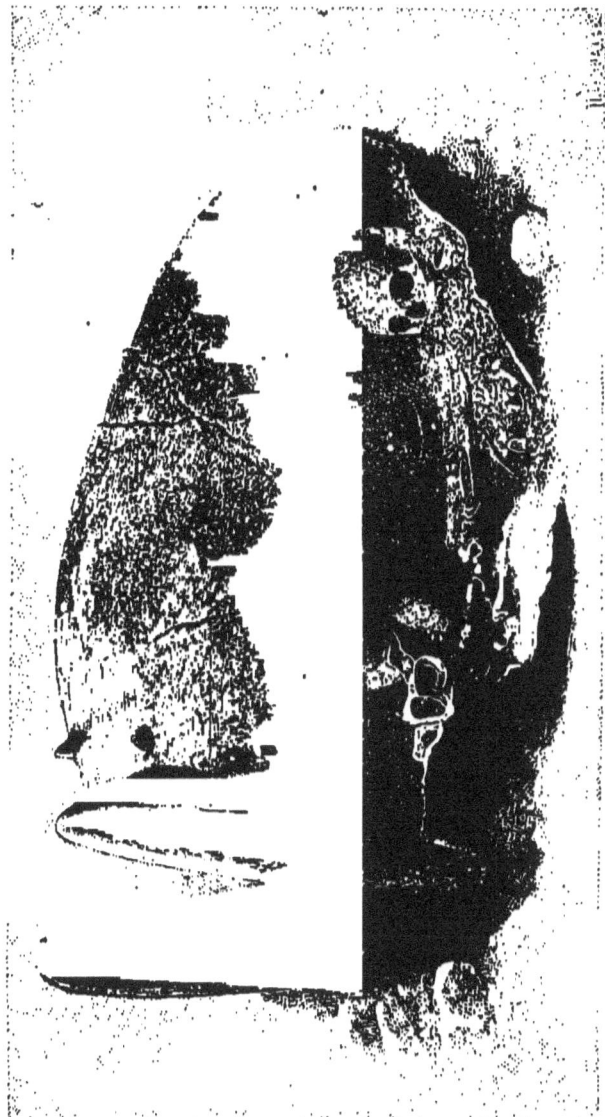

FIG. 108.—Example of burial in a jar.

Hove, in Sussex, the latter containing a splendid amber cup, evidence of the wealth of the man who had been buried in this primitive coffin.[1]

The ancient Caledonians sewed up their dead in the skins of oxen before burying them. The Egyptians also embalmed the ibis, the ox, the cat, the crocodile, and other animals deified by them, and the bodies of these creatures were then placed in vast subterranean chambers, where they have been discovered in the present day in great numbers. The Guanches of Teneriffe, the last representatives of the Iberians, and probably the most ancient race of Europe, took out the intestines of the corpse, dried the body in the air, painted it with a thick varnish, and finally wrapped it in the skin of a goat. This last custom was evidently a relic of the original idea of embalming, with a view to rendering the mummy as nearly as possible indestructible and, to use a happy expression of Michelet, to compel death to endure *(forcer la mort de durer)*. Our own contemporaries are thus able to look upon the very features of those who preceded them on the earth some forty centuries ago; and but yesterday photography reproduced in every detail what was once Ramses the Great, one of the most glorious kings of history.

Embalming was also practised in America. Recent travellers report[2] having seen in Upper Peru tombs of the shape of beehives, made of stones cemented with clay, each tomb containing one mummy or more in a crouching position (Figs. 109 and 110). This custom was still practised for many centuries; Garcilasso de la

---

[1] Stuart: "The Early Modes of Burial."
[2] Vidal Seneze: *Bul. Soc. Anth.*, 1877, p. 561.

Fig. 109.—Aymara mummy.

Vega tells us that the dead Incas were seated in a temple at Cuzco, wearing their royal ornaments as if they were still alive; their hands were crossed upon their breasts, and their heads were bending slightly forward.[1]

The facts enumerated above prove that burial was long practised, though it is impossible to say when it first came into use. About the time of the beginning of the Bronze age, or perhaps even earlier, however, a remarkable change took place in the ideas of man, and the dead instead of being buried intact were consumed by fire on the funeral pile.

What can have been the origin of this custom? What race first practised it? It has long been supposed by many archæologists that it was the Aryans from the lofty Hindoo Koosh Mountains who first introduced into Europe a civilization more advanced than that which had hitherto obtained there, and taught the people to cremate instead of bury their dead. This theory was accepted for a considerable time without question, but of late years a new school, headed by Penka, has arisen who claim that the reformers came not from the East but from the North. The Marquis de Saporta had indeed before suggested that the primitive races who were the contemporaries of the mammoth and the rhinoceros came originally from the polar regions, where the remains of a luxuriant vegetation prove that climatic conditions prevailed in remote times of a very different character to those of the present day. The lignites of Iceland are made up of tulip, plantain, and nut-trees, even the vine sometimes occurring. In the ferruginous sandstones, associated with the carboniferous deposits of

---

[1] "Histoire des Incas," Paris, 1744, chap. xviii.

Spitzberg, the beech, the poplar, the magnolia, the plum tree, the sequoia, and numerous coniferous trees can be made out. The sturdy sailors who dare the regions of perpetual ice come across masses of fossilized wood in Banks, Grinnell, and Francis Joseph's Lands, at 88° N. Lat. Among this fossil wood Heer made out the cypress, the silver pine, the poplar, the birch, and some dicotyledons with caducous leaves. These were not relics of wood which had drifted where it

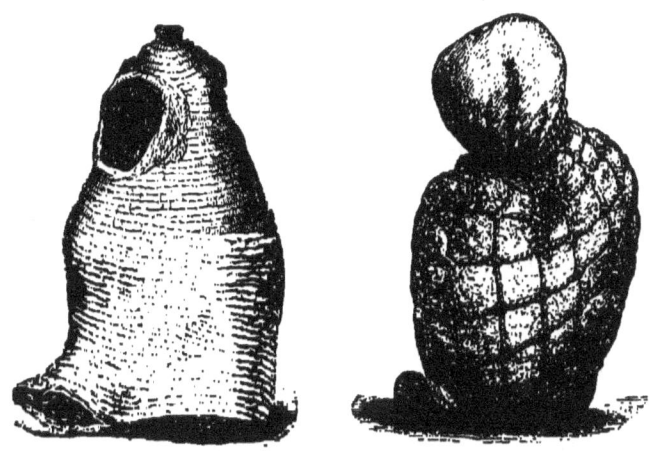

Fig. 110.—Peruvian mummies.

was found on floating ice, but of an actual local vegetation, as proved by trunks still erect in their original positions, buds, leaves, and flowers in every stage of growth, fruits in every stage of ripening. The very insects that had lived on honey from the flowers or on the leaves themselves could be identified. In those remote days, life, abundant life, similar to that now only found in the temperate countries farther south, flourished in those polar regions, so long supposed to have never been anything but lifeless deserts.

All this, plausible as it is, does not, however, appear to be conclusive on the point under discussion; and though we may have to abandon the idea of the Aryans having introduced cremation, we are scarcely, I think, in a position to say that races from the North were the first to practise it. I have dwelt more fully on the question of the origin of races and the evidence which language seems to give of a common source in two papers called "Les Premiers Populations de l'Europe," which appeared in the *Correspondent* for October 1 and November 25, 1889. Whatever may be the final decision on the much contested points involved in this controversy, one thing is certain that cremation, involving though it does a complete revolution in manners and customs, spread with very great rapidity. We meet with it from Greece to Scotland and Scandinavia, from Etruria to Poland and the south of Russia, in China as in Yucatan and certain parts of Central America.

In the early days of history, cremation was practised all over Europe. The Greeks attribute its inauguration to Hercules, and the funeral pile of Patrokles is described in the Iliad. The Pelasgians and the Proto-Etruscans burned their dead,[1] and we are told of the incineration of contemporaries of Jair, the third judge of Israel.

On the other hand, the earliest inhabitants of Latium buried their dead. Visitors, who probably came by way of the valley of the Danube, introduced the new custom, and for a long time the two rites were practised side by side. At Felsina and at Marzabotto we find instances alike of inhumation and cremation, and at

---

[1] Conestabile: "De l'Incinération chez les Etrusques."

Vilanova only half the tombs are those of corpses that had been cremated. In 365 of the tombs excavated in the Certosa, near Bologna, only 115 show signs of cremation having been practised. At Rome, the two rites were long both performed, probably, however, by the two distinct peoples who formed the primitive population of the town of Romulus. We know that Numa Pompilius forbade the burning of his corpse; Cicero relates that Marius was buried, and that Sulla, his fortunate rival, was the first of the Cornelia *gens* whose body was committed to the flames. We do not know how early cremation was introduced in Gaul; we can only say that Cæsar found it generally practised when he made his triumphal march across the country.[1] The celebrated excavations of Moreau prove that inhumation and incineration were both practised among the Gallo-Romans established in the eastern provinces of France. We may even assert that the two rites were practised long before the introduction of the use of metals. One thing is certain, the custom of cremation was but slowly abandoned as Christianity spread, for Charlemagne, in an edict dated 789, ordered the punishment of death for those who dared to burn dead bodies.

What we have just said about historic times applies equally to more remote epochs. Thanks to the learned researches of Dr. Prunières[2] we are able to trace for a great length of time the modes of sepulture adopted in Lozère. The cave men of the eroded limestone districts of Les Causses took their dead to the caves in which their ancestors had been laid, and the invaders, who were probably more civilized than those they

---

[1] A. Bertrand: "Arch. Celtique et Gauloise," Introduction.
[2] *Ass. française*, Nantes, 1875; Havre, 1877.

dispossessed, placed theirs beneath the dolmens which they erected in their honor. In the sepulchral caves of Rouquet and of *L'Homme Mort* we find inhumation; beneath the megalithic monuments dating from the end of the Neolithic period, we meet with the first traces of cremation, but so far of a very incomplete cremation; the action of the funeral fire had not been intense, and the bones were hard and resisted the heat. Noting beneath certain dolmens a few bones blackened by fire mixed with large quantities unaffected by it, one is inclined to think with the learned Doctor, that after practising cremation men had reverted to the old mode of burial. In the tumuli of the Bronze age, on the other hand, where the date can be determined with the aid of the ornaments and trinkets scattered about, the ustion was more complete; the bones are friable and porous, crumbling into dust when touched, and there is nothing to indicate that inhumation and cremation were both practised.

It is strange indeed to find that incineration was practised from Neolithic times in the wild mountains of Lozère. There can be no doubt on the point, however, and excavations beneath the dolmen of Marconnières strikingly confirm the earlier discoveries of Dr. Prunières. Beneath a layer of broken stones and a very thin pavement, was found a mass of human bones in the greatest confusion; some still retaining their natural color, others blackened and charred by fire. Among these bones was picked up an arrow of rock foreign to the country, three admirably polished lance-heads, and some finely cut flint-darts. The dolmen contained no metal objects, and there was no trace of metal on any of the bones.

At the same period the two rites appear to have been practised simultaneously in Armorica, but there incineration was the dominant custom. In one hundred and forty-five megalithic monuments supposed to date from the Neolithic period, seventy-two give proof of incineration and twenty of inhumation only. The others yielded a few cinders, but it was impossible to come to any definite conclusion. In many cases, as we have seen, the megalithic monument was surrounded by a double or triple *enceinte* of stones without mortar. Inside these *enceintes* were some small circular structures made of stones reddened by the action of heat. In the lower part of these structures were openings to admit a current of air to fan the flames. These strange structures, full of cinders and black greasy earth, bear the significant name of *Ruches de Crémation*.[1] Of thirty-nine sepulchres of the Bronze age twenty-seven gave evidence of incineration, two of inhumation, whilst ten decided nothing one way or the other.[2] The dolmen of Mont St.-Michel and that of Tumiac are separated by a short distance only; they were erected by the same race and probably about the same period, yet at Mont St.-Michel we find incineration, while inhumation was practised at Tumiac. How explain this difference in funeral customs? Does it imply a diversity of race, of caste, of religion, or of social position, or may it not rather be explained as being merely the result of those later displacements which upset the most careful reasoning?

---

[1] Luco: "Exposition de Trois Monuments Quadrilatères par feu James Miln," Vannes, 1883.

[2] P. du Chatellier: "Mém. Soc. d'Emulation des Côtes-du-Nord," Saint Brieuc, 1883.

Whatever may have been the cause of the different modes of burial, we meet with them in every country. In Scandinavia, during the Bronze age, cremation and burial were practised in about equal proportions. Similar facts are noticed in Germany, but in the North incineration predominates, while in the West it is inhumation. Beneath the cairns of Caithness in Scotland, we find some bodies lying at full length, while others are in a bent position, and large jars of coarse pottery filled with cinders and calcined bones which had belonged to men of medium height. One of the largest of these jars is fifteen or sixteen inches high by forty-nine wide at its largest part.[1] In excavating the barrows of the Orkney Islands, Petrie noted the practice of both modes of burial[2]; but were those buried in manners so different contemporaries? This is what we are not told, and what we have to find out.

At Blendowo in Poland, beneath a cromlech was found an urn filled with calcined bones, and thirty centimetres lower down a skeleton was discovered buried in the sand. Near this body was found a coin of Theodosius, and we wonder in vain whether both the individuals, whose remains are thus within a common tomb, lived at the same time. Throughout Prussia and in the Grand Duchy of Posen skeletons and jars containing human ashes are met with in the same tombs.[3] We must not forget to note, especially, the necropolis of Hallstadt, which was situated in the heart of the district of Bohemia occupied by the Boii.

---

[1] *Proceedings Soc. Anth. of Scotland*, January 11, 1886.

[2] "On the Ancient Modes of Sepulchre in the Orkneys" (*British Association*, 1877).

[3] Kohn and Mehlis: "Zür Vorgeschichte des Menschen im Ostlichen Europa," Iéna, 1879.

The most ancient of the tombs in these vast burial-places date from about two thousand years before the Christian era, and the Hallstadtian period, as it is sometimes called, culminated during the first half of the millennium immediately before the coming of Christ.[1] Nine hundred and ninety-three tombs have been excavated; all, to judge by the objects found with the human remains, belonging to the Bronze age; of these five hundred and twenty-seven contained buried bodies, and four hundred and fifty-three cremated relics.[2] This is a larger proportion than in the primitive necropoles of Italy.

In the tombs in which burial was practised, the bodies were laid in the trench without covering, and the remains of anything in the way of slabs or coffins or protecting planks are very rare; in those tombs in which cremation had been the rule, ustion had often been very incomplete, sometimes the head and sometimes the feet having escaped the flames.

Similar facts are noted at Watsch, at San Margarethen, and at Vermo in Styria, at Rovesche in Southern Carniola, and at Rosegg in the valley of the Drave. At Watsch, but ten skeletons were found, among two hundred examples of incineration. In the cremation sepulchres, if we may so call them, the cinerary urn was protected by large slabs; while in those where burial was practised, the bodies were simply confided to the earth as at Hallstadt; but by a singular contrast, the latter tombs contained much more important

---

[1] Hochstetter: "Die neueste Graber Funde von Watsch. und S. Margarethen und der Kultur Kreiss der Hallstadter Period," Wien, 1883. Siebenter: "Bericht der Prehistorischen Commission," Wien, 1884.

[2] In these tombs were found 64 gold objects, 5,574 bronze, 593 iron, 270 amber, 73 glass, and 1,813 terra-cotta. A. Bertrand: *Rev. d'Ethnographie*, 1883.

relics, the objects with the dead being more valuable and of finer workmanship. At Rovesche, the urn was placed in a square chest made of unhewn stones. The buried bodies lay with the head turned toward the east, an urn was placed at their feet, and their shrouds were kept in place by bronze fibulæ, while on the fingers were many rings of the same metal.

Lastly, to conclude this gloomy catalogue, excavations in the mounds of Ohio and Illinois[1] have shown that there too cremation and inhumation are met with in sepulchres which everything tends to assign to the same race and the same period.[2] The sepulchral crypts of Missouri contain several skeletons which had been subjected to intense heat. The human bones were mixed with the remains of animals, fragments of charcoal, and pieces of pottery, with some flint weapons. In a neighboring mound excavations revealed no trace of cremation; the bodies were stretched out upon the ground, and those who discovered them picked up near them a valuable collection of flints and of carefully made pottery. There is however nothing to show whether those who buried and those who burnt their dead belonged to the same race or lived at the same time. Cremation long survived among the most savage tribes of Alaska and California, where it is still practised, and the Indians of Florida preserve the ashes of their fathers in human skulls. In California, the relations of the deceased covered their faces with a thick paste of a kind of loam mixed with the ashes of the dead, and were compelled to wear this sign of their grief until it fell off naturally.

---

[1] *Smithsonian Report*, 1881.
[2] Putnam, xii. and xx. *Reports of the Peabody Museum.*

Although we meet with the burial of the dead either in a recumbent or a crouching position, everywhere the minor ceremonies connected with death are innumerable; each people, each race, indeed, having its own custom, handed down from one generation to another, and piously preserved intact by each successive family. Feasting was from the earliest times a feature of the funeral ceremonies. An edict of Charlemagne forbids eating and drinking on the tombs of the deceased, and Saint Boniface, the apostle of Germany, complains bitterly that the priests encouraged by their presence these feasts of death. We meet with the same kind of thing among the lower classes at the present day, and the cemeteries of Paris are surrounded with cafés and wine shops, where too often grief is drowned in wine. The custom of holding these feasts really comes down from the earliest inhabitants of Europe, and the savage cave man gorged himself with food upon the tombs of those belonging to him. At Aurignac, in the cave of *L'Homme Mort*, in the Trou du Frontal, broken bones and fragments of charcoal bear witness to the repast. Similar traces of feasts are met with beneath the dolmens and the tumuli. From the Long Barrows have been taken the skulls and feet of bovidæ, and it is probable that the other parts of the body had been devoured by the assistants, and that the head and feet were placed in the tomb as an offering either to the dead or to the divinities who are supposed to have presided at the death. In the ancient sepulchres of Wiltshire Sir R. Colt Hoare picked up the bones of boars, stags, sheep, horses, and dogs; which he too considered were the remains of funeral feasts.

Were feasts the only ceremonies connected with interments? We think not. The body was often placed in the centre of the sepulchral chamber, and around it were ranged the wives, servants, and slaves of the deceased, condemned to follow their chief into the unknown world to which he had gone. Beneath a dolmen of Algeria was found a crouching skeleton with two crania lying at his feet, which crania had doubtless belonged to victims immolated in his honor. The barrows of Great Britain preserve traces of human sacrifices, and Cæsar says in speaking of the Gauls: "Their funerals are magnificent and sumptuous. Everything supposed to have been dear to the defunct during his life was flung upon the funeral pile; even his animals were sacrificed, and until quite recently his slaves and the dependants he had loved were burnt with him."[1]

The facts we have been noticing prove that early man cherished hopes of immortality. All was not ended for him with death; a new life commences beyond the tomb, marked—for his ideas could go no farther—by joys similar to those he had known on earth, and events such as had occurred during his life. What else could be the meaning of the weapons, the tools of his craft, the vases filled with food placed near the defunct, the ornaments and colors intended for his adornment, the wives, slaves, and horses flung into the same tomb or consumed upon the same pile? It is pleasing to find this supreme hope among our remote ancestors; and clumsily as it was expressed, it implies a belief in a being superior to man, a protecting divinity according to some, but according to some few others a

---

[1] "De Bello Gallico," book vi., cap. xix. Consult also Pomponius Mela: "De Situ Orbis," book iii., cap. ii.

malignant and tyrannical spirit. The proofs so far to hand are not enough to justify us in seriously asserting that ancestors were worshipped by prehistoric man. But the subject is too important for us to refrain from putting before the reader such indications of this worship as have been collected, and which are necessarily connected with the moral and material condition of our remote ancestors.

The radius of a mammoth was discovered at Chaleux, occupying a place of honor on a large sandstone slab near the hearth. The Chaleux Cave dates from the Reindeer period; at which time the mammoth had long since been extinct in Belgium, so that there can be no doubt that the cave man had taken this bone from the alluvial deposits of the preceding epoch, and this huge relic of an unknown creature had been the object of his veneration, a lar or protective divinity of his home. A somewhat similar fact was discovered at Laugerie-Basse and, by a strange coincidence, certain tribes of North America of the present day preserve the bone of a mastodon or of a cetacean in their huts as a protection to their homes.

From Paleolithic times men were in the habit of cutting celts or hatchets in chalk, bitumen, and other fragile substances, which were certainly of no practical use. Thousands of similar objects in harder rock, but showing no sign of wear or tear, have also been found, and there is little doubt that they all alike served as amulets. This superstitious respect for certain objects lasted for many centuries, and was handed down from one generation to another. The tombs of the Bronze and Iron ages are often found to contain flint hatchets, some of them broken intentionally, a proof, as I have already said, that they were connected with funeral rites of the nature of which we are ignorant.

We also find votive hatchets beneath dolmens. By the side of some skeletons at Cissbury lay flint celts. A hatchet one and a quarter feet long was found in a Lake Station of Switzerland. It was of such friable rock that it can have been of no use but as a symbol; perhaps, indeed, it may have been a badge of office. Lastly, Merovingian tombs contain hundreds of small flint celts, the last pious offerings to the departed.[1]

We find hatchets engraved on the megalithic monuments of Brittany, on the walls of the caves of Marne, and we meet with them again on the other side of the Atlantic, evidently bearing the same signification, implying respect for them as means of protection. De Longpérier has published a description of a Chaldean cylinder, on which was represented a priest presenting his offering to a hatchet lying on a throne, and a ring was picked up at Mykenæ, on the stone of which was engraved a double-bladed celt. We find the same idea in many different mythologies. The word *Nouter* (God) is translated in Egyptian hieroglyphics by a sign resembling a celt, and the hatchet of Odin is engraved on the rocks of Kivrik. On a number of Gallo-Roman *cippi*, we find a hatchet beneath which we read the words, *Dis Manibus*, and lower down the dedication, *Sub Ascia dedicavit*. At all times and everywhere the hatchet appears as the emblem of force, and is the object of the respect of the people.

---

[1] In his fruitful excavations of Gallic, Gallo-Roman, and Merovingian tombs, Moreau collected no less than 31,515 flint celts or hatchets, which had evidently been votive offerings. See Album de Caranda ; " Fouilles de Sainte Restitute, de Trugny, d'Armentière, d'Arcy, de Brenny," etc.

The tradition of its value and importance is handed down from ancestors to descendants throughout many generations.

May we give a religious interpretation to the basins and cups hollowed out on rocks and erratic blocks and on the so-called *Roches Moutonnées*, with other monu-

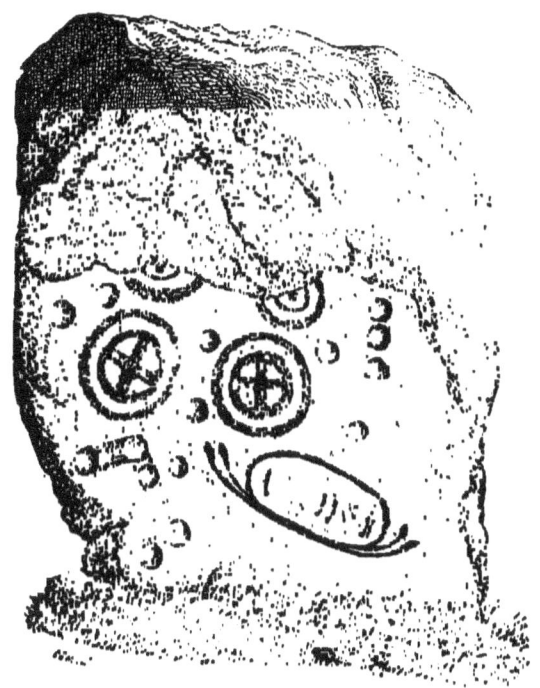

Fig. 111.—Erratic block from Scania, covered with carvings.

ments that have endured for many centuries (Figs. 111 and 112)? Or must we attribute them merely to passing caprice? Their number and importance we think forbid the latter idea. We find such blocks in Switzerland, in England, France, Italy, Portugal, and on the frozen shores of the Baltic. They are no less numerous in India, and they figure in the curious pictographs of the two Americas. There is no doubt that we have here a common idea, and one it is impossible not to recognize. How else can we account for the similarity of arrangement in the cup-shaped sculptures

Fig. 112.—Engraved rock from Massibert (Lozère).

from the tumuli of Schleswig-Holstein and those on the Indian rocks of Kamaou, or between those of Algeria and of England?

In Brittany and in Scotland these cup-like sculptures are found on rocks and menhirs, on the walls of sepulchral chambers, on stones forming the sides of *kistvœns*, accompanied in many instances with radiated circles, which do not, however, help us to understand them better. In Scandinavia they are known as *Elfen Stenars*, or elf stones, and the inhabitants come and place offerings on them for the *Little People*. According to a touching tradition, these little people are souls awaiting the time of their being clothed once more in human flesh. In Belgium these strangely decorated stones are attributed to the *Nutons*, dwarfs who are very helpful to mortals. In every country there is some legend sacred to the sculptured stones.

Such are the only facts we have been able to collect respecting the religious feeling of prehistoric races. They are not sufficient to authorize any final conclusion on the subject. At every turn we are compelled to admit our helplessness. But yesterday this past without a limit was absolutely unknown to us, and to-day we are but beginning to be able to obtain a glimpse into its secrets. We have been the laborers of the first hour, it will be for those who come after us to complete the task we have been able but to begin. May a genuine love of truth be to them, as we may justly claim it has been to us, the only guide.

INDEX.

Abbeville, 11, 14, 77
ABBOTT, on discoveries on the Delaware, 39
Abruzzi, the, 162
Acora (Peru), 178
Acorns, 151, 158
Acrotiri, island of, prehistoric houses under volcanic ashes, 311
ACY, D', on earliest tools and weapons, 82, 84
Ægean Sea, volcanic eruption in, 308-316
Africa, Stone age in, 30 ; human bones in, 45 ; Lake dwellings of, 165
—— Central, pile dwellings in, 145
—— North, dolmens the work of a powerful race, 196 ; *see also* "Algeria," "Morocco," and "Tunisia."
—— South, pottery and worked flints in, 34
Aggetelk (Hungary), 93
Ainos, the, 29, 90, 266
Alabama, kitchen-middings of, 142
Alaska, Quaternary mammals of, 66
Algeria, Stone age in, 32 ; dolmens and cromlechs, 33, 180 ; mammoth in, 57 ; ancient towers, 171 ; covered avenues, 188 ; a field for research, 195 ; megaliths of, 196 ; *djedas* of, 198 ; dolmens with circular openings, 211 ; rich in stone implements, 234 ; practice of trepanation in, 266 ; funeral jars of, 360 ; cup-stones in, 380

Alignments, 188-194 ; of menhirs in Northern India of present day, 222 ; in Kermario group, 224
Alpes-Maritimes, *enceintes* of, 286
Altamira cave (Santander), 122
Alt-Sammit, 216
Amber beads, 109 ; yellow amber from Baltic in tombs of Switzerland and France, 246 ; in Aurensan Cave (Bagnères-de-Bigorre), 247 ; amber cup at Hove, 364
Amelia Island, 142
America, Mound Builders and Cliff Dwellers of, 3 ; copper implements from mounds of, 21 ; antiquity of, 38 ; prehistoric races, 39 ; edentate and pachydermatous mammals, 39 ; fortifications, earthworks, temples, and sepulchres of, 40 ; shell heaps of, 40 ; stone weapons and pottery of Mound Builders, 41 ; cannibalism in, 57 ; pachyderms of, 57 ; fishing-tackle in, 63-65 ; absence of Chelléen implements in caves of, 139 ; kitchen-middings in, 140-142 ; fish food in, 143 ; horses extinct in, on arrival of Spaniards, 157 ; tumuli in, 176 ; great numbers of worked stones in, 234 ; instances of trepanation in, 267-270 ; colossal earthen fortifications of Mound Builders, 296, 297 ; brick buildings in, 320 ; similar modes of sepulture to those in Europe, 350 ; practice of embalming in, 364 ; cup-stones in, 380

Amiens, 11, 14
Amphoræ, 330
Amulets, *see* "Ornaments."
Anchors, 77
Ancress (Jersey), 216
Ancerty Point, 142
Angami-Nagas, the, of Northern India, 222
Animals of Stone age extinct in France, 11; edentate and pachydermatous mammals of America, 39; animals used for food, 47; plentiful as in South Africa at present time, 55; Quaternary animals in Europe, 56; tiger, elephant, rhinoceros, and hippopotamus in British Isles, 56; great number of bears, 56, 57; mammoth from North Europe to Greece, Spain, and Algeria, 57; in Asia from Altai Mountains to Arctic Ocean, 57; in America, in Mexico and Kentucky, mastodon in extreme North, Sonora and Columbia, 57; cervidæ in Gourdan Cave and at Hohlefels incalculable, 57; horses at Lunel-Viel and Solutré, 57; *horse-walls*, 58; no domestic animals, 58; from Moustier Cave (Dordogne), mammoth, *Rhinoceros tichorhinus*, elk, horse, aurochs, cave-lion, -hyena, and -bear; *Elephas antiquus* and *Rhinoceros Merckii* died out, 84; reindeer appears, 85; reindeer characteristic of Madeleine period, 86; mastodon, mammoth, rhinoceros, and cave-lion at Hohlefels, 96; at Ratisbon, hyenas, bears, and lions, 96; *Ursus spelæus* at Nabrigas Cave, 99; seal in cave near Périgueux of Quaternary period, 116; Quaternary animals extinct in kitchen-middings, 143; in Lake Stations, 156; in megalithic monuments, 222
—— of Neolithic period underwent complete transformation, the megaceros, mammoth, cave-bear, and large felidæ died out, domestic animals, ox, sheep, goat, and dog appear, 86; no domestic animals in Scandinavia, 137; earliest found in Lake Stations, 156; Lake fauna of Switzerland, 156, 157; progress of domestication, 157; mouse, rat, cat, and horse rare in pile dwellings, 157; Lake village of Nidau, wild animals rare, 157; horse extinct in America, 158; domestic animals of *terremares*, 159; wild animals very rare, 159; Neolithic animals in megalithic monuments, 222; boar, ox, sheep, and goat in Troy, horse and dog rare, cat unknown, 329; hippopotamus still known, 331
Anise, 315
Ankerstein, 77
Antas, of Portugal, 179
Apples at Lagozza, 151; in Lake Stations, Switzerland, 158
Arabia, cromlechs in, 181
ARCELIN, on Nile valley deposits, 30
—— on Boulder clays of Great Britain, 130
—— on manufacturing centre at Kalabshee, 240
Arctic fox, 253
Ardkellin Lough, crannoge at, 163
Argent (Basses-Alpes), 99
Argenteuil, 188
Ariège, 92
Arrayolos (Portugal), 178
Arrows, *see* "Weapons and Tools."
Art of prehistoric man at Sydney and Easter Island, 36-38; staves of office carved, 113; seals and eels carved on staff, 116; geometrical designs on ivory, 116; numerous engravings on stone and bone, 118, 119; art of cave-men at its zenith, 120; only found in

South France, and at Thayngen Cave, 120, 121; found with Quaternary animals, 122; carvings of human figure rare, 122-125; colored designs from Pyrenees, 126; carved and painted flints, 134; Sweno's pillar (Scotland), 185; carved and engraved dolmens, 207-209; colored ornamentation at prehistoric house at Santorin, 311; vases covered with arabesques and garlands of fruit and flowers, 312, 315; art in Troy, 337

Aryan race, 286, 339, 366, 368

Asia, Stone age in, 27-30

Asia Minor, gigantic bones found in, 5; manufacturing centre in Stone age, 240

Assyria, cromlechs in, 188

Atavism, 349

ATWATER, on fortifications at Old Fort (Kentucky), 299

Aumède dolmen, 250

Aurensan Cave, 247

Aurignac Cave, 47, 131

Aurochs, 47, 84, 122, 132

Australia, probable appearance of man before the continent attained its present configuration, 35; cromlechs in, 181; practice of trepanation in, 277

Austria, Lake Stations of, 25, 151-153

Avebury, cromlechs of, 182-184, 224

Avening, 213

Avenues, covered, 188-194, 197; *see also* "Megalithic Monuments."

Avenue des Mureaux, 261

Avrigny (Seine-et-Marne), 261

Aymaras, the, of Bolivia and Callao, 357

Aztalan (Wisconsin), 320

Aztecs, the, 18, 42

Balance-stones, 207

Balearic Islands, *talayoti* of, 165; *nanetas* of, 170

Baltic Sea, shores of, cup-stones on, 379

Baoussé-Roussé caves (Mentone, 49, 105, 108, 135, 345

Barbs, invention of, 90

Barley, 151, 158, 315

Barry Hill, vitrified fort at, 301

Barton Mere, Lake Station of, 154

Basina, 171

Baume-Chaude caves, 249, 258, 275

Bear, 56, 57, 84, 86, 96, 138

Bear's Point, 142

Beech, 367

Beech-nuts, 158

Bekoùr-Noz, 179

Belgium, pile dwellings in, 26; cannibalism in, 50; great number of bears in caves of, 57; harpoons from, 65; objects made of reindeer antler, 93; pottery from, 97; pieces of jet and ivory plaques from caves, 107; importance of discoveries in caves of, 233; cup-stones in, 381

Bellehaye (Normandy), 213

Berbers, the, 196

BERTRAND, on diversity of development in human races, 20; on megaliths of France, 194; on *enceintes* of France, 283

Betula alba, 150

Bienne Lake, 145, 265, 288

Birch, 367

Birds, bones of, 24; Dinornis of New Zealand, 35; remains of birds rarer than of animals, 48; great numbers in caves of France, and at Baoussé-Roussé, 49; moor-fowl, partridge, wild duck, and domestic fowl in Gourdan Cave, 49; thrush, duck, partridge, and pigeon in Frontal Cave, goose, swan, and grouse in other caves, 49; birds from kitchen-middings, 60; of Scandinavia, 138; wading birds in Brittany, 140; ostrich eggs at prehistoric workshop in Algeria, 234; wild swan and wild

goose in Troy, 329; also representations of the owl, 331; a large bird in sepulchral cave, 351
Bize Cave (Narbonne), 10
Black Sea, dolmens near, 179; dolmens with circular openings, 211
BLANCHARD, on origin of New Zealand, 35
Boar, 47, 137, 329
Boats, 68, 70-76. *See also* "Canoes."
BOETTICHER, on Hill of Hissarlik, 342
Bohemia, trepanation in, 265; vitrified forts in, 301
Bone and horn implements, 90; from sepulchral mounds, 93
Bones of animals, 47-49, 55-59
—— birds, 24, 35, 48, 49, 60, 140, 329
—— fish, 59, 60. *See also* "Kitchen-middings."
—— human, 36, 45, 49-52, 59, 249-256
Bos longifrons, from Lake Station at Kew, 155
BOUCHER DE PERTHES, on contemporaneity of men with extinct animals, 11-15
Bougon dolmen, 262
Bouicheta Cave, 131
BOULE, on early mining, 242
Bou-Merzoug, 197
Brachycephalic skull, 324
Brandenburg, 44
Brandon (Suffolk), flint quarries at, 237, 241, 242
Brazil, 17, 38, 53
Bream, 60
Breton dolmens, 215
British Isles, fauna of, in Quaternary times, 56; bronze and iron objects in, 219
Brittany, dolmens in, 180; menhirs in, 185; alignments in, 194; great number of menhirs, 194; highest development of dolmens in, 214; relics in dolmens, 214, 215; hatchets engraved on megalithic monuments of, 378

Brixham, 48
BROCA, on hunting implements, 48
—— on resemblance between dolmens of Europe, Africa, and America, 225
—— on trepanation, 258, 268, 274, 276
Bronze age, the, 19, 148, 258-260, 294, 334
Bronze, the first metal generally used, 64; in *terremares*, 160; weapons at Stonehenge, 184; in megaliths of France, 218; bronze beads, 258; idols, 296; bronze in Troy, 334
Bruniquel Cave, 50, 51, 59, 92, 111, 351, 354
Buccinum, 141
BUCKLAND, Miss, on resemblance between relics from Cornwall and Mycenæ, 248
Buenos Ayres, earthen dwellings near, covered with carapace of glyptodon, 128, 129
Burghs of Scotland, 165, 166
Burgwallen of Germany, 154
Burial-Mounds of Oberea, 36; of Otaheite, 36
Burial of chiefs in dolmens, 258
Burial of dead and cremation, 368-374. *See also* "Sepulture."
Burmah, 16
Burtneek, Lake, 139
Bury St. Edmunds, Lake Station near, 155
Buvards, earliest habitations, 127, 128
Bytchiskala, 265

Cabul, valley of, 201, 226
Caches, 64, 235
Cæsar's Camp, 285
Cæsar's Table, 185
Cairns, 180, 220, 302
Caledonians, the, 364
California, fishing-tackle used in, 63
Camp des cayeux, 236
CAMPER, on extinction of races, 6
Camps. *See* "*Enceintes*."

INDEX. 387

Canada, 40, 44
Canche, 140
Cannibalism, of cave-men, 49 ; practised in Belgium, 50 ; burnt human bones in Reggio Cave, 51 ; human bones fractured in same way as animals for food, 51 ; at Montesquieu-Avantès a hearth covered with human bones, 52; gnawed human bones from Kent's Hole of Stone age, 52 ; similar finds in Scotland, Portugal, Denmark, the Caucasus, near Jerusalem, in America, 52, 53 ; barbarity of Mexican sacrifices, 54 ; evidence of cannibalism in Trou d'Argent Cave, 253
Canoes, 69, 71–73, 164
Canstadt race, the, 344
CARL, on fossil bones, 6
Carnac, 193, 194, 205, 219, 223
Caroline Islands, pile dwellings in, 145
Carp, 60
CARTAILHAC, on discoveries in Portugal, 27
—— on similarity of implements at different periods, 88
—— on circular openings in dolmens, 214
—— on contents of dolmen of Grailhe, 215
—— on builders of megalithic monuments, 224
—— on early mining, 247
—— on trepanation, 263
—— on *citanias*, 292
—— on the *swastika*, 341
Carved and engraved dolmens, 207–210
Carved rocks at Sydney and Easter Island, 36
Carvings, *see* "Art of prehistoric man."
CASTELFRANCO, on pile dwelling at Lagozza, 150
Castellet Cave, 252
Castellieri of Istria, 172
Castelnuovo de Sotto, 162

Castione, 160
Castle Spynie, vitrified fort at, 301, 302
Castle Wellan, 178
Castrum Gredonense, 286
Cat, rare in pile dwellings, 157 ; unknown in Troy, 329
Catenoy (Oise), camp of, 284, 285
Caucasus, the, 52, 213, 219
Causses, les, 246
Cave-bear, 253, 344 ; -hyena, 116, 344 ; -lion, 96, 116, 253, *see also* "Animals"
Cave-men, *see* "Man, prehistoric."
Caves, remains of men and animals in, at San Ciro (Palermo), 6 ; at Hoxne (Suffolk), 9 ; at Nabrizas Cave, 10 ; near Cracow, 24 ; near Madrid, 26 ; at Santander, 27 ; near Nahr el Kelb, 28 ; Cave of Hercules (Morocco), 33 ; of Sureau (Belgium), 47 ; of Aurignac (France), 47 ; at Brixham, 48 ; at Thayngen, 48 ; at Chaleux, 48 ; at Moustier, 48 ; at Gourdan, 48; at Frontal, 49; caves of France, 49 ; of Baoussé-Roussé (Mentone), 49 ; of the Lesse, 50 ; of Reggio, 50 ; of Lourdes, Gourdan, and Bruniquel, 51; of Montesquieu-Avantès, 52 ; of Kent's Hole (Torquay), and Cesareda (Portugal), 52 ; of the Caucasus, 52 ; of Sentenheim (Alsace), 56 ; of Külock, 57 ; of Lherm, Belgium, Germany, Hungary, and Gourdan, 57 ; at Eyziès, and Nabrigas, 58 ; of the Vezère, 59 ; at Madeleine, Eyziès, and Bruniquel, 59 ; Madeleine, 60, 65 ; of South of France, Belgium, and Keyserloch (Germany), 65; at Kent's Hole, and near Settle (Yorkshire), 66 ; at Hoxne, 83 ; at Marsoulas, Picard, Eyziès, Laugerie-Basse, Bruniquel, Massat, the Madeleine, and Ariège, 92 ; at Kent's Hole, 93 ; at Aggetelk (Hungary), 93 ;

at Gourdan, 95; at Engis, 97; Frontal, 99; Argent (Basse-Alpes) and Nabrigas, 99; at Chaleux, 103; at Spy, 105; at Kent's Hole, 107; of Belgium, Roquemaure, 107; of Baoussé-Roussé, 108; at Eyziès, Schussenreid, Laugerie-Basse, and Chaffaud, 111; at Cottes, 112; of Périgord and Charante, 114; at Thayngen, 114; of Chaffaud (Vienna) and Lortet, 118; at Marsoulas and Feyjat, 119; at Thayngen, 120; at Goyet and Frontal, 121; at Altamira and Cresswell's Crags (Derbyshire), 122; at Madeleine, 123
— absence of Chelléen implements in caves of America, 129; caves in Wales in Glacial deposits, 130; distinction between caves of men and those of animals, 131; height of caves of Massat, Lherm, Moustier, Bouicheta, Loubens, Sauthenay, Eyziès, and Aurignac, 131; ooze in Montgaudier Cave, 132; eight different deposits in Placard Cave, 132; Neolithic caves hollowed out of limestone, 133; carvings in Coizard Cave, 134; household gods at Courjonnet Cave, 134; sepulchral caves, 134, 135, 246, 250, 370
Cayanes, 98
Celebes, pile dwellings in, 145
Cella, 355
Celts, the, 161, 195
Ceraunia, 5, 16–18, 34
Cervus megaceros, 59
Cesareda (Portugal), 52, 255
Cetati de pamentu of Roumania, 295, 296
Ceylon, cromlechs in, 181
Chaffaud Cave (Vienna), 111, 118
Chalacayo (Lima), 268
Chaldeans, the, mode of sepulture of,

Chaleux Cave, 48, 103, 105, 233, 377
Challas Cave (Savoy), 252
Chamant, 188
Chamber's Island, 269
Chamois, 47
CHAMPOLLION, on monuments of Egypt, 2
CHANTRE, on shell heaps in the Caucasus, 140
— on dolmens of South Russia, 179
— on ornaments of dolmens in the Caucasus, 219
Charante, 114
Chassey Camp, 95, 283, 284
Châteauvieux, vitrified fort at, 303
Chauvaux Cave, 255, 345
Chelléen period, 83, 84, 129
Cherry, 158
CHIERICI, on bones from Reggio Cave, 50
Chierici, *terremare* of, 161
Chili, 44
China, 16, 77
Chincas, the, 42
Chouchet of Algeria, 171
Chub, 60
Chulpas of Bolivia, 357
Circular openings in dolmens, 211-214, 346
Cissbury, Camp at, 288–291, 378
Citanias, 292
Cliff-Dwellers, 3, 41
CLOSMADEUC, on Island of Gavr'innis, 209
Clothing of prehistoric man, 103; cloth first woven in Neolithic age, 104; coarse hempen cloth from Lake Stations, Switzerland, 104
Cockleshells, 24, 107
Cod, 60
Coins, Gallic, 22; coins of later date than the monuments in which found, 220; Roman coins at Mané-er-H'roek, Finistère, Locmariaker, in Gloucestershire and Derbyshire, 220; silver coins of Caliphs of Bagdad in

Coins—Continued.
Scotch barrows, 221 ; Roman coins at Hastedon (Namur), 281; at Pont-de-Bonn (Namur), 282 ; coin of Theodosius in cromlech at Blendowo (Poland), 372
Coizard Cave, 134
COLANGES, DE, on Sepulture, 350
Coline des Mulets, *enceintes*, 287
Colombia, gold ornaments in, 338
Combs of reindeer-horn, 63 ; combs from Lake Stations, Switzerland, 146 ; bone comb from Lagozza, 150
Commerce, or barter, birth of, 244 ; shells taken long distances, 244 ; also hatchets, daggers, and nuclei, 246 ; coral and amber, 246 ; and minerals, 247 ; rapid development of, in Neolithic times, 247 ; gold cups from Cornwall and Mykenæ of similar workmanship, 248 ; shells, mica, and obsidian in tumuli of Ohio, from long distances, 248 ; jade celts and ornaments in America, 248 ; gold and obsidian in island of Santorin, 315
Comox (Vancouver Island), 255
Compans, 188
Concise, Lake Station, great number of worked stones at, 234 ; a manufacturing centre, 237 ; red coral from Mediterranean at, 246
CONDER, on megaliths in Syria, 199
Conflans-Sainte-Honorine, 188, 212
CONGREVE, on megalithic monuments in India, 29
Commana (Finistère), 207
Constance, Lake of, 148
Constantine, 353
Copiapo (Chili), 255
Copper, an age of, 21 ; in Hungary, 25, 65 ; prehistoric stations between Almeria and Carthagena of Copper age, 294
Copper mines, Lake Superior, 64
—— rings, 358 ; copper saw, 314

Coracles, 70
Coral, 106, 246
Coriander, 315
Cork float, 68 ; cork plug, 71
Corn, 151, 158, 295
Cornwall, 184, 213
Côtes-du-Nord, 194
Cottes Cave, 112
Couedic, 208
Coups de poing, 84
Courjonnet Cave, 134
Covered avenues, 188-194 ; *see also* "Megalithic Monuments."
Cracow, caves near, 24 ; bone implements, flints, and pottery found near, 233
Craig Phœdrick, vitrified cairn at, 302
Crania, of Lake Stations, Switzerland, 254 ; *see also* "Trepanation."
Crannoges of Scotland and Ireland, 162-164
Crécy-sur-Morin sepulchre, 261
Cremation, 218, 219, 324, 342, 366 ; practised all over Europe, 368 ; slowly abandoned, 369 ; *see also* "Sepulture."
Cresswell Crags (Derbyshire), 122
Crimea, 24, 225
Cro-Magnon caves, 106, 249
Cromlechs, 180-185 ; in Algeria, 195 ; still erected in India, 222 ; *see also* "Megalithic Monuments."
Crypts, 189, 190, 205
Cueva de Mengal (Malaga), 189
CUVIER, on antiquity of man, 12
Cypress, 367
Cyprina Islandica, 108
Cyprus, cromlechs in, 186

Dab, 60
Dahomey, pile dwellings in, 145
Dallas (Illinois), 269
Dampont (Dieppe), 262
Danubian Provinces, early civilization in, 25
Delaware, the, alluvial deposits of, 39

Denmark, kitchen-middings of, 24; cannibalism in, 52; cromlechs in, 180; covered avenues in and tombs of, 188; rich in flint implements, 234; trepanation in, 266; vitrified forts of, 301
Dessignac, 189
Devèzes, 258
Dinornis, 35
Discs, 107; of lava, 314; *see also* "Whorls."
Djedas, of Algeria, 198
Dog, 86, 137, 156, 329
Dol Varchant, 208
DOLGADO, on bones of the dead colored red, 348
Dolmens, rites in honor of, 18; in India, 30, 33; human bones in, 52.; types of implements in, 88; general description of, 177-180; in Algeria, 195-198; in Syria, 199; in India, 200; dolmens all tombs, 202; most numerous in France, 204; carved and engraved, 207; superstitious origin of, 212; pierced with circular openings, 211-214; human and industrial remains in, 214-221; variety of construction, 226; used for burial of chiefs, 258; circular openings in, 346; tombs, 355; *see also* "Megalithic Monuments."
Domestic animals, 49, 58, 86, 156-159
Donegal, 163, 164
Dolichocephalic skulls, 262, 265, 272, 324
DU CHATELLIER, on *enceinte* at Rosmeur, 283
Duck, 49, 138
DUCROS, on Palæolithic origin of Solutréen remains, 349
DUGDALE, on flint hatchets, 7
DUPONT, discoveries by, 94, 97, 345
Durfort Cave, 87, 88
Duruthy Cave (Sordes), 345
Dyke of Zeedyck, 282
Dykes in England, 288

Earliest habitations, 127, 128, 135
Earthern ramparts at Willem and Houlem, 282, 283
Earthworks in America, 40; in North America, 296-300
Easter Island, bust statues, engraved rocks, and human bones in, 36-38
Edentate mammals of America, 39
Eels, 116
Egyptian monuments, 21; worked flints in, 31; cromlechs in, 188
Elephant, 47, 56, 156
Elephas antiquus, 84
Elfen Stenars, 381
Elk, 84
Embalming, 364
Enceintes, 195, 197, 198, 224; a general term for camps and fortifications, 280; Neolithic examples at Hastedon (Namur), 280, 281; at Pont-de-Bonn (Namur), 282; in Limburg and Liège, 282, 283; numerous in France, 283; in the Vosges Mountains and at Rosmeur (Finistère), 283; at Chassey (Saône-et-Loire), 284; at Catenoy (Oise), 285; *Castrum Gredonense*, a Neolithic station, 286; pile dwellings and *terremares* fortified, 287; fortifications of Great Britain, 288; camp at Cissbury, 288-291; German fortifications, 291; at Potzrow and Zahnow on piles, 292; mounds between Thorn and the Baltic, 292; *citanias* in Portugal, 292; fortified town at Mouinho-da-Moura, 292; prehistoric stations of Stone, Copper, and Bronze ages, 294; *cetati de pamentu* of Roumania, 295, 296
—— colossal earthworks of America, 296; Mound-Builders, 297; Fort Hill, 297; Newark, 298, 299; Liberty (Ohio), 299; unique intrenchments at Old Fort (Kentucky), at Juigalpa (Nicaragua), 300
—— vitrified forts, 300; in Scotland,

Enceintes—Continued.
Bohemia, France, Denmark, and Norway, 301 ; the most celebrated at Barry Hill and Castle Spynie (Invernesshire), Top-O-Noth (Aberdeen), 301 ; vitrified cairns in Orkney Islands, Craig Phœdrick and Ord Hill of Kissock (Moray Firth), 302, 303 ; forts at Châteauvieux, 303 ; and Ribaudelle, 304 ; probably not prehistoric, 305 ; processes of vitrification, 305–308 ; vitrified walls at Hissarlik, 320 ; sarcophagi or *enceintes* near Constantine, 353
Engis Cave, 97, 98
England, pile-dwellings in, 26 ; harpoons in, 65 ; canoe in Devonshire, 71 ; tools of Chelléen type in, 83 ; absence of Palæolithic pottery in, 100 ; ancient pottery in North of, 142 ; Lake Stations in, 155 ; tumuli enclose tombs, 175 ; alignments of, lead to cromlechs, 183 ; alignments, 193 ; crypts, 205 ; circular openings in dolmens, 213 ; contents of, 217 ; discontinued in, 223 ; antiquity of, 224 ; cup-stones in, 379
Engraving, *see* "Art of prehistoric man."
Entre-Roches (Angoulême), 263
Erdeven, 194
Esquimaux, the, 22, 50
Essenam, 188
Esthonians, the, 195
Europe, Stone age in, 9–14, 24–27 ; animal life in, 56 ; fish food in, 143 ; iron rare in prehistoric times of, 219 ; cremation practised all over, 368
EVANS, on shell heaps in England, 140
Eyziès Cave, 58, 59, 92, 111, 131

FAIDHERBE, on division of Africa, 30
—— on dolmens of Algeria, 180
Feasts of death, 375
Feder-See, 68

FERAUD, on megaliths of Algeria, 197
FERGUSSON, on megalithic architecture, 203
Ferns, 151
Feyjet (Dordogne), 119
Finistère, 188, 202, 207, 210, 218, 220, 283
FINLAY, researches in Greece by, 27
Finns, the, 195
Fire, prehistoric use of, proved, 101 ; used in mining, 241 ; surprising skill in management of, 306
Fish, skeletons of, and shells of oysters and cockles in kitchen-middings, 24 ; shell heaps in America, 40 : fresh-water and marine fish used as food, 59 ; in French caves bones of the jack, carp, bream, chub, trout, and tench, 60 ; from Lake Stations, Switzerland, remains of mollusca, turtle, and goldfish, 60 ; Scandinavians caught mackerel, dab, and herring, 60 ; in kitchen-midding near the Oka (Nijni-Novgorod) remains of salt-water mollusca, 139 ; similar remains all over Europe, 140 ; shell heap, St. Simon's Island (Georgia), of oyster shells, 141 ; many others similar, 142, 143
Fishing-tackle, the earliest hooks of bone or wood, 60 ; of teeth of animals, 61 ; flint fish-hooks, 62 ; also of horn and boars' tusks, 62 ; stone hooks rare in America, 63 ; bone the most ancient there, 63 ; a fish-hook manufactory on Santa Cruz Island, shells used by Californians, 63 ; bronze hooks, 64 ; a few of copper in America, gold hooks more numerous in New Granada, 64, 65
—— harpoons of bone in France, Belgium, Germany, England, Switzerland, and Scandinavia, 65, 66 ; in Alaska, one found beside most ancient mammals of America, 66

Fishing-nets of hemp from Lake Stations of Switzerland, 67, 68 ; weights of stone, and floats of wood and cork from Lake Stations of the Stone age, 68
Flax, at Lagozza, 151
Flints, *see* "Weapons and Tools."
FLOQUET, on dolmens as tombs, 202
Florida, kitchen-middings in, 142
Flute, 111, 112
Fondi di Cabane of Italy, 162
FONDOUCE, on megaliths as the produce of progressive civilization, 225 ; by various races, but all of one type, 227
Fontabert Cave, 132
Food of prehistoric man chiefly meat, 47 ; bones split open by cave-men, 48 ; large mammals preferred, rodents also eaten, 48 ; bones of birds rarer, 48 ; remains of birds in Gourdan Cave, 49 ; fifty-one species of birds in caves of France, and great numbers at Baoussé-Roussé, 49 ; brains and marrow dainties, 49 (*see* "Cannibalism") ; horseflesh favorite diet at Solutré, 58 ; in caves of Vezère, Madeleine, Eyziès, and Bruniquel bones of the jack, carp, bream, chub, trout, and tench, 60 ; Lake Stations (Switzerland), all kinds of fish, 60 ; salt-water fish from kitchen-middings, 60 ; mammals, birds, and fish from kitchen-middings, 138 ; fish food in Brittany, 140 ; in England and America, 143 ; Lagozza a vegetarian settlement, 151 ; domestic animals in Lake Stations, 156 ; stag and ox most numerous, 157 ; corn, millet, peas, nuts, plums, and other fruit from pile dwellings, 158 ; from Cortaillod barley, cherry-stones, acorns, and beech-nuts, 158 ; water-chestnuts, from Laybach, 158 ; stores of grain in fortified camps of Spain, 295 ; stores of millet in *cetati de pamentu* of Roumania, 296 ; barley, millet, lentils, peas, coriander, and anise in island of Santorin, 315 ; fish, mollusca and cereals chief food in Troy, 329
Fort Hill, 297, 298
Fortifications, *see* "*Enceintes.*"
Fossés de Trajan, 295
Foundry of Larnaud, 64
Fowl, domestic, 49
Fox, 47
FRAAS, on pottery found with remains of giant mammals, 96
France, caves of, 49 ; harpoons found in, 65 ; caves of, 90 ; in caves of South of, needles with eyes, barbed arrows, and stilettos of deer antler, 92 ; ornaments of bright colored shells in caves of, 107 ; carved and engraved stones and bones of, 120 ; Lake Stations of, 155, 156 ; few cromlechs in, 180 ; megaliths in, 194 ; crypts in, 205 ; dolmens with circular openings, 211–213 ; contents of dolmens, 216, 217 ; gold ornaments in, 217 ; megaliths discontinued, 223 ; antiquity of, 224 ; prehistoric workshops of, 238 ; implements of rocks foreign to the country, 246 ; trepanation in, 258–264 ; *enceintes* in, 280–283 ; vitrified forts in, 301 ; cup-stones in, 379
FRÈRE, on worked flints, 8, 9
FRIEDEL, on *Ankerstein*, 77
Frontal Cave, 49, 98, 121, 244, 354, 375
Funen, island of, 64
Funeral rites, 53 ; similar in all countries, 228 ; trepanation a rite, 269, 270 ; possible rites, 345, 346 ; bones of adults colored red, 347–349 ; funeral customs and feasts, 375 ; *see also* "Cremation" and "Sepulture."
—— vases, 220, 295, 360

Fusaïoles, 160, 322, 324, 326, 339; see also "Whorls."

Galgals of Brittany, 180
GALLES, on hatchets from dolmens of Brittany, 214
Game played with knuckle bones, 328
Gang Graben, of Denmark, 188
Gangraben, of Germany, 355
Garenne de Verneuil (Marne), 354
GAUDRY, on hatchets from the Somme, 15
Gavr'innis, Isle of, 190, 205, 209
Gendron Cave, 345, 347
Germany, remains of bears in caves of, 57; harpoons found in, 65; pottery in caves of, 96; fortifications in, 291; burial and cremation in, 372
Giant mammals, *see* "Animals."
Gibraltar, 255
Gironde, department of, subterranean storing-places for grain, 158
Glacial epoch in England, 71, 130, 131
Glass bowls, 169
Glutton, 253
Glyptodon, 39, 128
Goat, 47, 86, 156, 217, 329
Gods, 134, 322
Gold buckle at Aspatria (Cumberland), 220
—— chains in dolmen at Finistère, and Leys dolmen (Inverness), 218
—— cups from Cornwall, Mycenæ, and Troy, 248, 337
—— diadem from Troy, 337
—— fish-hooks, 64-66
—— necklaces and other gold ornaments from New Grange (Ireland) and dolmens of France, 218
—— ornaments at Ojcow, 25; in great variety from Troy, 337, 338
—— plate, and gold olives from dolmens of France, 217
—— rings at Santorin, 314

Goldfish, 60
Goose, 49, 138, 329
Gourdan Cave, 48, 51, 57, 95, 251
Goyet Cave (Belgium), 111, 114, 121
Grain, stores of, 158, 295
Grand Pressigny, 235, 246, 296
Great Britain, age of deposits in caves of, 130; highest development of cromlechs in, 182; fortifications in, 288
Grez, 233, 286
Grindstone for crushing grain, 51, 296
Grottes-des-Fées, 191
Grouse, 49
Guanches, the, 364
Gubernaculum, 77
Guérin mound (Paris), 260
Guisseny tumulus (Finistère), 259, 272

Hallstadt (Bohemia), necropolis of, 362, 372
Hallstadtian period, 373
HAMY, on scarcity of human remains in Palæolithic caves and mounds, 231
—— on wounds in bones, 249
Hare, 47, 48
Harpoons, 65-67
Hartmannsweiller Kopf (Alsace) *enceinte* of, 301
Hastedon (Namur), 280, 281
Hatchet, the, a sacred symbol, 378; *see also* "*Ceraunia*."
Hatchets, *see* "Weapons and Tools."
Havelse, 137
HAXTHAUSEN, on *kurganes*, of Russia, 195
Hearths, 101, 136, 284, 349
Heidenmauer of Saint Odila (Hermeskiel), 291
HEILBIG, on *terremarecolli*, 161
Hellstone (Dorsetshire), 178
Helvetians, proto-, 149
Hemp used for fishing-nets, 67; for coarsely-woven cloth, 104

Hercules, caves of, 33
HERODOTUS, on pile dwellings, 145
Herring, 60
Hindoo Koosh Mountains, 201
Hippopotamus, 9, 11, 56, 86, 156, 331
Hissarlik, Hill of, 317-338
HOARE, on earliest habitations, 127
—— on remains of funeral feasts, 375
Hohlefels, 57, 96
Holderness (Yorkshire) Lake Station, 154
Holed stones, 213
Homicidal struggles, commencement of, 59
Hordeum hexastichum, 151
Horses, 47, 58, 132, 157, 158, 329
Horse-walls, 58
Hove, 364
Hoxne, 9, 83, 237
Human sacrifices, 51, 54, 376
Hungary peopled in Neolithic times, 25; bears in caves of, 57; bone daggers and amulets, 93; Lake Stations of, 151
Hünengräber of Germany, 179, 191
Hunting implements, 48
Hyena, 84, 96, 116, 344

Iberians, the, 286, 361, 364
Iceland, 45
Idols, 296, 322
Incas, the, 366
India, Stone age in, 29; Chelléen tools and weapons in, 83; great number of megaliths in, and legends connected with them, 200, 201; dolmens with circular openings, 211-213; megalithic monuments still erected in, 222; cup-stones in, 379
Industrial arts, progress in, 86
—— centres, *see* "Workshops."
Inscriptions, cuneiform, 2
—— in old Irish cipher on megaliths, 222, 341
Insects, 367

Ireland, pile dwellings in, 26; a stone hammer in head of a *Cervus megaceros*, 58; bronze fish-hooks, 64; boats from bogs, 70; crannoges in, 162-164; round towers of, 167; cromlechs of, 184, 185; crypts in, 205; iron knives and rings, bone needles, copper pins, and glass and amber beads in Cairn of Dowth, 120; great number of bone implements in cairn near Lough Crew, 120; rich in flint implements, 324
Irish cipher writing on megalithic monuments, 222, 341
Iron age, 19, 377
—— found at Carnac, and in Megaliths of England and Scotland, 219; rarer than bronze in Europe and America, 219; iron knives, 220
Istria, 165, 172
ISSEL, on sepulture in Italy, 346
Italy, flint weapons in, 26; pottery in, 97; Lake Stations of, 104, 149-151; *terremares* of, 159-162; great number of *truddhi* in, 171; cromlechs in, 180; bones of the dead colored red in Neolithic times, 347, 348; funeral pits in, 356; cup-stones in, 379

Jack, 60
Jade, hatchets and hammers, 81; from pile dwellings, 146; celts and ornaments in America, 248
Japan, use of stone implements in, 22, 29; dolmens in, 179; trepanation in, 266; sepulture in decorated vases, 362
Japanese, the, 17
Java, pile dwellings, 145
Javelins, 87
Jellalabad, 201
Jersey, contents of dolmens in, 216
Jet, 107, 109
Jeuilly, 263

Joigny, 127
JOLY, on contemporaneity of man with cave-bear, 10
—— on human bones, pottery, and skeleton of *Ursus spelæus* in Nabrigas cave, 99
JOUANNET, on stone weapons near Périgord, 9
Juigalpa (Nicaragua), 300
Jura Mountains, pile dwellings in, 155

Kabyles, the, 196, 277
Kamena baba, 195
Kent's Hole (Torquay) 52, 66, 93, 105, 107
Kern, 301
Kew, 155
Keyserloch, 65
Khassias, the, 222
Kherson, 181
Kistvaens, 175, 220, 381
Kitchen-middings, in Denmark, 24; in Florida, 53; in Scandinavia, 54; in Long Island, 63; on Atlantic and Pacific Coasts, 94; in Scandinavia, 136, 138; in France, 139; at Canche, 140; in America, 140–143; Quaternary animals disappeared in, and similarity of, in Europe and America, 143
Kit's Cotty House, 213
Klementz, on Valley of the Yenesei, 28
Kůloch, 57
Kurganes, the, 181, 195, 348

La Justice (near Paris), 188
LA MARMORA, on age of *nurhags*, 169
La Mouline (Charante), 201
La Muela de Cherte (Maeztrago), 294
LA PÉROUSE, on sculptures of Easter Island, 36
Lagozza, 94, 104, 150
Lake Bienne, 145, 265, 288
—— Burtneek, 139
—— Constance, 145, 148

Lake Geneva, 145
—— Maggiore, 149
—— Salpi, 149
—— Stations of Austria and Hungary, 25; of Switzerland, 25; of Belgium, 26; fish in stations in Switzerland, 60; bone fish-hooks at Wangen, Moosseedorf, and St. Aubin, 62; bronze hooks in Switzerland, 64; Lake Stations of Switzerland from Stone age to time of Romans, 67; fishing in, 68; boats in, 74; first discovered, 200; stations in Switzerland, 145; pile dwellings still used, 145; of Switzerland of three periods, 145; general description, 146–149; local names for, 147; great numbers at Wangen and at Robenhausen, 148; stations of Italy, 149; at Lagozza, 150; a vegetarian station, 151; of Austria and Hungary, 151; near Laybach, 152; construction of Lake Stations of Pomerania, 153; station in Scotland, 154; in England at Holderness, Thetford, Barton Mere, near Bury St. Edmunds, near Kew, and in London, 154, 155; in France at Vatan, the Jura Mountains, Pyrenean valleys, and in the department of Landes, 155; in Bourget Lake, Saint-Dos, and Lake Paladru, more recent stations, 156; Lake fauna, 156; in Lake village of Nidau domestic animals more general and wild animals rarer, 157; Lake dwellings probable in Asia and Africa, 165; amber from Baltic in Lake dwellings of Switzerland, 246; village of Lake Bienne of Stone age fortified, 288; sepulchral chest Lake Station of Auvernier (Switzerland), 360
—— Zurich, 144
Lares penates, 134, 377; *see also*, "Idols."

Larnaud, 64
Laugerie-Basse, 92, 111
Laybach, 151–153
Lechevalier, on site of Troy, 318
Lechs of Brittany, 185
Lenormant, on use of *specchie*, 171
Lentils, 315
Les Causses, 369
Lesse, caves of the, 50
Lestridiou (Finistère), 192
LEWIS, on fortifications at Old Fort (Kentucky), 299
Lherm Cave (Belgium), 57, 131
L'Homme Mort Cave, 250, 258, 272, 273, 354, 375
Liberty (Ohio), 299
Liège, caves, 10
—— *enceintes*, 283
Limburg, 282
Limpets, 108
Lion, 84, 96, 156
Little People, 381
Littorina littorea, 136
Livingstone, on South Africa, 31, 55
Livres de beurre, 246
Lizières, 262
Loaves of bread, 159
Loch Stemster (Westmoreland), 182
Locmariaker (Brittany), 185
Lombardy, Lake Stations of, 149; *terremares* of, 159
London, 7, 155
Long Barrows, 190; at Moustoir-Carnac, 205; West Kenret, 216; nearly all buried in long barrows had met with a violent death, 254; bones and flints in, 346; remains of funeral feasts in, 375
Long Meg and her daughters, 182
Long-Nick Branch, 142
LONGPÉRIER, on ancient vases, 316
—— on hatchets as sacred symbols, 378
Lortet, 118
Loubens Cave, 131
Lourdes Caves, 51

Lozère, 88, 99, 215, 218, 246, 257, 258, 369, 370
LUBBOCK, on prehistoric sculpture, 38
—— on worked flints from Chili and New Zealand, 44
—— on absence in England of Palæolithic pottery, 100
—— on settlement at Havelse, 137
—— on *burghs* of Scotland, 165, 166
—— on ancient fortifications of Great Britain, 288
LUND, on scarcity of human bones in caves of Brazil, 231
—— on crania pierced by a tool, 255
—— Museum of, 62
—— University of, 59
LYELL, on flints from bed of Somme, 14
—— on shell heaps of Georgia, 141

Mackerel, 60
Madeleine Cave, 59, 60, 65, 85, 92, 93, 123
—— period or type, 85, 132, 351
Madisonville (Ohio), 255
Madras, 201
Madrid, caves near, 26
Magnolia, 367
MAHUDEL, on worked stones, 7
Malabar, iron used in, 219; mode of sepulture in, 361
Mammals, *see* "Animals."
Mammoth, 57, 84, 86, 96, 253, 344, 377
Mamoas, or *maminhas*, of Portugal, 175
Man, prehistoric, 7; flints found at Hoxne, 8, 9; contemporaneity of man with extinct mammals doubted, 7–13; established by Boucher de Perthes, and confirmed by Falconer and others, 14, 15; diversity of development in human races, 20; implements similar to prehistoric still used by uncivilized races, 22, 23; extreme North peopled, 24; kitchen-middings in Denmark, 24; discov-

INDEX.

Man, prehistoric—*Continued.*
eries in Poland, Russia, and Austria confirm the great antiquity of man, 25; in Hungary of Neolithic times, Lake Stations of extinct races, 25; pile dwellings in France, Italy, Germany, Ireland, England, and Belgium, 26; signs of man in South of Europe, 26, 27; Stone age in Europe, 27; in Siberia and Palestine, 28; in Japan, Egypt, Isle of Melos, and India, 29, 30; worked flints in North and South Africa, 30-34; ruins in the Transvaal, 35; man appeared in all countries about the same time, 35; worked flints with bones of Dinornis in New Zealand, 35; megalith and trilithon at Tonga-Taboo, pyramid in Otaheite, 36; bust statues and tools of obsidian in Easter Island, 36-38; man contemporary with edentate and pachydermatous mammals in America, 39

—— huge earthworks of, throughout North America, 40; Mound-Builders, 41; *pueblos*, 41; Cliff Dwellers, 41; succeeded by Toltecs, Aztecs, Chibcas, and Peruvians, 42; in every part of the world, worked flints and megalithic monuments, 43-45; gradual development of man, 46

—— food of, chiefly animal, 47; the horse, 47; large mammals and rodents, 48; birds rarer, 48, 49; cannibalism, 49-53; fish food, 59, 60; ancient Scandinavians deep-sea fishermen, 60, 69

—— early use of boats by, 69-76; gradual use of oars, mast, rudder, and anchor, 76, 77, *see also* "Fishing-tackle," and "Boats."

—— first weapon of a knotty branch, 79; instinct taught, 80, 81; most ancient tools, 81; gradual development of skill and ingenuity, 82, 83; Chelléen period, 83, 84; Moustérien period, 84; Solutréen period, 85; Madeleine period, 85

—— in Neolithic period abandoned a nomad for a sedentary life, ceased to be a hunter, became an agriculturist and shepherd, 86; metals still unknown, but stone polished, 86; handles to tools, 88; use of bone and horn, 90; needles with eyes and barbed arrows, 92; unexpected civilization of Neolithic times, 94; earthenware spoons, 94; vases, 98; use of fire proved by baked pottery, 101; family hearths, 101; Lake Stations of Italy, cultivated hemp, 104; at Wangen and Robenhausen coarsely woven cloth, 104; in Périgord caves needles too fine to sew skins, 104; tatooing, 104, 105; use of ornaments of teeth or jet, 106; shells, ivory, amber, crystal, coral, and human bones, 106-110; whistles and flutes, 111, 112; carved and engraved bone for staves of office, 113-116; hilt of dagger and other objects, 116, 118; art of cave-men at its zenith, 120; engraving on wood, 123; colored designs, 126

—— in caves of Great Britain before Glacial epoch, 130; progress in Neolithic times, 133; huts of clay, and tents of skins, 135; intelligence of primeval man, 136

—— of Scandinavia renounced nomadic life, 138; metals unknown to them, 138; man of kitchen-middings fixed abodes, 144; proto-Helvetians well-developed men, 149; pastoral life, 157; agriculturists, 158; *terremarecolli* of Italy agriculturists, 159; of uncertain origin, 160, 161; emigration of races, 161; crannoges in Ireland, 162; huts in Ireland under peat 164; construction of crannoges

Man, prehistoric—*Continued*.
in Scotland, 164; of Stone age, 164; probably occupied by successive generations, 165; *burghs* of Scotland, 165; *Picts' houses*, 166; *nurhags* of Sardinia, 167, 168; *talayoti* of Minorca, 170; *nanetas* of Balearic Isles, 170; *truddhi* and *specchie* of Italy, 171; *castellicri* of Istria, 172; progress of civilization, 172
—— builders of megalithic monuments, 174; human bones at Stonehenge, 184; at Moen, 191; at Mureaux, 192; vanished races of Yenesei, 195; powerful races in North Africa, 196; skeletons at La Mouline, 201; at Maupas, 202; earliest inhabitants of tombs removed, 203; intelligent workmen, 206; skulls at Vauréal, 216; rich offerings in tombs, 217, 218; progress in industrial arts, 220; in architecture, 225; similarity of aspirations and powers in all men, 225; no certain knowledge of the builders of megalithic monuments, 227–230
—— bones of, scarce, worked flints very abundant, 231–235; growth of populations in Palæolithic times, 231–235; the extreme North more populous then than now, 236; more civilized than Lake dwellings, and megalithic monuments of South, 236; all the continents peopled, civilization almost identical, 240; signs of division of labor, 240; of long travel, 244–248; daily life of Stone age, 248; struggle for existence, 249; skulls and bones with scars and flint points still in them, 249–256; early attempts at surgery, 252; skill in, and nursing, 256, 257; trepanation, 257–278; a possible funeral rite, 269; still practised, 270; as a treatment of diseases, 271; long continuance of practice, 272
—— first made weapons, then fortifications, 279; Neolithic *enceintes*, 280–286; of Portugal, 293; and of Spain, of Stone, Copper, and Bronze ages, 294; inhabited by agriculturists, 295; coarse pottery, grindstones for crushing grain and bronze idols from *cetati de pamentu* of Roumania, 296; strongholds of Mound-Builders of America, 297; intelligence shown in choice of sites, 297; fortifications a proof of combined action, 308
—— at Santorin (Ægean Sea), 310; two gold rings and a little copper the only metals found, 314; advanced civilization, 315; solidly built houses, and other signs of, 315; one human skull, 316; gradual progress, 317; Hill of Hissarlik a witness of, 319; hunting a favorite pastime, 329; pottery of infinite variety, decoration inferior, 330; figure of hippopotamus, and busts of women with heads of owls, 331; the *swastika*, sacred symbol of Aryan race, found in all parts of the world, 339–341; proves identity of origin, 341
—— skeletons of, at Spy (Namur) with implements of Moustérien type, and Quaternary fauna, 344; two in Chauvaux Cave, 345; in Gendron Cave seventeen skeletons, in Duruthy Cave thirty, with Palæolithic implements, and at Baoussé-Roussé, 345; dead buried in caves still inhabited, 346; openings in dolmens used for throwing in bones, when separated from flesh, 346; successive inhumations in dolmens, 347; bones of adults colored red in Neolithic Italy, 347; in Portugal, Russia, Poland, and North America, 348, 349; earliest tombs on the

Man, prehistoric—*Continued*.
hearth, 350; modes of sepulture of Neolithic age, 351-354; caves and tombs closed, 355; urns from Italy imitating human dwellings, 355; forty skeletons at Tours-sur-Marne, of transition period between Stone and Bronze age, 355, 356; five human bodies in good preservation at Floyd (Iowa) of very low grade, 358 (*see also* "Sepulture"); cremation first practised, 366; continued side by side with burial, 368, 374; feasts at funerals, 375; human sacrifices at funerals, 376; signs of belief in immortality, 376; sacred symbols, bones of extinct animals, and hatchets, 377, 378; cup-sculptures, 379; legends sacred to, 381
Mané-Lud dolmen, 204
Mantegazza, on trepanation in Peru, 267
Marconnières dolmen, 370
Marne, caves, 246-259
—— funeral pits, 355
—— megalithic monuments, 378
Marsoulas Cave, 92, 119
Marzobotta, 360
Massat, 92, 131
Mastodon, 39, 57, 96
Masts, 77
Maupas, 201, 202
MAYENFISCH, VON, on pile dwellings, 148
Mecklenburg, megalithic monuments in, 191; crypts in, 205; contents of dolmens, 216
Megaceros, 86
Megalithic Monuments, in India, 29; in Algeria, 32; in Tonga-Taboo, 35, 36; in all countries, 44, 45
—— witnesses of the remote past, 74; tumuli of England enclose a *histvaen*, 175; *mamoas* of Portugal, 175; tumuli in Poland, 175; Edwin-Harness Mound (Ohio), 176
—— dolmens, 77; of Persia, near

Megalithic Monuments—*Continued*.
Mykenæ, of New Grange (Ireland) Arrayolos (Portugal), Hellstone (Dorsetshire), Castle Wellan (Ireland), and Acora (Peru), 178; of Bekour-Noz, in the Kouban basin, and coasts of Black Sea, of Stone age, 179; in Yezo (Japan) and Puerto Descado (Patagonia), 179; general description of, 180
—— cromlechs common in Algeria, Sweden, Denmark, 180; few in France and Italy, 180; at Tyre, in Persia, Arabia, and between Mourzouk and Ghât, 181; of Anajapoura (Ceylon), at Peshawur, in Peru, and Australia, 181; at Myzora (Morocco), 181; highest development of, in Great Britain, 182; at Salkeld (Cumberland), Loch Stemster (Caithness), *Long Meg and her daughters* (Westmoreland), 182; of Avebury, 182, 183; of Stonehenge, 183, 184; of Ireland, of Cornwall, at Upland (Gloucestershire), 185
—— menhirs of Brittany, 185; Sweno's pillar (Scotland), in memory of victories, 185, 186; in France, Cyprus, and Yucatan, 186; in Egypt, Assyria, Persia, and Mexico, 188
—— alignments, or covered avenues, called *essenam* by Arabs, 188; often built beneath masses of earth, such near Paris, the *Gang-Graben* of Denmark similar, 188; covered avenues at tumulus of Dessignac, 189; at *Cueva de Mengal* (Malaga), at crypt at Pastora (Seville), at Gavr'innis, and the Long Barrows at West Kennet, Littleton, Nempnitt, and Uley, 189, 190; sepulchral chamber of oval shape in island of Moen, 190, 191; megaliths of Mecklenburg of two kinds, 191; the *Grotte des Fées* of Provençe, 191; Neolithic covered avenue of Mureaux, 192

Megalithic Monuments—*Continued.*
—— different forms and modes of megalithic monuments found in juxtaposition, as at Mané-Lud and at Lestridion (Finistère), 192; in England and Moab alignments lead to cromlechs, 193; one of most important monuments at Carnac, 193; in Brittany, 194
—— number of, incalculable, 194; in France, 194; the Orkney Islands, north of Scania, and in Otranto, 195; kurganes in Russia, 195; Algeria a field for research, 195-198; *djedas* of, 198; monuments of Tunisia, 198; tumuli in Syria, 198; great numbers in Moab, 199; megaliths in India, 200; legends connected with them, 201; numerous at Jellalabad, Nagpore, valley of Cabul, and in Madras Presidency, 201
—— are either tombs or in honor of the dead, 201; at Mugen, the Cabeco d'Aruda (Portugal), at Monastier (Lozère), the Mas de l'Aveugle (Garde), and La Mouline (Charante), skeletons found, 201; at Maupas crypts of Neolithic age, 201, 202; in Morbihan bodies and cists, 202; cremation in Finistère, 202; all dolmens tombs, 202, 203; crypts in Mecklenburg, England, Wales, Ireland, Orkney Islands, and France, 205; long barrow of Moustoir-Carnac, 205; difficulties of construction, 206, 207; balanced stones of Martine and Castle Wellan, 207; granite dolmens carved and engraved, 207-209; orientation of megaliths, 210; dolmens with circular openings, 211-13
—— of Brittany, relics in, 214, 215; contents of other dolmens of France, Mecklenburg, and Jersey, 216; of England, Spain, and Algeria, 217;
gold ornaments found in France, Scotland, and Ireland, 217, 218; bronze in France and Algeria, 218; iron rare in Europe and America, 219; stone, bronze, and iron at Carnac and Rocher, 219; bronze and iron in British Isles, 219; iron sword inlaid with silver in cist at Aspatria (Cumberland), 220; in cairn of Dowth (Ireland) iron knives and rings and copper pins, 220
—— to do honor to the dead, 221; only bones of Neolithic animals in them, 221; erected from Stone age to present day, 222; discontinued in France and England in 8th or 9th century, in Scotland and Scandinavia later, 223; not mentioned by Roman historians of Britain, Gaul, or Germany, or by early French writers, 224; proofs of antiquity in France and England, 224
—— difficulty of ascertaining by whom built, 224; megalithic zones, 225, 226; dolmens vary in construction, 226; all of one general type, 227; use of circular openings in, 346; Port-Blanc dolmen, 347; megaliths near Constantine, 353; dolmen of Maconnières, 370; of Mont St. Michel and Tumiac, 371
Meilgaard, 137
Menhirs, 18, 180-188, 197, 199, 222; *see also* "Megalithic Monuments."
Mentone, 345, 347
Merovingian tombs, 22, 264, 272, 349, 378
Mesaticephalic skull, 265
Metallurgy, 161, 294, 315, 334
Metals unknown to prehistoric Scandinavians, 138, 143
Meudon, 188
Mexicans, the, 22
Mexico, earthworks in, 41; barbarity of sacrifices in, 54; polished flints in, 87; cromlechs in, 188

Michigan, 248
Midjana, megaliths at, 197
Millet, 158, 296, 315
MILNE-EDWARDS, on birds in French caves, 49
Minano, pile dwellings of, 145
Minerals foreign to the country in which found, 247
Miners and mining, 28, 241, 242, 290
Moab, alignments in, 193; menhirs in, 199
Mobile, 143
Moen, island of, 190, 191
Mollusca, in pile-dwellings of Switzerland, 60; fish-hooks of *Mytilus Californicus* and *Haliotis* in California, 63; in caves of France, fossil and recent shells, 107; *Cyprina Islandica* in French cave, and *Nassa nerita* at Baoussé-Roussé, 108; salt-water shells at Oka (Russia), scallops, oysters, limpets, and pectens in Brittany, 139, 140; shells at mouth of the Somme, 140; oyster shells at St. Simon's Island, 141; in mound near St. John River, *Mya, Venus, Pecten, Buccinum,* and *Natica*, 141; pearl oyster shells at Chaleux, Frontal, and Nuton caves, at Thayngen, and in Italy, 244; arctic marine mollusca in caves of Cro-Magnon, Madeleine, Bize, and Solutré, 244; fossil shells of cretaceous strata, South of France, 244; specimens from Isle of Wight at Laugerie-Basse, 244; pearl oysters of Indian Ocean in South of France, 244
Monastier (Lozère), 201
MONTAIGLON, DE, on vitrification, 307
Montesquieu-Avantès Cave, 52
Montgaudier Cave, 132
Monuments, *see* "Megalithic Monuments."
Moor-fowl, 49, 138
Mooseedorf, 64, 145

Morbihan, 180, 194, 202, 209, 210, 212, 213, 215, 260, 347
Moreau, 369
Morges, Lake, 148
Morocco, cromlechs in, 180
Mortars, for crushing grain, 34; for grinding paint, 105, 106
MORTILLET, on inhumation at Solutré, 350
Mother Grundy's Parlor, 122
Mouinho-da-Moura, 292
Mound-Builders, 3, 41, 297–299, 320
Mouse, 157
Moussa (Shetland), 166
Moustérien period, 84, 132, 344
Moustier Cave, 48, 83, 84, 131
Moustoir-Carnac, 205
Mur de Barrez, flint quarries, 241, 242
Mureaux, 192
Mussels, 136
Mya, 141
Mykenæ, 90, 178, 248, 338, 378
Mytilus Californicus, 63

Nabrigas Cave (Lozère), 10, 58, 99
Nœs dolmen, 266
Nagpore, 201
Nanetas of Balearic Islands, 170
Nassa, 108
Natal, 34
Natica, 141
Navigation, 69, 70
Neanderthal skull, 359
Necklaces, *see* "Ornaments."
Needles of bone, with eyes, 90; in Lake Stations, 145, 146
NÉLATON, on trepanation, 268
Neolithic period, 20, 31; giant animals died out, and domestic animals appeared, 86; man adopted sedentary life, 86; weapons of, in Moustier Cave, and rounded stones, 88; pile dwelling of, 90; civilization of, 94; clothing in, 104; megaliths of, 191, 202, 222; rapid development of commerce in, 247; trepanation

Neolithic period—*Continued.*
in, 257–259, 261; sepulchres of, 261, 262; modes of sepulture in, 351, 356
Nerita, 108, 109
Neuchâtel Lake, 145
Nevada, 39
Newark (America), 298, 299
New Grange (Ireland), 178, 205, 218
New Guinea, pile dwellings of, 145
New Zealand a portion of a submerged continent, 35; Stone age in, 35; worked flints from, 44
Nicaragua, jade celts and ornaments in, 248
Nile valley, implements of flint and porphyry in, 30
Nogent-les-Vierges, 250
NORDENSKIÖLD, on stone weapons of the Tchoutchis, 22
—— on women of, 103
—— on shell heaps at Cape North, 140
NORDMANN, on bones from cave near Odessa, 56
Normandy, *enceintes* in, 283
North, the, peopled in most remote times, 24; abundant life in, 367
Northumberland, megaliths in, 209
Norway, boat in tumulus in, 72; vitrified forts in, 301
Nuclei, 28, 246, 281
Nurhags, of Sardinia, 165; construction of, 167, 168; great antiquity and uncertain origin of, 169; tombs side by side with them of uncertain date, 170
Nuts, 151, 158

Oars, 77
Ogham, 222, 341
Ogris, the, 195
Ohio, mounds of, 269, 357, 358
Old Fort (Kentucky), 299, 300
Oleron, Isle of, 218, 232
Ord Hill of Kissock, 302, 303

Orkney Islands, dolmens in, 180; megaliths in, 195; crypts in, 205; vitrified forts in, 302
Ornaments, from Wirzchow Cave, amulets and fish cut in ivory, 25; fringed cloth from Lake Stations of Italy, 104; fine needles for (possible) embroidery, 104; love of ornaments a natural instinct, 106; cave-men wore fossil coral, beads of clay, teeth, tusks, fish-bones, and belemnites as amulets, 106; necklace of bears' and lions' teeth, 106; ivory plaques with three holes from Cro-Magnon, 106; delicate oval discs from Kent's Hole, 107; slices of jet and ivory plaques from Belgian caves, 107; bright colored shells from French caves, necklace of three hundred, 107; shells brought from a distance, 108; necklaces of nerites and limpets in Scotland, shells used to fasten clothes, 108; at Baoussé-Roussé a necklace, bracelet, amulet, garter, and net for head of nerite shells, 108, 109; beads of jet, crystal, gray schist, amber, and hyaline quartz, also polished balls of calx, 109; necklaces of human teeth, 109; pendants of human bone, 110; staves of office of antlers engraved, 113–116; staff with geometrical designs found with Quaternary fauna, 116; beads and other ornaments in sepulchral caves, 135; dolmens carved and engraved, 207–210; amber beads and necklace of calaïte, and ivory ring from dolmens of Brittany, 214; glass beads and amber bowls, 215; beads of blue glass, enamel, and amber, 215; gold ornaments in France, Scotland, and Ireland, 217, 218; in the Caucasus, blue glass beads and bronze rings, 219; at Aspatria, gold buckle, 220; in

Ornaments—*Continued*.
Posen, silver and gold ornaments, 220; stone and bronze beads in Lozère caves, 258; gold ornaments in great variety in Troy, 337, 338; similar ornaments at Mykenæ, near Bologna, in Lake dwellings, and in Colombia, 338; necklace of bits of limestone from Neolithic funeral pit at Tours-sur-Marne, 356; copper rings and shell beads in mound in Ohio, 358; amber cup in rough plank coffin at Hove, 364
Orry's Grave (Isle of Man), 213
Ors (Isle of Oleron), 218, 232
Ossuaries, 347, 354
Osteitis and caries, possible treatment of, 271
Ostrich, 234
Otaheite, 36
Otranto, 171, 195
Otter, 138
OUVAROFF, on Siberia, 28
—— on bone spear, 66
—— on excavations at Oka (Russia), 138
Ovibos moschatus, 121
Owl, 331
Ox, 86, 156, 157, 217, 329
Oyes Cave, 251
Oyster, 24, 136, 290

Pachydermatous mammals of North America, 39
Palæolithic period, 20; caves of, in Poland, 24; worked flints of, 31; chipped flints of, 87; an ornamented bone implement of, 94; pottery unknown in, 100; Scandinavia not peopled in, 137; finds of human bones in, 231, 232; valley of the Seine inhabited in, 233; workshop of, 237; trepanation in, 263; *see also* "Quaternary period" and "Stone age."
Palestine, Stone age in, 28

PALLAS, on kurganes of Russia, 195
Papaver somniferum, 151
Paris, covered avenues near, 188; environs of, rich in deposits, 233
Park Cwn (Wales), 205
Parma, *terremares* in, 159
Partridge, 49
Pastora (Seville), 190
Patagonia, dolmens in, 179
Pears, 158
PEARSE, on tumulus at Nagpore, 177
Peas, 158, 315
Pecten, 140, 141
Pedras fittas of Sardinia, 195
Penguin, 138
PENKA, on Northern origin of European civilization, 366
Périgord Caves, 9, 104, 114, 246
Persia, dolmens in, 178; cromlechs in, 181, 188
Peru, cromlechs in, 181; trepanation in, 267; sepulchre in, 341; embalmed bodies in, 364
Peruvians, the, 42
Pesons de fuseau, 160
Petit-Morin Caves, 134, 135, 251, 354
Pfahlbauten, *Palafittes*, 147
Phoca grænlandica, 116
Piacenza, 159
Picard Cave, 92
Picts' houses, or *Weems*, 166
Pig, 156, 217
Pigeon, 49
PIGORIN, on mode of sepulture, 346
Pile dwellings, 26, 144, 145, 147–149, 153, 159, 163, 287
Pinus picea, 150
Pinus sylvestris, 150
PITT-RIVERS, on ancient fortifications of Sussex, 288
Placard Cave, 105, 107, 132
Plouhennec, tumulus of, 346
Plourouses, 202
Plum, 158, 367
Poisons, 92

Poland, caves of, 24; tumuli in, 175; trepanation in, 266; burial and cremation in, 372
POMEL, on man and the cave-bear, 10
Pomerania, Lake stations of, 153
POMMEROL, on rounded stones, 88
Pont-de-Bonn (Namur), 282
Poplar, 367
Poppy, Indian, 151, 158
Porpoise, 138
Portugal, caves in, 52; *mamoas of*, 175; dolmens in, 178; *antas* in, 179; *citanias* in, 292; cup-stones in, 379
Posen, tumuli in, 220
Pottery, hand-made, 34; from cliff dwellings, 41, at French Exhibition, 1878, 44; of Neolithic period, 51; spoon of black earthenware, 94; others of brown, 95; pottery of great variety, 96–101; most ancient found in England, 142; almost identical in Europe and America, 143; of Lake dwellings of Switzerland, 146; earthenware spindlewhorls, 150; little figures and black vases, 153; terra-cotta ware, 156; *fusaïoles* in *terremares*, 160; vases with handles and ornaments from *fondi*, 162; vases from dolmens, 215; ornamented pottery from Alt-Sammit 216; Neolithic vases, 216; fragments of pottery at West Kennet, with tusks of extinct boars, 217; glass beads in Ireland, 220; funeral vases in Posen, and Prussia, 220; pottery hand-made and mixed with crushed shells, 285; fragments at Cissbury, 290; terra-cotta vases at Santorin, 312–314; coarse pottery from colonies at Hissarlik succeeding the Trojan, 324; superior in first town, 325; ornamented with flowers and fruit, 326; vases of great size, 330; jars, basins, and *amphoræ* used as funeral urns, 362;

jars of coarse pottery filled with bones at Caithness, 372
Potzrow, 292
POUCHET, on hatchets from the Somme, 15
PRESTWICH, on flints from the Somme, 14
PRÉVOT, on vitrification, 307
PROUST, on megaliths of France, 195
PRUNIÈRE, on human bones bearing scars, 250
—— on skill of Neolithic bone-setters, 257
—— on trepanation, 257, 258
—— on implied belief in future life, 275
—— on operation on the forehead, 277
—— on Neolithic station at Grez, 286
—— on sepulture of cave-men, 369
Prussia, funeral vases, silver and gold ornaments, and tumuli in, 220; burial and cremation in, 372
PULLIGNY, DE, on *enceintes* of Normandy, 283
Pyrenean valleys, Lake Stations of, 155
Pyrenees, the, 126

Quaternary period, deposits of, 10; of the Somme, 15; in South Africa, 34; animal life in, 56; mammals of, 66; huge animals of, 80; flint tools and weapons of, 90; pottery unknown in, 101; great cold of, 116; animals of, 116, 122; deposits of, 130; floods of, 131; animals of, extinct, 143, 156, 222; existence of man in, 234; trepanation in, 263; *see also* "Palæolithic period" and "Stone age."
QUATREFAGES, DE, on Quaternary deposits of the Somme, 15
—— on prehistoric races, 45

QUATREFAGES, DE, on kitchen-middings facing south, 137
—— on fortification on the Nive, 285, 286

Races, prehistoric, 42, 45
Raspberry, 158
Rat, 157
Reggio, 162
REINACH, on sepulture, 350
Reindeer, 47, 84, 85, 86, 132, 344
Reindeer period, 27, 35, 50, 63, 111, 113, 377
Religious rites in which flint knives were used, 17, 18; condemned by church, 18, 19; used by sorcerers in England, 19; barbarity of sacrifices in Mexico, 54; respect for the dead, 217; offerings in tombs, 216-218; portions cut from the skull after death, a rite, 274; *see also* "Sepulture."
Résille, 108, 135
Rhinoceros, 56, 96, 156
—— *incisivus*, 11
—— *Merckii*, 84
—— *tichorhinus*, 84, 116, 344
RIALLE, DE, on monuments of Tunisia, 198
Ribandelle, 304
Riesenbetten, 191
Rivatella, 162
Robenhausen, 148
Rochebertier, 124
Roches Moutonnées, 379
Rodents, 48
Rodmarden, 213
Roe-deer, 217
Roknia (Algeria), 266
Rondelles, 258, 259, 262, 263, 266, 274, 275
Roquemaure Cave, 107
ROSA, on *fondi*, 162
Rosmeur (Finistére), 283
ROSSI, DE, on Palæolithic workshop at Ponte-Molle, 237

ROUGÉ, DE, on monuments of Egypt, 2
Roumania, earthworks in, 294-296
Round towers of Ireland, 167
Rounded stones of granite or sandstone, 88
Rovesche, 373
Ruches de Crémation, 371
Rudders, 77
Ruins in the Transvaal, 35
Run-Aour (Finistère), 188
Rundyssers, 180
Runes, 291
Russia, dwellings above flood line in, 137; kitchen-middings in, 138; kurganes of, 195; *valla* in, 295

Sacred symbols, 339, 377
Sahara, desert of, 30-32
Saint-Acheul, 83, 233
St. Affrique dolmen, 263
St. Andrew (Winnipeg), a manufacturing centre, 240
St. John River, 141
Saint-Martin-la-Rivière, 262
Saint-Pierre-en-Chatre, 64
St. Quentin, 263
St. Simon's Island, 141
Salkeld (Cumberland), 182
Salzbourg, 290
San Ciro Cave (Palermo), 6
San Margarethan, 378
Santa Cruz, island of, 63
Santandar Caves, 27
Santhenay Cave, 131, 134
Santorin, Island of, 134, 308-316
SAPORTA, DE, on Northern origin of European civilization, 366
Sardinia, *nurhags* of, 165
Saturnia (Italy), 178
SAUVAGÈRE, on megaliths of France, 224
Saw-bladed knives, 29
Scandinavia, worked flints in, 44; human bones in, 45; deep-sea fish in kitchen-middings of, 60; har-

Scandinavia—*Continued*.
poons in, 66; attempts at navigation in, 69; polished flints in, 87; not peopled in Palæolithic times, no domestic animals, 137; orientation of houses in, 137; nomadic life in, 138; dead buried in crouching position, 351; burial and cremation in, 372; *Elfen Stenars* of, 381
Sceptre, 111
Schaafhausen, vitrified ramparts at, 301
Schlaken Wälle, 301
SCHLIEMANN, on Hill of Hissarlik and Troy, 317-339, 342
SCHMERLING, researches of, near Liège, 10
—— discovery of pottery and Moustèrien flints in Engis Cave, 97
—— on scarcity of human bones in Belgian caves, 231
Schussenreid Cave, 111, 148
Science, prehistoric, starting-point of, 4
Scotland, bronze fish-hooks in, 64; pirogue from ancient bed of the Clyde, 70; shell necklaces found in, 108; Lake stations of, 154; crannoges of, 164; *burghs* of, 165, 166; *Picts' houses* of, 166; dolmens in, 180; gold ornaments found in, 217; iron in monuments of, 219; megalithic monuments discontinued in, 223; vitrified forts in, 301-303; burial and cremation in, 372; cup-sculptures on menhirs in, 380
Seal, 116, 138
Sentenheim Cave, 56
Sepolture dei Giganti, of Sardinia, 170
Sepulchral caves, objects found in, 134, 135, 246; human remains in *L'Homme Mort* Cave, and a cave at Nogent-les-Vierges, 250; inhumation in caves of Roquet and *L'Homme Mort*, 370

Sepulchral chambers, or crypts, 188-192, 205, 261, 262
—— mounds in America, 93, 357, 374; *see also* "Megalithic Monuments" and "Tombs"
Sepulchre, Neolithic, at Crécy-sur-Morin, 261; and at Dampont (Dieppe), 262
Sepulture, similarity of, at Solutré and in Merovingian times, 360; stone chests for sepulture, 360; earthenware jars used by ancient Iberians, Chaldeans, W. coast of Malabar, in Thracia, and at Troy, 361; similar custom in Peru, Mexico, and on shores of the Mississippi, 362; trunks of trees used as coffins at Apremont, Hallstadt, in the cairns of Scania, at Gristhorpe, and Hove, 362, 364; ancient Caledonians sewed up their dead in skins, 364; embalming in Teneriffe, Egypt, and Peru, 364; burial and cremation proceeded side by side all over Europe, 368-378; burial customs, 373, 374; mounds of Ohio and Illinois, 374; cremation still practised by savages of Alaska, California, and Florida, with other strange customs, 374; feasts of death, 375; human sacrifices in honor of dead, 376; belief in immortality by cave-men, 376; bones of extinct animals venerated in succeeding epochs, 377; flint hatchets intentionally broken in tombs of Bronze age, 377
Settle (Yorkshire), 66
Sheep, 86, 156, 217, 329
Shell-heaps of America, 40, 140; at St. Simon's Island (Georgia), near St. John River, 141, and in Florida and Alabama, 142; in California and at Mobile, 143; at Hill of Hissarlik, 322, 329; *see also* "Kitchen-middings."

Shells of *Mytilus Californicus* and *Haliotes* made into fish-hooks, 63; necklaces of *Nassa* and *Nerita*, 108; pendants of scales of unio shells, 110; *see also* "Mollusca," and "Shell-heaps"
Siberia, flints in, 28; Stone age in, 28; mammoth in, 57; prehistoric civilization of, 236
Silver ornaments, 220; vase, 337
Solutré Cave, 57, 58, 85, 98, 108, 112, 232, 244, 349, 350, 360
Solutréen period, 85, 87, 132
Somme, the, bones and flints found near, 11, 14; kitchen-midding at mouth of, 140
Sordes Cave, 87, 106, 249, 345
Spain, pottery in, 97; circular openings in dolmens in, 211; prehistoric stations in, 294
Spiennes, 241, 242
Spindle-whorls, 28, 150, *see also* "*Fusaïoles*" and "Whorls."
SPRING, on human bones at Chauvaux, 49
Spy Cave (Namur), 97, 105, 343, 344
SQUIER, on fortifications at Old Fort (Kentucky), 299
Stag, 47, 137, 156, 157
Staves of office, 111-116
Stazzona of Corsico, 179
STEENSTRUP, on kitchen-middings, 135
Stendos of Sweden, 179
Stone age, 19; not a fixed period, 23; in Western Europe, 27; in Palestine, 28; in Algeria, 32; in Tunisia, 33; cannibalism in, 51; human bones of, 52; Lake stations of, 68; boats of, 71; ornaments of, 109; staves of office, 113, 116; art of, 126; Lake dwellings of, 147, 149; monuments of, 169; mode of life in, 248; places of refuge in, 279; successive Stone ages, 294, *see also* "Neolithic period," and "Quaternary period."

Stonehenge, 183, 185, 254
Store-houses for grain, 158, 295
Sureau Cave (Belgium), 47
Surgery, early attempts at, 252, 256, 271, *see also* "Trepanation."
Swan, 49, 329
Swastika, 339-341
Sweden, bronze fish-hooks in, 64; cromlechs in, 180; alignments in, 188; dolmens with circular openings in, 211
Sweno's pillar (Scotland), 185
Switzerland, Lake Stations of, remains of fish in, 60; bronze fish-hooks, 64; harpoons at Concise, 65; of Stone and Bronze ages, 67, 68; boats used in, 68, 69, 74; discovery of, 144; of three periods, 145; construction of, 147-149
—— Lake fauna of, 156, 157; fortified village in, 287, 288; cup-stones in, 379
Sydney, 36
Syria, tumuli in, 198

Talayoti of Balearic Islands, 165, 170
Tantama marca of Peru, 355
Tatooing in early times, 104; red chalk, red iron ore, and a fine red powder, also a pebble used to grind it, found in France, 105; fragments of ochre, manganese, red chalk, and black lead frequent, also hollowed stones in which to crush them, 106; an engraving of a tatooed man, on a bone, 106
TAYLOR, on megaliths of India, 200
Tchoudes, the, 195
Temples, rock hewn, 2; in America, 40, 42; at Hissarlik, 320, 324
Tench, 60
Terremares, of Italy, construction of, 159; bronze objects found in them, 160; *fusaïoles*, uncertain use of, 160; at Castione *terremares* in artificially hollowed basins, 160; un-

Terremares—Continued.
certain origin of *terremarecolli*, 160; *terremares* at Toszig in Hungary, 161; fortified *terremares*, 286
Thayngen Cave (Belgium), 48, 107, 114, 120, 233, 244
Therasia, Island of, prehistoric houses under volcanic ashes and tufa, 310
Thetford, Lake Station, 154
Thrush, 49
Thunder-stones, 17, 34, *see also* "*Ceraunia.*"
THUOT, on vitrification, 307
THURMAM, on burials in long barrows, 254
Tiger, 56
Toltecs, the, 42
Tombs, in Sardinia, 170; kurganes of Russia, 195; megalithic monuments either tombs or in honor of the dead, 201; all dolmens tombs, 202, 203, 246; burial of chiefs in dolmens, 258; tombs at Trüpschutz (Poland), 266; at Spy (Namur), 344; at Chauvaux, Gendron, and Duruthy, 345; at Baoussé-Roussé, 345, 346; in Italy, Sicily, Belgium, the Pyrenees, and in Brittany, and Long Barrows of England, 346; Port-Blanc dolmen (Morbihan) and Grand Compans (Luzarches), 347; cave of Stone age near Rome, 347; sepulchre at Solutré, 349; at Schwann (Mecklenburg), Oxevalla (East Gothland), Vence Cave (Alpes-Maritimes), 351; dolmens of Aveyron, 351; tombs at Mané-Lud, Luzarches, Cape Blanc-Nez, and Equehen, 352; Cravanche Cave (Belfort), 353; at Aurignac, Bruniquel, Frontal Cave, and caves of *L'Homme Mort*, 354; *Tantama Marca*, of Peru, 354; funeral pits of bottle shape at Tours-sur-Marne, 355

Tombs of transition period between Stone and Bronze Ages, 356; others of later date in Italy, 356; Aymaras of Bolivia buried beneath megalithic monuments resembling dolmens, or in *chulpas*, 357; mounds of Ohio cover sepulchres, 357, 358; remarkable discovery at Floyd (Iowa), 358; inhumation, 370; first traces of cremation, 370, 371; beneath cairn at Caithness large jars, at Blendowo (Poland) an urn filled with burnt bones, 372; necropolis of Hallstadt (Bohemia) of Bronze age, 373
TOPINARD, on trepanation, 272
Top-O-Hoth (Aberdeen), 302
Torquay, 14
Toszig (Hungary), 161
TOURNAL, researches by, near Narbonne, 10
Tours-sur-Marne, 355
Trepanation, early practice of, discovered, 257; examples, 258-268; a funeral rite, 269, 270; North American instances posthumous, 270; possible reason for practice as treatment of diseases, 271; examples from early Neolithic to Merovingian times, 272; subjects operated on young, 273; a religious rite, 274, 275; modes of operation, 276; spoken of by ancient historians, 277; still practised, 277
Triticum vulgare antiquarum, 151
—— *vulgare hibernum*, 151
Trou d'Argent Cave (Basses-Alpes), 253
Trout, 60
Troy, 134, 317-320, 324-338, 361
TROYON, on crannoges of Scotland, 164
Truddhi and *specchie*, of Otranto, 171
Tumuli, 45, 175, 176, 188, 197, 198, 201-203, 295, *see also* "Tombs."
Tunisia, workshops of, 33; megalithic monuments in, 198
Turtle, 60, 138

Turtle Mound, near Smyrna (America), 142
Tygelso (Scandinavia), 255

UJFALVY, researches by, in Siberia, 27
Uley (Gloucestershire), 190, 205, 254
Upland, 185
Ursus spelæus, 48, 59, 99

Valla of Roumania, 295
Varano, *terremare* of, 161
Vauréal, 250
Vegetable products used in Lake dwellings, comb of yew wood, pile dwellings at Lagozza made of silver birch, pines, and larch, 150; probably a vegetarian settlement, no remains of animals, but two kinds of corn, mosses, ferns, flax, the Indian poppy, acorns, nuts, and apples, 151; in Swiss Lake Stations, corn, millet, peas, poppy-heads, nuts, plums, raspberries, and dried apples and pears, 158; from Cortaillod, barley, cherry-stones, acorns, and beech-nuts, 158; at Laybach, water-chestnuts, 158; from some places loaves of bread, 159; corn, beans, vines, and various fruits cultivated by dwellers in *terremares*, 160; stores of grain in fortified camps of. Spain, 295; stores of millet in *cetati de pamentu* of Roumania, 296; in island of Santorin barley, millet, lentils, peas, coriander, and anise, 315; wheat known in Troy, 329; lignites of Iceland formed of tulip, plantain, and nut-trees, 366; in Spitzberg the beech, poplar, magnolia, plum, sequoia, and numerous coniferous trees, 167; in Banks, Grinnell, and Francis Joseph's Lands the cypress, poplar, silver-pine, and birch, in every stage of growth, 367

Vence Cave (Alpes-Maritimes), 351
Venezuela, 145
Venus, 141
Vezère Cave, 59, 134
Vilanova, 360
Villevenard Cave, 251
Villers-Saint-Sépulchre (Oise), 212
VIRCHOW, on kitchen-midding at Lake Burtneck, 139
—— on age of Lake stations, 154
—— on trepanation, 266
—— on vitrified forts, 301
—— on Hill of Hissarlik, 319
—— on Bronze age in Troy, 334
Vitrified forts, *see "Enceintes."*
Vivarais Cave, 252
Volcanic eruption in Ægean Sea, 308
Vosges Mountains, *enceinte* on, 283

Wading birds, 140
Wales, caves in, 130; crypts in, 205
WANKEL, on deposit at Prerau (Olmutz), 253
—— on trepanation, 265, 272
Water-chestnuts, 158
Watsch, 373
Weapons and tools of earliest man, 4; rock hatchets from Capri, 5; human origin of worked-stones recognized, 6, 7; worked flints at Hoxne (Suffolk), 9; stone weapons in Périgord, 9; worked flints near Narbonne, 10; near Liège, and Abbeville, and at Amiens, 11; at Torquay, and from the Somme, 14, 15; universally believed to be of supernatural origin, 15-17; stone weapons still used, 22; thousands of worked flints in France, 23; crescent-shaped flints in Crimea, 24; implements of schist and slate in Russia and Finland, 24; in kitchen-middings of Denmark, knives and hatchets of stone, horn, and bone, 24; in Wirzchow Cave amulets, fish cut in ivory, and four

Weapons—*Continued*.
thousand stone objects, 25; flint tools and bone spatulæ at Ojcow, in many Lake stations none but stone implements, 25; flint weapons in Italy, 26; in Portugal, 27; worked bones in Spain, 27; serpentine hatchets and wedges from Siberia, 27, 28; hammers, hatchets, pestles, and spindle-whorls from Ural Mountains, flints from Nahr el Kelb, Lebanon, and Sinai, 28; flint weapons from Japan, 29; worked agates, ancient javelin heads, in basalt and quartz, from Godavery, saw-bladed knives from Isle of Melas, and stone implements from Northwest India, 29

—— Stone age in Africa, 30; series of stone weapons and implements in Boulak Museum, 31; no bones with flints of Lower Egypt, 31; worked stones in Algeria, 32; stone objects and workshops in Tunisia, and worked flints in Morocco, 33; stone hatchets in Southern Africa, roughly-hewn flints, arrow-heads, mortars for crushing grain, at Natal, stone weapons of Cliff Dwellers, 41; in all countries, worked flints, 43, 44

—— construction and materials of, hatchets, wedges, and hammers of jade, fibrolite, and basalt, sharp-pointed and cutting tools of quartz, jasper, agate, and obsidian, 81; Moustier flints almond-shaped and pointed, 83; Chelléen type abundant in France and England, found in Italy, Spain, Algeria, Hindostan, and America, 83, 84; Moustérien epoch more varied forms, 84; Solutréen period stalked arrow-head, and more elegant forms, 85; Madeleine period great variety of shapes and materials, 85; Neolithic period polished weapons and tools, 86; fine specimens from Scandinavia, Brittany, and Mexico, 87; rounded stones the weapons peculiar to Neolithic period, 88; flint arrows triangular, or oval, 90; a bow from pile dwelling, Robenhausen, and one from Lutz, 90; bone and horn implements, 90; invention of barbs, 90; bevelled arrow, 92; possible use of poison, 92; needles with eyes, barbed arrows, bodkins, and amulets of bone, 92, 93; numbers of bone implements at San Francisco, Madisonville (Ohio), and in kitchen-middings of Atlantic and Pacific coasts, 93, 94; processes of cave-men simple, Neolithic progress, 94; earthenware spoons in Germany and Italy, 94; narrow spoons of bone and horn, 95; in Spain Neolithic implements of dorite and serpentine, 97; workshops with highly polished hatchets, 97

—— in sepulchral caves, 135; tools with horn handles from Swiss Lake Stations, 146; polished stone implements, arrows with transverse cutting edges, earthenware spindle-whorls, and bone combs from Lagozza, 150; lozenge-shaped worked flints from *fondi*, 162; unpolished flints and quartz wedge from hut in Donegal, 164; at Moen tomb a flint hatchet, balls of amber, and vases, 191; tools of quartzite, granite, schist, and diorite in alignments of Brittany, 194; polishing stone and cup-stones from megaliths of France, 194; hatchets of quartzite, fibrolite, diorite, nephrite, and jadeite from Brittany, 214; hatchets and celts of foreign stone, 215; polished stone weapons from West Gothland, 217; iron sword, inlaid

Weapons—*Continued*.
with silver, fragments of shield and battle axe, and iron bridle-bit from Aspatria (Cumberland), 220; in Ireland, iron knives and rings, copper pins, and a great number of bone implements, 220; hatchets vary in different districts, 227
—— immense numbers of, 231; at Solutré 4,000 flints, at Ors 8,000 objects, 232; in Thayngen Cave 12,000 chipped stones, in caves of Belgium 80,000, at Grez 60,000 worked stones, and arrows of every known type, 233; environs of Paris rich in deposits, 233; also Ireland, Denmark, Algeria, and America, 234; flints of Grand-Pressigny, 235; *caches*, 235; bronze hatchets, daggers, and bridle-bits from Siberia, 236; from Concise knives, stilettos, arrow-heads, and chisels of boars' tusks, 237; at St. Julien-du-Saut stone implements of every epoch, 238 (*see* "Workshops"); polishers at Loing (Nemours), 238; mining implements, 241, 243; in France implements of rock foreign to the localities, 246; hatchets and nuclei from Pressigny le Grand, in bed of the Seine, in Brittany on banks of the Meuse, and in Scotland, 246; pick-hammers from Lake of Bienne, 255; beautiful darts and polished boars' tusks from Lozère Cave, 258; hatchets of coralline limestone, jade, fibrolite, and serpentine, flint knives, arrows feathered or stalked, from Saint-Martin-la-Rivière, 262; marrow spoon and button from Lake Station, Switzerland, 288; weapons of Moustérien type at Cissbury, also wooden picks, 290; similar picks in copper mines of Asturias, salt mines of Salzburg, and petroleum well, United States, 290; from Roumania

grindstones for crushing grain, 296; from Santorin (Ægean Sea) troughs for crushed grain, lava discs used in weaving, lava weights, flint arrowhead and saw, obsidian arrows and knives, and small copper saw, 314; stone implements from 3d, 4th, and 5th colonies of Hill of Hissarlik, 322; stone and bronze implements from Troy, 324; celts and saws of rock, with handles of wood or bone, awls and pins of bone and ivory, 326; hæmatite and diorite projectiles, 334; Bronze age in Troy, spits and nails of copper, 335; metal shields, vases, and dishes, 336; *fusaïoles*, construction of, 339
—— from funeral pits at Tours-sur-Marne, 355, 356; celts and hatchets as amulets, 377; flint hatchets intentionally broken a funeral rite, 377; votive hatchets beneath dolmens, 378; hatchets engraved on megaliths, 378
Weaving, 314
WEBSTER, on sepulchral mound at Floyd (Iowa), 358
WEISGERBER, on Algerian megaliths, 197
West Kennet, 190, 216, 217, 254
Whistles, 112
Whittlesey (America), 299
Whorles of flint, 28; of earthenware, 150; *see also* "*Fusaïoles*"
Wiltshire, dolmens with circular openings, 213
Wirzchow Cave, 25
Wolf, 47
Wooden picks, 290
Workshops of Stone age in Tunisia, 33; at Argecilla, 96, 97; in Algeria, 197; at Wargla (Algeria), 234; at Grand-Pressigny, 235; on shores of the Bay of Kiel, and in other places, 236; at Spiennes, Hoxne, Brandon, Bellaria, and

Workshops—*Continued.*
Rome, 236, 237; Concise a manufacturing centre, 237; manufactories of France, 238; of Algeria, Asia Minor, and America, 240; at flint quarries at Spiennes, Brandon, and Mur Barrez, 241-243; of Neolithic date, 244; camp at Cissbury. 290; in Spain workshops of metallurgists, 295
WORSAAE, on age of shell heaps of America, 143

Written characters at Cissbury, 291
WURMBRAND, on Lake Stations of Austria and Hungary, 151
WYLDE, on Irish crannoges, 163

Yenesei, the, 195, 236; valleys of, 28
Yezo (Japan), dolmens of, 179
Yucatan, cromlechs of, 186; temples of, 341

Zahnow (Posen), 292
Zeedyck, 282

www.ingramcontent.com/pod-product-compliance
Lightning Source LLC
Chambersburg PA
CBHW030552300426
44111CB00009B/946